Resources for Teaching

The Bedford
INTRODUCTION TO
LITERATURE

The Bedford
INTRODUCTION TO
LITERATURE

Second Edition

MICHAEL MEYER
University of Connecticut, Storrs

ELLEN DARION

CHRISTINE FRANCIS
University of Connecticut, Storrs

ANNE PHILLIPS
University of Connecticut, Storrs

JOHN REPP
Mount Ida College

DAWN SKORCZEWSKI
Rutgers University

A Bedford Book *of* St. Martin's Press
Boston

PREFACE

This instructor's manual is designed to be a resource of commentaries, interpretations, and suggestions for teaching the works included in *The Bedford Introduction to Literature,* Second Edition. The entries offer advice about how to approach individual selections and suggests possible answers to many of the questions raised in the text. No attempt has been made to generate definitive readings of the works; the text selections are rich enough to accommodate multiple approaches and interpretations. Our hope is that instructors will take what they find useful and leave the rest behind. Inevitably, instructors will disagree with some of the commentaries, but perhaps those disagreements will be helpful starting points for class discussions too.

In addition to offering approaches to the selections, many of these entries suggest additional topics for writing, particularly comparisons with other works. The format of the entries varies from itemized responses that cover specific questions to essays that present overviews of individual works. There are also additional "Connections" questions in the manual for a number of selections. This flexibility allows each entry to be more responsive to the nature of the work and the questions asked about it. Suggested critical readings are included for authors treated in-depth and elsewhere when they are deemed especially appropriate means of teaching a work. These are highly selective. For more general bibliographic guides, see the annotated list of reference sources for fiction, poetry, and drama on pages 1842–1843 of the text.

The manual is conveniently arranged by genre and in the order that the selections appear in the text. Following the title of each entry is the page number on which it appears in the text.

For the second edition of the manual we have added an extensive list of film, video, and audiocassette resources for teaching the selections in *The Bedford Introduction to Literature.* There is also a list of the selections linked by "Connections" questions in the text for easy reference. Finally, at the end of the manual, you will find the list of works included on a new audio recording of poems from the text and information on how to obtain a copy of this recording.

We are indebted to J. Michael O'Neill for writing the entries for *Hamlet* and Contexts for Reading Shakespeare.

CONTENTS

APPENDICES

FICTION

1. Reading Fiction

KATE CHOPIN, *The Story of an Hour* (p. 12)

As you begin to consider this story, lead the class into a discussion of Mrs. Mallard's character. What do they think of her? Even for the 1990s, this is in certain ways a bold story, and there are likely to be students who will describe the protagonist as callous, selfish, unnatural — even, in Mrs. Mallard's own words, "monstrous" — because of her joyous feeling of freedom after her initial grief and shock.

Go through the text with the class, finding evidence that this radical shift in feeling is genuine. To demonstrate her grief and subsequent numbness you might point to Mrs. Mallard's weeping with "sudden, wild abandonment" (paragraph 3), the "physical exhaustion that haunted her body . . . and soul" (4), the way she sat "motionless, except when a sob came up into her throat and shook her, as a child who has cried itself to sleep continues to sob in its dreams" (7), and her look, that "indicated a suspension of all intelligent thought" (8). Especially important to the defense of Mrs. Mallard's character is her effort to fight off "this thing that was approaching to possess her": "she was striving to beat it back with her will" (9–10).

Ask students to discuss (or write about) what they imagine Mrs. Mallard's marriage was like. If her husband "had never looked save with love upon her" (13), what was wrong with the marriage? The answer can be found in the lines "She had loved him — sometimes. Often she had not . . . What could love, the unsolved mystery, count for in the face of this possession of self-assertion which she suddenly realized as the strongest impulse of her being!" (15). The surprise ending (which some readers may find manipulative) aside, this story is basically about a woman awakening to the idea that all the love and stability in the world can't compensate for her lack of control over her own life.

Ask the class if they can locate any symbols in the story. "The tops of trees that were all aquiver with the new spring life," sparrows "twittering" (5), "patches of blue sky showing . . . through the clouds" (6), "the sounds, the scents, the color that filled the air" (9) — all suggest the renewal and rebirth that follow.

Students could also write about the ending of the story, specifically the last three paragraphs. What is the tone here? (Ironic. First, Mrs. Mallard suffers a heart attack when she *sees* her husband, rather than when she learned of his death, which is when everyone originally feared she would have an attack. Second, she does not die of joy, as the doctors claim, but of shock — the shock of having to go back to her old way of life once she has realized there is another way to live.)

Chopin's story offers an opportunity to demonstrate how a reader's own values and assumptions are relevant to literary interpretation. Responses to Mrs. Mallard are — for better or worse — often informed by readers' attitudes toward marriage. Similar issues can also be engaged in the Van Der Zee and Godwin stories that follow Chopin's.

Chapter 32, "Critical Strategies for Reading," includes a variety of approaches to "The Story of an Hour." Students who are exposed to this chapter early in the course will be likely to

1

generate more pointed and sophisticated kinds of questions about the subsequent texts they read.

A Composite of a Romance Tip Sheet (p. 18)

This tip sheet offers an opportunity to begin discussions of the elements of fiction. Reading a romance novel is not a prerequisite for discussion, because most of us have experienced similar formulas in magazines, popular television programs, or films; also, an excerpt from a romance novel begins on page 22. Students are usually delighted to recognize the patterns prescribed in the tip sheet and have no trouble recalling stories that fit this description. This gets class discussions off to a good start, provided the emphasis is on why readers derive pleasure from romance formulas rather than on a denigration of such reading.

Recent criticism has focused considerable attention on the audience and appeal of romance novels. (See, for example, Tania Modleski, *Loving with a Vengeance: Mass-Produced Fantasies for Women* [New York: Archon, 1982]; Janice A. Radway, *Reading the Romance: Women, Patriarchy, and Popular Literature* [Chapel Hill: University of North Carolina Press, 1984]; and the excerpt from Kay Mussell's *Fantasy and Reconciliation: Contemporary Formulas of Women's Romance Fiction* on p. 35.) Romance readers are typically housewives ranging in age from their twenties to midforties. Not surprisingly, the age of the heroine usually determines the approximate age of the reader, because the protagonists of Harlequin and Silhouette romances — to name only the two most popular series — are created so that consumers will readily identify with the heroines' romantic adventures in exciting settings as a means of escaping the loneliness and tedium of domesticity. (It's worth emphasizing, of course, that male readers engage in similar fantasies; Philip Larkin's "A Study of Reading Habits" [p. 503] suggests some possibilities.) The heroine is "attractive" rather than "glamorous" because she is likely to appeal to more readers who might describe themselves that way.

Romance readers are often treated to a veritable fashion show, with detailed descriptions of the heroines' clothes. This kind of window-shopping is especially apparent in television soap operas, in which the clothes and sets resemble Bloomingdale's displays more than they do real life. In a very real sense their audience is shopping for images of success, courtship, and marriage. The hero is a man who may initially seem to be cold and cruel but ultimately provides warmth, love, and security. He is as virtuous as the heroine (if he's divorced his ex-wife is to blame) but stronger. His being "about ten years" older emphasizes male dominance over female submissiveness, a theme that implicitly looms large in many romances.

The use of sex varies in romances, especially recent ones, in which explicitness seems to be more popular. Nevertheless, suspense and tension are produced in all romances by the teasing complications that keep lovers apart until the end. The major requirement in love scenes between the hero and heroine is that they be culminations of romantic feelings — love — rather than merely graphic.

The simplified writing style of romances is geared for relatively inexperienced, unsophisticated readers. Probably not very many romance readers cross over to *Pride and Prejudice* or *Jane Eyre*, although some of Austen's and Brontë's readers have certainly been known to enjoy romances. Instructors who share their own reading habits with a class might reassure students that popular and high culture aren't necessarily mutually exclusive while simultaneously whetting students' appetites for the stories to come.

KAREN VAN DER ZEE, *From* A Secret Sorrow (p. 22)

Karen Van Der Zee was born and grew up in Holland. She published a number of short stories there early in her career. Although the United States is her permanent home, she and her husband, a consultant in agriculture to developing countries, often live abroad. The couple was married in Kenya, their first child was born in Ghana, and their second child arrived in the United States. Van Der Zee has contributed ten books so far to the Harlequin line.

The excerpt from *A Secret Sorrow* subscribes to much of the plotting and characterization described in the composite tip sheet. Kai and Faye are not definitively brought together until the final chapter, after Faye's secret is revealed and Kai expresses his unconditional love for her. Students should have no difficulty understanding how the heroine's and hero's love for each other inevitably earns them domestic bliss in the "low white ranch house under the blue skies of Texas," where the family "flourished like the crops in the fields" (paragraph 137). Kai is the traditional dominant, protective male who takes charge of their relationship (albeit tenderly). A good many prepackaged phrases describe him: he has a "hard body," and he kisses her with a "hard, desperate passion" when he isn't speaking "huskily" or lifting her face with his "bronzed hand." In contrast, Faye is "like a terrified animal" and no match for his "hot, fuming fury" when he accuses her of jeopardizing their love.

Despite the predictable action, stereotyped characterizations, clichéd language, and flaccid descriptions of making love (see paragraph 108), some students (perhaps many) will prefer *A Secret Sorrow* to Godwin's "A Sorrowful Woman." But that's natural enough. Van Der Zee's story is accessible and familiar material, while Godwin's is puzzling and vaguely threatening, because "A Sorrowful Woman" raises questions instead of resolving them. Rather than directly challenging students' preferences and forcing them to be defensive, demonstrate how Godwin's story can be reread several times and still be interesting. *A Secret Sorrow* certainly does not stand up to that test, because it is written to be consumed on a first reading so that readers will buy the next book in the series.

GAIL GODWIN, *A Sorrowful Woman* (p. 30)

Gail Godwin traces her beginnings as a writer to her mother, a teacher and writer herself, who read stories out of a blank address book, "the special book," as Godwin has called it, "a tiny book with no writing at all in it." Although she frequently contributes essays and stories to publications such as *Harper's, Esquire, Cosmopolitan,* and *Ms.* and has written four librettos, Godwin is primarily known as a novelist, whose books include *The Perfectionists* (1970), *The Odd Woman* (1974), *Violet Clay* (1978), *A Mother and Two Daughters* (1982), and *The Finishing School* (1985). Born in 1937 in Birmingham, Alabama, Godwin was educated at the University of North Carolina and the University of Iowa. She worked as a reporter for the *Miami Herald* and as a travel consultant with the U.S. Embassy in London before pursuing a career as a full-time writer and teacher of writing. She has received a National Endowment for the Arts grant, a Guggenheim Fellowship, and an Award in Literature from the American Institute and Academy of Arts and Letters. She was coeditor of *Best American Short Stories* in 1985 and has had her short stories collected in *Dream Children* (1976), *Real Life* (1981), and *Mr. Bedford and the Muses* (1983).

"A Sorrowful Woman" challenges the assumptions that inform romance novels. The central point of *A Secret Sorrow* is that love conquers all and that marriage and motherhood make women "beautiful, complete, [and] whole." In contrast, Godwin's story begins with an epigraph that suggests a dark fairy tale: "Once upon a time there was a wife and mother one too many times." The story opens with a pleasant description of the woman's husband ("durable, receptive, gentle") and child ("a tender golden three"), but she is saddened and sickened by the sight of them. These unnamed characters (they are offered as types) seem to have the kind of life that allows Kai and Faye to live happily ever after, but in Godwin's world this domestic arrangement turns out to be a deadly trap for "the woman." The opening paragraph shocks us into wanting to read the rest of the story to find out why the woman is repulsed by her seemingly perfect life.

It may be tempting to accept the husband's assessment that "Mommy is sick." Students might be eager to see her as mad or suffering from a nervous breakdown, but if we settle for one of those explanations, the meaning of the story is flattened. We simply don't know enough about the woman to diagnose her behavior in psychological terms. She is, after all, presented as a type, not as an individual. She does appear mentally ill, and she becomes progressively unstable until she withdraws from life completely, but Godwin portrays her as desperate, not

3

simply insane, and focuses our attention on the larger question of why the sole role of wife and mother may not be fulfilling.

The woman rejects life on the terms it is offered to her and no one — including her — knows what to make of her refusal. (For a discussion of the nature of the conflict in the story see pp. 45–46 of the text.) What is clear, however, is that she cannot live in the traditional role that her husband and son (and we) expect of her. She finds that motherhood doesn't fit her and makes her feel absurd (consider the "vertical bra" in paragraph 5). When she retreats from the family, her husband accommodates her with sympathy and an "understanding" that Godwin reveals to be a means of control rather than genuine care. He tells her he wants "to be big enough to contain whatever you must do" (22). And that's the problem. What he cannot comprehend is that she needs an identity that goes beyond being his wife and his child's mother. Instead, he gives her a nightly sleeping draught; his remedy is to anesthetize his Sleeping Beauty rather than to awaken her to some other possibilities.

Neither the husband nor the wife is capable of taking any effective action. The husband can replace his wife with the "perfect girl" to help around the house, and he can even manage quite well on his own, but he has no more sense of what to do about her refusal to go on with her life than she does. Her own understanding of her situation goes no further than her realization that her life did not have to take a defined shape any more than a poem does (23). Her story is a twentieth-century female version of Herman Melville's "Bartleby, the Scrivener" (p. 80); both characters prefer not to live their lives, but neither attempts to change anything or offer alternatives. Instead, they are messengers whose behavior makes us vaguely troubled. The two stories warrant close comparison.

In the end, when spring arrives, the woman uses herself up in a final burst of domestic energy that provides the husband and son with laundry, hand-knitted sweaters, drawings, stories, love sonnets, and a feast that resembles a Thanksgiving dinner. But neither renewal nor thanks is forthcoming. Instead, the boy, unaware of his mother's death, asks, "Can we eat the turkey for supper?" (39). The irony reveals that the woman has been totally consumed by her role.

Ask students why this story appeared in *Esquire,* a magazine for men, rather than, say, *Good Housekeeping.* The discussion can sensitize them to the idea of literary markets and create an awareness of audiences as well as texts. Surely a romance writer for *Good Housekeeping* would have ended this story differently. Students will know what to suggest for such an ending.

For a discussion of Godwin's treatment of traditional role models in the story, see Judith K. Gardiner, "'A Sorrowful Woman': Gail Godwin's Feminist Parable," *Studies in Short Fiction* 12 (1975): 286–290.

PERSPECTIVE

KAY MUSSELL, *A Defense of Formula Romances* (p. 35)

Ask students whether they read any formula fiction, and if so whether they find any one genre (western, romance, mystery) more satisfying than any other. If so, why? Do they agree that formula romances try "to invest women's lives with significance"? Ask those students who read formula fiction if they read it for "significance" at all — or if they instead read it for sheer pleasure or escapism.

2. Plot

EDGAR RICE BURROUGHS, *From* Tarzan of the Apes (p. 40)

Discussed in text, 43–46.

Most of the sixty books Edgar Rice Burroughs wrote recorded bedtime stories he had told his children. In addition to the enormously popular Tarzan series, Burroughs wrote a good deal of science fiction, most notably a series of books that chronicle the adventures of John Carter of Mars. Before making his fortune as a writer, Burroughs was a cowboy, gold miner, policeman, and store manager. His books include *The Princess of Mars* (1917), *Tanar of Pellucidar* (1930), and *Tarzan and the Foreign Legion* (1947). *Tarzan of the Apes,* published in 1914 and the first of the Tarzan series, has been translated into more than fifty languages.

WILLIAM FAULKNER, *A Rose for Emily* (p. 47)

The ending of this mystery story is as chillingly gruesome as it is surprising. Just when we think that the discovery of Homer Barron's body ("what was left of him") is the awful revelation that the narrator has been leading up to, we realize in the final climactic paragraph (and particularly in the last three words) that the strand of "iron-gray hair" on the indented pillow belongs to Emily. The details indicate that she has slept with Homer since she murdered him, because we are told in paragraph 48 that her hair hadn't turned gray until after Homer disappeared. The closing paragraph produces a gasp of horror in most readers, but by withholding this information until the very end, Faulkner allows us to develop a sympathetic understanding of Emily before we are revolted by her necrophilia.

The conclusion is skillfully foreshadowed: Emily denies her father's death; she buys arsenic; Homer disappears; and there is a terrible smell around the house. These clues are muted, however, by the narrator's rearrangement of the order of events. We learn about the smell before we know that Emily bought arsenic and that Homer disappeared. Hence, these details seem less related to one another than if they had been presented chronologically. Faulkner's plotting allows him to preserve suspense in a first reading. On subsequent readings we take delight in realizing how all the pieces fit together and point to the conclusion.

The gothic elements provide an appropriate atmosphere of mystery and are directly related to the conflicts in the story. Emily's decrepit house evokes an older, defunct South that resists the change imposed by garages, gasoline pumps, new construction, paved sidewalks, and a Yankee carpetbagger such as Homer. This exposition is essential to the story's theme, because it explains Emily's antagonists. Emily rejects newness and change; her house smells of "dust and disuse." Her refusal to let go of the past is indicated by her insistence that her father did not die and by her necrophilia with Homer. She attempts to stop time, and although the narrator's collective "we" suggests the town's tolerance for and sympathy with such an attitude (as a representative of the North, Homer is powerful but vulgar), the story finally makes clear that living in a dead past means living with death. As much as the narrator realizes that Emily's illusions caused her to reject the changing realities of her life, he — like his fellow citizens — admires Emily with "a sort of respectful affection" (1). She is like a "fallen monument," a reminder of an Old South that could not survive the new order of Reconstruction. Even though she murders Homer, Emily cannot stop the changes brought by the urbanization associated with him.

This story, minus its concerns about change in the South and its tribute — a rose — to Emily's strong sensibilities (in spite of her illusions and eccentricities), fits into the gothic horror tradition, but it would be a far less intriguing work of fiction if the formula were to supersede Faulkner's complex imaginative treatment.

Connections (p. 54)

1–3. A number of useful connections can be made between "A Rose for Emily" and Mishima's "Patriotism" (p. 412). Mishima's plot contains no surprises while the incidents in Faulkner's story are arranged to lead up to the final ghastly scene. Students might be asked to write about how they respond to the plotting of each story; this will encourage them to keep track of their responses and to connect them to specific events in the stories. Additionally, although Faulkner and Mishima focus on radically different cultures, they both use concepts of honor and tradition to develop conflict and reveal character. Students should be encouraged to see how important a role dignity plays in the lives of Reiko and Rose. Moreover, it is worth pointing out that death in these stories — whether suicide or murder — is, at least from the central character's point of view, a means of preserving dignity.

See also Judith Fetterley's "A Feminist Reading of 'A Rose for Emily'" (p. 1799) and the sample student research paper on "A Rose for Emily" (p. 1853).

In the "Perspective" that follows the story, Faulkner discusses the title of the story, what inspired it, and the story's conflicts.

PERSPECTIVE

WILLIAM FAULKNER, *On* A Rose for Emily (p. 54)

Ask students to consider Faulkner's statement "I was simply trying to write about people," which was made in response to a question about symbolism in this story. Have the class look at other stories in which symbols are prevalent, or at least obvious. Are the characters always realistic and convincing? Have you come across any characters who serve a symbolic function but are not entirely credible as far as motivation or behavior goes?

GRACE PALEY, *A Conversation with My Father* (p. 56)

Students' attention may be drawn to the stories which the daughter tells for her father in "A Conversation with My Father." However, they should recognize the primary subject: the relationship between the writer-daughter and her dying father.

At the beginning of the story, the father questions his daughter's talent by comparing it with the stories of de Maupassant, Chekhov, and Turgenev — three male, renowned, European storytellers. There's a sharp contrast between them and the young, female, American daughter who writes stories in her own style. To please her father, who asks for "a simple story just once more" (2) before he dies, she tries to work with a style that is not her own: to subvert her own artistry. Her first version isn't acceptable because it's too simple. Her father points this out as he requests more detail, demonstrating that in this relationship, the daughter seems to please her father the most by providing him with opportunities to criticize her and her work. Her second story is closer to her own style, and instead of criticizing the details, her father discusses its ending. The story is a success because it involves the father; he cares enough to debate its ending and meaning with her. In providing him with a topic that moves him and allows him an opportunity for the argument that he so loves, the daughter has achieved her goal.

How do the stories within this story develop the characters of the father and the daughter? Both versions of the inner story involve a parent and a child. The mother, taking part in her son's life and art, is left alone and sad at the end of the story. Having devoted herself only to his development, she has nothing left when he leaves her. This is analogous to the father in the primary story, who focuses almost entirely on his daughter's writing. Whether he does so from genuine interest or from his physical inability to develop other interests, his conversation concerns her telling of stories. In another sense, the mother of the inner story is like the writer-daughter. Both are caught up in caring for other members of their families. Like the mother, the daughter will soon be abandoned. The debatable point of the inner story is whether the mother will develop a new life after her abandonment. The writer insists that the mother will: "That woman lives across the street. She's my knowledge and my invention. I'm sorry for her. I'm not going to leave her there in that house crying" (37). The writer may feel the need to add hope to the mother's story because she too faces abandonment. The father insists that the mother won't create a new life: "Truth first. She will slide back. A person must have character. She does not" (41). His criticism of the mother sounds suspiciously like his criticism of his daughter. He also claims that the writer won't accept reality: "As a writer that's your main trouble. You don't want to recognize it. Tragedy! Plain tragedy! Historical tragedy! No hope. The end" (34). Perhaps he needs to know that she accepts his own dying. He may also be trying to ease his own guilt at abandoning her .

The son in the inner story can also be associated with the father and the daughter. The son educates his mother in drug use, and accustoms her to a communal, intellectual way of life. He then leaves her for a younger, clearer-headed, intellectual woman. Like the son, the father is training his daughter to write a certain kind of story; she is becoming accustomed to a life in which she caters to his literary needs. The father will then leave her by dying. On the other hand, the daughter is like the son. She will accustom her father to her attention, involve him in her artistic zeal, and eventually leave him by succeeding with her own style. If he were not dying, she might eventually leave him to pursue her own career as well as her own development of a family. Although the son and the mother of the inner story are at a different stage in their story than the father and daughter, their story parallels the outer plot.

The stories we tell reveal us. The daughter and the father reveal their characters, their fears and their concerns, in their discussion about the story. They also unify their family, which would appear to consist of only two members, although others are referred to by the daughter, by creating a story about a mother and a son. The story within the story of "A Conversation with My Father" isolates each member of this multi-level fiction, reveals a little something about each character, and then unifies them through discussion. In the end, the innermost story of the mother and son demonstrates the outer characters' preparations for the father's death.

3. Character

CHARLES DICKENS, *From* **Hard Times** (p. 62)

Discussed in text, 62–64.

WILLIAM FAULKNER, *Barn Burning* (p. 66)

In William Faulkner's "Barn Burning," a boy is continually placed in situations where he must decide whether to support his family and deny his conscience or to uphold society's conventions and act according to his convictions. Within this plot, Faulkner also reveals the concerns and stylistic traits most characteristic of his fiction by emphasizing the innermost thoughts, impressions, and urges of human beings, or as he identifies them in his Nobel Prize acceptance speech, "the problems of the human heart in conflict with itself."

The boy, Colonel Sartoris Snopes, is faced with three distinct moments when he must decide whether to stand with his family or with the society that Abner continually battles. The first trial occurs in a small town general store, the courtroom where Abner is accused of setting fire to another man's property. The boy's initial response is animal: He convinces himself that he and his father face a mutual enemy in the judge. When he is called forward to testify, he realizes that he is in an impossible position, caught between his father and the judge. *"He aims for me to lie,* he thought, again with that frantic grief and despair. *And I will have to do it"* (7). He has no choice practically; his psychological and economic security stem from his father's favor. All he knows is that he must fight for his father. Yet when the moment to speak arrives, he cannot lie. Both the judge and his father realize this, and the judge settles the trial without forcing the boy to answer. That night, after the family has left the area, Abner hits Sarty, but the real blow is caused by his words: "You were fixing to tell them. You would have told him. . . . You're getting to be a man. You got to learn. You got to learn to stick to your own blood or you ain't going to have any blood to stick to you" (28–29).

Sarty can only hope that he won't be put in such a situation in the next town, but life there is no simpler. The second trial occurs when Abner sues Major de Spain over the value of the rug that he has spitefully ruined. In that courtroom scene, Sarty is hardly considered one of the family. Although he tries to help, he is banished to the back of the room, where he can watch the proceedings with other strangers. This strengthens his own sense of justice because it releases him from the restricted perception of the family. After this incident, his father addresses him as he might a stranger. His honeyed response to Sarty's attempted reassurance is even more distancing, and dangerous, than his normally harsh treatment of the boy: "his father glanced for an instant down at him, the face absolutely calm, the grizzled eyebrows tangled above the cold eyes, the voice almost pleasant, almost gentle: 'You think so? Well, we'll wait till October anyway'" (81). The father immediately mends the wagon, indicating that the family will be making another move long before harvest. His actions completely contradict the comment he has addressed to the son he no longer trusts.

Sarty's third crisis of conscience occurs in the evening, when he knows that his father is about to burn Major de Spain's barn. Finally, he is able to break free from all of his family loyalties and alert the Major. He acts according to his conscience, but he must sacrifice his family ties as a result. As he experiences each psychological ordeal during this short period of time, Sarty matures from a scared, dependent child to a young man capable of making moral distinctions and acting on them.

The conflict between this son and his father is indicative of the clash Faulkner saw between the rising, mechanistic, materialistic "New South" and the receding, chivalric "Old South." Abner Snopes is representative of the new breed of Southerner. A scavenger in the Civil War, fighting only for his own gain, he is associated with machines and material gain. Faulkner consistently describes him in industrial terms: "the stiff black back, the stiff and implacable limp of the figure which was not dwarfed by the house . . . the impervious quality of something cut ruthlessly from tin, depthless, as though, sidewise to the sun, it would cast no shadow" (41). He clearly displays animosity toward the wealth and gentility of the fading upper classes. His son, on the other hand, feels an inward loyalty to the upper classes, and demonstrates that affinity at the end of the story when he alerts Major de Spain. Named for Colonel Sartoris, an honorable Southern warrior, Sarty is of the Old South. His immediate response to seeing the de Spain house is relief that his father cannot reach these people: *"They are safe from him. People whose lives are a part of this peace and dignity are beyond his touch"*(41). The affluence of the house and its furnishings speaks directly to the boy's soul. "The boy, deluged as by a warm wave by a suave turn of the carpeted stair and a pendant glitter of chandeliers and a mute gleam of gold frames, heard the swift feet and saw her too, a lady" (43). Nothing else in Sarty's "poor white trash" existence has had this effect on him. At heart, Sarty is more a descendant of Major de Spain (a link indicated as well by their names) than he is of the Snopes's lineage.

The matter of the de Spain carpet also illustrates this conflict between the Old South and the New South. Abner ruins the valuable rug to show his defiance of de Spain wealth. The Major enforces the cleansing, and the penalty for ruining the carpet, not as a genuine response to its destruction but to teach Abner some Southern manners: "That won't keep Mrs. de Spain quiet but maybe it will teach you to wipe your feet before you enter her house again" (63).

Does the mechanistic southerner succeed, or does old southern gentility prevail? It may be a mixed solution: Sarty escapes, and can finally begin living according to his conscience. On the other hand, a blaze has been set, and there are other Snopeses to continue these acts of arson. If students are interested in reading more about the fortunes of the Snopes family, including Abner's horsetrading career and the effect of the spotted horses on the town in which Sarty has seen them advertised, they should be directed to Faulkner's Snopes trilogy: *The Hamlet, The Town,* and *The Mansion.*

Students who recognize Abner Snopes's instinctual rebellion against an economic system that builds wealth for a few individuals at the expense of black and white labor — "He stood for a moment, planted stiffly on the stiff foot, looking back at the house. 'Pretty and white, ain't it?' he said. 'That's sweat. Nigger sweat. Maybe it ain't white enough yet to suit him. Maybe he wants to mix some white sweat with it.'" (46) — might find themselves in sympathy with Abner's defiance. You might raise this as a topic for discussion.

HERMAN MELVILLE, *Bartleby, the Scrivener* (p. 80)

Although students are usually intrigued by Bartleby's bizarre behavior, they are likely to respond to the "inscrutable scrivener" in much the same way that Ginger Nut assesses him: "I think, sir, he's a little *luny.*" But to dismiss Bartleby as, say, a catatonic schizophrenic reduces the story to merely a prescient case study and tends to ignore the narrator-lawyer, the other major character. Besides, we don't learn enough about Bartleby to make anything approaching a clinical judgment because, as the lawyer tells us in the first paragraph, "no materials exist, for a full and satisfying biography of this man." He is as disturbingly mysterious as Godwin's protagonist in "A Sorrowful Woman."

What makes the story so weird — a term that nearly always comes up in discussions of Bartleby — is that the lawyer and the scrivener occupy two radically different fictional worlds. We recognize the lawyer as a character from the kind of fictions that convey at least some of the realistic textures of life, but Bartleby seems to be an allegorical or symbolic intruder in that world. Melville uses Bartleby to disrupt the lawyer's assumptions about life. It's as if a Kafka character suddenly turned up in a novel by Dickens or James. Melville makes us as much as the lawyer feel that Bartleby is somehow out of place. The following answers to the questions in the text offer some suggestions about how to place him.

Considerations (p. 104)

1. Melville has the lawyer characterize himself in the first few paragraphs so that we understand the point of view from which we will see Bartleby. No champion of truth and justice, the lawyer makes his living doing a "snug business among rich men's bonds, and mortgages, and title-deeds" (paragraph 2). He is convinced that "the easiest way of life is best"; he is an "eminently *safe* man" who takes pride in his "prudence," "method," and status. It is significant that he is a lawyer rather than simply a businessman, because the law is founded on precedents and assumptions; Bartleby, however, is "more a man of preferences than assumptions" (149). Because Bartleby is beyond the lawyer's experience, the lawyer does not know how to respond to the scrivener's passive refusal to "come forth" and do "his duty." The lawyer's reliability as a narrator is discussed in the text on pages 131–132.

2. Turkey, Nippers, and Ginger Nut are introduced to the reader before Bartleby is in order to make credible the lawyer's tolerance for eccentric behavior. So long as the lawyer gets some work out of these human copying machines, he'll put up with just about anything — provided they don't publicly embarrass him or jeopardize his reputation.

3. Bartleby's physical characteristics foreshadow his death. When we first meet him (17) he already seems to have withdrawn from life. He is "motionless" and "pallidly neat, pitiably respectable, incurably forlorn!" He seems scarcely alive and is described as "cadaverous." With nearly all the life gone out of him, he is capable of nothing more than "silently, palely, [and] mechanically" (20) copying until he prefers not to; this refusal marks the beginning of his increasing insistence on not living.

4. Bartleby's "I would prefer not to" confuses and enrages the lawyer and his employees. This simple declaration (the tone of which is discussed in the text, pp. 231–232) takes on more power and significance as the story progresses (not unlike Edgar Allan Poe's use of "nevermore" in "The Raven"). Bartleby's seemingly mild statement carries with it considerable heft, because "some paramount consideration prevailed with him to reply as he did" (39). His declaration is both humorous and deadly serious.

5. This is "A Story of Wall Street" because Bartleby's "dead-wall reveries" (the symbolic walls are discussed on pp. 174–175 of the text) represents a rejection of the materialistic values that inform the center of American financial interests. Business and money mean nothing to Bartleby, but they essentially constitute the sum total of the lawyer's life until his encounter with him.

6–7. The protagonist is the lawyer; he is a dynamic character who changes while Bartleby, the antagonist, remains static throughout. Despite the title, the story is the lawyer's, because his sense of humanity enlarges as a result of his experience with Bartleby. "The bond of a common humanity" creates "presentiments of strange discoveries [which] hovered round me" (91). In a sense the lawyer discovers what Emily Dickinson's speaker describes in "There's a certain Slant of light" (p. 1825), a poem that can help students understand the significance of the lawyer's final comment: "Ah Bartleby! Ah, humanity!" Some critics, however, see Bartleby as the story's central character. For alternative readings see the article by Stern cited at the end of this discussion.

8–9. The Dead Letter Office is essential to understanding what motivates Bartleby's behavior. Although Melville is not specific, he suggests enough about the nature of the thwarted hopes and desires that the scrivener daily encountered in the Dead Letter Office to account for Bartleby's rejection of life. Somehow it was all too painful for him and rendered life barren and meaningless — hence his "dead-wall reveries." The lawyer makes the connection between this experience and Bartleby. But Melville has him withhold that information so that we focus on the *effect* Bartleby has on the narrator rather than on the causes of

Bartleby's rejection of life. By the end of the story the lawyer has a chastened view of life that challenges his assumption that "the easiest way of life is best."

10. Melville sympathizes with the characters while rejecting their responses to life. He clearly does not endorse the lawyer's smug materialism, but neither does he offer Bartleby's unrelenting vision of death as an answer to the dehumanizing, mechanical meaninglessness that walls the characters in. In this story Melville presents issues not solutions; it is exploratory rather than definitive.

11. The lawyer moves beyond his initial incredulity, confusion, anger, and frustration and begins to understand that Bartleby represents a challenge to all his assumptions about life. Finally, he invests meaning in Bartleby instead of dismissing him as eccentric or mad. Melville expects the reader to puzzle out his meaning too.

12. This story can be usefully regarded as a kind of sit-in protest — at least on a metaphysical level with nonnegotiable demands. Bartleby is a stubborn reminder that the lawyer's world is driven by expediency rather than principle — that the lawyer's satisfaction with life has been based on his previous avoidance of the big issues.

13. Surprisingly, there is some delightful humor in the story as the characters' exasperation with Bartleby's behavior develops. We know that the scrivener is going to get a rise out of them. There is also humor in Bartleby's reply to the lawyer that he is "sitting upon the banister" when the lawyer asks him what he's doing in his office building. And consider the lawyer's suggestions that Bartleby be a bartender, a bill collector, or a traveling companion "to entertain some young gentleman with your conversation" (195–210). A student once suggested that a dramatization of the story should feature Richard Nixon as the lawyer and Woody Allen as Bartleby. Ask students for their own suggestions on who might play these roles; the question encourages them to think of what goes into a characterization.

14. Students might be asked to trace their reactions to Bartleby while they read and then to compare them with how they respond to him after class discussion of his character.

For an excellent survey of the many varied critical approaches to the story, see Milton R. Stern, "Towards 'Bartleby the Scrivener,'" in *The Stoic Strain in American Literature*, ed. Duane J. MacMillan (Toronto: University of Toronto Press, 1979), 19–41.

PERSPECTIVE

NATHANIEL HAWTHORNE, *On Herman Melville's Philosophic Stance* (p. 105)

Assign consideration 1 as a writing topic.

4. Setting

EUDORA WELTY, *Livvie* (p. 109)

In this story Solomon's Bible and his bottle trees indicate that he is a pious man. But his house and yard reveal much more: He is a man preoccupied with symmetry and order, with having as much control over his environment as possible. His kitchen table is always spotless, and "there were four baited mousetraps in the kitchen, one in every corner" (paragraph 2). There is a lamp with three feet atop a three-legged table, and even the palmettos on his wallpaper are spaced at "careful intervals" over the walls. Outside, this "even balance" continues. There is an easy chair on either side of the porch, and bushes and trees appear in equal numbers on each side of the steps. "A clean dirt yard with every vestige of grass patiently uprooted" further represents Solomon's obsession with order and control; he is trying to conquer the forces of nature (3–4).

Solomon's watch is another symbol of his attempt to control and organize the world he lives in: "He might be dreaming of what time it was, for even through his sleep he kept track of it like a clock, and knew how much of it went by, and waked up knowing where the hands were even before he consulted the silver watch that he never let go" (15). On his deathbed Solomon offers the watch to Livvie as an act of love; it is his most prized possession. But at the same time he is giving her much more, and knows it. He is giving her her life back, relinquishing his control over time and over her. When, in Cash's embrace, Livvie drops the watch, she is freeing herself from Solomon's values. She succumbs to spontaneity, to passion, to all the things Solomon feared. (The class might be interested to know that this story was originally published under the title "Livvie Is Back.")

As Solomon's wife, Livvie is lonely and homesick, but not consciously aware that she is unfulfilled. It is apparent to us, if not to Livvie, that she represents a life force; even her name suggests the word *life*. And consider how she is drawn to the workers in the field: "But what if she would walk now into the heart of the fields and take a hoe and work until she fell stretched out and drenched with her efforts, like other girls, and laid her cheek against the laid-open earth, and shamed the old man with her humbleness and delight?" (14). Instead of recognizing herself as repressed, however, Livvie believes such thoughts are cruel and evil, and is ashamed of her envy of the life and sense of community she sees in the field. For Livvie is a dutiful, respectful girl; she honors Solomon's wishes and customs (one of which is continuing to think of herself as a "girl" rather than a woman, despite the fact that she is twenty-five years old). She knows what she is good at (waiting on people, keeping house, and so on), and she is proud of her ability to do these things well.

Miss Baby Marie's visit is the catalyst for Livvie's awakening to her situation and subsequent rebirth. The simple application of lipstick brings Livvie to life; although she hasn't ventured out of the house since Solomon took to his bed, she goes out now — and meets Cash. Dressed in vibrant, vital pinks and greens — the colors of spring, a traditional symbol of rebirth — Cash is the opposite of the pious, discreet, controlled Solomon. His very clothes clash loudly, and he demonstrates no respect in the house of a dying man; he even raises his fist as if to strike Solomon. Like Livvie, Cash represents a life force, but a not entirely beneficial one, for he brings destruction in his wake. His shattering of the bottle trees represents a destruction of Solomon's values — and simultaneously brings the possibility of evil into Livvie's life, since she, like Solomon, believes in the trees' power. Still, no rebirth occurs without a struggle, and the story's end should be read optimistically. While Solomon may have been morally upright in conventional ways, he did not live a very happy life, a fact he acknowledges on his deathbed. At least with Cash, Livvie can begin to live as a young person should.

Cash's name suggests not just money but the freedom that comes from being able to enjoy it. (Livvie and Solomon were not poor, but still Livvie didn't have fine clothes or lipstick.) The "Baby" in Miss Baby Marie's name suggests just what Livvie is when she picks up the chinaberry lipstick: a baby delighted in the discovery of a new world. The name *Solomon* has traditional associations with wisdom and keeping the peace, as Solomon did, but to a fault.

ERNEST HEMINGWAY, *Soldier's Home* (p. 121)

This is a war story that includes no physical violence because Hemingway focuses on the war's psychological effects on the protagonist. A truce ended the wholesale butchery of youth fighting during World War I, but the painful memory of it has made Krebs a prisoner of war. Although the story's setting is a peaceful small town in Oklahoma, Hemingway evokes the horrors that Krebs endured and brought back home with him. In a sense the real setting of this story is Belleau Wood as well as the sites of the other bloody battles Krebs experienced. (A brief student report summarizing the nature of these battles and the casualties they produced can provide a vivid context for class discussion of the story.)

But Krebs cannot talk about his experiences at home because people in town have "heard too many atrocity stories to be thrilled by actualities" (paragraph 4). He has been affected as a result of his experiences in a way they'll never be, and therein lies the story's conflict. The fraternity brother who went off to war in 1917 with romantic expectations returns knowing what the real picture is (consider the ironic deflation produced by the two photographs in paragraphs 1 and 2). Krebs knows that popular visions of the glory of war are illusions and that the reality consists more typically of sickening fear. An inadvertent hint of that comes from his sister, who calls him "Hare," a nickname that suggests fright and flight. (For a poem with a similar theme see Wilfred Owen's "Dulce et Decorum Est," p. 552.) Krebs prefers silence to lying.

Krebs refuses to engage in the familiar domestic patterns of life expected of him. He also rejects the "complicated" world of the young girls in town. (Krebs's rejection of whatever is "complicated" is related to Hemingway's style on pp. 229–230 in the text.) Nothing really matters very much to him; he appears numb and unwilling to commit himself to what he regards as meaningless, trivial games. He feels more at home remembering Germany and France than living in his parents' house. Reading a history of the battles he's been in gives him a feeling of something more real than his life at home, which strikes him as petty, repressive, and blind. His father's permission to use the family car, for example, is neither wanted nor needed. (For a discussion of the symbolic significance of home in the story see p. 174 in the text.)

Krebs's mother brings the conflict to a climax. She speaks for the family and community, urging Krebs to get back to a normal life of work, marriage, and "being really a credit to the community" (Hemingway's use of point of view in this scene [58–70] is discussed in the text on pp. 130–131). Krebs finds his mother's values little more than sentimental presuppositions that in no way relate to the person he has become. The only solution to the suffocating unreality imposed on him by his family and town is to leave home. He can neither love nor pray; he's no longer in "His Kingdom" (63). There's no going back to that prewar identity as an innocent fraternity brother from a Methodist college. The story's title, then, is ironic, for Krebs cannot go home again, because home seems to be either a lie or stunningly ignorant of what he discovered in the war.

A writing assignment based on a comparison of how settings are used in "Soldier's Home" and Welty's "Livvie" or Tim O'Brien's "How to Tell a True War Story" will encourage students to relate the characters and themes to each story's setting. The landscape of home in each story is equally important but radically different in its significance.

5. Point of View

ALICE MUNRO, *How I Met My Husband* (p. 133)

Alice Munro's fiction explores the problems experienced by women who have high aspirations and few opportunities because of provincial Canadian values. Born in 1931 in Wingham, Ontario, Munro attended the University of Western Ontario, then moved to Victoria, British Columbia, where she managed a bookstore with her first husband. She began publishing her stories in the 1950s, and her first collection, *Dance of the Happy Shades,* won the Governor-General's Literary Award, the highest honor given to Canadian writers, in 1968. Her work has since won two more Governor-General's Awards: in 1978 for *Who Do You Think You Are?* (published as *The Beggar Maid* the next year in the United States) and in 1987 for her most recent collection, *The Progress of Love.* Munro has lived with her second husband since 1972 in Clinton, Ontario. Her other books include *Lives of Girls and Women* (1971), *Something I've Been Meaning to Tell You* (1974), and *The Moons of Jupiter* (1982).

Most students will recognize and appreciate this straightforward, realistic, first-person coming-of-age story as exactly that. The narrator is looking back on herself at age fifteen, presenting these events (which do lead up to her meeting the man who will become her husband) as she remembers them, adding occasional adult insights in retrospect.

Ask the class whether the title is in any way misleading. It suggests that we will read a story about a courtship or romantic encounter — which will involve the narrator and a man the narrator will eventually marry. And we believe this is what we're reading about, just as Edie believes Chris will write to her, until the day she suddenly realizes he won't. (Most readers, especially those older and wiser than Edie, realize Chris won't write to her a little sooner than she does.) So the title becomes gently ironic, since Edie meets her husband by waiting for the mail every day, smiling not for Carmichael the mailman but in anticipation of a letter from Chris.

Direct students' attention to the last sentence of the story, particularly the last phrase: "because I like for people to think what pleases them and makes them happy." The narrator is able to speak this line now — but did she always feel this way?

Edie can feel generous because she is a mature and happy adult. But she wasn't this giving as a naive and definitely opinionated adolescent. She didn't think highly of the Peebleses, especially Mrs. Peebles, who didn't bake, had only two children and no barn work, complained about living in the country, and generally, as Edie saw it, didn't know the meaning of good hard work. And Edie certainly didn't want Alice Kelling to be happy. But in retrospect Edie disapproves of her own behavior. "You'd think I'd be ashamed of myself, setting her on the wrong track . . . Women should stick together and not do things like that. I see that now, but didn't then" (paragraph 157). It is Edie's maturity, along with her own happiness, that gives her this warmer, more accepting attitude toward other people and toward life.

Questions for Discussion and Writing

1. *Ask the class what, besides a warning lesson about untrustworthy men, Edie learns in this story.*

   She learns a lot about the complexity of human relationships; hers is not just a sexual awakening. She learns "the way people feel when you are working for them. . . . They like to feel you don't notice things, that you don't think or wonder about anything but what they liked to eat and how they liked things ironed" (50). And she learns that adults talk to each other differently than they talk to fifteen-year-olds, and that fifteen-year-olds think differently than adults: "Sometimes [Mrs. Peebles] came out and had a conversation with [Chris]. He told her things he hadn't bothered to tell me. But then I hadn't thought to ask" (86). And Edie learns that good looks aren't everything:

> This Alice Kelling had on a pair of brown and white checked slacks and a yellow top. Her bust looked to me rather low and bumpy. She had a worried face . . . . Nothing in the least pretty or even young-looking about her. But you could tell from how she talked she was from the city, or educated, or both (94).

Edie may be prettier, but Alice Kelling has a sophistication she'll never have.

2. *Another good paper topic would be to compare this story to Tony Cade Bambara's "The Lesson" (p. 364) and John Updike's "A & P" (p. 407), two other first-person stories about initiations into the adult world. Sylvia, Sammy, and Edie all learn lessons about how unfair life can be, but each of the stories has a very different tone. What accounts for these differences? Does "initiation into the adult world" accurately and completely describe the theme of each of these stories? Or does each author focus on different aspects of the theme? Do any of them introduce additional conflicts or themes, which are perhaps more important? (Suggest that students read Mordecai Marcus's "What Is an Initiation Story?" on page 481 before answering these questions.)*

ANTON CHEKHOV, *The Lady with the Pet Dog* (p. 146)

It would be useful to assign Chekhov's statement "On Morality in Fiction" (p. 158) at the same time you assign this story; the commentary makes an excellent springboard for discussion of the story. Ask the class whether they think Chekhov does "all the time speak and think" in Gurov's tone and spirit, as the author says he must, in order to show what kind of a person his character is.

The story is told from Gurov's point of view, which Chekhov refuses to comment on, morally or otherwise. His aim is simply to portray Gurov as accurately as he can; here is a man who does certain things, feels certain feelings, and so on. It is by this constant exposure to Gurov's thoughts and actions that we get to know, and eventually care about, the protagonist. Initially, he is not a sympathetic character; he speaks ill of his wife and of women in general. He considers women inferior because of "bitter experience" (paragraph 5) with them, but later thoughts reveal that it is *he* who has treated *them* badly. For evidence of this, direct the class to paragraph 28: "From the past he preserved the memory of carefree, good-natured women whom love made gay and who were grateful to him for the happiness he gave them . . . and of women like his wife who loved without sincerity . . . and of very beautiful, frigid women, across whose faces would suddenly flit a rapacious expression — an obstinate desire to take more from life than it could give . . . and when Gurov grew cold to them their beauty aroused his hatred, and the lace on their lingerie seemed to him to resemble scales."

The fact is that he is afraid of women, afraid of their power over him. (See the end of paragraph 5: "Some force seemed to draw him to them [the women], too.") Gurov calls women inferior to empower himself against them, so that he can control them, instead of the other way around. Yalta's atmosphere, which is deceptively festive, is the perfect place for Gurov to play his games with women and himself. It is a resort town, a place people visit for vacations, or, as in Anna's case, to escape their daily lives. Since everyone is there on a temporary basis, nothing that happens there is permanent or matters in the "real" world to which the vacationers must all eventually return.

Chekhov sticks to Gurov's consciousness so closely that while we may or may not sympathize with him, we cannot help but begin to understand him. For instance, many readers will not be kindly disposed to Gurov when he becomes annoyed by Anna's distressed reaction to committing adultery (37), but even then we can comprehend what is going on in his mind. (All the other women he has had affairs with were old hands at the game; he is not used to women like Anna, who is genuinely disturbed by what she has done.) But in the story's third section, we see Gurov changing; he realizes that Anna is different (63), that he is unable to forget her the way he forgot the others, and that she is "the only happiness that he now desired for himself" (84). Finally, he realizes that "only now when his head was gray he had fallen in love, really, truly — for the first time in his life" (115). If the story had been told from Anna's perspective, we would miss the crucial insights and transitions Gurov experiences in the last two sections.

Chekhov's objectivity makes it possible for us to understand Gurov and Anna; his presentation of his characters is so compassionate it is clear he sympathizes with them, and their situation. This is not to say he condones their actions; he is simply able to see (and to make us see) how this relationship has come about, and why these characters behave the way they do. Both married young, perhaps too young to know any better, and apparently neither of their marriages is based on love. This information helps explain the characters' motivations, as well as their plight at the end of the story. Living in a society where divorce was not considered an acceptable alternative, and having recognized their love for each other as too powerful to deny, they can have no resolution to this conflict. For as long as Anna and Gurov love each other, life will remain "complicated and difficult."

PERSPECTIVE

ANTON CHEKHOV, *On Morality in Fiction* (p. 158)

Chekhov suggests that the result of combining art with "a sermon" would be bad art (or at least bad technique). Ask students whether they agree with this statement. Have them select a story that either does or does not "combine art with a sermon," and ask them to discuss whether it succeeds — both on their terms and on Chekhov's.

JOYCE CAROL OATES, *The Lady with the Pet Dog* (p. 159)

In retelling Chekhov's story, Oates is paying homage to this classic tale of adulterous love. While Oates sets her own story in twentieth-century America, she has deliberately retained many aspects of Chekhov's version. The couple meet at a renowned vacation spot, complete with beach; the woman is alone because she wanted to get away from her husband for a while; the man has children and the woman doesn't; months after their initial parting, the man seeks out the woman at a local performance she is attending with her husband. All these details evoke certain associations for a reader who knows Chekhov's story; we expect that parallel events and emotions will unfold. But Oates's version certainly stands on its own; she has integrated all the details she borrowed into a story that makes sense even if you are not familiar with Chekhov's predecessor.

Of course there are differences between the two versions, the most obvious being the perspective from which the story is told. Oates went beyond paying her respects to Chekhov, for to change the point of view is to change the story being told. (Remind the class how different Melville's "Bartleby, the Scrivener" [p. 80] would be if Bartleby's were the central consciousness.) Oates's version is Anna's story; it is her heart and mind we see here, and it is her character we begin to understand.

When the lovers first separate, Anna tells herself (in paragraph 30) that she is glad: "she understood that she was free of him . . . she would leave him soon, safely, and within a few days he would have fallen into the past, the impersonal past. . . ." He had threatened her with love, something she had grown used to living without. For here is what passed for love, or at least for conjugal relations, in her marriage (see paragraph 126): "sometimes he failed at loving her, sometimes he succeeded, it had nothing to do with her or her pity or her ten years of love for him, it had nothing to do with a woman at all. It was a private act accomplished by a man, a husband, or a lover, in communion with his own soul, his manhood." Experiences like this having formed her attitude toward love and sex, it is easy to see why she is not eager to embark on another relationship — why, in other words, she is relieved to be parting from her lover. But in the end she realizes that her lover is different, and she lets herself love, understanding that believing in and accepting her lover are far better than the sterile life she has with her husband, and the "clumsiness" (17) of his love.

This story may initially be confusing to students because of the order in which it is told. But the order is actually quite strategic. In the first two parts, we learn the profound effect Anna's lover, and indeed the very concept of the affair, has on her. A good example is this sentence in paragraph 10: "She was still panicked. . . . it made her think of mucus, of something thick and gray and congested inside her, stuck to her, that was herself and yet not herself — a poison." In paragraph 12 we learn that Anna is not happy with her husband: "for years now they had not been comfortable together." And in paragraph 20 we learn that "she did not really trust men."

In the first two sections of the story we are also given some specific history about the lovers. Anna tells her lover she believes in him (69), and we realize the significance of this statement since Anna said earlier that she did not trust men. But her lover replies by speaking "of his wife, her ambitions, her intelligence, her use of the children against him"; in other words, he speaks of his unwillingness to get a divorce. So Anna's trust is shattered; she thinks about killing him, as she thought, earlier, about killing herself. If the story was told chronologically, starting with the couple meeting, all of this information would have to be provided in the exposition, thus interrupting the narrative and lessening the tension that precedes and pervades the beginning of the affair.

6. Symbolism

COLETTE, *The Hand* (p. 176)

In "The Hand," Colette's description of one night in the life of a woman and her sleeping husband forces readers to rely on the imagery associated with the husband's hand and on the wife's limited actions for meaning. By contrasting the wife's initial observations of the husband's hand with her later perceptions of it, students can clearly see her changing awareness of her lover. The husband's hand is a microcosm of the whole man, isolated as it is among the sheets. Initially, the wife focuses on its manicure, representative of the man's breeding and elegance: "the flat nails, whose ridges the nail buffer had not smoothed out, gleamed, coated with pink varnish" (13). The glazed nails are a symbol of his refinement. However, she is distracted by the color of the nails, a too feminine touch, which clashes with the size and strength — the masculinity — of the hand. As she discovers this incongruity, her conception of the hand, and of the man, rapidly changes from idealization to realization. She focuses primarily on male qualities of the hand, associating them with uncivilized, inhuman imagery: "the hand suddenly took on a vile, apelike appearance" (15). Her following observations of it are filled with references to its animal qualities: "tensed up in the shape of a crab," "the hand . . . lowered its claws, and became a pliant beast," "red fur" (17, 17, 19). Her husband is no longer a handsome lover; he has become a beast.

The wife's changing awareness of the hand affects her behavior. At the beginning of the story, as she gazes around the bedroom and at her sleeping lover, the hand rests next to her right elbow, and she is content. At the end of her story, her initial response is to shrink from contact with it or with anything it touches, including the piece of toast it has buttered. Her change in attitude toward the hand and its owner is presented in two stages. As she gazes at the hand and its nails, she feels in control: She makes a mental note to convince the husband not to use pink varnish. Then the hand moves, revealing the thumb as "horribly long and spatulate" (15), and she responds with a single word: "'Oh!' whispered the young woman, as though faced with something slightly indecent" (16). The hand's altered appearance forces her beyond blissful, romantic, honeymoon notions of it, and into a more realistic inspection. The setting reinforces this intrusion of reality. As she utters the first "Oh!" she suddenly becomes aware of the world outside the bedroom: "The sound of a passing car pierced the silence with a shrillness that seemed luminous" (17). As she studies the hand, she becomes more aware not only of its appearance, but of its potential for destruction. It is described in militaristic, warlike terms: "ready for battle," "It regrouped its forces" (17, 19). These images are reinforced by the association of the hand's power with a criminal act: "slowly drawing itself in again, [it] grabbed a fistful of the sheet, dug into it with its curved fingers, and squeezed, squeezed with the methodical pleasure of a strangler" (19). The wife's realization of the hand's (and therefore the husband's) absolute power causes her to utter a second "Oh!" Her first, whispered response has become a cry of terror. The hand is not only capable of evil, and of harming the wife; it appears to take great pleasure in such acts of cruelty, reinforcing the ultimate representation of the husband as a beast.

At the beginning of "The Hand," the wife is like a character in a fairy tale. A whirlwind romance led to her marrying a man whom she really didn't know well. After her one-night encounter with the hand, representative of her husband in a truly unconscious, natural state, details of the husband's background that previously seemed innocent take on sinister connotations: He is "recently widowed" and her involvement with him "had been little more than a kidnapping" (3). In the end, she is Beauty married to her Beast, legally and eternally. Her expectation of living life "happily ever after" has been defeated; instead, she is preparing for "her life of duplicity, of resignation, and of a lowly, delicate diplomacy" (25). Symbolizing her helplessness, she can only kiss his hand, the "monstrous hand" of the beast to whom she has entrusted her fate.

RALPH ELLISON, *Battle Royal* (p. 179)

The opening paragraph of this story is fairly abstract and may be difficult for some students to grasp on first reading. But by the story's end the narrator's comments in this paragraph should have become very clear. Throughout this story Ellison is concerned with the masks, roles, and labels people impose on one another in this society. The narrator is invisible because the town's white citizens don't see him (or anyone else black) for what he is — which is, simply, a human being. What they see is a black man, or, in their vocabulary, a "nigger," "coon," or "shine." And niggers, to their minds, are to be treated a certain way; mainly, they are to be publicly humiliated and abused. It is bitterly ironic that these men can bestow a great honor on this boy (the college scholarship) and simultaneously treat him worse than they would treat their pet dogs. It is equally ironic that, despite the brutal treatment the narrator receives at the hands of these men, he still wants to give his speech, and is still proud to receive their gift. Neither the behavior of the white men nor that of the narrator makes any sense.

The horrifying battle royal can be seen as a metaphor for the society the narrator lives in, in which nothing makes sense. Ten black boys are viciously used by some of the most important men of the town; they are forced to provide a freak show — first in the boxing ring, later on the electrified rug. In both cases they are jerked around like puppets on a string. They are, in fact, puppets; the white men are the puppeteers. If the boys refuse to fight one another, or grab for the money with sufficient enthusiasm, it is clear the drunken white mob will hurt them much worse than they will hurt one another. White men have the power and make the decisions in this society, so the boys do as they are told. And not once do any white men — the very source of all this angry violence and confusion — get hurt.

The boys are brought in front of the naked blonde in an attempt to make them feel as uncomfortable as possible; they are not supposed to look at white women, and, left to their own devices, they wouldn't, especially in a room full of drunken white men. The blonde, with her ironic American flag tattoo, suggests all the things the boys (who are supposed to be Americans too) can't have simply because they are black: dignity, self-respect, freedom of choice, the freedom not to beat each other up or be beaten up by the white citizens present.

The blonde also serves another, very different function: at the same time that she is superior to the boys by virtue of the color of her skin, she is being used by the men; she too is a puppet. In paragraph 9, when she is being tossed into the air, the narrator sees the same "terror and disgust in her eyes" that he and the other boys are feeling.

As a high-school graduate, the narrator is extremely naive and believes that these men really respect him as he gives his speech after the battle, barely able to talk because he is choking on his own blood. In retrospect, as an educated adult, he realizes that he could not possibly have got an ounce of respect from any of them, just as, if he had known better at the time, he would not have respected himself. He realizes now that he was a laughing stock, and that the white men were sending him the very message he read in his dream: "Keep This Nigger-Boy Running." In retrospect, too, he is able to understand his grandfather's dying words. His grandfather meant that a black man in this society didn't stand a chance by fighting racism openly. Instead, he believed blacks should *pretend* to play the game; white people had so much power that it was only by working within their system (by receiving scholarships to black colleges, for example, and then leading black people "in the proper paths") that blacks could hope to accomplish anything in the fight for equality. Dignity and self-respect, meanwhile, could come from within, since you would know you were agreeing them "to death and destruction" (2).

PERSPECTIVE

RALPH ELLISON, *On Fiction as an Oblique Process* (p. 189)

You might ask students to look for other stories in the text that exemplify Ellison's belief that "deep down we believe in the underdog, even though we give him hell" (para. 3). How does Flannery O'Connor make use of this belief in "Revelation" (p. 327), for example? You might also ask students if they agree with Ellison's conviction that this belief in the underdog "provides a rhetoric through which the writer can communicate with a reader beyond any questions of their disagreements over class values, race, or anything else" (3). Once the writer communicates with a reader, does this change the reader's beliefs about class values or race?

KATHERINE ANNE PORTER, *The Grave* (p. 191)

Students should be encouraged to read Katherine Anne Porter's "The Grave" more than once in order to recognize Miranda's transformation as it results from the events described in the story. Both the ring and the rabbit have significant impact on Miranda's sense of herself and the world. A rite-of-passage story, "The Grave" concerns a young girl's achievement of knowledge and her loss of innocence.

Porter reveals contrasting aspects of Miranda's character in "The Grave." Initially, Miranda is clad in male clothing — "dark blue overalls, a light blue shirt, a hired-man's straw hat, and thick brown sandals" (10). She scandalizes the older women of the community by her masculine appearance, and her behavior is equally censured because, like the boys, she goes hunting and rides "astride barebacked horses" (10). Yet in spirit, Miranda is not suited to these activities. She goes shooting with Paul, but her heart is not in the hunt: "'What I like about shooting,' said Miranda, with exasperating inconsequence, 'is pulling the trigger and hearing the noise'" (4).

The ring Miranda acquires from Paul serves as a catalyst for her inner, more feminine self. Once the ring is firmly on her thumb, she envisions a different exterior. The ring "turned her feelings against her overalls and sockless feet, toes sticking through the thick brown leather straps. She wanted to go back to the farmhouse, take a good cold bath, dust herself with plenty of Maria's violet talcum powder — provided Maria was not present to object, of course — put on the thinnest, most becoming dress she owned, with a big sash, and set in a wicker chair under the trees" (11). The ring, associated throughout the story with the ties that bind together men and women, causes Miranda to consider the proper appearance of women. Once she has physically linked herself with it, the ring influences her psychological state as well.

Miranda is also child-like at the beginning of the story. Even though she has a natural understanding of how creatures are born, live, and die, it is an unconscious one. While Paul skins the rabbit, she is interested in acquiring the fur only as a coat for one of her dolls. After he cuts open the rabbit's body, Miranda is still innocently interested: when she says "Oh, I want to *see*" (14), she means that she wants literally to look at the baby rabbits. They seem pretty to her. Only after she has touched the baby rabbits — after she has felt the blood and the flesh — does she truly begin to understand the process of life. She "began to tremble without knowing why. Yet she wanted most deeply to see and to know. Having seen, she felt at once as if she had known all along. The very memory of her former ignorance faded" (14). From a more knowledgeable, adult perspective, she is consciously aware of her own ability to bear children, and her own responsibilities as a woman. As Porter writes, Miranda "understood a little of the secret, formless intuitions in her own mind and body which had been clearing up, taking form, so gradually and steadily she had not realized that she was learning what she had to know" (14). Articulating the connections she has made, Miranda equates the baby rabbits with human babies. Although Paul throws away the corpse of the rabbit and its skin, it has forced Miranda into a more mature view of the world.

The graves at the beginning of the story are echoed in the burial of the baby rabbits within their mother and in the way Miranda buries her memories of the incident. Like the grandmother who unearths her husband in order to ensure their unity, Miranda brings her memories of the ring and the rabbit to the surface. Porter's powerful description appeals to all five senses, but it emphasizes smell, first of the graveyard — a pleasantly sweet, corrupt smell, being mixed with cedar needles and small leaves" (3) — and then of the marketplace — "it was a very hot day and the smell in the market, with its piles of raw flesh and wilting flowers, was like the mingled sweetness and corruption she had smelled that other day in the empty cemetery at home" (15). Porter's description also emphasizes the importance of touch, as Miranda reaches out to both the ring and the rabbit.

In its natural setting, and with such emphasis on innocence and experience, "The Grave" evokes a comparison between Miranda and Eve. Highlighting this comparison is Miranda's casual inquiry: "'What about snakes?' asked Miranda idly. 'Can I have the first snake?'" (10). As women, as innocents who become wiser through experience, Miranda and Eve are sisters.

7. Theme

STEPHEN CRANE, *The Bride Comes to Yellow Sky* (p. 200)

In this story Jack Potter is conflicted between the love and duty he feels toward his new wife and the love and duty he feels toward Yellow Sky. As town marshal, protector and defender of, and friend to, Yellow Sky, he feels he has betrayed the town not only by marrying a stranger but by marrying without the town's knowledge as well. Crane is playing with some traditional western myths here — most notably the idea of the lawman's loyalty to his territory above anything else, even personal happiness.

In fact, the title and first paragraph of this story set up our expectations for a typical western. The bride coming to Yellow Sky supplies the element of adventure and a little bit of tension (how will she react to her new home, and how will the town react to her?). The train and the plains, with their mesquite, cactus, "little groups of frame houses," and the "sweeping" vista, all provide the setting we associate with western adventures. But Crane is quick to let us know that he is playing off these traditions rather than adopting them conventionally. Notice that the bride is not pretty or young, and that while the newlywed couple is ostensibly very happy, they are practically tortured by embarrassment.

As far as traditional westerns go, something is definitely askew here. Marshals don't usually have brides, because women only get in the way in the wild world of gunslingers and Indians. And if there is a wife, she is decidedly young and pretty. She is also in the house, where she belongs, rather than in San Antonio, dragging the marshal miles away from where *he* belongs, taking care of the local drunk bully. Finally, while we expect this story to end in a shoot-out (though because of the comic tone we don't really expect anyone to get killed), words are exchanged instead of bullets and Scratchy Wilson is "disarmed" by the incredible fact (and sight of) Jack Potter's bride. For all we know, if Mrs. Potter hadn't been standing there, Wilson might not have believed Potter's claim that he had just gotten married (which was also his explanation for why he didn't have a gun). So Mrs. Potter actually serves as a weapon more powerful than a gun; Wilson takes one look at her and loses interest in shooting.

What kind of shoot-out is this, where no shots are fired? What kind of West is this, with a bride in a cashmere dress (attire we can't imagine women wearing, or even having access to, in that setting)? And we're explicitly told that Scratchy Wilson's gaudy outfit is inauthentic western garb; the shirt came from New York City and the inappropriate boots are, we learn in paragraph 63, "the kind beloved in winter by little sledding boys on the hillsides of New England." The suggestion is that the romantic West of the storybooks is dead, or at least dying fast. Edwin H. Cady, in *Stephen Crane* (New York: Twayne, 1962), notes that "'The Bride Comes to Yellow Sky' is a hilariously funny parody of neo-romantic lamentations over 'The Passing of the West.' The last marshal is tamed by a prosaic marriage and exempted from playing The Game so absurdly romanticized. . . . His occupation gone, the last Bad Man, a part-time worker anyhow, shuffles off into the sunset dragging boot tracks through the dust like the tracks of the last dinosaur" (102). When Scratchy Wilson says, "I s'pose it's all off now" (88), the specific reference is to his rampage on the town, but the larger implication is that the whole myth of the West is over as well.

Scratchy's comic and ineffective qualities are meant to suggest those same qualities in Yellow Sky, and in any part or member of the West that still adheres to this myth. The drummer in the saloon reinforces this concept; as an outsider to Yellow Sky, he helps dramatize this episode. The fact that he has been many places but hasn't encountered such a situation before suggests how ridiculous this little scene really is; people just don't go around shooting up a town this way anymore (if they ever really did), and Yellow Sky seems to be one of the last places to find this out.

Crane creates suspense by delaying the inevitable meeting between Potter and Wilson; he alternates scenes of the bride and groom en route to Yellow Sky with scenes of what is going on in Yellow Sky at the same moment. But it is a teasing rather than gripping suspense; Crane's tone is sufficiently mocking and ironic that we don't really believe Wilson, or anybody else, is actually going to kill anyone.

JOSEPH CONRAD, *An Outpost of Progress* (p. 208)

In "An Outpost of Progress," Joseph Conrad displays the breakdown of humanity and society, first through the erosion of Kayerts's and Carlier's morality and ultimately, by their deaths. In his setting, characterization, and asides to the reader, Conrad presents a damning judgment of the vision and moral fiber of human beings.

"An Outpost of Progress" is set at an ivory trading station in the deep jungle. Not only is the location remote; it is also primitive. Conrad describes a portion of the house inhabited by the main characters: "the plank floor was littered with the belongings of the white men; open half-empty boxes, torn wearing apparel, old boots; all the things dirty, and all the things broken, that accumulate mysteriously round untidy men" (para. 1). The seedy station matches the characters who are assigned to run it. As the director of the company remarks, "Look at those two imbeciles. They must be mad at home to send me such specimens. I told those fellows to plant a vegetable garden, build new storehouses and fences, and construct a landing stage. I bet nothing will be done! They won't know how to begin. I always thought the station on this river useless, and they just fit the station!" (2).

The two men, Kayerts and Carlier, begin their term of duty most genially. Both have taken this position through family pressures: one to save money for his daughter's dowry and the other because his brother-in-law is tired of supporting him. As the steamer leaves them, they join together: "ascending arm in arm the slope of the bank, [they] returned to the station" (5). Each is secure in his sense of himself as a good, hard-working man. Shortly thereafter, however, each considers the possibility of having to bury the other. Throughout the first part of the story, they remain polite on the surface. In the second part of the story, catalyzed by the murder and abduction of the men from their station and Gobila's tribe, their superficial friendship disintegrates. Conrad clearly reveals the reason for the difference in their regard for each other: "It was not the absolute and dumb solitude of the post that impressed them so much as an inarticulate feeling that something from within them was gone, something that worked for their safety, and had kept the wilderness from interfering with their hearts" (64). Whether that "something" is Gobila's favor, or the realization that they are truly isolated, or the discovery that their moral systems will accept the duplicity with which Makola arranges the slave trade, neither of the men is willing to continue extending the courtesy they originally expressed. Finally, they quarrel over a meaningless issue — whether or not to use sugar in their coffee — and reveal their true opinions of each other, using such phrases as "pot-bellied ass" (80), "scoundrel" (81), and "flabby, good-for-nothing civilian" (82). These characters are not significantly different; hence, Kayerts's confusion over his identity is entirely appropriate: "then he tried to imagine himself dead, and Carlier sitting in his chair watching him; and his attempt met with such unexpected success, that in a very few moments he became not at all sure who was dead and who was alive. This extraordinary achievement of his fancy startled him, however, and by a clever and timely effort of mind he saved himself just in time from becoming Carlier" (96). Indeed, readers may find it difficult to distinguish between Carlier and Kayerts throughout the story. This supports Conrad's suggestion that all men, given identical situations, are alike.

In his ironic statements, Conrad presents a pessimistic if realistic view of human beings and civilization. According to Conrad, civilization and progress are really means for hiding ineptitude. Commenting on his characters, Conrad writes, "they were two perfectly insignificant and incapable individuals, whose existence is only rendered possible through the high organization of civilized crowds" (5). He continues his remarks on society throughout the story, adding that "society, not from any tenderness, but because of its strange needs, had taken care of those two men, forbidding them all independent thought, all initiative, all departure from routine; and forbidding it under pain of death" (7). Civilization controls human beings in Conrad's society, particularly the white humans, rather than human beings commanding society. It is fitting, therefore, that the story should end with Kayerts's irreverent gesture toward the Managing Director.

Students should examine the contents of Parts I and II carefully. Why has Conrad made such a definite separation within his story? How do the events and details in Part I foreshadow and emphasize the events of Part II? Students might also compare Conrad's discussions about society and humanity with the thoughts and actions of the characters. Do the white characters significantly differ in their thoughts, actions, and principles from the black characters? Is Conrad condescending toward his characters? Students might also define "civilization" and "progress" according to their own experience, and then redefine them according to Conrad's illustration of them. In contrasting traditional notions of these terms with Conrad's, students may more clearly understand "An Outpost of Progress."

PERSPECTIVE

THOMAS MCCORMACK, *On the Problem of Teaching Theme* (p. 226)

As a writing assignment, ask students to analyze a character in Conrad's story (or any other story) using McCormack's questions about character on page 227:

For example, each character has a certain impact on us, the readers. To clarify how that impact is achieved, certainly notice what he [or she] says and does, what we're told about him [or her]; even ask crafty questions: What does he want or promise? What does he do to get it? What result does he cause? Why do we like or dislike him?

8. Style, Tone, and Irony

GABRIEL GARCÍA MÁRQUEZ, *A Very Old Man with Enormous Wings* (p. 234)

Students will immediately notice that something out of the ordinary is occurring in Gabriel García Márquez's "A Very Old Man with Enormous Wings." Márquez captures their belief in stages. The rain which has fallen for three days may seem unusual, but realistic; less conceivable are the crabs, so numerous inside the house that they have to be slaughtered with clubs and thrown back into the sea. Most unbelievable, and yet acceptable in the world of reality and absurdity that Márquez has created, is the presence of the very old man with enormous wings. No character questions his existence; in fact, the characters believe readily that the old man is an angel. Because they accept him, readers also are more willing to suspend their disbelief.

Although he is identified as a supernatural being, the old man seems so real and so human that readers are drawn into accepting his existence. The old man is bald, with very few teeth, and broken, dirty wings. He also smells like a human being rather than a celestial being: "seen close up he was much too human: he had an unbearable smell of the outdoors, the back side of his wings were strewn with parasites and his main feathers had been mistreated by terrestrial winds, and nothing about him measured up to the proud dignity of angels" (5). Angels are expected to perform miracles, and while this old man does so, his miracles produce unexpected results: "the few miracles attributed to the angel showed a certain mental disorder, like the blind man who didn't recover his sight but grew three new teeth, or the paralytic who didn't get to walk but almost won the lottery, and the leper whose sores sprouted sunflowers" (10). Whether or not the old man is an angel, he isn't shaping himself to conform to the people's expectations. Because he's so outrageously non-angelic in the traditional sense, he becomes a humorous figure.

Márquez reinforces the outrageous nature of his humor in this story with constant references to carnivals and the behavior associated with them. The angel provides the people with a chance to leave their "normal" existence behind and gawk. At sunrise on the day after the angel appears, Pelayo and Elisenda discover that their courtyard has become an arena: "they found the whole neighborhood in front of the chicken coop having fun with the angel, without the slightest reverence, tossing him things to eat through the openings in the wire as if he weren't a supernatural creature but a circus animal" (4). Pelayo and Elisenda have put him into the coop, equating him with the other feathered animals of their world. The neighbors are responding as they would to the caged animals in the zoo. All of the people in this story seem to snatch any opportunity to behave in extraordinary ways. Not only does a traveling carnival instantly appear to take advantage of the old man's popularity, but he loses his value as a curiosity because the spider woman at the carnival is more ready to discuss her deformity with all who pay to view her. She manipulates the crowd, while the old man seems to prefer his solitude. In a sense, he seems more angelic because he holds himself above the crude sensationalism of those around him.

Father Gonzaga debates whether or not the old man is an angel after he attempts to communicate with him. He also contributes to the underlying circus theme as he speaks to the angel-watchers: "He reminded them that the devil had the bad habit of making use of carnival tricks in order to confuse the unwary" (5). This is ironic: The old man is supposed to be an angel, yet the representative of organized religion cannot recognize him. Father Gonzaga fits the old man into his pre-established world view; he cannot expand that world view to admit the old man. Márquez pokes fun at organized religion in this story. Father Gonzaga cannot recognize this "angel" through his own spirituality. Instead, he must obey the instructions of some far-off human leader: "he promised to write a letter to his bishop so that the latter would write to his primate so that the latter would write to the Supreme Pontiff in order to get the final verdict from the highest courts" (5).

You might ask students to discuss if and how Márquez's presentation varies in its themes and concerns from stories written by American writers. You might also ask students to discuss fairy tale elements in the story — a straightforward explanation of fabulous events. Its happy ending, in which the angel's wings have regenerated enough to allow him to fly off, is one element conforming to the fairy tale tradition. Are there others? Are there elements that subvert this tradition?

TILLIE OLSEN, *I Stand Here Ironing* (p. 239)

This story, narrated in the first person by Emily's mother, records a mother's attempt to come to terms with several aspects of her relationship with her daughter: how the mother raised Emily, who Emily is now, why her teacher wants the mother to come in to talk about Emily. (The speaker in the second paragraph is never explicitly identified as Emily's teacher, but it is suggested again in paragraph 18 — "You must have seen it in her pantomimes" — and in paragraph 46, where the narrator recalls suggesting to Emily that she enter the school amateur show.)

Some students may initially think the narrator is a bad mother because she doesn't want to talk to her daughter's teacher, because she thinks there is nothing she can do to help her daughter at this late date. But is soon becomes painfully clear that the mother had no choice, for instance, about sending Emily away, and that when she did have choices, the ones she made were always well intentioned. This is a deeply moving story, and one in which the mother expresses a great deal of sorrow, but is is clear that the author sympathizes with both mother and daughter and is not trying to assign blame.

Emily was treated differently from her brothers and sisters for a number of reasons. First, she was the oldest; she was nursed and raised "with all the fierce rigidity of first motherhood" (6), her mother always doing everything exactly as the books and experts said she should. (By the time the later children came along, she had learned, the hard way, that sometimes the experts are wrong.) Second, Emily's father deserted her mother when Emily was just eight months old, and the child had first to be left with the woman downstairs and then sent to her father's family for more than a year. Third, Emily got the measles exactly when her sister Susan was born, and though Emily was very ill, she could not be comforted by her mother or even see the new baby because her disease was so contagious. After that she was sent away again, this time to a convalescent home. None of these things could have been helped, but they did contribute to the difficult, tense, unhappy environment in which she grew up. Emily's stepbrothers and stepsisters were all born later, when there was a little more money, their mother was older, and times were not quite so hard. Emily's talent for comedy is quite ironic, since she of all the children grew up with so little laughter.

The story's next-to-last paragraph provides a capsule version of most of what has come before, with one big difference: the tone here is cold rather than warm. In this paragraph the diction is much more straightforward, the sentence structure much more conventional than elsewhere in the story. There is no attempt to portray the way people really talk, the way life really is. The information appears almost in the form of an itemized list — as it would in some teacher's, doctor's, or social worker's notebook, to be transferred onto an official form. Emily's mother feels that these experts helped to do her daughter serious damage in the first place, and she's sure they are the last people who could help her now.

The mother's ironing suggests larger meanings. She has been a housewife all her life (except for a couple of menial jobs she was forced to take to support herself and her child), and she is in effect a housewife still. The suggestion here is not that there's anything wrong with being a housewife per se, but that, if she had it to do over again, the mother would live her life differently — and that she hopes her daughter *will* do so. Note the strain of optimism here, since Emily is nineteen when the story is being told — and, so far, has not repeated any of her mother's mistakes. The story ends with the mother's desperate hope that her daughter will know she is and can become "more than this dress on the ironing board, helpless before the iron." The narrator wants her daughter to know that she is not helpless, that she is not bound to the same life of drudgery and poverty that her mother led, that she can, and should, fight her way out.

MARK TWAIN, *The Story of the Bad Little Boy* (p. 245)

Twain's message here is that life as we live it, as it *really* happens, has nothing to do with life as depicted in books, Sunday school, or elsewhere. Not only are the bad not necessarily punished for their wrongdoings, but the good are often punished unjustly. (For example, the model, moral George Wilson gets thrashed for a theft the bad boy Jim committed.) More important, bad people often get rewarded for their wrongdoing. Students should have no trouble citing the story's next-to-last paragraph as an example of this: "and now he is the infernalest wickedest scoundrel in his native village, and is universally respected, and belongs to the legislature." "Nice guys finish last" (see question 7) is only the half of it; the rest is that thieves and murderers often finish first.

Twain's tone here becomes more and more sarcastic as he tells us not just about "the bad little boy" but also about the hypocritical society that simultaneously condemns and praises such boys. Society says people like Jim are bad and then turns around and elects them to public office. By contrasting his own cynical style with the mawkish one of Sunday-school books, Twain illustrates how ridiculous those books and attitudes really are. For example, have the class examine the first sentence in the story's second paragraph. The beginning of the sentence — "He didn't have any sick mother, either" — is vintage Twain, mocking everything from sentimentality to religion. The second half, though, could be straight out of a Sunday-school lesson: "a sick mother who was pious and had the consumption, and would be glad to lie down in the grave and be at rest but for the strong love she bore her boy, and the anxiety she felt that the world might be harsh and cold toward him when she was gone." Another typically cynical Twain statement can be found in paragraph 4: "Oh, no; he stole as many apples as he wanted and came down all right; and he was all ready for the dog, too, and knocked him endways with a brick when he came to tear him."

Examples of verbal irony also abound: consider the excerpt from the next-to-last paragraph quoted earlier, along with the narrator's statements "This Jim bore a charmed life — that must have been the way of it" (7) and "It was very strange — nothing like it ever happened in those mild little books with marbled backs, and with pictures in them of men with swallow-tailed coats and bell-crowned hats, and pantaloons that are short in the legs" (4).

PERSPECTIVE

MARK TWAIN, *The Art of Authorship* (p. 248)

Here Twain responds to a letter asking him to describe his writing process by saying that he can't. He believes that, at least in his case, writing is an unconscious and spontaneous process rather than a conscious and analytic one, and that the best way to learn to write is to keep doing it.

9. A Study of Two Authors: Nathaniel Hawthorne and Flannery O'Connor

NATHANIEL HAWTHORNE, *The Wives of the Dead* (p. 253)

Students may have more questions than answers about Nathaniel Hawthorne's "The Wives of the Dead." Certainly the final sentence of the story suggests possible double meanings with its ambiguous reference to "she." Are the husbands still alive, as the title of this story implies, with its emphasis on "wives" rather than "widows"? Are both women merely dreaming of their husbands' resurrections? Is Margaret's husband the only survivor? Has Mary only dreamed that her husband lives? In the process of answering these questions, students can examine the characterizations of the wives. In addition, they can be directed to possible interpretations of the story based on Hawthorne's use of light and dark imagery.

The characterizations of the wives of the dead, Mary and Margaret, are reflected in the plot, setting, and imagery of this story. Like Mary and Martha, the New Testament sisters whose brother Lazarus is raised from the dead by Jesus, these sisters mourn the deaths of the brothers who are their husbands. Mary is the quiet, pious sister, married to the sea-faring brother. Recovering first from her grief, Mary arranges the meal and the grace: "let us ask a blessing on that which is provided for us" (2). While she continues to grieve for her loss, she appears to accept her fate. Margaret, on the other hand, is fiery, rebellious, and unable to accept recent events either as her fate or God's will. "There is no blessing left for me, neither will I ask it" (4). Like her husband, who has gone to battle in Canada, Margaret fights against acceptance. The sisters' responses to their tragedies are mirrored by their behavior during the night. Mary soon falls asleep; Margaret "became more disturbed and feverish, in proportion as the night advanced with its deepest and stillest hours" (5). Later in the story, Margaret describes Mary's sleeping attitude: "Her face was turned partly inward to the pillow, and had been hidden there to weep; but a look of motionless contentment was now visible upon it, as if her heart, like a deep lake, had grown calm because its dead had sunk down so far within" (16). In a complementary passage, Mary later describes Margaret's repose: "Margaret lay in unquiet sleep, and the drapery was displaced around her; her young cheek was rosy-tinted, and her lips half opened in a vivid smile; an expression of joy, debarred its passage by her sealed eyelids, struggled forth like incense from the whole countenance" (26). In their conscious or unconscious behavior, Mary is associated with water, while Margaret is linked with fire.

The events of the night extend these associations with water and fire. Mary's messenger is the former suitor who makes his living along the shore: "A young man in a sailor's dress, wet as if he had come out of the depths of the sea, stood alone under the window" (19). Her response to Stephen's message is "a blessed flood of conviction" (26). The calls of Margaret's messenger, a local innkeeper, cause her to seize the lamp from the hearth. His appearance outside her house is not unlike her feverish wakefulness: "A lantern was reddening the front of the house, and melting its light in the neighboring puddles, while a deluge of darkness overwhelmed every other object" (9). Margaret's reaction to her messenger differs from Mary's: "Joy flashed in her heart, and lighted it up at once" (14). In this imagery, Margaret is like the lantern brightening the house; Mary can be linked to the nearby water.

Hawthorne relies heavily on imagery of light and darkness in this fairly short story. Ask students what they associate with "light" and "dark." Do the references to light and dark in this story uphold or conflict with their notions? Lights, fires, and illuminations constantly appear in "The Wives of the Dead." The fire burns in the main room. During the night, a lamp casts light into both bedrooms. The lamp provides the reader with a picture of the sisters' and brothers' unity: "The cold light of the lamp threw the shadows of the furniture up against the wall, stamping them immovably there, except when they were shaken by a sudden flicker of the flame. Two vacant arm-chairs were in their old position on opposite sides of the hearth . . . two humbler seats were near them, the true thrones of that little empire" (5). Both messengers are associated with light: Margaret's carries a lantern and Mary's stands in the moonlight, announcing that her husband will be home by daylight. Her belief in the messenger and the truth of his message is strongest when she can see him in the moonlight.

Darkness is also mentioned frequently in the story. The story begins in "The rainy twilight of an autumn day" (1), and continues throughout the night. Wherever light appears, darkness surrounds it, as in the innkeeper's contrast with the darkened street and the sailor's recurrent appearance and disappearance among the moonbeams and the shadows of other houses. In the sisters' house, the corners of their rooms are dark, and each sister's use of the lamp affects the other's physical and spiritual darkness.

As Hawthorne reminds us, "It is difficult to be convinced of the death of one whom we have deemed another self " (7). Are the messengers merely inventions of the sisters' imaginations? Is one a figment while the other exists? How are the windows and doors mysteriously opened and shut in this story? On perhaps a more tangible level, students might characterize the sisters' relationship to each other. Exactly how do their responses to the messengers differ? How might the sisters have responded if they had received each other's message? Because there are no definitive answers to these questions, students should find it easy to generate lively discussions of "The Wives of the Dead."

NATHANIEL HAWTHORNE, *Young Goodman Brown* (p. 258)

Brown's name conveys several meanings that can be determined *after* reading this story. This is a point worth stressing with students so they do not mistakenly assume that they should perceive the following meanings on a first reading. *Young* suggests the protagonist's innocent, simple nature at the beginning of the story, when he has an as yet untested, abstract faith in life. *Goodman,* in addition to being a seventeenth-century honorific somewhat like *mister,* takes on an ironic meaning when Brown meets the devil. *Brown* is a common name that perhaps serves to universalize this character's experience. If Hawthorne had chosen the name *White* or *Black,* he would have cast the protagonist in too absolute a moral role. *Gray* would do, but *Brown* has the additional advantage of associating the protagonist with the forest, particularly in the fall, an appropriate season for the story's movement from innocence to experience.

The opening paragraphs provide important contrasts between the village and the forest. The village represents the safe, predictable landscape of home, associated with light, faith, goodness, and community. In paragraph 8 the forest is dreary, dark, gloomy, narrow, and threatening; it represents a moral wilderness in which skepticism and evil flourish.

Brown journeys into the forest to meet the devil. No specific reason is given for the journey, but most of us can understand Eve's curiosity about biting into the apple. Brown assumes that he will be able to cling to "Faith" after his encounter with the devil (although students may never have heard of this story, most will grasp its allegorical nature very quickly). But of course Brown turns out to be wrong, because when he sees that the rest of the community — from all the respectable deacons, selectmen, and religious leaders to his family and beloved Faith — share the impulses he has acted on, his faith is shattered.

We know that Brown's meeting is with a supernatural figure because the old man explains that he had been in Boston only fifteen minutes before his meeting in the forest outside Salem village. His devilish nature is conveyed by his serpentine staff; indeed, he even sits under "an old tree" (10) that suggests the tree of knowledge in Genesis. We don't have to believe, however, that Brown has a literal encounter with the devil. Hawthorne tells us that the staff's wriggling like a snake probably was only an "ocular deception" (13). This kind of calculated ambiguity is used a number of times in the story to accommodate readers who are wary of supernatural events and prefer "reality" in their fiction.

Students should be asked to locate other instances of ambiguity — such as Faith's ribbons and the question at the end concerning whether Brown simply dreamed the entire sequence of events. It seems that the answer to this question doesn't really matter because in the final paragraph Hawthorne dismisses such questions and instead emphasizes the terrible results of Brown's *belief* that he has been betrayed by everyone in the community. Brown's life is ruined; he becomes as stern and dark as the moral wilderness he abhors. Because he turned away from life and lost faith, "his dying hour was gloom." There is no absolute evidence either to relieve the community of responsibility for its involvement with evil or to pronounce it innocent. (A reader can, however, draw on Hawthorne's other works to demonstrate that he viewed humankind as neither wholly corrupt nor perfect; see, for example "The Birthmark.")

Even if Faith has some knowledge of evil or is tempted by it, that does not mean that "evil is the nature of mankind" (65) as the devil (not Hawthorne) falsely claims. When she joyfully meets her husband on the village street, Hawthorne paints on Faith's face no ironic smile, which would indicate hypocrisy or deception. And she has her pink ribbons. There is no actual reason for Brown to shrink "from the bosom of Faith" (72). He does so because he refuses to tolerate any kind of ambiguity. He is a moral absolutist who mistakenly accepts the devil's view of humanity. In a psychological sense his rejection of the world may be seen as a projection of his own feelings of guilt, and so he repudiates all trust, love, and especially faith, because he now sees faith as a satanic joke.

Hawthorne's built-in ambiguities in "Young Goodman Brown" have encouraged many readings of the story. (See Frederick Crews's "A Psychological Reading of 'Young Goodman Brown'" on p. 295.) For a convenient sample of twelve different readings see Thomas E. Connolly, ed., *Nathaniel Hawthorne: Young Goodman Brown* (Columbus, Ohio: Merrill, 1968). If a half dozen students are asked to read and summarize varying interpretations, the class will have an opportunity to debate the story in detail and develop an idea of what makes one interpretation more valid than another. It's also useful for them to realize that critics can disagree.

NATHANIEL HAWTHORNE, *The Birthmark* (p. 268)

Aylmer (a variant of *Elmer,* meaning "noble") in this story is neither evil nor mad. An eighteenth-century scientist, he embodies the period's devotion to science and reason. However, his studies supersede all else in his life; they are his first love — even before his wife. His choice of science over love identifies him as the kind of Hawthorne character who displays an imbalance of head and heart. His intellect usurps his common sense and feelings. He loses sight of Georgiana's humanity in his monomaniacal quest to achieve an ideal perfection in her person.

Aylmer is shocked by Georgiana's birthmark because he sees it as a "visible mark of earthly imperfection" (paragraph 5). To him the "crimson hand" (a sign perhaps that humankind's fallen nature is imprinted by the devil [original sin] on all human beings) symbolizes the "fatal flaw of humanity" and is a sign of mortality, "toil and pain" (8). This extreme perspective differs from the more normal views of the birthmark in paragraph 7.

Georgiana (whose name is appropriately associated with the earthy rather than the ideal) loves her husband so completely that she is willing to risk her life to win his approval. Her feelings serve as a foil to his obsessive efforts to perfect her; she loves him despite his willingness to dehumanize her. She is unaware of his blasphemous pride, which the reader sees clearly: "what will be my triumph when I shall have corrected what Nature left imperfect in her fairest work!" (19). Georgiana, like many nineteenth-century female characters, is passive and incapable of changing the course of events that will inevitably destroy her. She becomes a martyr to her love for Aylmer. Students are likely to see her as hopelessly weak rather than nearly perfect. When Georgiana reads Aylmer's journal and observes that "his most splendid successes were almost invariably failures, if compared with the ideal at which he aimed" (51), many readers wonder why this and other grim foreshadowings about the nature of his work (see 32–37) do not alarm her. Hawthorne, however, stresses her loyal devotion to her husband more as a virtue than as a weakness.

Aminadab is also an obvious foil to Aylmer. His name spelled backward is, interestingly enough, *bad anima* (bad soul or life principle). He represents the opposite of Aylmer's aspirations for the ideal: "he seemed to represent man's physical nature." His physical features — his grimy, shaggy, low stature and "indescribable earthiness" — are in stark contrast to Aylmer's "slender figure, and pale, intellectual face," which make him "a type of the spiritual element" (25). Aminadab's "smoky aspect" is the result of his tending Aylmer's "hot and feverish" furnace, which seems demonic and evokes the destructive nature of Aylmer's efforts to spiritualize matter (57).

Although Aylmer's motives are noble, his egotism blinds him to a central fact that his science ignores, for, according to Hawthorne, there can be no such thing as mortal perfection. The story's theme argues that the nature of mortal existence necessarily means humanity's "liability to sin, sorrow, decay, and death" (8). For Hawthorne, no science can change that fact of life. As soon as the birthmark fades from Georgiana's face, her life fades, because mortality and perfection do not coexist. Aylmer lacks the profound wisdom to embrace the human condition. Like Young Goodman Brown, he fails to accept the terms on which life offers itself.

Students may find provocative a discussion (or writing assignment) about this story as a modern version of our obsession with attaining physical perfection, through exercise, cosmetic surgery, or some other means. Hawthorne's theme of human imperfection is largely a philosophical issue, but it can also be addressed through psychological and sociological perspectives.

Judith Fetterley offers "A Feminist Reading of 'The Birthmark'" on page 297.

NATHANIEL HAWTHORNE, *The Minister's Black Veil* (p. 279)

Like "The Wives of the Dead," Nathaniel Hawthorne's "The Minister's Black Veil" presents readers with unanswerable questions: Why does the minister wear the black veil? What does the veil represent? A first-person point of view would destroy the ambiguity, and therefore the intellectual challenge, of the tale. If Mr. Hooper told his congregation and Hawthorne's readers why he made the choice to wear the veil, it is likely that neither group would be affected by his action. Because Mr. Hooper does not reveal his motivation, students are forced to propose their own theories for it.

If, as Edgar Allan Poe and other critics have suggested, Mr. Hooper wears the veil as a penance for a specific sin, possibly in connection with the young woman whose funeral he conducts, he exacts a heavy toll from his parishioners. From the first moment he appears wearing the veil, "two folds of crape, which entirely concealed his features, except the mouth and chin, but probably did not intercept his sight, farther than to give a darkened aspect to all living and inanimate things" (6), he casts a cloud upon his parishioners' faces and spirits. They cannot return his greeting. The traditional atmosphere of the church is disrupted by the congregation's horror, and after church many of Mr. Hooper's listeners reverse their normally decorous behavior to gawk or gossip: "Some talked loudly, and profaned the Sabbath-day with ostentatious laughter" (13). Later the same day, even the corpse in the coffin shudders as Mr. Hooper bends over it, though a black veil is appropriate for the occasion. The minister then officiates at a wedding, but "the same horrible black veil which had added deeper gloom to the funeral . . . could portend nothing but evil to the wedding" (22). The groom shivers, and the bride is so pale that she is associated with the dead maiden of the earlier funeral. These are short-term effects of the minister's decision to wear the black veil; a long-term effect of it on his parishioners is the breakdown of his communication with them. The good people of his church are accustomed to guiding him in church matters as well as to being led by him: "Hitherto, whenever there appeared the slightest call for such interference, he had never lacked advisors, nor shown himself averse to be guided by their judgment" (24). Yet when they approach him to discuss his reason for wearing the veil and call his attention to its adverse effect on the church, they are unable to reach him. Not even his wife-to-be, Elizabeth, can convince him to remove his mask, even for a moment. Though she is noted for her "calm energy" (25) and "firmer character than his own" (36), she too is affected by the veil. "But in an instant, as it were, a new feeling took the place of sorrow: her eyes were fixed insensibly on the black veil, when, like a sudden twilight in the air, its terrors fell around her" (36). If the minister dons the black veil as a penance for his unknown sin, the fear, distrust, and isolation it inspires are greater evils which seem to defeat his purpose.

If Mr. Hooper dons the black veil to symbolize the sins of his secretive flock, he exacts a heavier toll upon himself. On the first Sunday of its appearance, the veil isolates him not only from his parishioners but from God: "it threw its obscurity between him and the holy page, as he read the Scriptures; and while he prayed, the veil lay heavily on his uplifted countenance" (10). God cannot reach him, and his congregation chooses to avoid him. "None, as on former occasions, aspired to the honor of walking by their pastor's side. Old Squire Saunders, doubtless by an accidental lapse of memory, neglected to invite Mr. Hooper to his table, where the good clergyman had been wont to bless the food, almost every Sunday since his settlement" (13). As he continues to wear the veil, the people not only avoid him but express their opinions of him in bewilderment and scorn: "Our parson has gone mad!" (9); "it was reckoned merely an eccentric whim" (44); "But with the multitude, good Mr. Hooper was irreparably a bugbear" (44). Even though he becomes a renowned speaker, and people come from great distances to hear his church services, they come for dubious, clearly not religious, reasons: "with the mere idle purpose of gazing at his figure, because it was forbidden them to behold his face" (46). The people in his village go out of their way to avoid him in the streets, while children flee at his approach. Far from being a holy man, he has become a monster. His personal life is in no better condition after his bride-to-be leaves him. He himself is frightened at his reflection in the mirror. In the end, the black veil has cost him his link with humanity: "it had separated him from cheerful brotherhood and woman's love, and kept him in that saddest of all prisons, his own heart" (47). Mr. Hooper addresses this awful personal cost on his deathbed when he cries, "Why do you tremble at me alone? . . . Tremble also at each other" (58). This is his final intimation that the wearing of the veil is connected with his parishioners' spiritual welfare.

One other possible motive is a self-righteous and total obsession with wearing the black veil — he is unable to give it up for his lover, his congregation, or his God. He speaks on his deathbed of the supposed meaning of the veil, and of man's fundamental tendency to hide sins. If he is purely self-motivated, this deathbed speech is hypocritical. He has worn the black veil at an inestimable cost.

Hawthorne suggests that at the funeral over which Mr. Hooper presides, the veil is "an appropriate emblem" (18). Does Mr. Hooper's life-long appearance in the veil suggest an on-going funeral for the town's spirituality? What is the meaning of the minister's constant smile? Is it genuine, ironic, or the sign of a crazed intellect? In what real-life situations do people wear veils? How does Mr. Hooper's application of the black crape conform to or contrast with these traditional uses? As students attempt to answer these questions, ask them to explain how "The Minister's Black Veil" is, as Hawthorne claims, a parable. Students' definitions of the term may lead them to their own answers to these questions and interpretations of the story.

PERSPECTIVES ON HAWTHORNE

Hawthorne on Solitude (p. 289)

Students can use this letter to get a sense of how Hawthorne worried about his self-imposed solitude and how he used "nothing but thin air to concoct my stories." Ask students if tensions in the letter are manifested in any of the Hawthorne stories included in this chapter.

EDGAR ALLAN POE, *On a Story's Single Effect* (p. 290)

Poe's pronouncements about the nature of the short story and how it should be written are worth having students test, in both his work and others'. Probably students will prefer either Poe's or O'Connor's method of short story writing (see "O'Connor on Theme and Symbol" [p. 356]), depending on their temperaments. Those inclined to be analytic will find Poe more convincing, while those who cultivate their intuitions will side with O'Connor. This can lead to a discussion of how a writer's personality inevitably informs his or her work.

Hawthorne on the Power of the Writer's Imagination (p. 291)

The light of a writer's imagination cast on familiar objects and events changes our perceptions of things. Good writing causes us to encounter not merely observable facts but also meanings supplied by the author. Hawthorne's purposes as a writer go beyond a realistic presentation of the world; he sought to invest his work with his own reading of "the truth of the human heart."

HERMAN MELVILLE, *On Nathaniel Hawthorne's Tragic Vision* (p. 292)

Melville admired Hawthorne's exploration of the darker side of human potential. He dedicated *Moby-Dick* to Hawthorne because he recognized in him a kindred spirit willing to risk an outward-bound voyage, even if it meant the possibility of being lost.

Hawthorne on His Short Stories (p. 293)

Hawthorne seems a bit nervous and uncertain about characterizing his stories because he anticipates his public's objection to their ambiguities and sometimes puzzling themes. He is aware that a weird tale such as "The Minister's Black Veil" is radically different from the popular sunny magazine sketches of robust American life contemporary to it.

HYATT H. WAGGONER, *Hawthorne's Style* (p. 294)

Waggoner is correct in noting that the themes Hawthorne offers are "modern." The inner conflicts his characters experience carry with them the kind of social and psychological implications that continue to fascinate and trouble twentieth-century readers. Hawthorne's style, however, is quite remote from us. Ask students to rewrite a paragraph by Hawthorne in the style of Hemingway or one of the authors in the Album of Contemporary Stories.

FLANNERY O'CONNOR, *Good Country People* (p. 302)

The central conflict in this story is between Hulga, who believes herself to be vastly superior to everyone around her, and the Bible salesman, Manley Pointer, whom Hulga and her mother at first take to be simple, naive "good country people." Hulga wants to seduce Pointer to shatter his alleged innocence, both physical and spiritual. She wants him to believe in nothing, as she does. Her initial impulse is mean spirited, but even her first thoughts of seducing him include a fantasy of being with him once she has enlightened him about her version of the truth. "She imagined that she took his remorse in hand and changed it into a deeper understanding of life. She took all his shame away and turned it into something useful" (paragraph 91). Despite her facade of nastiness, which she uses as a sort of defense mechanism, Hulga really does want warmth, respect, admiration, and even love. She begins to recognize these feelings in herself, ironically, as Pointer is convincing her to show him her artificial leg. She is moved by what she perceives to be his innocence, which has enabled him (she thinks) to see the truth about her: that she "ain't like anybody else" (128).

But the joke is on Hulga. No sooner does Pointer get his hands on her leg than all his apparent innocence and tenderness disappear. It was the leg he wanted all along, for his collection; the sexual activity would have been a nice fringe benefit, but he is perfectly willing to leave without it. When Hulga asks him, in paragraph 136, "aren't you just good country people?" she is, ironically, clinging to the very values that she previously denounced and satirized. She is forced to acknowledge that civility and common decency (which Pointer has flouted, by taking her leg) do matter. She has been deceiving herself by pretending that these things are dispensable, that she does not need affection, and that she does not believe in, or need to believe in, anything. It has taken someone more cynical and evil than herself to make her aware of the truth.

Hulga now realizes that, compared with Pointer, she is the innocent one. O'Connor's suggestion is that Hulga will soon get the same message we do from Pointer's last words: the result of "believing in nothing" is the kind of depravity of spirit Pointer exhibits, and if she wants to save herself from that she'd better start believing.

Hulga's two names represent her inner conflict between everything she is and everything she is repressing. The name *Joy,* of course, is just another of her mother's empty clichés, so she changes it to Hulga (which suggests some combination of the words *ugly, huge,* and *hulk*). By denying the "nice" name her mother gave her, she can deny the "niceness" in herself. She can, in fact, create a new self: hostile, angry, and abusive — all to hide the pain she feels because of what she is repressing. Mrs. Hopewell's name emphasizes the shallowness of her beliefs that "nothing is perfect" (11) and that "people who looked on the bright side of things would be beautiful even if they were not" (17). And Mrs. Freeman's name suggests that she is free in a way that both Joy and her mother are not.

Mrs. Freeman sees through Hulga as her mother can't; direct the class to paragraph 16, where we learn that Mrs. Freeman calls the girl "Hulga" rather than "Joy." "Mrs. Freeman's relish for using the name only irritated [Hulga]. It was as if Mrs. Freeman's beady steel-pointed eyes had penetrated far enough behind her face to reach some secret fact." This secret fact is that, as the author says in "O'Connor on Theme and Symbol" (p. 356), "there is a wooden part of [Hulga's] soul that corresponds to her wooden leg." Mrs. Freeman's statement at the story's end, "Some can't be that simple," suggests that she has seen through the Bible salesman as well. That Mrs. Hopewell repeatedly refers to Mrs. Freeman with condescension as "good country people" becomes increasingly ironic in light of the fact that Mrs. Freeman is much smarter and a much better judge of human nature than either her employer or her employer's daughter.

The older women are introduced before Hulga so that her character can be developed in relation to theirs. By the time Hulga appears, we are as alienated by her mother's insipid thoughts and conversation as Hulga is, so we can empathize with the girl somewhat. The last two paragraphs of the story depict an unchanged, vapidly optimistic Mrs. Hopewell, who knows nothing of what has gone on between Hulga and Pointer in the barn. Her cheerful ignorance contrasts sharply with Hulga's "churning face" and emotions in the preceding paragraph; it is Mrs. Hopewell who has the most to learn.

The limited omniscient point of view lets O'Connor alternate between Mrs. Hopewell's and Hulga's perspectives, giving us access to the actions and thoughts of both characters and allowing us to make informed judgments that we would not be able to make if we were limited to Hulga's point of view.

FLANNERY O'CONNOR, *Everything That Rises Must Converge* (p. 316)

This story opens in what "had been a fashionable neighborhood forty years ago" (paragraph 5) and moves to a bus Julian's mother would not ride "by herself at night since they had been integrated" (1). Julian and his mother's destination is the Y, where very few members "arrived in hat and gloves and . . . had a son who had been to college" (9). The scene is the post-World War II South, where O'Connor lived and set almost all her work, work often concerned with the social and economic change in the region.

Julian's mother cannot adjust to or accept this new world, so she clings to her past, in which everyone had his or her place and knew what it was — a world in which she knew who she was. Although she claims to know who she is now, the life-style and circumstances she grew up with no longer exist.

For all his claims to liberality, Julian can't adjust either. His great-great-grandfather's house

> remained in his mind as his mother had known it. It appeared in his dreams regularly.
> . . . It occurred to him that it was he, not [his mother], who could have appreciated
> it. He preferred its threadbare elegance to anything he could name and it was because
> of it that all the neighborhoods they had lived in had been a torment to him. (31)

Julian's inability to recognize his attachment to the past is symptomatic of his overwhelming lack of self-knowledge; he doesn't realize that his contempt for his mother's views reveals his own prejudices or that he is completely dependent on his mother, emotionally and financially. Julian has no trouble observing that "everything that gave [his mother] pleasure was small and depressed him" (3), but he doesn't realize that the only thing that gives him pleasure is tormenting his mother — an impulse which is certainly small and depressing.

Julian wants to teach his mother that the genteel, gracious world she grew up in no longer exists, that "knowing who you are is good for one generation only" (17), that it is no longer acceptable to coo over little black children and offer them pennies, that Negroes are an integral, inescapable part of the world she lives in now, and that she had better learn to accept them. When the black woman boards the bus wearing the hat his mother thought was unique, Julian gleefully interprets this as a made-to-order lesson in race relations; this woman not only could afford the same extravagance his mother did but she could parade it on the bus. Julian's triumphant attitude belies his real feelings about blacks; he is not interested in them as people (if he were he might not have found it so difficult to make friends with them); he is interested in them only insofar as he can use them to upset his mother. Julian mistreats his mother in an attempt to distance himself from everything she stands for, everything he claims to hate.

Julian's mother's stroke is foreshadowed by several signals, all of which Julian is too wrapped up in his fantasies to see. In paragraph 71 Julian observes that his mother's "eyes retained their battered look. Her face seemed to be unnaturally red, as if her blood pressure had risen." In paragraph 74 Julian fantasizes about bringing home "some distinguished Negro professor or lawyer," but realizes that his mother's "blood pressure would rise to 300. He could not push her to the extent of making her have a stroke." In paragraph 79 Julian's mother's "face seemed almost gray and there was a look of dull recognition in her eyes," and in paragraph 83 her "mouth began to twitch slightly at one corner."

The black woman knocks Julian's mother down because Julian's mother had been condescending to her and her son ever since they boarded the bus. This action can also be seen as one manifestation of the story's title; the blacks have been rising, and this physical contact can be seen as a convergence of whites and blacks.

The most common interpretation of the title, however, traces it to its source: the writings of Pierre Teilhard de Chardin, a French Jesuit philosopher whose work O'Connor had been reading. Many critics agree with the following interpretation:

> Since it is Julian, not the Negro mother, who is the main character, it is his rising and
> converging which is central. . . . Julian's calamity will eventually lead, so all the
> evidence indicates, to "growth of consciousness," to raised sight, to a risen spirit.
> According to Teilhard de Chardin, growth toward unity with others is the spiritual
> direction of evolution and is a process to which those with "expanded consciousness"
> contribute. It is, moreover, the true end of man. . . . In so far as Julian is able to . . .
> [obviate] the necessity of belittling others in order to enhance the value of the self, to
> this extent will it be possible for him to attain personhood, a "true ego" capable of
> proper self-love and proper love of others. The capacity to develop such an ego is
> the psychological equivalent of the Christian's faith in man's ability to be radically
> altered by grace. (Peter M. Browning, Jr., *Flannery O'Connor* [Carbondale: Southern
> Illinois University Press, 1974], 107–108)

Julian, of course, is not conscious of any of this at the story's end. He is only aware suddenly, piercingly, of how much he really does love and need his mother — and this awareness does, for him, constitute an expanded consciousness.

FLANNERY O'CONNOR, *Revelation* (p. 327)

Mrs. Turpin in this story has much in common with Julian's mother in "Everything That Rises Must Converge." As a member of "the home-and-land owner" class, she believes herself to be superior to "niggers," "white-trash," and mere "home-owners" (paragraph 24). She takes pride in her position in the community, and, far worse in O'Connor's credo, Mrs. Turpin takes pride in what she perceives to be her privileged position in relation to God. In paragraph 74 she thinks, "He had not made her a nigger or white-trash or ugly! He had made her herself and given her a little of everything. Jesus, thank you! she said. Thank you thank you thank you!" She believes that she was singled out to have this high station, along with her other virtues. In other words, she believes that she is saved, and has nothing to worry about on Judgment Day. The gospel music on the radio in the doctor's office adds an extra ironic twist. Note, in paragraph 21, that Mrs. Turpin can supply the song's "last line mentally"; this is a gesture of routine rather than one that comes from the heart. Mrs. Turpin takes God and his mercy for granted; she might as well be singing along with a toothpaste commercial.

Among the signals Mrs. Turpin misses but we comprehend is the parallel between the doctor's waiting room and Mrs. Turpin's pig parlor. A close reading of paragraphs 173–181 will reveal that Mrs. Turpin sees the hogs as interchangeable rather than individuals. She is unable, however, to make the connection to the group of people in the doctor's office, or to humanity in general — which she still, this late in the story, insists on dividing into classes. It is in this context, too, that we understand Mrs. Turpin's hired woman's comment "You just had you a little fall" (147). It suggests that she has fallen from God's grace, at least in part because she thought she could earn and control it.

In paragraphs 178–186 Mrs. Turpin is addressing God; her anger and confusion stem from the fact that she really does believe herself to be a good person; it is not until the end of the story that she realizes her prideful hypocrisy. So at this point she feels that the message that she is a warthog from Hell is unwarranted, that God has tricked her somehow and is being cruel and unfair. The truth is revealed to her in the story's last two paragraphs, when "a visionary light settled in her eyes" (191). According to Frederick Asals, the "abysmal" knowledge Mrs. Turpin receives is that "those like herself, who had possessed 'good order and common sense and respectable behavior,' who had been blessed with a 'God-given wit,' discover that although these gifts are apparently their worldly responsibility, they have no final value in themselves." But the message is also "life-giving," or at least has the potential to be so:

> The visionary procession of "Revelation" clearly carried into eternity . . . the purifying action of the fire itself. Indeed . . . the imaginary fire in O'Connor's fiction . . . is most often purgatorial . . . and what it signals is the infliction of a searing grace, the onset of a saving pain. (Frederick Asals, *Flannery O'Connor: The Imagination of Extremity* [Athens: University of Georgia Press, 1982], 225–226)

We see that Mrs. Turpin has at least a chance for redemption, although there will be a high price to pay.

Mary Grace attacks Mrs. Turpin partly because she is a messenger from God, partly because she is a lunatic, and partly, we suspect, because she recognizes (perhaps through her God-given vision as a lunatic) Mrs. Turpin for the hypocrite she is. Mary Grace's name, of course, suggests redemption. Because she is ugly and nasty, Mrs. Turpin feels superior to her, so it is fitting that Mary Grace deliver the divine message: that Mrs. Turpin might as well be a warthog from Hell for all the good her "virtues" will do her on Judgment Day. Further irony comes from the title of Mary Grace's textbook; in O'Connor's Catholic vision, human development can't be studied, or controlled, by humans; it is all in the hands of God. (If it could be controlled, why would the little boy have an ulcer? Why would Mary Grace be a lunatic?)

The humor in this story (as well as in the rest of O'Connor's work) is bitter, but it helps to cut the pain of the characters by introducing a measure of buoyancy, a light at the end of the tunnel. O'Connor's is a tragicomic vision; she recognized that while humanity's folly is great, it is also funny. But humor, in literature and in life, has always operated as a defense mechanism, to help people bear their trials and tragedies. This is one of the reasons O'Connor's work resonates even for readers with no religious faith. (See question 3 after "O'Connor on the Use of Exaggeration and Distortion" [p. 356]). Humor is universal, as are O'Connor's concerns with hypocrisy and truth.

Dorothy T. McFarland offers "A Formalist Reading of 'Revelation'" on page 359.

FLANNERY O'CONNOR, *A Good Man Is Hard to Find* (p. 342)

This story may initially puzzle students. It certainly defies easy interpretation. As they analyze the grandmother's and the Misfit's characters, they may understand more of the story, but even after discussion, students might have more questions than answers.

At the beginning of the story, the grandmother dwells on the past. Her manners and attire are lady-like: "the grandmother had on a navy blue straw sailor hat with a bunch of white violets on the brim and a navy blue dress with a small white dot in the print. Her collars and cuffs were white organdy trimmed with lace and at her neckline she had pinned a purple spray of cloth violets containing a sachet" (12). She is a hard contrast to the mother, a young woman in slacks who represents contemporary woman, and the rude granddaughter, June Star, the woman of the future. The grandmother's stories, about former beaus, lost opportunities, and secret panels in houses long gone, emphasize her preoccupation with the past. Even her humor involves the past: "'Where's the plantation?' John Wesley asked. 'Gone with the Wind,' said the grandmother. 'Ha. Ha'" (23–24). She seems incapable of accepting the present or preparing for the future. She can only focus on her personal affairs and desires.

The Misfit is striking because he forces the grandmother beyond her obsession with herself and her past. As soon as she sees him, she focuses on identifying him. Then, trying to save herself and her family, she attempts to convince him that he *is* (note present tense) a good man. The Misfit and the grandmother are similar in one sense: he too dwells on his past. His grievances about his criminal record highlight his human past, and his observations about Jesus reflect a more universal human past. After hearing his "confession," the grandmother attempts to preserve both of their futures by "saving" the Misfit: "If you would pray . . . Jesus would help you" (118). Even though the Misfit refuses her help, they are both shaken out of their selfish memories. The grandmother becomes a more Christian woman because of her encounter with the Misfit. In truth, as the Misfit explains, "She would of been a good woman, . . . if it had been somebody there to shoot her every minute of her life" (140). Jesus taught the people by his good example and his raising of the dead; the Misfit enlightens the woman by his evil example and his execution of her.

This story obviously foreshadows its violent ending by its constant references to death in the plot, the dialogue, and the setting. The grandmother dresses up for the journey so that if she is in an accident, "anyone seeing her dead on the highway would know at once that she was a lady" (12). The last city that the family drives through is Toombsboro. The Misfit and his henchmen drive a car associated with funerals: "a big black battered hearse-like automobile" (70). Is the Misfit the Death the story foreshadows, or is O'Connor simply leading up to the deaths of the family?

Does "A Good Man Is Hard to Find" seem like a genuine story, or is the plot too coincidental? Are the characters and events believable? The power of surface appearances is constantly emphasized: the old woman is a lady because of the way she dresses; she recognizes the Misfit as one of her children only after he dons the shirt worn previously by Bailey Boy. Why does O'Connor call attention to these surface appearances and their effects? If this story is an allegory, what do the Misfit and the grandmother (for whom other, more specific names are never indicated) represent? What is the effect of the epigram at the beginning of the story? It may merely warn the reader about the journey this family is making; there may, however, be added significance to the source and the religious nature of its message. What might the dragon represent?

Students may be able to make meaningful connections between this story and Faulkner's "Barn Burning" (p. 66). What kind of people survive and prevail at the ends of these stories? Is there a distinctly Southern flavor to them? How might O'Connor have been influenced by Faulkner?

PERSPECTIVES ON O'CONNOR

O'Connor on Faith (p. 354)

At the end of "Good Country People" and "Everything That Rises Must Converge," Hulga and Julian each appear to be likely candidates to "cherish the world at the same time [they] struggle to endure it." Ask the students to explain how and why this change comes about.

O'Connor on the Materials of Fiction (p. 354)

Passages that appeal through the senses, that dwell on "those concrete details of life that make actual the mystery of our position on earth" abound in O'Connor's stories. Some examples you might cite, or direct the class to, include the descriptions of Mrs. Freeman's facial expressions in the first paragraph of "Good Country People"; Hulga's appreciation of the sound of her own name in "Good Country People" (16); Hulga's perceptions of taste and touch in paragraph 113, when she and Pointer are kissing in the loft; Julian's descriptions of the huge black woman in "Everything That Rises Must Converge" (77 and 102); Mrs. Turpin's visual perceptions immediately after being struck by Mary Grace's book in "Revelation" (102); the passage describing the road supposedly leading to the house with the secret panel in "A Good Man Is Hard to Find" (60).

O'Connor on the Use of Exaggeration and Distortion (p. 355)

The theft of Hulga's leg, the death of Julian's mother, and Mrs. Turpin's vision can all be seen as events or actions that purify the main characters.

For a specific response as to whether O'Connor's stories have anything to offer a reader without religious faith see the comments in the last paragraph of this manual's entry for "Revelation" (p. 37).

O'Connor on Theme and Symbol (p. 356)

Ask students to consider the hogs in "Revelation" as objects that accumulate meaning through the story.

CLAIRE KAHANE, *The Function of Violence in O'Connor's Fiction* (p. 358)

Mrs. Turpin in "Revelation" is a good example of a character transformed through a divine influence. For further discussion of her transformation, see the individual entry for "Revelation."

10. A Collection of Stories

TONI CADE BAMBARA, *The Lesson* (p. 364)

"So I deal in straight-up fiction myself, 'cause I value my family and friends, and mostly 'cause I lie a lot anyway." Toni Cade Bambara's "straight-up fiction" has been collected in *Gorilla, My Love* (1972) and *The Sea Birds Are Still Alive* (1977), and in 1980 she published her first novel, *The Salt Eaters*. A number of her screenplays have been produced, including "Zora" (1971), "The Johnson Girls" (1972), "Epitaph for Willie" (1982), "Tar Baby" (1984), "The Bombing of Osage" (winner of the 1986 Best Documentary Award from the Pennsylvania Association of Broadcasters and a Documentary Award from the National Black Programming Consortium), and "Cecil B. Moore: Master Tactician of Direct Action" (1987). Born in New York City in 1939, Bambara graduated from Queens College in 1959, studied at the University of Florence and the École de Mime Étienne Decroux in Paris and New York between 1961 and 1963, and earned her M.A. from City College, New York, in 1964. She has also studied dance, linguistics, and filmmaking. Her working life demonstrates similar variety: Bambara has been employed by the New York State Department of Welfare, directed recreation programs in the psychiatry department of Metropolitan Hospital, New York City, served as program director of Colony House Community Center, New York City, and taught at various colleges and universities, including Rutgers University and Spelman College.

The title is a good way to start discussion of this story: What is the lesson Miss Moore is trying to teach Sylvia (the narrator) and her friends? Is she successful?

Miss Moore is trying to get her charges to see that they live in "a society . . . in which some people can spend on a toy what it would cost to feed a family of six or seven" (paragraph 50), and that, in Sylvia's words, "poor people have to wake up and demand their share of the pie" (44). But despite Sylvia's ability to paraphrase Miss Moore's lecture, it is clear she hasn't completely taken it in when she goes on to say, "Don't none of us know what kind of pie she talking about in the first damn place." Miss Moore has, however, had some success: Sugar provides her with precisely the answer she was hoping to hear: "You know, Miss Moore, I don't think all of us here put together eat in a year what that sailboat costs. . . . This is not much of a democracy if you ask me. Equal chance to pursue happiness means an equal crack at the dough, don't it?" (49 and 51).

Still, the fact that Miss Moore can sense Sylvia's anger assures her that at least some of her point has gotten across. We (the readers) can sense it too, when Sylvia thinks things such as "I sure want to punch somebody in the mouth" (41), "Who are these people that spend that much for performing clowns and $1000 for toy sailboats? What kinda work they do and how they live and how come we ain't in on it?" (44), and finally "I'm going . . . to think this day through. . . . Ain't nobody gonna beat me at nuthin" (58).

Ask the class what they think the last line of the story means. Does Sylvia think Sugar is smarter than she is because Sugar knew the answer to Miss Moore's question and she didn't? Could the "nobody" in that line refer to anyone other than Sugar?

Sylvia is annoyed and feels betrayed partly because Sugar is suddenly playing into the student/teacher game Miss Moore creates on these occasions, which the kids all usually hate; Sylvia feels Sugar shouldn't be giving Miss Moore the time of day. But Sylvia is also unhappy because to identify the problem (the unequal distribution of wealth), as Sugar has done, is to admit that there *is* a problem — and this is something Sylvia hasn't come to terms with. We know this from her earlier comments about Miss Moore's lecture: "And then she gets to the part about we all poor and live in the slums, which I don't feature" (3). So the last line of the story refers not only to Sugar but to Sylvia's position (and that of black people in general) in society.

Clearly Bambara intends this story to be instructive to her readers as well as to the children in Miss Moore's charge. It is not easy to make a social comment of this nature without sounding preachy; how does she manage it?

Humor is one of the hallmarks of Bambara's style, and the accuracy with which she renders her characters' speech is marvelous. Her language is charged with enough energy to snare even the most lethargic reader, and she captures the rhythm and idioms of her characters' dialect precisely, brilliantly contrasting the children's "street" talk against Miss Moore's "proper speech."

Questions for Discussion and Writing

What is the conflict in this story? Is there more than one? How are these conflicts resolved?

Initially the conflict is between Sylvia (and her friends) and Miss Moore, who "was always planning these boring-ass things for us to do" (1). The kids resist Miss Moore's educational efforts precisely because they are kids; it is a normal response, at their age, to talk back, to want to break rules for the sake of breaking them, and generally to horse around. This is why Sylvia is disgusted with Sugar's "treachery" when Sugar answers Miss Moore. To Sylvia it seems that Sugar has turned into a Goody Two-Shoes, gone over to the other side. But what Sugar has realized during the course of the story (and what Sylvia will realize eventually, perhaps even as soon as she "think[s] this day through") is that Miss Moore is not the enemy. There are much more important things to rebel against.

JOHN CHEEVER, *Reunion* (p. 369)

In "Reunion," John Cheever shows the disparity between a father's appearance and his character. As he is seen by the young son, the father is incapable of fitting into any environment. The son, who cherishes dreams of a father who can control the world, learns during a short visit with him that the dreams cannot come true.

At the beginning of the story, the son steps off the train with a romantic ideal of his father in mind. His father is an important man; after all, a secretary keeps track of his appointments. The son describes the father as "a big, good-looking man, and I was terribly happy to see him again" (1), and he reveals his fantasy that "someone would see us together. I wished that we could be photographed. I wanted some record of our having been together" (1). Even his physical contact with the father is phrased in romantic terms: "I smelled my father the way my mother sniffs a rose. It was a rich compound of whiskey, after-shave lotion, shoe polish, woolens, and the rankness of a mature male" (1). At first impression, the father seems to live up to the son's dreams.

A short time later, after the father has embarrassed himself and his son in four bars with four very different atmospheres and at the newsstand, the son has a much more realistic awareness of his father. Dependent on alcohol and imaginary authority over other people, the father cannot even control himself. He has potential to succeed, in his appearance and his knowledge, but he insists on offending everyone around him. As he tells the son, "Just wait a second. I want to get a rise out of this chap" (34). Instead of displaying his most positive traits for his son, he impresses him with his worst behavior. The reader can imagine why the narrator's mother left the father. Instead of wishing for a memento of the occasion, the son willingly goes to his train without accepting even a newspaper.

"Reunion" reveals the way a character can expose his true self by his actions. Were the son to rely solely on his father's appearance, he would retain an entirely different picture of the man. Knowing more about the father, the narrator (and thus the reader) must alter his perceptions — or rather, the son must remember the father he has, no doubt, seen many times before. The narrator's remark on first seeing his father suggests this knowledge: "as soon as I saw him I felt that he was my father, my flesh and blood, my future and my doom. I knew that when I was grown I would be something like him; I would have to plan my campaigns within his limitations" (1). Students might find it useful to write about this comment. What does the future hold for the narrator? How will his lunch engagement with his father affect him? Can children ever totally escape their parents' influence?

JAMES JOYCE, *Araby* (p. 372)

James Joyce was born in Dublin, Ireland, in 1882 and, in an imaginative sense, he never left that city. He received a strict Jesuit education and was quite religious as a boy, but once he began to doubt his faith during his final year at Belvedere College, Dublin, he felt his calling as a writer more and more strongly. Further, he came to believe that this calling inevitably involved living in exile. Joyce studied modern languages at University College, Dublin, and taught himself Norwegian so he could read the plays of Henrik Ibsen in their original language. Ibsen's depiction of individual rebellion against community values resonated deeply for Joyce and contributed to his resolution to leave Ireland for Paris after he received his B.A. degree in 1902.

Joyce returned to Dublin when his mother contracted a fatal illness, and he stayed on for a brief time, working as a schoolteacher. He departed for Switzerland, leaving Ireland for good, in 1904. Nora Barnacle, an uneducated young woman with little interest in literature, came with him. The couple lived in Trieste and Zurich, where Joyce taught school and wrote. He published *Dubliners* in 1914, after a seven-year battle with his English and Irish publishers over the uncomfortably pointed descriptions of certain citizens of the city. *A Portrait of the Artist as a Young Man* followed in 1916. Joyce then began to secure several well-to-do patrons, especially Harriet Shaw Weaver, who subsidized him from 1917 onward and also helped publish his work. Joyce and Nora moved to Paris in 1920 and remained there until World War II forced them back to Switzerland. He published *Ulysses* in Paris in 1922, but the book was banned in America and Britain until 1933. *Finnegan's Wake,* which Joyce considered his crowning achievement, took fourteen years to write and was published in 1939. Joyce died in 1941.

In the beginning of Joyce's "Araby," the narrator attempts to distance himself from the general paralysis that affects his city and his society. By romanticizing his relationship with Mangan's sister, the narrator temporarily adds vision, color, and hope to his environment. Yet in the end, the narrator's passion cools, and he succumbs to his society's paralysis, rather than defeating it.

Joyce carefully describes the initial setting of "Araby" — the narrator's street and house — to convey Dublin's limitations. The street is "blind" (1); here, "the houses had grown somber" (3). The area is "silent" and lit only by "feeble lanterns" (3). The house is no more healthy: "Air, musty from having long been enclosed, hung in all the rooms, and the waste room behind the kitchen was littered with old useless papers" (2). Previously inhabited by a priest, the house is associated with self-denial. The narrator's and the priest's lives are not substantially different.

The narrator perceives Mangan's sister as beautiful and exotic. His infatuation with her helps him escape his priest-like life. Fascinated by her appearance — the "white curve of her neck, . . . the white border of a petticoat" (9), he watches her from behind the blinds of his house, follows her on her way to school, and, appropriately, promises her a gift from the bazaar. Mangan's sister is like Araby in the narrator's eyes: Both are exotic and desirable. Going to Araby is, for the narrator, a simple substitution for associating with Mangan's sister.

By the time the narrator has wheedled his uncle into giving him money, however, the bazaar is closing for the night. It becomes more like the society he is familiar with than a pleasure oasis. Joyce chooses words that will indicate the link between the narrator's city and Araby. Dublin is "thronged with buyers and glaring with gas" (24), but for all its bustle, it is unhealthy. The special train, heading straight to Araby, is "deserted" (24), yet it "crept onward among ruinous houses" (24). Emphasizing isolation, the narrator tells us, "I remained alone in the bare carriage" (24). Like the scenery he has viewed through the window of the train, the bazaar is closing for the evening. The narrator finds that "nearly all the stalls were closed and the greater part of the hall was in darkness. I recognized a silence like that which pervades a church after a service" (25). If this is Araby, it is a disappointment. Associated with Araby in the narrator's mind, Mangan's sister is also something less than he had imagined. His infatuation, which initially changes him into a passionate creature, fades, leaving him distraught: "Gazing into the darkness I saw myself as a creature driven and derided by vanity; and my eyes burned with anguish and anger" (37).

The power of Joyce's fiction lies not in dialogue or convoluted plots, but in deceptively simple description. It is a useful exercise to have students compare the opening description of the street with the ending description of the bazaar. How does the blindness of the narrator's street and house connect with his description of himself? You might also direct students to think about the significance of bazaar stalls operated and patronized by people with "English accents" (26) — in other words, the tensions between the Irish people and the English overseers of Ireland. How does this shed light on Joyce's portrait of Irish society?

FRANZ KAFKA, *A Hunger Artist* (p. 376)

Although he died (in 1924, in Vienna) relatively early in the century, many consider Franz Kafka the quintessential twentieth-century writer. Influenced by the philosophers Søren Kierkegaard and Friedrich Nietzsche, and by the Jewish Talmud, Kafka's portrayals of alienation and what came to be called existential *angst* prefigure the particular horrors of our time with uncanny accuracy. The conflicts and ironies of Kafka's life read like some of his fiction: He was born Jewish in Catholic Czechoslovakia (Prague, 1883). His father, a German-speaking shopkeeper who dominated family life, pushed his son toward a career in business despite knowing of his love for literature. Kafka lived with his parents for most of his life in spite of deep disappointment with them. He was a passionate man who seemed cold and strange to those around him. He took a degree in law and worked as an executive in an insurance company until tuberculosis forced him to quit in 1922. The two novellas (*The Metamorphosis*, 1915, and *In the Penal Colony*, 1919) and the collection of stories (*The Country Doctor*, 1919) published during his lifetime, as well as three novels (*The Trial*, 1925; *The Castle*, 1926; *Amerika*, 1927) and one collection of stories (*The Hunger Artist*, 1924) published posthumously repeatedly show individuals caught in meaningless, ironic, oppressive, unrelentingly grim circumstances. Kafka's work has been an enormous influence on later writers such as Samuel Beckett, Harold Pinter, Alain Robbe-Grillet, and Gabriel García Márquez, among many others. The facts that he wished at the end of his life to have all his work burned, that his three sisters died in concentration camps, and that he thought himself an abject failure all can be described as Kafkaesque.

Kafka's symbolism in this fantastic story can be interpreted on several levels. Instead of outlining these directly, it is probably more profitable to let the discussion of symbolism spring from answers to more concrete questions. You might begin with the hunger artist himself. Ask the class why he is fasting. Why do people usually fast? Do these reasons apply to the protagonist in any way?

The hunger artist is fasting for the same reason a painter paints or a writer writes: it is his art. It is also, of course, his profession. Fasting is what he excels at and what he gets paid for. Since the usual motives for fasting are religious or spiritual, on the surface the hunger artist is *not* fasting for the usual reasons. A person fasting with the aim of religious purification would not be concerned with being "cheated of the fame he would get for fasting longer" or being "the record hunger artist of all time" (paragraph 3). This is not to paint the artist as a completely vain creature; his "capacity for fasting" is more than a matter of pride for him. He is "too frantically devoted to fasting" to consider another profession (5). Self-denial is his art, and it does have a nonmaterial, spiritual value for him.

Discuss the protagonist's change in attitude toward his art during the course of the story. While he seems initially to be fasting for some greater glory, by the end he claims he is fasting only because he "couldn't find the food" he liked (9). Is this statement merely the reflection of a deranged mind (which the protagonist possesses by now, because he has been starving himself to death), or does it suggest any deeper meaning?

One possible reading of this statement is to interpret "the food he liked" metaphorically. Perhaps he made no such claim earlier in his career because he *had* "the food he liked": public acclaim, respect, approval, even reverence. In those days the public shared and appreciated his values. By the end of the story, however, the audience's interests and values have changed; the nourishment he needs simply does not exist any longer; there is no place for someone with the hunger artist's talents and beliefs.

Many critics believe the hunger artist represents the fate of the artist in the twentieth century: what was once an honored and respected position is now considered frivolous and irrelevant. Other critics believe that the artist represents the spiritual side of human beings, while the panther represents the physical. (Regardless of the strength of the spiritual side, the physical wins. The artist dies because he denied his physical needs, and he is replaced by the pure life force of the panther.) Most critics also perceive the hunger artist as a religious figure — mystic, holy man, saint, or priest. This interpretation holds that the story is about the decline of religion in the modern world.

The story provides ample evidence to support all these theories; a symbolic analysis would be an excellent writing assignment. Another writing assignment might be to discuss the tone of the story. What is it (ironic), and how does Kafka establish it? (Through the voice of this omniscient narrator, who is sufficiently detached from the artist that we can tell he doesn't share or even understand all of the artist's feelings.)

JAMAICA KINCAID, *Girl* (p. 382)

In this story two voices engage in what is actually a dialogue. The majority of the lines are instructions from a mother to her daughter about proper behavior. Whether the mother is training her daughter to carry out the traditional duties of women on various days of the week, explaining cooking tips, or warning her about growing up to be a "loose" woman, her advice can be taken in two ways. In one view, she is a typically scolding mother, who must nag her daughter in order to communicate with her. In another view, the entire speech is a harangue designed to entertain the reader. This double level of interpretation applies to the daughter's italicized responses as well. In one view, she can only internalize her responses because her mother gives her no opportunity to present her own views. In the other, more humorous interpretation, the daughter acts as the "straight-man," responding with lines designed to set up the punchline, the ending line, of her mother's joke. Whether genuine scolding or parody, the effect is at the daughter's expense.

Encourage students to read this short piece aloud. "Girl" may prompt them to write about the differences between American teenagers' responsibilities and Kincaid's character's duties. They may also be inspired to consider their own relationships with their parents or children. No matter how the students respond to the piece, they should view the "conflict" from both points of view to fully appreciate it.

D. H. LAWRENCE, *The Horse Dealer's Daughter* (p. 383)

D. H. Lawrence was born in 1885 in the Nottinghamshire village of Eastwood, in England's industrial Midlands. Although he grew up feeling closer to his book-loving mother, Lawrence would finally regard his miner-father's rough vitality with deep respect, and he imbued a number of his male characters with his father's qualities of mind and behavior, which qualities he came to see as essentially masculine. Further, the depictions of marriage in his mature work echo the "union of opposites" embodied in his parents' relationship. No "true marriage" — no true relationship, really — could exist, Lawrence thought, without fundamental conflict.

After finishing high school, Lawrence became a clerk, then an elementary-school teacher; he spent two years at Nottingham University College, earning a teacher's certificate in 1908. During this time he worked on his first novel (*The White Peacock,* published in 1911), wrote poetry and short fiction, and read constantly. He got a job as a schoolteacher in a suburb of London and stayed for four years, until he fell in love with Frieda von Richthofen, the German wife of a professor at Nottingham. They married in Germany in 1914, by which time Lawrence's autobiographical second novel, *Sons and Lovers,* had been published to both good reviews and good sales.

The couple returned to England early in World War I. Lawrence's vehement opposition to the war (it didn't help that Frieda was German) led to trouble with the English authorities. This was, in fact, only the first in what was to become a lifelong series of conflicts with the established order. *The Rainbow* was banned soon after its publication in 1915 because of its depictions (frank for the time) of sexuality. When the war ended, Lawrence left England with his wife, only to spend the rest of his life looking for a community where he felt welcome. Often very ill with the tuberculosis that eventually killed him, Lawrence lived and wrote in Italy, Australia, Mexico, France, and New Mexico. After his death his ashes were scattered near the ranch house where he had lived outside Taos, New Mexico.

Lawrence's works include *Women in Love* (1920), *Aaron's Rod* (1922), *Kangaroo* (1923), *The Plumed Serpent* (1926), *Lady Chatterley's Lover* (1928), and *Studies in Classical American Literature* (1923). Some students will be confused or even disturbed by Lawrence's vision of love, life, and death as presented in this story. For this reason an attempt to answer the concrete question Why does Mabel attempt suicide? might be a good way to move toward a discussion of the themes. What about Mabel's life is so oppressive, unbearable, and meaningless? What, prior to the opening of the story, had made her life worthwhile?

Mabel's life has been grim since her widowed father remarried, an action that set Mabel "hard against him." (Presumably Mabel felt the marriage violated her father's original love for her mother, who had died thirteen years before this story takes place.) Before he remarried, Mabel had been contented enough, attending her father and living "in the memory of her mother, . . . whom she had loved." But with her father's death went the family fortune — the one thing that had made Mabel feel "established," "proud," and "confident." Her brothers had always been "brutal and coarse" and had never shown any interest in her. She had no friends or acquaintances, both her parents were dead, and her poverty made her feel completely degraded. The only place she felt secure was in the churchyard where her mother was buried; her only source of happiness was tending her mother's grave and anticipating "her own glorification, approaching her dead mother, who was glorified." The fact is, Mabel has been leading a sort of living death (paragraphs 96–98).

This analysis of Mabel's situation should give students better insight into her character and can lead to a more sophisticated discussion of or writing assignment on the use of symbols in the story. Students should now be able to identify many of the symbolic aspects of the setting: the large house, servantless and desolate; the empty stables; the "gray, wintry day, with saddened . . . fields and an atmosphere blackened by the smoke of foundries not far off"; and "a slow, moist, heavy coldness sinking in and deadening all the faculties" (99 and 106). Yet while all of these suggest death, the story contains as many symbols of life: the horses, with their "swinging . . . great rounded haunches" and their "massive, slumbrous strength" (6); "the working people," who provide Fergusson with excitement, stimulation, and gratification (106), and Mabel herself, who is literally brought back to life by Fergusson, but who also, figuratively, brings *him* to life. "He could never let her go again. . . . He wanted to remain like that forever, with his heart hurting him in a pain that was also life to him" (154).

This introduction to the interrelated themes of life and death and love should enable students to discuss the story more fully. You could also ask students to write about the main characters: Do they change during the course of the story, and if so, how? What brings about these changes? Why does Mabel ask Fergusson if he loves her when she does? Why does he react to her question "amazed, bewildered, and afraid" (146)? What does the last paragraph of the story suggest about Mabel and Fergusson's future, and about Lawrence's vision of relationships between men and women?

A third writing topic might be a discussion of point of view. Ask students to identify and discuss the type of narration used. Could the story have been told exclusively from Mabel's point of view, or Fergusson's? Why or why not?

KATHERINE MANSFIELD, *Miss Brill* (p. 394)

Born in New Zealand in 1888, Katherine Mansfield moved to London when she was a young woman and began writing short stories. Her first collection, *In a German Pension*, appeared in 1911. subsequent publications which include *Bliss and Other Stories* (1920) and *The Garden Party* (1922), secured her reputation as an important writer. The full range of her short stories is available in *The Collected Short Stories of Katherine Mansfield* (1945). Mansfield tends to focus her stories on intelligent, sensitive protagonists who undergo subtle but important changes in their lives. In "Miss Brill," an aging Englishwoman spends the afternoon in a park located in an unnamed French vacation town watching the activities of the people around her. Through those observations, Mansfield characterizes Miss Brill and permits us to see her experience a moment that changes her view of the world as well as of herself.

Mansfield's characterization of Miss Brill is a portrait of an elderly woman alone. We never learn her first name because there is no one to address her familiarly. She carefully observes the crowds in the park because they are the only people in her life, aside from the students she tutors or the old gentleman for whom she reads the newspaper. She notices that the band conductor wears a new coat, and she looks forward to her special seat in the park, which is for "sitting in other people's lives just for a minute while they talked around her" (paragraph 3). By silent participation in other people's lives — even if they are only a husband and wife quarreling over whether one of them should wear spectacles — her life is enriched.

Miss Brill is content with her solitary life of observations. She is not merely a stock characterization of a frail old lady. She prides herself on her ability to hear and watch others. She sorts out the children, parents, lovers, and old people and vicariously participates in their lives, but she does not see herself in the same light as the other people who sit on the benches: "They were odd, silent, nearly all old, and from the way they stared they looked as though they'd just come from dark little rooms or even — even cupboards!" (5). Miss Brill believes she is more vital and alive than that.

Life in the park offers all the exciting variety of a theater production to Miss Brill. She regards herself as part of a large cast, every member of which plays an important role. She feels a sense of community with them that makes her want to sing with the band. The music seems to be a confirmation of her connection with people and a fitting expression of her abiding concern that kindnesses be observed: she wants to rebuke a complaining wife; she disapproves of the haughty woman who rejects the violets picked up for her by a little boy; and she regards the man who blows smoke in the face of the woman with the ermine toque as a brute. Her reactions to these minor characters reveal her decency and sensitivity.

At the climatic moment, when she feels elated by the band's music, she is suddenly and unexpectedly made to realize that the young "hero and heroine" (actually the story's antagonists) who sit nearby regard her as an unwelcome intrusion in their lives. She hears herself described as a "stupid old thing" and the fur that she so fondly wears is dismissed as merely "funny" (11–14). This insensitive slight produces the conflict in the story and changes Miss Brill because she is suddenly made aware of how she is like the other old people in the park. She returns home defeated, no longer able to delight in the simple pleasure of a honeycake. "Her room [is] like a cupboard," where she places her fur in a box. When "she put the lid on she thought she heard something crying" (18). Her fur — Miss Brill's sense of herself — expresses for her the painful, puzzled sense that she is less vitally a part of the world than she had assumed. Her life appears to be closed down — boxed up — at the end. Having denied herself the honeycake, it seems unlikely that she'll return to the park the following Sunday. If she does, her role in the "play" she imagined will have been significantly diminished, because she no longer perceives herself as an astute observer of other characters but as one of them, "odd, silent," and "old."

As a writing assignment, you might ask students to discuss the function of the minor characters mentioned in the story. They can analyze the way Mansfield uses these characters to reveal Miss Brill's character.

There is almost no physical description of Miss Brill in the story. Another writing assignment might be to develop a detailed description that is consistent with Miss Brill's behavior.

EDGAR ALLAN POE, *The Pit and the Pendulum* (p. 398)

Even stripped of the embellishment and inaccuracy that have plagued accounts of his life almost from the day it ended, the real life of Edgar Allan Poe seems too lurid to be true. Depending on one's point of view or literary bias, Poe can appear as any one of a gallery of writer/artist stereotypes: Doomed Genius, Self-promoting Fraud, Alcoholic Wild Man, Misunderstood Revolutionary, Prolific Artist Despite Appalling Odds.

Indeed, the odds were against him from the start. Poe's parents were itinerant actors Shortly after the writer's birth in Boston in 1809, his father left his wife and child. His mother died in 1811 in Richmond, Virginia, whereupon John Allan, a wealthy tobacco merchant, took the child into his household. The Allans never legally adopted Poe, but they gave him every benefit of an uppper-class Virginia upbringing and education. After a year at the University of Virginia, where he accumulated gambling debts and girlfriends, Poe had a falling-out with Allan because he had no interest in entering Allan's business. Poe traveled to Boston, where he self-published *Tamarlane and Other Poems* in 1827.

While doing a stint in the army (under the name Edgar A. Perry), Poe made up with Allan. He entered West Point in 1830, not quite a year after his second collection of poems appeared. The authorities tossed him out of "The Point" for lack of attendance at classes. Now 22, and having broken with Allan for good, Poe became an editor, an occupation that provided a decidedly marginal living in various cities until he died. He lived in Baltimore from 1831 to 1835 with relatives from his father's family, including his aunt and her daughter, Virginia, whom Poe married in 1836, when she was fourteen. By this time the three had relocated to Richmond so Poe could take a job with the *Southern Literary Messenger*.

After a brief time in New York (where his novel *The Narrative of Arthur Gordon Pym* was published in 1838), Poe moved to Philadelphia. His reputation as a poet, critic, and writer of fiction had been slowly growing since his stories had begun appearing in newspapers in the early 1830s. Many of these were collected in *Tales of the Grotesque and Arabesque* in 1840.

Poe had some success in the mid-1840s (praise for *The Raven and Other Poems* ; a position as lead reviewer for an influential publication), but his life went into precipitous decline after his wife died of tuberculosis in 1847. His drinking, which plagued him throughout his adulthood, became worse, his behavior became more "eccentric," and he worked at an even more frantic pace. In October 1849 he was found unconscious on a Baltimore street, having gotten off the train that was taking him to a job in Philadelphia. He died on October 7 and was buried in an unmarked grave. When a tombstone was placed there in 1875, Walt Whitman was the only literary light present. Poe has, of course, been claimed since as an important influence on various writers and types of fiction and poetry: Baudelaire, Mallarmé, and Valéry saw him as a Symbolist precursor, and the detective and horror genres show his particular influence.

"The Pit and the Pendulum," a story of death and rebirth, is generally considered one of Poe's most harrowing tales. Before plunging into any symbolic analysis, make sure the class understands the actual circumstances of the story. The narrator is a victim of the Spanish Inquisition who has been accused of heresy, then sentenced to torture and death. The tale is literally his account of what happens to him in the chamber in which he is imprisoned. Initially the narrator is overwhelmed by terror. Gradually, however, he calms down enough to examine his situation more closely and to see if there is a way to avert the fate his tormentors have planned.

Ask the class to analyze the tone and mood of the story, and to discuss how Poe created its atmosphere.

The closely attached first-person narration is the key: the narrator is not only the protagonist but also the only character, save a few brief mentions and sightings of his torturers. Since everything we are told is filtered through his narrative consciousness, his claustrophobic terror becomes ours, just as we share his delirium, his hopes, and his desperate horror. We know only what the narrator knows — and in this case the more our half-crazed narrator knows, the worse his situation gets.

A topic for writing or discussion is the story's surprise ending. (This is a good opportunity to introduce the term *deus ex machina*.) Ask the class how they feel about such intervention. Did the ending satisfy them? Compare the conclusions of this story and Chopin's "The Story of an Hour" (p. 12), which also has a surprise ending. Was one more appropriate, or satisfying? (Ultimately, of course, there is no "right" answer, since this is a matter of aesthetics — but the questions raised could lead to interesting insights about both stories and about what readers expect from fiction.) Objectively, the ending of Chopin's story is probably more prepared for, since the first line of the story warns us about Mrs. Mallard's heart condition. But it is still an ending like Poe's, in that the protagonist is not in control of the resolution.

It is common to analyze Poe's work in psychoanalytic terms. While it is perfectly possible (and, many teachers and students feel, preferable) to discuss, understand, and enjoy Poe's work without this frame of reference, here is one such interpretation of this story from Bettina L. Knapp's *Edgar Allan Poe* (New York: F. Ungar, 1984):

> The narrator is imprisoned in his archaic world which may be thought of as the collective unconscious. . . . The original predicament of the narrator symbolizes that of the inner being which at first is unable to see any lighter areas in the primal blackness. As he explores his situation as rationally as he can, he is in effect encountering his shadow and attempts to deal with it. . . . The potion inserted in his food . . . makes him sleep. The profound sleep which he is now experiencing enables him to come into contact with the deepest levels of his psyche, endowing him with the strength to deal with the awesome dangers that threaten his life. Upon awakening, the narrator's fear of losing his life is viewed more logically; he divides his problems into segments, analyzes his plight, and determines the best way out of it. (pp. 170–171)

JOHN UPDIKE, *A & P* (p. 407)

John Updike is one of those rare writers who command both popular acclaim and critical respect. The prolific novelist, short story writer, and poet was born in Shillington, Pennsylvania, in 1932, completed a bachelor's degree at Harvard University (where he worked for a time as a cartoonist for the *Harvard Lampoon*), and spent a year at Oxford University studying at the Ruskin School of Drawing and Fine Arts. After returning from England in 1955, he worked at *The New Yorker*, where he began publishing his short fiction. He left the magazine in 1957 to pursue writing full-time.

Updike's great subject is the relationship between men and women, especially in marriage. The Rabbit novels (*Rabbit, Run*, 1960; *Rabbit Redux*, 1971; and *Rabbit Is Rich*, 1981; named for their protagonist, Harry "Rabbit" Angstrom) constitute perhaps the best-known examples of this preoccupation. Updike has received numerous awards, including the National Book Award, the Pulitzer Prize, and the Creative Arts Medal for Lifetime Achievement from Brandeis University. His collections of stories include *Pigeon Feathers* (1962) and *Trust Me* (1987); his novels include *The Centaur* (1963), *The Coup* (1978), and, most recently, *S.* (1988). His poetry collections include *The Carpentered Hen and Other Tame Creatures* (1958) and *Tossing and Turning* (1977); his nonfiction works include a collection of essays and criticism, *Hugging the Shore* (1983), and the memoir *Self-consciousness* (1989).

Sammy's voice is what pulls us into "A & P," thanks to his engaging first-person narration. Ask the class to describe his voice — the tone he uses, the things he thinks and says, the way he says them. What kind of a person is Sammy?

While Sammy is not exactly an all-American boy — he's too much of a smart aleck and somewhat disrespectful to his elders and women (when he's not telling us about "sheep" or "houseslaves," he's focused on someone's belly or shoulders or "sweet broad soft-looking can") — he is funny, and we excuse most of his prejudices on the ground of youth. (He *is* young. It is difficult to imagine the more mature, responsible Stokesie, for example, quitting his job over this incident.) Updike's mastery of the vernacular makes Sammy all the more appealing: we enjoy hearing him talk and think, and his observations about protocol in the A & P and his small town are mercilessly accurate. At the same time Sammy is critical of this context, however, he is also a part of it: "We're [the A & P is] right in the middle of town, and the women generally put on a shirt or shorts or something before they get out of the car into the street. . . . Poor kids, I began to feel sorry for them, they couldn't help it" (paragraphs 10–11). He understands how the little world he lives in works, and he knows it is inappropriate for the girls to be wearing bathing suits in the A & P.

Ask the class to identify the climax of the story (Sammy quitting his job), and to discuss why Sammy quits.

Sammy hasn't given us any evidence that he hates his job. He has a friend there, and his wonderful description of using the cash register suggests he gets a certain amount of pleasure from his mastery of the machine. He *is* bored, however. (His descriptions of the store's regular clientele and the view from the front of the store demonstrate this.) And, without realizing it, he's probably looking for a cause, or at least something to react to. He does, after a while, feel bad for the girls, and quitting becomes a heroic gesture. In his mind, he isn't defending the honor and dignity of just these three embarrassed girls but of everyone including himself, who feels humiliated or restricted by the narrow parameters of the silly, limited, limiting town or society in which they live.

Ask the class what Sammy gains from quitting. In acting on what has suddenly become principle, does he gain anything?

On the surface he certainly loses more than he gains. The gesture is lost on the girls, who hightail it out of the store too fast even to hear him. And, of course, he loses his job. But for the moment, anyway, he retains his dignity — and the last line of the story suggests he has already gained some perspective.

Ask the class whether they think Sammy should have quit, and whether they agree that "once you begin a gesture it's fatal not to go through with it" (31). How do they imagine Updike feels about this statement?

The relatively somber tone of the story's last three paragraphs, along with the narrator's dramatic last line, suggests that Updike does not agree with Sammy on this point. Sammy's going to learn from this experience, but he's learning the hard way. (This can lead to an interesting paper, exploring the roles and attitudes of the two minor characters, Stokesie and Lengel, by comparing them with Sammy.)

Another good writing assignment would be to compare this story with Bambara's "The Lesson" (p. 364), a story with a similarly humorous and personable first-person narrator. Both narrator/protagonists have many critical things to say about the people around them. Both are young, use slang, and come from a different social class than some of the people they encounter, or have to think about, during the course of their respective stories. Both learn something unpleasant about the way the world works and experience a certain initiation into maturity. In what ways are Sammy's and Sylvia's experiences different? Is one story more concerned with the issue of growing up, while the other focuses more on social and political issues? In what other ways are the stories similar or different?

AN ALBUM OF WORLD LITERATURE

YUKIO MISHIMA, *Patriotism* (p. 412)

On the afternoon of November 25, 1970, the day he completed what is usually considered his masterpiece (the tetralogy *The Sea of Fertility*), Yukio Mishima and several members of his private "army" captured the headquarters of Japan's Eastern Ground Self-defense Forces. The group issued a series of demands that went unmet, leading to Mishima's ritual suicide, or *seppuku*, a part of the samurai tradition. For most of his life he had felt that Japan was drifting too far from its classic traditions.

Mishima was born Kimitake Hiraoka in Tokyo in 1925 to a family with samurai antecedents. When World War II began, he became convinced that he would die for his emperor, but he failed the army physical, a dishonor that may explain his lifelong devotion to bodybuilding and the martial arts. After the war he attended law school at Tokyo University and worked for a short time at the Finance Ministry. *Confessions of a Mask*, his first novel, was published in 1949.

In addition to being an enormously prolific writer, Mishima sang, acted, modeled, designed the uniforms for his "army," and became an expert in karate and kendo. He wrote poetry, stories, plays, novels, travel books, and articles, and translated a number of *No* dramas. In addition to the *Sea of Fertility Tetralogy*, some of his best-known novels in English translation include *The Sound of Waves* (1954), *The Temple of the Golden Pavilion* (1956), and *The Sailor Who Fell from Grace with the Sea* (1963).

Plot (or structure) is a good opening into "Patriotism": Why does Mishima choose to reveal the entire sequence of events in the story's first paragraph? How does knowing the outcome of the story affect the reader? Suspense is clearly not important to the author here; by summarizing the story in the first paragraph, he eliminates any possibility for suspense (or even curiosity) about what happened next or how the conflict will be resolved. Ask the class what *is* the most important element in this story. How does Mishima hope to snare his readers and maintain their interest?

Character and theme are the heart of this story — understanding who these people are and why they do what they do. The biggest question, of course, is motivation: Why does the protagonist commit suicide? The factual answer to this question can be found in the story's first paragraph. He was "profoundly disturbed by the knowledge that his closest colleagues had been with the mutineers from the beginning, and indignant at the imminent prospect of Imperial troops attacking Imperial troops." His colleagues had mutinied, and, because he had been completely uninvolved and unaware, he was about to be put "in command of a unit with orders to attack them. . . . I can't do it. It's impossible to do a thing like that."

In other words, this is a matter of honor, pure and simple. Implicit in Takeyama's statement "I knew nothing. They hadn't asked me to join" (paragraph 23) is the suggestion that he might have joined the mutiny had he been asked. Ironically, having been denied the opportunity to take a stand, he is forced into the position of defending the status quo and opposing the mutineers. He cannot make himself attack his own colleagues, but refusing to do so would mark him as a mutineer, unfaithful to the imperial troops as well. He sees himself as doomed and chooses the only honorable death — honorable for himself and for his country. (Hence the title, "Patriotism.")

This analysis helps explain the lieutenant's motivation for killing himself. Reiko's suicide may be more difficult for some students to accept. Her decision to "accompany" her husband cannot be explained as solely romantic; it must also be seen as a reflection of Mishima's belief in "traditional" Japanese values and attitudes toward women: her husband was the "sun about which her whole world revolved" (9), and "husband and life should be harmonious" (10).

The bulk of the story consists of a lengthy scene in which the couple makes love, and then a lengthy scene depicting the suicides. Why does Mishima devote so much space to these scenes, and what is the effect of juxtaposing these two intensely physical activities?

The author seems to draw a parallel between the lovemaking and the suicides. Both activities are, strictly speaking, "sensual" experiences. When the lieutenant is waiting for his wife to join him on the bedding, he wonders, "Was it death he was now waiting for? Or a wild ecstasy of the senses? The two seemed to overlap, almost as if the object of this bodily desire was death itself " (62). In a review of Mishima's work, Hortense Calisher wrote that Mishima "is telling us that death is one of life's satisfactions" (*New York Times Book Review*, 12 Nov. 1972: 56–60).

This is a disturbing story, and it may be helpful to provide the class with some biographical information early in the discussion. Particularly interesting is the fact that when this story was made into a movie shortly after its publication, Mishima played the role of Takeyama. While it is important, in reading fiction, not to equate the narrator with the author, biographical facts do help explain how Mishima came to write such a story. Apparently he revered the values of austerity, loyalty, and allegiance practiced by the ancient samurai, from whom his grandmother descended. (This accounts for the symbolic use of *seppuku* in the story.) Mishima was reportedly deeply disturbed by the corruption and materialism so prevalent in modern Japan. According to the critic Donald Richie, "a romantic such as Mishima is a man who compares things as they are with things as they have been or could be and who, in the face of public indifference and private doubt, has the strength of character to live by those standards" (*Harper's*, Sept. 1972).

Questions for Discussion and Writing

1. *Ask the class to identify the various rituals in the story. (In addition to the lovemaking and seppuku, there are, among others, the morning worship, preparing and drinking sake, bathing and shaving.) What do these rituals tell us about the characters of the protagonist and his wife? (If there were some way out of his predicament besides suicide, he probably wouldn't recognize it, as locked into his rituals as he is. But he is locked into them by choice [as is his wife]: if he is living in the past, he is doing so because he wants to.)*

2. *Locate the contrasting images in the story. (Heat and cold, dark and light, control — spiritual and physical — and lack of control.) Discuss how these help illustrate the story's theme.*

R. K. NARAYAN, *Trail of the Green Blazer* (p. 428)

Although he has published a memoir and prose versions of a number of classic Indian texts, such as *The Mahabharata*, R. K. Narayan is best known for his novels and short stories. Readers and critics alike have noted in particular the Malgudi novels, about the people of a mythical Indian village. Narayan's realistic descriptions, his ability to work universal themes while retaining a convincing sense of place and character, and the sometimes comic tone of his writing have led to comparisons between Malgudi and William Faulkner's Yoknapatawpha County.

Narayan was born in Madras, India, in 1906, and educated at Maharaja's College, where he received an undergraduate degree in 1930. He has won a number of honors, including the National Prize of the Indian Literary Academy (in 1958, for *The Guide*) and the English-speaking Union Book Award (for *My Days: A Memoir*, 1975). He owns Indian Thought Publications in Mysore, India, and, from 1959 until his election to the Indian parliament in 1986, had spent considerable time in New York City. The American Academy and Institute of Arts and Letters named him an honorary member in 1981. His books include *Swami and Friends: A Novel of Malgudi* (1935), *The Dark Room: A Novel* (1938), *An Astrologer's Day and Other Stories* (1947),

The Financial Expert: A Novel (1952), and, more recently, *Under The Banyan Tree and Other Stories* (1985), and *Talkative Man: A Novel of Malgudi* (1986).

In Narayan's "Trail of the Green Blazer," Raju, the pickpocket, survives by denying his humanity. As long as he can objectify his victims and view his activity as nothing more than a livelihood, he succeeds. Yet when he pauses to consider the feelings of his victims and their loved ones — to apply his sense of a common humanity — he fails as a thief.

Raju has carefully developed a method of pickpocketing. First, the victim cannot be viewed as a person, or the pickpocket will feel too much sympathy. As long as Raju can refer to his prey as a nameless "Green Blazer," he is distanced enough to complete his operation. Next, there is an art to mingling with the crowd: "He kept himself half-aloof from the crowd; he could not afford to remain completely aloof or keep himself in it too conspicuously" (1). The process of following the victim is also an exact science: Raju "followed the Green Blazer, always keeping himself three steps behind. It was a nicely calculated distance, acquired by intuition and practice. The distance must not be so much as to obscure the movement of the other's hand to and from his purse, nor so close as to become a nuisance and create suspicion. It has to be finely balanced and calculated" (4). As long as he relies on his system instead of seeing the victim as a human being, Raju can successfully pick his pocket. Rationalizing his act by deciding that the Green Blazer is unpleasant, Raju steals the purse.

In following the Green Blazer, however, Raju learns too much about him. Overhearing the victim haggle with a merchant over a balloon for his motherless child, Raju begins to associate himself with the Green Blazer and to sympathize for the motherless family as if it were his own: "Raju almost sobbed at the thought of the disappointed child" (9). Once his emotions are enlisted on the victim's behalf, he is trapped by both his conscience and by the Green Blazer, who catches him putting back the purse and the balloon, but not the money. He suffers a physical assault and personal shame simply because he tries to perform a good deed.

This ironic twist is related in such a matter-of-fact tone that readers do not worry about Raju's fate. Throughout the story, in fact, Narayan implies that nothing should be taken too seriously. Raju sees his occupation not as a life or death matter, but as "a gamble, of course. Sometimes he got nothing out of a venture, counting himself lucky if he came out with his fingers intact" (2). His immoral acts cause no serious consequences if he fails; if he succeeds, his sin seems to be erased as soon as he throws away the empty purse. The lighter tone of the story contributes to the conclusion, in which it is entirely appropriate that the crowd and the police view his failure to put back the purse, as well as his capture, as a huge joke. Like the "wax model of Mahatma Gandhi reading a newspaper" (6), the events of "Trail of the Green Blazer" seem both humorous and somewhat absurd.

LILIANA HEKER, *The Stolen Party* (p. 432)

Born in Argentina in 1943, Liliana Heker edited *El ornitorrinco (The Platypus),* an influential literary magazine, during Argentina's years of military dictatorship. In 1966 she published *Los que vieron la zarza (Those Who Beheld the Burning Bush),* her first collection of short stories, and it established her reputation. She has since published *Acuario* (1972), *Las peras del mal* (1982), and a novel, *Un resplandor que se apago en el mundo* (1977). Her second novel, *Zona de clivaje,* was published in 1988 and won the Buenos Aires Municipal Prize.

In Liliana Heker's "The Stolen Party," the reality of the birthday celebration, and Rosaura's role in that celebration, is clear to both Rosaura and the reader only at the end of the story. Until the moment when Señora Ines extends the money to Rosaura, the girl can act out a very different scenario.

In the experience she has chosen to create, Rosaura commands an elevated status. Although she must admit to the girl with the bow that she is "the daughter of the employee" (32), her actions and conversations with the other characters establish, in her own mind, her superiority. Rosaura feels important because she can enter portions of the house such as the kitchen, where the other children are not allowed to go. She is also asked by an adult to assist with serving refreshments, whereas the other children are seemingly not to be trusted. "She wasn't a butterfingers, like the others" (19). She wins the sack race, and excels at tag. When no one else is brave enough to participate, Rosaura holds the monkey for the magician. The magician appears to recognize her elevated status: "Thank you very much, my little countess" (53). In Rosaura's construction of events, she is empowered by her success and by the other children's recognition of that success. Her favorite moment of the party fulfills her desire for power:

> But the best was still to come. The best came after Luciana blew out the candles. First the cake. Señora Ines had asked her to help pass the cake around, and Rosaura had enjoyed the task immensely, because everyone called out to her, shouting "Me, me!" Rosaura remembered a story in which there was a queen who had the power of life or death over her subjects. She had always loved that, having the power of life or death. To Luciana and the boys she gave the largest pieces, and to the girl with the bow she gave a slice so thin one could see through it (39).

This party matters so much to her because it makes her feel important; her associations with Luciana and with words like "countess," and "queen" prove that she is more than just the "employee's daughter."

The conclusion of the party forces her to realize not only that she is the employee's daughter but that she has become the employee. In reality, her starched dress, game-victories, and fancied powers are insignificant. Instead of using the party to gain prominence, she has been used by Señora Ines. Her desire for friendship with Luciana and her dream of owning a big house are shown to be not only false, but foolish.

Heker ends the story with the words, "an infinitely delicate balance" (73). What is literally being balanced? What else could the phrase refer to? Ask students to describe what might happen to this 'delicate balance' after the story's conclusion. What actions might the characters take? What are the implications of those actions? In addition, students might characterize Rosaura's relationship with her mother at the beginning of the story (and the party). How do the events of the party affect that relationship? How are Rosaura and her mother posed at the conclusion?

"The Stolen Party" provokes discussion about social status, economic reality, and the contrast between child and adult world views. How do these themes relate to the title of the story? Do readers recognize Rosaura's real position in this story before she does? Why is the monkey an appropriate entertainment for this party? Are there any textual connections between the monkey and Rosaura? By analyzing Rosaura's experience at this party, students may recall their clashes between imagination and reality, and identify more closely with her.

AN ALBUM OF CONTEMPORARY STORIES

RAYMOND CARVER, *Boxes* (p. 436)

Raymond Carver died in August 1988 knowing he was widely considered the most influential writer of short fiction of our time. Born in 1938 in Clatskanie, Oregon, to working-class parents, Carver grew up in Yakima, Washington, was educated at Humbolt State College, and did graduate work at the University of Iowa. He had married at age nineteen and during his college years, worked at a series of low-paying jobs to help support his family.

"I begin a story with an urge to write the story, but I don't know quite where it's going," he told the *Boston Globe*. "Usually I'll find out what I want to say in the act of saying it." This approach often results in surprise in the reading, and a quality of bemusement inhabits many of Carver's stories and leavens their often grim proceedings.

Carver's collections of stories include *Will You Please Be Quiet, Please?* (1976), *What We Talk About When We Talk About Love* (1981), *Cathedral* (1984), and *Where I'm Calling From: New and Selected Stories* (1988). His poetry collections include *Where Water Comes Together With Other Water* (1985) and *Ultramarine* (1986). Carver edited *Best American Short Stories* in 1986 and *American Short Story Masterpieces* in 1987. He taught at a number of universities, including the University of California at Berkeley, the University of Iowa, the University of Texas at El Paso, and Syracuse University.

The title of Carver's "Boxes" aptly represents its plot, characters, and themes. In his title and his story, Carver suggests the awkward, alienated feelings people have about each other, and the way they may or may not reveal those feelings.

Literally, the boxes of the title might refer to moving boxes. The narrator's mother, constantly on the move, surrounds herself with boxes. They are her portable fortress. When she is tired or threatened by her circumstances, all she has to do is fill up her boxes and move to a new location. Because she so often finds fault with her surroundings — with the weather, the people, or the attention she may or may not receive — her boxes are constantly in use.

"Boxes" may also refer to the way Carver's characters keep their feelings tightly enclosed. They rarely speak absolute truth to each other. Of the main characters, Jill is most capable of opening up, as she does when she tells the narrator's mother, "You know what? Your son is worried sick about you" (55). The other characters have more trouble sharing their feelings. The mother could be opening up when she threatens to kill herself, but she might also be trying to get the son's attention. The narrator knows that this may be the last encounter with his mother — evoking an association between coffins and boxes — but he is unable to articulate his response to the realization. Instead, as the narrator explains, "I lean forward in the chair and cover my face with my hands. I sit like that for a minute, feeling bad and stupid for doing it. But I can't help it" (70). The narrator reveals his thoughts to the reader, but he remains "boxed" off from the other characters.

In its verb form, "Boxes" indicates the way these characters spar with one another. The mother, with her constant complaints and bids for attention, seeks her son's devotion; the son seems to desire a quiet, unmolested life. Jill is caught between the other characters, as the person who can articulate the narrator's feelings and feel comfortable in approaching the mother. As the narrator's spokesperson, she is as involved in the matter as the other characters. The narrator describes Jill's verbal assault on the mother: "'You're driving him crazy. He's going crazy with worry over you.' She is on one side of my chair, and my mother is on the other side. They could tear me apart in no time at all" (74). In their stance and their dialogue, these characters are boxers, striking out in an attempt to express themselves and resolve their situation.

The characters are chronically unhappy, trapped in a situation with no resolution. The narrator cannot satisfy his mother's need for attention without losing his independence, and his mother cannot accept responsibility for making a better life for herself. The narrator comes closest to pleasing and soothing his mother when he addresses her, as his father used to, as "Dear": "I don't know why, but it's then I recall the affectionate name my dad used sometimes when he was talking nice to my mother — those times, that is, when he wasn't drunk. It was a long time ago, and I was a kid, but always hearing it, I felt better, less afraid, more hopeful about the future" (84). In this form of address — a small but sincere gesture — the narrator takes the initiative in reaching out to his mother, instead of relying on Jill to speak for him. The act reveals a little development of the narrator's character and acceptance of his role in the world of this story.

Students may generate additional associations with the word "Boxes" that might add meaning to their interpretations of this story. Are any other boxes, of any sort, depicted in the story? Are there any additional interpretations of the meaning of the ending? Has the narrator begun to deal with his mother, or is he merely giving in to her desire for male companionship by addressing her, in the way that his father used to, as "Dear"? Is the situation described by Carver resolvable?

LOUISE ERDRICH, *Fleur* (p. 444)

Louise Erdrich is of Chippewa Indian and German heritage. Born in 1954 in Little Falls, Minnesota, she grew up as part of the Turtle Mountain Band of Chippewa in Wahpeton, North Dakota. After graduating from Dartmouth College (where her poetry and fiction won several awards, including the American Academy of Poets Prize), she moved back to North Dakota to teach in the Poetry in the Schools Program. She completed an M.A. in creative writing at Johns Hopkins University in 1979.

Her first novel, *Love Medicine,* winner of the 1984 National Book Critics Circle Award, is part of an interlocking series of novels concerning Native American life in North Dakota. She is presently at work on the fourth of these books, having published *The Beet Queen* in 1986 and *Tracks* in 1988. She enjoys a very close professional relationship with her husband, Michael Dorris, a professor of Native American Studies at Dartmouth: the two worked together on Dorris's *The Broken Card: A Family's Ongoing Struggle with Fetal Alcohol Syndrome* (1989) and are collaborating on a novel called "The Crown of Columbus," which concerns a Native American woman who discovers Christopher Columbus.

You might begin by discussing the powerful threads of magic and myth in "Fleur." Erdrich's subject — the lives of contemporary Chippewas on and around a North Dakota reservation — is likely to be new to most of your students, but they should have no trouble recognizing the magical elements here. Identify some of these and discuss their purpose. Ask students whether they can imagine this story without them.

We are set up for mystery and magic from the very start of the story, with the phrase "The first time [Fleur] drowned. . . ." Immediately we know she drowned more than once, which means she didn't really drown (as we understand the word) the first time — or, if she did, she came back to life. This fact is magical not just to readers but to the narrator and the whole town; drowning is ostensibly "the death a Chippewa cannot survive" (paragraph 5). The suggestion is that the people on the reservation, narrator included, expect, accept, and allow for a certain amount or a certain kind of magic: they believe Chippewas can survive *other* deaths — but not death by drowning. For them, this is what makes Fleur different, suspect. We (the readers — most of whom are generally conditioned to expect solid realism from contemporary American fiction) accept these beliefs because of the matter-of-fact tone in which the narrator presents them. There is no question about cause and effect. The information is all presented as factual: Fleur Pillager drowned twice; a Chippewa cannot survive death by drowning; "it was clear that Misshepeshu, the waterman, the monster, wanted her for himself" (4); Fleur Pillager "kill[ed] men off by drowning in the lake" (6). Ask the class to identify other magical qualities about Fleur. (She could stand heat no one else could; her hips were "fishlike, slippery, narrow"; "her braids were thick like the tails of animals"; her fifth toes were missing; she was "half-tamed, but only half" [17].)

Clearly, the people in this story live by these myths; such beliefs are an integral part of their lives. These stories define and explain their lives. To remove the myth and magic in this story would be impossible; it would remove the world in which the story takes place.

An evaluation of point of view in this story would make an excellent paper topic. Technically, the story has a first-person narrator who is a minor character. Pauline is an ideal narrator in this respect. She is there to set the scene for us in the story's first section, but, as the title indicates, this is Fleur's story: subsequently Pauline acts primarily as an observer. She makes a few brief comments about herself that apply not only to her life in Argus but to her function as a narrator in this story: "I was a good one to have around because . . . I was invisible . . . Because I could fade into a corner . . . I knew everything" (11). (Note the suggestion of magic — Pauline's invisibility — here as well.)

But the narration doesn't remain strictly first person; the speaker frequently shifts from "I" to "we," because she is telling us not just what she thinks and feels but what the entire reservation thinks and feels. For example, when Pauline is talking about Misshepeshu, the waterman, she says, "Our mothers warn us that we'll think he's handsome, for he appears with green eyes, copper skin, a mouth tender as a child's" (5). And when she talks about Fleur she says, "After the first time, we thought she'd keep the good ways. But then, after the second drowning, we knew that we were dealing with something much more serious. She was haywire, out of control. She messed with evil, laughed at the old women's advice" (6). The members of this society all agree on what "the good ways" are; they all know, for instance that laughing at old women's advice is crazy, even damning. This collective consciousness, this joint observation and analysis of Fleur's behavior and the havoc it wreaks, makes the story even more powerful.

Questions for Discussion and Writing

1. *Examine the incidents in which Fleur is responsible (according to the beliefs of the narrator and everyone on the reservation) for people coming to harm. Was she really responsible for these things, and, if so, why did she do them? Was she ever provoked?*

   Obviously Fleur was provoked in the town of Argus; the suggestion is that she was responsible for the tornado, which was her means of revenge. Whether she was really capable of bringing on a tornado — or was really responsible for the deaths earlier in the story — is impossible to know. Such logical analysis is completely beside the point in this rich story, which is based on the power of myth, not facts.

2. *Discuss the relationship between magic and nature and the title character in "Fleur."*

   While it may be Misshepeshu who keeps Fleur alive after drowning, what about her footprints turning into claw marks or paw prints at night? And what about the tornado that kills the three men who raped her but harms no one else? Clearly there is some benevolent relationship between nature and Fleur.

TIM O'BRIEN, *How to Tell a True War Story* (p. 454)

Tim O'Brien's work is heavily influenced by his service in Vietnam and by the "war writing" of Ernest Hemingway and Joseph Heller. His first book, *If I Die in a Combat Zone, Box Me Up and Ship Me Home* (1973) collects anecdotes of O'Brien's tour of duty, and *Going After Cacciato*, which won the National Book Award in 1978, revolves around a vision in which one of the characters decides to leave the war and walk to Paris. O'Brien was born in 1946 in Austin, Minnesota, graduated summa cum laude from Macalester College, and did graduate work at Harvard University. He has written for the *Washington Post, Esquire,* and *Playboy,* among other publications, and his books include *Northern Lights* (1974) and *The Nuclear Age* (1985).

In "How to Tell a True War Story," O'Brien establishes the pattern of his narrative in the first seven paragraphs. The vignette about Rat, his friend, and the sister who doesn't write back is a microcosm of the story as a whole. It establishes a sequence — introduction of characters, narration of details, topped by a punchline — that the following portions of the story closely parallel, incorporating specific terminology and black humor, as well as metanarration in which instructions about how to write and tell war stories are conveyed, the story is realistic. In its inability to identify a single moral or a distinct meaning, "How to Tell a True War Story" parallels American reaction to the Vietnam War.

In the opening sequence, the narrator introduces his characters: Bob "Rat" Kiley, the friend who is killed, and the dead soldier's sister — the "dumb cooze" who "never writes back" (7). O'Brien's later amplifications of the story also rely on immediate characterization: "the dead guy's name was Curt Lemon" (11); "I heard this one, for example, from Mitchell Sanders" (21); and finally, affecting the narrator most directly, "This one wakes me up" (97). Even the commentaries about telling war stories focus most immediately on the people who listen to them and respond — "Now and then, when I tell this story, someone will come up to me afterward and say she liked it. It's always a woman. Usually it's an older woman of kindly temperament and humane politics" (106). Through his characters, O'Brien can reach his readers. More importantly, O'Brien reminds us that stories cannot exist without storytellers and audiences.

Within the narratives, O'Brien fills the readers' minds with graphic, brutal details and terminology appropriate to the war situation. In the opening section, Rat describes how his friend's courage caused him to "volunteer for stuff nobody else would volunteer for in a million years, dangerous stuff, like doing recon or going out on these really badass night patrols" (3). In later sections, the details reveal the way Curt Lemon explodes in the sunlight, the bewilderment of the patrol on the mountain, or the gruesome horror of Rat's slow, deliberate destruction of the baby buffalo. Each of the sections builds on the trauma of previous ones: The buffalo sequence is far more tortuously laid out than the story about Rat's friend.

The final sentences of each portion of the story invariably build to punchlines. They either depend on black humor for their power, or they reveal the seeming meaninglessness of the war effort. The punchlines also indicate some build-up of power — some exaggeration — leading to ironic endings in which little is actually accomplished. The first section, told in a tone of incredulity and cynicism, involves silence on the part of a soldier's family. Later story lines end with the ominous silence of the mountain after the patrol has expanded its force to destroy sound, and with Rat's meaningless annihilation of a mute animal. Each narrative points to the soldiers' frustrations in a variety of different situations — frustrations that affect them not only during the war, but years later: "Often in a true war story there is not even a point, or else the point doesn't hit you until twenty years later, in your sleep, and you wake up and shake your wife and start telling the story to her, except when you get to the end you've forgotten the point again" (96). Like America's involvement in Vietnam, which its citizens are still questioning, the episodes in "How to Tell a True War Story" do not deliver any neatly packaged truisms.

Students should compare the sections of the story that contain the narratives with those that tell about the narratives. Why has O'Brien included both types of narrative in his story? Students might also trace the progression of each type of narration: To what point does each build? Finally, O'Brien's artistry should be recognized. His words are forceful, but they convey the beauty and grandeur of war as well. He writes that war "is grotesque. But in truth war is also beauty. For all its horror, you can't help but gape at the awful majesty of combat" (92). Like the war it describes, O'Brien's story combines the grotesque and the beautiful to create a powerful statement about conflict.

FAY WELDON, *IND AFF, or Out of Love in Sarajevo* (p. 463)

Fay Weldon, whose most recent books include *The Hearts of the Country* (1987), *The Rules of Life* (1987), *The Shrapnel Academy* (1987), and *The Hearts and Lives of Men* (1988), was born in 1933 in Alvechurch, Worcestershire, England. She wrote advertising copy for various companies and was a propaganda writer for the British Foreign Office before turning to fiction. Like many English writers, she works in a variety of forms: novel, play, television and radio script. In fact, her script for an episode in the "Upstairs, Downstairs" television series won an award in 1971 from the Society of Film and Television Arts. Although some critics think that Weldon's fiction is too tied to stereotypical portrayals of women, she is usually considered a feminist writer, "an expert chronicler," as one critic put it, "of the minutiae of women's lives, good at putting their case and pleading their cause." Novels such as *The Fat Woman's Joke* (1967), *Down Among the Women* (1971), *Praxis* (1978), and *The Life and Loves of a She-Devil* (1983) often use ironic humor to portray carefully drawn female characters coming to terms with the facts of their lives.

In this brief cautionary tale, Weldon manages to question the nature of fate and individual will, desire and imagination, as well as question the relationship between the apparently political and the apparently personal. It is not so much the "sad story" promised by the first line as it is a fable about taking responsibilities for one's actions and understanding the essentially interconnected nature of all events.

When the twenty-five year old unnamed narrator fell in love with her forty-six year old thesis director (who was already married and the father of three children), she fell in love with her idea of him rather than falling in love with him as a man. The narrator, who tells her story from the perspective of one who has learned her lesson and is now simply imparting it, has come to understand that she had confused "mere passing academic ambition with love" (48), believing this man's assessment of the world and of herself ("He said I had a good mind but not a first-class mind and somehow I didn't take it as an insult" [4]) when she should have been coming up with her own conclusions. Weldon comments in another story concerned with a young woman's infatuation with a much older man that "it was not her desire that was stirred, it was her imagination. But how is she to know this?" What the narrator wishes to believe about her lover — that this is "not just any old professor-student romance" — and what she actually feels about him are two different things.

Peter Piper (the name itself should indicate a certain lack of respect on the part of the author for such characters), the Cambridge professor who has been married to a swimming coach for twenty-four years, likes to "luxuriate in guilt and indecision," and has taken his student/mistress with him on a holiday to see whether they are "really, truly suited," to make sure that it is "the Real Thing" before they "shack up, as he put it." The narrator is desperately drawn to her teacher because he represents much more than he actually offers. To maintain her affection for Peter, she overlooks his stinginess ("Peter felt it was less confusing if we each paid our own way" [43]), his whining ("I noticed I had become used to his complaining. I supposed that when you had been married a little you simply wouldn't hear it" [12]), the fact that often when she spoke "he wasn't listening," the fact that he might not want her to go topless at the beach ("this might be the area where the age difference showed") as well as overlooking his "thinning hair" because he seems authoritative (speaking in "quasi-Serbo-Croatian") and powerful. He "liked to be asked questions," and obviously adores the adoration of his student. She loves him with "inordinate Affection," she claims. "Your Ind Aff is my wife's sorrow" (27) Peter moans, blaming a girl who was born the first year of his marriage for his wife's unhappiness, absolving himself from any blame.

The question of whether particular events happen because of the inevitable build-up of insurmountable forces or, instead, because of a series of particular moments that might have been avoided with care, caution or consideration is brought to bear not only on the narrator's relationship with Peter but on the question of World War I. With the background material effortlessly supplied by Weldon, even readers unfamiliar with the story of Princip's assassination of the archduke will be able to see the way Princip's tale parallels that of the narrator. Was the war inevitable? Was it, as Peter Piper claimed, bound to "start sooner or later," because of the "social and economic tensions" that had to find "some release"? Along the same lines of reasoning, was the twenty-four year marriage between Peter and the woman who is known only as Mrs. Piper doomed to failure, or was it instead pressured into failure by the husband's infidelity? Was it, as the narrator's sister Clare (herself married to a much older professor) claimed, a fact that "if you can unhinge a marriage, it's ripe for unhinging, it would happen sooner or later, it might as well be you" (36)? Is it, in other words, the narrator who is assassinating the Piper marriage?

The climax of the story occurs when the narrator and Peter are waiting to be served wild boar in a private restaurant. She notices a waiter whom she describes as being "about my age" (showing her keenly felt awareness of the difference in age between herself and Peter). She has felt desire for Peter in her mind, and has learned to feel "a pain in her heart" as an "erotic sensation" but in looking at the virile, handsome man her own age she feels "quite violently, an associated yet different pang which got my lower stomach." She describes this desire as the "true, the real pain of Ind Aff!" Her desire for the waiter has nothing to do with his position, his authority or his power. It has to do with his "flashing eyes, hooked nose, luxuriant black hair, sensuous mouth." She thinks to herself in a moment of clear vision "what was I doing with this man with thinning hair?" She thinks to herself, when she automatically tells Peter that she loves him, "how much I lied." She has freed herself from the confines of his authority, and declares in opposition to his theory, that, "If Princip hadn't shot the archduke, something else, some undisclosed, unsuspected variable, might have come along and defused the whole political/military situation, and neither World War I nor II ever happened" (43). She then gets up to go "home."

"This is how I fell out of love with my professor," declares the narrator, describing their affair as "a silly, sad episode, which I regret." She sees herself as silly for having confused her career ambitions with desire, and silly for trying to "outdo my sister Clare" who had married her professor (but has to live in Brussels as a sort of cosmic penance). Piper eventually proved spiteful and tried to refuse the narrator's thesis, but she won her appeal and, delightfully, can confirm for herself that she does indeed have a "first-class mind" after all. She feels, finally, a connection to poor Princip, who should have "hung on a bit, there in Sarajevo" because he might have "come to his senses. People do, sometimes quite quickly."

Questions for Discussion and Writing:

1. *Henry Kissinger once said that "power is the ultimate aphrodisiac," and Weldon's story takes up the notion that, especially for young women, it can often be a man's position rather than his personal attractions that spark her desire. What changes does the narrator go through in order to arrive at the "true, the real" Ind Aff she feels for the waiter? Why can she finally see Peter Piper for what he is?*

2. *Discuss the importance of the definition of Ind Aff offered by Piper. Consider the fact that it was felt by an aging minister for a young parishioner, and discuss the implications for the relationship between the narrator and her professor.*

3. *It would be interesting to hear this story told from the perspective of another character in the tale. What would the wife's version be like? What would Clare say about the relationship? How would the young waiter describe the events of the day? How would their voices and perspectives differ from the narrator's?*

4. *Consider the importance of the details Weldon uses to delineate the finer points of her story. Consider the importance of the general and the immediate setting, of the description of the hotel room, of the food when it finally arrives, of the mistake Peter makes when he says "Hungro-Austrarian" instead of "Austro-Hungarian." How do these details work to set the tone, mildly ironic and cautionary, of the tale?*

11. Perspectives on Fiction

THOMAS JEFFERSON, *On the Dangers of Reading Fiction* (p. 470)

Draw on any story that was popular in class to argue that reading fiction is time spent "instructively employed" and that reason and good judgment can be improved by reading fiction — in short, to refute Jefferson's argument. Have students tell you what they learned from any of the stories in the anthology, and state why they were worth reading. Jefferson's views could also be discussed in light of the book banning and censorship going on in this country today.

KATHERINE MANSFIELD, *On the Style of* **Miss Brill** (p. 471)

Consideration 2 would make an excellent writing assignment.

F. SCOTT FITZGERALD, *On the Continuity of a Writer's Works* (p. 471)

Fitzgerald suggests that each writer has "two or three great and moving experiences" in his or her life, and that he or she tells those "two or three stories — each time in a new disguise — maybe ten times, maybe a hundred, as long as people will listen." Ask the class whether this statement might have broader implications — isn't there a "certain family resemblance," for instance, between most stories about growing up, or about death, or about divorce? Ask students to try to group stories in this anthology into such families. If they are thematically similar, then what makes the stories different?

WARREN BECK, *Sentimentality in Formula Fiction* (p. 472)

Just as Chekhov said that preaching a sermon in fiction would result in bad art, Beck is suggesting that sentimentality usually leads to bad art. Have students identify the stories in this text they found most moving. Is there any "deceptive sentimentalizing of reality" in them? If not, what in the stories moved students?

A. L. BADER, *Nothing Happens in Modern Short Stories* (p. 474)

Ask students to read through relatively recent issues of *The New Yorker,* the *Atlantic,* or *Esquire* until they find a short story they really like. Does anything "happen" in the story? Is there a character change? If not, what do they like about the story?

EUDORA WELTY, *On the Plots of* **The Bride Comes to Yellow Sky** *and* **Miss Brill** (p. 475)

Welty asserts that "considerably more of a story is attempted" in "Miss Brill" than in "The Bride Comes to Yellow Sky"; she describes Crane's story as "playful" and a "comedy." Ask the class first whether they agree with this assessment and second whether they think that because something is playful or funny it is necessarily "less" of a story, or a less serious piece of work. Ask students whether they can cite works that are both funny and serious. (Bambara's "The Lesson" [p. 364] is a good example.)

ELIZABETH BOWEN, *The Writer's Roving Eye* (p. 478)

Bowen writes, "the writer, in fact, first knows he has found his subject by finding himself already obsessed by it. . . . He must . . . share, make known, communicate what he has seen, or knows. The urgency of what is real to him demands that it should be realized by other people." This quotation is an excellent context in which to discuss any story the class finds odd or disturbing — but especially those by Mishima and O'Connor. Mishima's "Patriotism" (p. 412) is very clearly an instance in which the author desperately wants his readers to understand how passionately he feels about something. In O'Connor, the revelation of the real is violent and upsetting.

ERNEST HEMINGWAY, *On What Every Writer Needs* (p. 478)

Assign consideration 2 as part of a writing topic. For the rest of the assignment, ask students to discuss a character (from any story) who does *not* have a "shit detector." How might this character think and behave differently if he or she did have such a "radar"?

VLADIMIR NABOKOV, *On How to Be a Good Reader* (p. 479)

Nabokov values "imagination" and "artistic sense" quite highly. But he also agrees these values are subjective ("you . . . may be merely my dream, and I may be your nightmare"). A fascinating discussion could ensue on which of the stories in this anthology require the most "imagination" and/or "artistic sense" to read. Ask students whether these criteria are the same as their criteria for a good story.

WILLIAM FAULKNER, *On the Demands of Writing Short Stories* (p. 481)

A good topic for a paper could spring from this statement; you could ask students to write a stylistic analysis of the story of their choice. Have them examine the language line by line, and explain why they think the author phrased things as he or she did — in other words, demonstrate how every word is "almost exactly right." (Such an assignment could easily become too lengthy; perhaps students could concentrate on the opening paragraph, or section, of a story.)

MORDECAI MARCUS, *What Is an Initiation Story?* (p. 481)

To the list of stories suggested for categorization in consideration 2, add Bambara's "The Lesson" (p. 364), Lawrence's "The Horse Dealer's Daughter" (p. 383), and Munro's "How I Met My Husband" (p. 133).

GORE VIDAL, *The Popularity of the Tarzan Books* (p. 482)

In light of Vidal's statement that "action" is so hard to write, ask students to compare the action in the excerpt from *Tarzan of the Apes* (p. 40) with the action in any story they think might stand up well against "Tarzan." Particularly good choices would be Mishima's "Patriotism" (p. 412) and Poe's "The Pit and the Pendulum" (p. 398).

MODY C. BOATRIGHT, *A Typical Western Plot Formula* (p. 484)

Have students compare this western plot formula with the "Composite Romance Tip Sheet" (p. 18). How do these formulas differ? What do they have in common? Can students make any connection between the formulas and Beck's essay "Sentimentality in Formula Fiction" (p. 472)?

JOHN CHEEVER, *On Morals in Fiction* (p. 485)

Ask students whether there are any stories in this anthology that they think would be better described as philosophy than as fiction.

E. L. DOCTOROW, *The Importance of Fiction* (p. 486)

Compare Doctorow's beliefs about fiction with Jefferson's (p. 470). While Doctorow clearly thinks fiction is good and Jefferson, for the most part, does not, is there anything the two men have in common? (Quite a bit: they both believe in the power of fiction, and that it can be a dangerous thing. Doctorow, however, believes that the dangerous things fiction can do should, and must, be done.)

POETRY

Brief biographical notes for major poets are included in the first entry for each poet. Check the Index of Authors and Titles (in the text) for page numbers of first entries.

12. Reading Poetry

MARGE PIERCY, *The Secretary Chant* (p. 493)

This poem provides an opportunity to discuss point of view in poetry. The secretary's view of herself mirrors the way she is treated. She has become a variety of objects, a list of useful items, because she is looked at as an object by people outside her. Her attitude toward herself is framed by other people's perspectives on her, although we must assume that she is aware of her ability to write satire. We get an inkling of her "real" self in the last three lines; the misspelled "wonce" mocks misperceptions of her intellect, while "woman" indicates that there is much more to be learned about the speaker.

In a writing assignment, you might ask students to discuss the metaphors in this poem. What assumptions about women and secretaries do the metaphors satirize? How do sound patterns such as "Zing. Tinkle" (line 14) affect the satire?

Connection

1. *Compare the speaker's attitude toward women in this poem with the attitude in E. E. Cummings's "she being Brand" (p. 527). What might Piercy say about Cummings's poem?*

ROBERT HAYDEN, *Those Winter Sundays* (p. 494)

Useful comparisons can be made between any of the poems in this book that speak of love's transcendence or amplitude and any others, like this one and Theodore Roethke's "My Papa's Waltz" (p. 637), that speak of its difficulty, the time it sometimes takes to recognize love. Hayden's speaker looks back at his father's unappreciated Sunday labor, at last knowing it for what it was and knowing, too, that the chance for gratitude has long passed. The poem gives a strong sense, especially in its final two lines, that the speaker has tended to "love's austere and lonely offices." The repetition of "What did I know?" seems to be a cry into the silence not only of the past but of the poet's present situation as well. The poem plays the music of the father's furnace work, the hard consonant sounds "splintering, breaking" as the poem unfolds and disappearing entirely by the poem's end.

JOHN UPDIKE, *Dog's Death* (p. 496)

This poem is a narrative. Ask students to find the events that lead to the dog's death. How does the speaker relate these events to us? He tells us the dog's age when he talks about her toilet training and immediately establishes the family's relationship to her by repeating their words: "Good dog! Good dog!" (line 4). Alliteration and assonance soften the story; after they have identified these sound patterns, ask students why the repeated sounds are appropriate to the subject matter. Direct their attention to the enjambment in lines 12–13. Why does the sentence span two stanzas? Might the speaker be reluctant to tell us the dog died?

When he relates his wife's reaction to the death, the speaker describes her voice as "imperious with tears" (14). After they have established a definition of the word imperious, ask students to determine why it would be used here. The ambiguous "her" and "she" in the final two lines of the stanza make us puzzle out for a moment the pronouns' referent. Is the speaker talking about his wife or the dog? Are both implied? How does this distortion of identity work in a discussion of death?

The final stanza reads as a eulogy; the consonants become harder — "drawing," "dissolution," "diarrhoea," "dragged" — perhaps because the speaker is working at closing off the experience. In a writing assignment, you might ask students to discuss the three uses of "Good Dog." How does the last one differ from the first two? How does the poem prepare us for the change?

Connection

1. *Richard Eberhart's "The Groundhog" (p. 592) offers an extended and difficult treatment of the death of an animal. His tone is quite different from Updike's, because Updike talks about a house pet, not a strange, discovered animal. A longer writing assignment might ask students to compare the two poems, exploring the speaker's relationship to his subject in each. How does the diction of each speaker fit his subject? How would Eberhart's subject sound if it were articulated in Updike's words?*

WILLIAM HATHAWAY, *Oh, Oh* (p. 498)

Discussed in text.

ROBERT FRANCIS, *Catch* (p. 499)

Encourage students to enjoy listening to this poem. Like a good pitcher, Francis finds various ways of throwing strikes. Consider, for example, line 3, with its "attitudes, latitudes, interludes, altitudes," or "prosy" and "posy" later in the poem.

CONRAD HILBERRY, *Tongue* (p. 500)

Students should have no trouble articulating what happens in this poem, but take some time to go over the imagery. Consider, for example, the steely, inescapable quality of "the cold clanged shut" (line 8), especially with the *cl*-sounds following so closely the mention of the Cyclone fence. Observe "shame that tasted like blood" (16), a simile that joins an emotion with the physical fact that gives rise to it. The repetition of "He swallowed" in the final line not only recreates a sense of the repeated act but also provides a sense of closure. Without relying very heavily at all on descriptive language, Hilberry makes us feel the boy's pain and shame.

You might ask students to write a one- to two-page paper in which they discuss two or three images in the poem and how each elicits sensory response in the reader.

ELIZABETH BISHOP, *The Fish* (p. 501)

Born in Worcester, Massachusetts, Elizabeth Bishop knew displacement early: her father died when she was an infant, and her mother was committed to an asylum when she was five. Bishop lived with relatives during her childhood and adolescence in Nova Scotia and New England; after completing a degree at Vassar College, she lived in New York City, Key West, and for sixteen years in Brazil. Travel and exile, as well as the insistent yet alien presence of the "things of the world," figure prominently in her work.

The most arresting feature of "The Fish" is its imagery. Consider, for example, the brown skin that "hung in strips / like ancient wall-paper" (lines 10–11), the ornamentation of "fine rosettes of lime" (17), or the pause to mention and comment again on "the frightening gills" (24). Not only does Bishop have an eye for the particular, even the minute, but in this poem *(text pages) 501–505*

she exhibits an ability to dissect imaginatively flesh, bones, bladder, the interior of the fish's eyes.

After you review the appearance of the fish, it might be a good idea to glance back at the syntax of the poem. Note, for example, the syntactic simplicity and parallelism of lines 5–7, conveying with their flat factuality the fish's implacable "thereness." The syntax becomes a little more complex later on, as Bishop's vision penetrates into the interior of the fish's anatomy and, eventually, into its being. The fish is no longer a mere member of its species but a kind of military hero and a survivor that has escaped at least five attempts on its life.

Bishop's skill transforms the fish into a thing of beauty and an object of admiration, almost without our realizing it. At this point in the discussion, though, it would be a good idea to step back and see what she is looking at. The scene is simply an old fish, brown and battle-scarred, with sullen jaw, staring back at the speaker (Bishop, we assume). Not an ideal setting for the epiphanic moment.

But that is, of course, what occurs — signaled to us by the repetition of the word *rainbow*. In a sense, both fish and poet have transcended themselves — the one by surviving, the other by seeing beyond the ugliness. Victory, indeed, fills up the boat.

You might teach this poem in connection with Robert Lowell's "Skunk Hour" (p. 553). A writing assignment could be organized around an analysis and comparison of the poems' endings or around the themes of survival and victory.

PHILIP LARKIN, *A Study of Reading Habits* (p. 503)

Discussed in text.

ROBERT MORGAN, *Mountain Graveyard* (p. 504)

Discussed in text.

This poem might be used to demonstrate the rewards of active reading. One must "construct" a meaning here more deliberately than when reading many other poems. Some students might like to try writing their own anagram poem, using as a starting point a word pair from this poem, or striking out on their own.

E. E. CUMMINGS, *l(a* (p. 505)

E. E. Cummings was born in Cambridge, Massachusetts, the son of a Congregationalist minister. He earned a degree from Harvard University and began writing his iconoclastic poems after coming upon the work of Ezra Pound. His experimentation with syntax and punctuation reflects a seriously playful attitude toward language and meaning and a skepticism about institutional authority.

At first glance, "l(a" seems to be a poem spewed out by a closemouthed computer held in solitary confinement. As with Morgan's "Mountain Graveyard," however, the poem comes into its own as the reader not only deciphers but brings meaning to the text. Implied here is a simile between a falling leaf and loneliness. The natural image used to suggest an emotion recalls Japanese haiku (see Chapter 19).

The vertical quality of the poem illustrates the motion of a single leaf falling. Students might also point out the repetition of the digit *one* (indistinguishable in some texts from the letter *l*), along with other "aloneness" words, such as *a* and *one*. If ever a poem's medium enhanced its message, this one surely does.

65

ANONYMOUS, *Western Wind* (p. 506)

Discussed in text.

REGINA BARRECA, *Nighttime Fires* (p. 507)

This narrative poem has a recurrent theme, indicated by the repetitions of the word "smoke." Smoke is the end of the father's quest, but what, exactly, is he looking for? His daughter, the speaker, provides a clue when she tells us that her father lost his job, so he had time to pursue fires. Smoke is the father's assurance that there is justice in the world, because fires destroy rich and poor people alike. Ask students to look at the images the speaker uses to describe her father: What kind of man is he? What is the daughter's relationship to him? Does the mother also think of these drives as "festival, carnival"? In some respect, the carnival is the father's performance before his family, in which the "wolf whine of the siren" is matched by his "mad" expression.

In a writing assignment, you might ask students to examine the metaphors describing the father. What do these figures tell us about his life? For example, in the final image of the father, his eyes are compared to "hallways filled with smoke" (line 31). Why is he likened to a house? What might this image tell us about his life?

Connection

1. *Compare the speaker's diction in this poem with the diction in Robert Creeley's "Fathers" (p. 891). What is the relationship of speaking child to father in each case? How do the speakers' attitudes to their fathers compare? What might account for the differences or similarities in diction and tone between these two poems?*

HELEN FARRIES, *Magic of Love* (p. 511)

Note the ways in which this poem fulfills the greeting-card formula, especially with its "lilting" anapests, internal rhymes, and tried-and-true (and terribly trite) metaphors, all designed to lift the reader's spirits.

JOHN FREDERICK NIMS, *Love Poem* (p. 512)

Greeting cards must speak to the anonymous mass. Nims's poem, while maintaining a simplicity of diction and a directness of sentiment, is far stronger than the greeting-card verse, in part because it is addressing a specific person.

The poem is obviously not a piece to be carved on the pedestal of some faceless ideal; students will probably have at least some curiosity about a poem that begins "My clumsiest dear." After they have become accustomed to this violating of poetic convention, ask them to review the poem for other refreshing and surprising uses of language. They might mention, for example, the use of "shipwreck" as a verb in line 1, the play on "bull in a china shop" (3), or the projective quality of "undulant" in line 8 to describe the floor as it appears to the drunk. Again, unlike conventional verse, this poem concludes with an almost paradoxical twist to the most salient feature of this woman who breaks things: her absence would cause "all the toys of the world [to] break."

In a writing assignment, you might ask students to compare this poem with Shakespeare's sonnet "My mistress' eyes . . ." (p. 648).

TRACY CHAPMAN, *Fast Car* (p. 513)

Considerations (p. 514)

1. The third stanza gives a good indication of what the speaker's life is like. Her poverty and loneliness drive her to the desperate solution she comes up with. She hopes a "fast car"

will move her out of the shelter, out of the city, and into a house, a good job, and tolerable living conditions.

2. The speaker's desperation and hopes resound in the repetitions of "You got a fast car." These repetitions also give the lyric the coherence a song requires, making it appeal to the listener's ear. The man described is a lot like the speaker's father; he drinks heavily and ignores his responsibilities to his children. Rather than find a way to escape his situation, he chooses the temporary pleasures of alcohol and a fast car. Like his car, the speaker goes at a high speed, but in no particular direction.

3. One of the reasons we don't require punctuation to read these lyrics must be our familiarity with the song. We hear the music in the background as we read. But another reason is that the poem organizes itself around the repetitions of the line "You got a fast car"; this short sentence makes sense of all the rest.

4. In that it tells the story of the speaker's life, this is a narrative poem.

PERSPECTIVE

ROBERT FRANCIS, *On "Hard" Poetry* (p. 515)

Considerations (p. 515)

1. Hard poetry is best defined through its opposite, soft poetry. Hard poetry does not use excess words, does not lapse into sentimentality, does not have an undefined or loose form. The hard poem sustains tension between poet and speaker, reader and text.

3. Chapman's poem is probably not tense enough to be called "hard" in Frost's sense of the term. Her narrative is accessible and uncomplicated so the reader can digest it immediately; the repetitions give the poem a loose but orderly form. The essential, timeless ambiguity that Frost seems to call for does not exist here, perhaps because this is a song. Music lyrics are a genre requiring both listener and author to undertake different tasks.

TED KOOSER, *Selecting a Reader* (p. 516)

The irony in the title of this poem is that although Kooser imaginatively projects his "ideal" reader, she in fact selects — and then rejects — him. The act bespeaks a sort of cool control over her world, a resistance to being swept up by romantic values. These apparently are traits that Kooser admires in this attractive woman, who at least stops momentarily to look at his poems. You might ask students to imagine the kind of poetic style Kooser's book would be written in. Very likely, it would resemble this poem — an ambling, naturally falling free verse (a little like the woman's hair, perhaps), with few adornments of image or metaphor and a fairly heavy reliance on the cadences of everyday conversation.

MARY OLIVER, *The Black Snake* (p. 516)

You might begin by asking the class whether they accept Oliver's assurance in this poem that the prevailing story is of "endless good fortune." Through the archetypally powerful image of the snake, which makes reflection on death possible, Oliver asserts that the pulse of life (and light) "at the center of every cell" is the force that drives us through the "green leaves," season to season, as we seem to meet our natural calling. Oliver ascribes reflection on death to reason, not to this "brighter fire" urging us onward.

Connections (p. 517)

1. Contrasts between the attitudes expressed in Stafford's poem and in this poem are striking and could be addressed in a three-page paper. Clearly, Oliver's voice is the more optimistic, whereas Stafford is more likely to characterize our consciousness of death as a visceral knowledge that probably goes deeper than Oliver's "reason." Life for Stafford,

on the other hand, is a Dantesque journey through a dark wood, beset by doom and the continuous accompaniment of death. For Stafford, it is possible in this world to be "alive, still, never to be born."

2. Whereas Dickinson's presentation gives us the "essence" of snake through a riddling poem, Oliver's presentation of the same animal provides an opportunity for thinking about death. Dickinson's is a more imagistic poem; we might call Oliver's poem symbolic. Of course, given the symbolic importance of the snake since the story of Adam and Eve in the Garden of Eden, Dickinson's poem cannot help but have those connotations as well; Oliver, though, explores the image of death much more deliberately.

ANONYMOUS, *Sir Patrick Spens* (p. 517)

Poetry should, according to a long-standing critical tradition, instruct and delight. Narrative poetry (with "Sir Patrick Spens" as an example) clearly meets those demands. Originating and continuing as an oral tradition, narrative poems were rhythmic poems recited with musical accompaniment or sung. Such poetry took on a communal nature in at least two senses. An individual heard and shared the poem within his or her group, and whatever anxieties or tragedies were told in the poem became a part of that group's cultural history. In a second and larger sense, the narrative poem created links between generations as it was passed down, often with modifications. Despite its "folk" origins, this is a fairly sophisticated narrative poem and raises some interesting questions.

Considerations (p. 518)

1. Sir Patrick Spens is a man of honor who obeys his king as part of the chivalric code, even though to do so courts disaster. The poem indicates that the nobles do not advise the king wisely and seem to have no sense of sea conditions.

2. The development of this poem does not show the usual gradual unfolding of events that we might expect from any narrative, whether story or verse. Instead, events shift suddenly, in a manner similar to the film technique of splicing.

3. Ballads often depend on a storytelling community that already knows their plots. Omitting the details of the shipwreck speeds up the narrative, helps emphasize the morality of the king's order, and preserves an almost Greek decorum in the presentation of the tale.

4. As long as there are political hierarchies, one will be able to sympathize with and relate to a story describing a good and competent person who gets trapped in the machinery of blind authority.

JOHN DONNE, *The Sun Rising* (p. 519)

John Donne was born Roman Catholic when England was staunchly anti-Catholic, a circumstance that made his pursuit of worldly success significantly more difficult than it might otherwise have been for one with his intelligence, energy, and wit. Donne attended Oxford and Cambridge universities and trained in the law for a time. After a youth and young manhood full of worldly pleasure, Donne became an Anglican preacher in 1615.

You might begin a discussion of this poem by reading aloud (or having a member of the class read aloud) at least the first stanza. Donne excels in the fine art of poetic vituperation and argument. Here he ranges from complaint to lover's hyperbole, and from regard for an individual to conversation with the cosmos.

The poem opens with the speaker lying in bed with his beloved as the sun streams in. The speaker's blunt message to the sun is to leave the lovers alone and bother other people who need waking to get on with the work of their ordinary lives. The tone softens in the second stanza, as Donne thinks more of his beloved. When he is with her, the world seems to be concentered in their presence. If the sun were to shine only on their room, it would be everywhere.

In the final stanza the speaker continues to expound on how, when you are in love, your heaven, earth, and kingdom are contained in your beloved. As he writes in the opening of this stanza, "She is all states, and all princes I," and later, "All honor's mimic, all wealth alchemy." Some students might point out that the idea that true love is a treasure worth far more than any amount of money still persists.

The "Connection" question following this poem, which suggests a comparison between the poem and Richard Wilbur's "A Late Aubade," would make a good writing topic for a three-page paper. The language in the two poems is certainly different, and the world that Wilbur describes is secular and less hierarchical, but the delight in lying in bed after sunrise is shared.

NIKKI GIOVANNI, *Nikki-Rosa* (p. 520)

"Black love is Black wealth," Giovanni tells us near the end of this poem, and you might want to take that phrase and refer back to Donne's "The Sun Rising" with a comment on how love as wealth possesses a universal currency. This lyric puts any saccharine sentimentality at bay by telling both good and bad childhood remembrances in a natural, direct style. Giovanni presents this poem as though she were speaking it and all the memories, as well as what those memories would mean to her and to an outsider listening in, came to her in a rush. The lack of punctuation reflects this near-simultaneous process of association. The poem, though, probably has a rhetorical purpose beyond mere narration. Giovanni seems to be writing for both black and white readers, warning the latter that they will never fully understand her and the former that their experience is not likely to be perceived accurately.

Connections (p. 520)

1. In Barreca's poem the speaker recounts a horrible childhood memory that makes her father appear almost insane. The speaker's exploration of her father through the fire-chasing experiences details the difficulties of living in his social class, being unemployed, and trying to take care of his family. The speaker in "Nikki-Rosa" also has difficult past experiences to talk about, but her emphasis is on a racial difference that would lead her audience to assume and to dwell on the aspects of her life that are most grim. she resists those racist readings, insisting on the power of "Black love" to create a kind of wealth that it would be difficult for her (white, wealthier) critics to understand.

2. The speaker in Holman's poem criticizes Mr. Z for denying his culture, whereas Giovanni's poem celebrates her cultural background in the vivid details of what it was like to live in her house. Mr. Z denies his past, whereas Giovanni's speaker shows that her past has made her who she is. The poems share a similar attitude toward white interpreters of black people's lives. Mr. Z is revered for having turned himself into a white man ("One of the most distinguished members of his race"), but Giovanni's speaker warns her critics to look at the details of her life in a less condescending way, to try to understand that "Black love is Black wealth."

EMILY DICKINSON, *To make a prairie it takes a clover and one bee* (p. 521)

With the exception of one year at the South Hadley Female Seminary (which later became Mount Holyoke College) and several brief visits to Boston, Philadelphia, and Washington, D.C., Emily Dickinson spent her entire life in or near her father's house in Amherst, Massachusetts. Her work's rhythms (which often exactly reproduce those in Protestant hymns), subject matter, and characteristic tone derive from her upbringing in the Congregational church.

"To make a prairie" reads like a recipe — add this to that and you will get the desired result. But it could just as well be a call for props in a theater production: Take these items and add a little reflective imagination and the result will be a prairie, itself a symbol of open-endedness and freedom of spirit. What wondrous things can be achieved through lushness, industry, and the alchemy of the seeing (and singing) spirit.

To enable students to understand the poem more clearly, you might ask them in a brief writing assignment to specify as broadly and clearly as possible the suggestion inherent in "bee," "clover," "prairie," and the notion of "revery."

13. Word Choice, Word Order, and Tone

RANDALL JARRELL, *The Death of the Ball Turret Gunner* (p. 525)

Discussed in text.

E. E. CUMMINGS, *she being Brand* (p. 527)

This poem is a naughtily playful allegory of a young man's attempt to initiate a sexual experience with his girlfriend. Language accommodates the situation of the poem nicely since men of a certain age seem to respond to cars and women with equal measures of affection and caretaking and refer to both cars and women as "she." Cummings drops innuendos of his witty double entendres early on. Listen, for example, to the opening eight lines, in which the poet seems to pause over words like "stiff," "universal," and even "springs," which could suggest springs of affection. Knowing the "secret" of the poem, the class should enjoy lines such as "next / minute i was back in neutral tried and / again slo-wly; bare,ly nudg. ing (my" (13–15). This work also offers good opportunities to discuss the function of punctuation in poetry.

KATHARYN MACHAN AAL, *Hazel Tells LaVerne* (p. 529)

You might begin discussing this poem by talking about names and how they too have connotative value. Would our expectations be the same if the poem were titled "Sybil Speaks with Jacqueline"? By and large this poem does a good job at getting across its meaning through denotative language. But the fact that Hazel does use language almost exclusively in denotative terms is in itself a sign of her personality. As in a dramatic monologue by Robert Browning, Hazel tells more about herself, her social class, and her impenetrably matter-of-fact outlook on life than she does about her encounter with the frog. We as readers then fill in the gaps of the speaker's perceptions as well as piece together her outlook and attitude.

You might ask students to respond to Hazel's personality. She is likable; her matter-of-factness cuts through any of the fairy tales the world might try to sell her, and she's funny. Students can probably provide examples of characters from TV shows who are like Hazel and whose humor derives from their plainspoken concreteness. We all admire the survivor who cannot be duped.

EMILY DICKINSON, *If I can stop one Heart from breaking* and *If I shouldn't be alive* (p. 530)

You might begin discussion of "If I can stop . . ." by recalling comments on sentimentality and the greeting-card tradition (pp. 510–511). Dickinson's relation to such popular occasional verse is, after all, not so farfetched, since she is reputed to have honored birthdays and other social occasions by composing poems. This poem, though, exhausts the limits of the well-intentioned. It is a fine idea to help others, but to adopt that principle as the only rule of conduct seems self-effacing — and sentimental.

Why this poem succeeded in the world of popular letters is readily apparent. The idea contains the cant of what we think we should think, and it is simply stated. You might speculate with students on why the least common denominator of a poet's work is so often what the popular mind accepts. Recall as a parallel Walt Whitman's poem on Lincoln, "O Captain! My Captain!" — a rhymed lyric that still finds its way into many high-school anthologies.

"If I shouldn't be alive," is much more in keeping with Dickinson's usual ironic mode. Here the speaker's capacity for an undermining wit is hinted at in the circuitous expression of the opening/title line. The first stanza and most of the second, though, seem to echo the kindly if unthinking benevolent spirit of "If I can stop. . . ." The speaker playfully singles out and personifies a robin to receive a token remembrance ("a crumb") as "Memorial," presumably of her.

The final line, however, abruptly and irreversibly deflects the poem from its course of saccharine gentility. We are no longer smiling indulgently at this fanciful and excessively polite person (a lady, we assume); instead, she forces us to face death by asserting her desire to fulfill her obligation, even from the "other side." As a way of enabling students to appreciate this masterstroke, you might have them rewrite the final line so that it steers the poem back toward a more conventional expression.

Here is another writing assignment: We often like a poem because we like, or at least have a sense of, its speaker. Compare in a one-page paper the speakers in these two poems, and pay special attention to their diction. Which speaker is the more engaging and likable and why?

MAXINE KUMIN, *Woodchucks* (p. 531)

Kumin has a farm in southern New Hampshire, and many of her poems describe her experiences with the land and with raising and training her horses. To anyone familiar with farming, especially in New England, woodchucks are pesky creatures that seem to do their best to make a peaceable coexistence between animals and humans difficult. In her efforts to get rid of the woodchucks, notice how Kumin arranges language as an armor to justify her acts. Like a good attorney, she has an "airtight" legal and moral case against the woodchucks. But when you read line 5, you see that her action amounts to entrapment. Language drawn from a religious sphere is also used to bolster her resolve to kill the woodchucks. The knockout bomb is described as "merciful" (3), and as the speaker picks up the .22, she "righteously" thrills to its feel (13). Even in her personal estimation, she is "a lapsed pacifist fallen from grace / puffed with Darwinian pieties for killing" (15–16). Where religion hesitates, science, with its promise of salvation for the fittest, moves in. What surprises Kumin is her newfound awareness that she can kill, one-on-one, with the dispatch of "murderer," or "hawkeye killer" (23–24). She thrills to the act and yet is haunted by it. Observe with the class how particular are her memories of each woodchuck she shoots and how, afterward, she has an unquiet dream of killing.

The final lines of the poem, "If only they'd all consented to die unseen / gassed underground the quiet Nazi way," are disquieting and filled with implications. An essay topic could be organized around an evaluation of Kumin's attitude toward her act, particularly with reference to these lines. Initially, Kumin did attempt to gas the woodchucks. Now that she has shot them, does she somehow feel implicated in the mindset that fueled the Jewish Holocaust? Aside from learning that she can kill, what has she learned from this experience?

ROBERT HERRICK, *To the Virgins, to Make Much of Time* (p. 532)

Robert Herrick, son of a well-to-do London goldsmith, rather halfheartedly became an Anglican clergyman assigned to Dean Prior in Devonshire, in the west of England. He wrote poems secretly, making up for many of them alluring, exotic, phantom mistresses. After losing his position when the Puritans rose to power, Herrick published his only book, containing some twelve hundred poems, in 1648.

This is one of the better-known poems of the *carpe diem* (seize the day) tradition. Here, Herrick is advising young women in a tone of straightforward urging to make the most of their opportunities for pleasure while they are in the prime of youth and beauty. These "virgins," Herrick implies, are like the sun at its zenith or a flower in full bloom; they will soon begin to decline and may never have the same opportunities for marriage again. The word *virgins*, rather than *women*, accommodates the advice in the last stanza to "go marry" and carries with it as well the connotation of sought-for sexual fulfillment. Some of your students might point out how a young woman's situation is much more complex today than it apparently was in Herrick's time, since "seizing the day" can and often does mean pursuing opportunities for career over those for marriage.

ANDREW MARVELL, *To His Coy Mistress* (p. 534)

After graduating from Cambridge University in 1639, Andrew Marvell left England to travel in Europe. Almost nothing is known of his life from this time until he became the tutor of the daughter of a powerful Yorkshire nobleman in 1650. Most of his poems seem to have been written during the next seven years. He served for a short time as John Milton's assistant when Milton was Latin secretary for the Commonwealth, and he represented Hull, his hometown, in Parliament from 1659 until he died.

Considerations (p. 535)

1. The poem is structured with flawless logic. Marvell begins with a hypothetical conjecture, "Had we but world enough, and time," which he then disproves with hyperbole, promising his "mistress" that he would devote "an age at least" to praising her every part. Time is, of course, far more limited, and the second section of the poem makes clear time's ravages on beauty. The third section expounds the *carpe diem* theme: if time is limited, then seize the day and triumph over life's difficulties with love.

2.,3. From his initial tone of teasing hyperbole, the poet modulates to a much more somber tone, employing the metaphysically startling imagery of the grave to underscore human mortality. Lines 31–32 are an example of understatement, calculated to make the listener react and acknowledge this world as the time and place for embracing.

4. Some classes may need help in recognizing that the verbs in the first part of the poem are in the subjunctive mood, while those in the last are often in the imperative. At any rate, students should easily recognize that the last section contains verbs that all imply a physical vigor that would seize time, mold it to the lovers' uses, and thus "make [time] run" according to the clock of their own desires.

5. The poem seems far more than a simple celebration of the flesh. It confronts human mortality and suggests a psychological stance that would seize life (and face death) so that fulfilling of one's time would be a strategy of confronting time's passing.

As a writing topic you might ask students to explain the radical and somewhat abrupt change in tone between the opening twenty lines and the rest of the poem. Marvell offers more than one reason to temper his initial levity.

Refer students to Bernard Duyfhuizen's "'To His Coy Mistress': On How a Female Might Respond", for a contemporary perspective on the poem.

PERSPECTIVE

BERNARD DUYFHUIZEN, *"To His Coy Mistress": On How a Female Might Respond* (p. 535)

You might ask your students in a writing assignment to use Duyfhuizen's analysis as a model in writing their own description of a female's response to a male poet's address. They could use the poems in this section (Robert Herrick's "To the Virgins, to Make Much of Time" and Richard Wilbur's "A Late Aubade"), or they might choose a poem like Shakespeare's "Shall I compare thee to a summer's day?" (p. 647). Students could also choose an address by a female poet to a male — Margaret Atwood's "you fit into me" (p. 563), for example — or a poem by a woman about a relationship with a man — Adrienne Rich's "Living in Sin" (p. 839) — and analyze the male's response.

RICHARD WILBUR, *A Late Aubade* (p. 536)

It is difficult to translate the forms of Renaissance charm and wit into the more hurried, less mannered tones of the twentieth century. So Wilbur seems to find as he writes his "late" aubade ("late," one supposes, as in "late Corinthian," as well as late in the day), in which going means staying and seizing the day dictates staying in bed. Despite the turnabout in manners and customs, this poem achieves its own special charm. You might begin discussion, though, by asking the class to evaluate the speaker here as rhetorician or persuader. Does he keep to the rules of logic, or does he beg some questions and employ loaded language in other instances? Obviously, he has no admiration for women who spend hours in either libraries or shopping malls, and with deadpan doggerel he sets up a rhyme in stanza I between "carrel" and "Ladies' Apparel" that devalues both activities. Likewise, he colors the attitude of the person being addressed by talking of planting a "raucous" bed of salvia (which yield bright blue or red flowers) or lunching through a "screed" (the archaism is deliberate here) of someone's loves.

The poem is an appeal to the assumed and presumed sensuality of both the speaker and the woman he addresses. Thus the Matisselike still life of chilled white wine, blue cheese, and ruddy-skinned pears with which Wilbur concludes the poem is a fitting tricolor tribute to the senses, even though the woman here is still the one who serves and waits.

A writing assignment could be organized around a comparison of Herrick's "To the Virgins, to Make Much of Time," Marvell's "To His Coy Mistress," and this poem. Wilbur's poem is more conversational and relaxed, reflecting a commonality of spirit between the lovers. The speaker here dwells more on the prolonged moment than on the bleak foreknowledge of death.

EDNA ST. VINCENT MILLAY, *Never May the Fruit Be Plucked* (p. 538)

Edna St. Vincent Millay wrote her first poem when she was only five years old. Her mother, divorced when Edna was very young, strongly encouraged her writing, and Millay published her first important poem, "Renascence," in 1912. She graduated from Vassar in 1917 and moved to Greenwich Village in New York, where she continued to write poetry and created verse dramas for the Provincetown Players. *A Few Figs from Thistles,* Millay's second volume of poetry, was published in 1920, and she won the Pulitzer Prize in 1923 for *The Harp Weaver.* She was involved in politics as well as the arts: she participated in the crusade to save Sacco and Vanzetti in 1927, and used her poetry for political expression from that time through World War II. Her shockingly blunt poems helped to debunk traditional notions of femininity, ushering in the "New Woman" of the 1920's. Millay died in 1950.

Considerations (p. 538)

1. The fruit is the end product of growth, while the rosebud represents the promise of a beautiful flower (and fruit) to come. Herrick's speaker urges his listener to pluck the bud from its stem before it has bloomed. In a similar vein, Millay's speaker encourages her listeners to enjoy love while it is ripe. She adds a warning to lovers that they cannot take the fruit with them. Both speakers characterize love as flourishing in the present. It should not be stored for some uncertain future or avoided to preserve a questionable virtue.

   You might ask students about the difference between Herrick's and Millay's images for love (a rosebud on the verge of blooming versus ripe fruit). Do they feel it reflects a general difference between male and female visions of love?

2. We may think of "eat[ing]" as consumption for nutrition or for sensuous pleasure. The distinction is implied in line 3; for this speaker love must be consumed out of physical need, not greed. There is an urgency to the image of eating in these lines. Of course, the sexual connotations of desire and fulfillment are also implied. The act of eating may harm the tree, or cause one to encounter unappetizing fruit, but the speaker claims these as the inevitable conditions of loving.

3. Love cannot be gathered or harvested into barrels because it cannot survive in unnatural surroundings, away from its source. The speaker defines love as ephemeral and immediate. It is an experience requiring the lover's active participation to keep it alive. This is a *carpe diem* poem in its urging for immediate consumption of the fruit. This poem defines seizing as experiencing, living, feeling.

4. "Never May the Fruit Be Plucked" could very well be addressed to men or women or both. But the message may not be the same for each. To men in the tradition of the *carpe diem* poem, who urge their lovers to forsake their virginity for a moment's pleasure, this poem offers a gentle corrective reminder of their own mortality. To both women and men, the poem offers a new definition of love, requiring much more than physical desire for its sustenance.

5. The last two lines are visually graphic, slightly threatening, and intellectually sobering. There is no hope for love to last forever; it must, by its nature, die. Comparing the death of love to the changing of seasons, the speaker stresses both the inevitability and the rapidity of its demise. The speaker's tone most resembles Marvell's in its sensitivity to physical decay.

Connections (p. 538)

1. Cummings and Millay seem to have similar notions of the spontaneous and ephemeral nature of love, although Millay does not seem to go as far as Cummings does when he writes "kisses are a better fate / than wisdom." Cummings's speaker humorously compares language to death, whereas Millay's speaker chooses more ominous images to remind her listeners of love's mortality.

2. Dickinson's tone is more expectant than Millay's. In "Wild Nights — Wild Nights!" the speaker looks forward to the completion that will come from her union with her beloved, whereas Millay's speaker warns would-be lovers that they must be careful or they will destroy love, even before it dies a natural death. Far more optimistic than Millay's poem, Dickinson's anticipates eternal love.

3. You might direct students to focus on the images of the urn and the tree as they contrast these poems. Ask them to consider the tree as an organic representation of love and the urn as an artifact. This distinction identifies the crucial differences between the poems. Keats's speaker is far more interested in the art of writing about love than in prescribing the proper way to love. Both speakers agree that love is fleeting, but Millay suggests a physical consuming as a way to appreciate it, whereas Keats implies that the best part of loving is the anticipation of first kissing the beloved. Keats's urn is "still unravished"; Millay's tree offers the promise of ravishing until the lovers are satiated.

THOMAS HARDY, *The Convergence of the Twain* (p. 539)

Between the ages of fifteen and twenty-one, Thomas Hardy was apprenticed to an architect in his native Dorchester, an area in southwest England that he was to transform into the "Wessex" of his novels. He went to London in 1862 to practice as an architect and pursue a growing interest in writing. Though he enjoyed a successful career as a novelist, Hardy stopped writing fiction after publishing *Jude the Obscure* in 1895, concentrating instead on the poetry that ranks him among the major English poets.

Considerations (p. 540)

1. The *Titanic* is described in this poem as "gaily great" in its luxurious opulence, but Hardy also stresses the ship's "vaingloriousness," planned by the "Pride of Life." It is as though in this dramatic gesture of invention and design humanity became the tragic overreacher. In a writing assignment you might ask the class to compare the tones of the speakers in this poem and in Percy Bysshe Shelley's "Ozymandias" (p. 848).

2.   The "marriage" between ship and iceberg is suggested in this poem through the use of several words and phrases, such as "sinister mate," (line 19), "intimate welding," as in "wedding" (27), and "consummation" in the final line.

3.   Hardy, the master celebrator of "Hap" (see p. 792), assigns the disaster to Fate, or as he allegorizes it — the "Immanent Will" that directs all things and the "Spinner of the Years," who decides when time has run out.

DAVID R. SLAVITT, *Titanic* (p. 540)

Although Slavitt's poem acknowledges the power of fate, it focuses on human attitudes rather than cosmic forces. The first stanza, for example, calls attention to our gullibility, its weary, yet affectionate tone originating in the "this is how we are" shrug of the two *who* clauses. The speaker ponders death, deciding that since "we all go down," it would be better to do so with some company and some notice from the rest of the world. But the speaker's gentle urging that it wouldn't be "so bad, after all" to go "first-class" includes some simple, unambiguous description of what such a mass loss of life would actually be like: "The cold water," which would be "anesthetic and very quick"; the "cries on all sides." Death always wins, "we all go down, mostly / alone," so wouldn't it be fine to die "with crowds of people, friends, servants, / well fed, with music"?

You might ask students to compare in a short paper the attitudes toward fate in "Titanic" and Hardy's "The Convergence of the Twain" and how each poem's diction and tone contribute to the communication of these attitudes.

GWENDOLYN BROOKS, *We Real Cool* (p. 541)

Gwendolyn Brooks, who grew up in Chicago and who won the Pulitzer Prize in 1950, has been a deeply respected and influential poet for more than forty years. As do many poets, she keeps witnessing her books going out of print.

Considerations

1.   *The repeated "we" sounds the menacing note of the communal pack, its members secure perhaps only when they are together. The truncated syntax reflects both a lack of and a disdain for education, yet the poem celebrates the music of its vernacular, a quality that would be mostly lost were the pronouns to appear at the beginnings of lines.*

2.   *Brooks's attitude toward this chorus that finds strength in numbers is a measured anger against its self-destructiveness. The absence of "we" in the final line is a silent prophecy of their future.*

3.   *The theme of the poem is death (burial/shovel) at an early age and the corruption of a golden opportunity to spend youth more wisely. The "Golden Shovel" also bespeaks an ironic promise that the events of the last line sadly belie.*

MARGE PIERCY, *A Work of Artifice* (p. 541)

Considerations (p. 542)

1.   A bonsai tree is a potted tree or shrub that has been dwarfed by pruning. Piercy suggests that women, like the bonsai trees, have been dwarfed by their "gardeners" — presumably, men. The gardener's crooning makes this comparison apparent; his words dictate the plant's "nature," convincing it that its environment is suited to its function.

2.   The gardener's song condescends to the bonsai tree. Words such as "small and cozy, / domestic and weak" (lines 13 –14) invoke the small stature into which the gardener's hands mold the plant. The gardener clearly thinks himself superior to the plant, as he tells it how "lucky" it is to have a pot. For the plant, we can imagine, the pot is a prison. The

adjectives in the final lines ("dwarf," "bound," "crippled") offer another perspective on the gardener's song; his verbal and physical pruning hideously distorts the tree.

3. Images and words in advertisements often imply that women are sexual objects without brains or physical stamina. Commercials such as the soap advertisement alluded to in the final two lines work like the gardener's song; they tell women that it is natural for them to worry about their appearances and leave the thinking to men. The poem implicitly criticizes a culture whose women are continually limited in this way. Piercy's poem urges a rethinking, both of images of women in our culture and of the roles they are encouraged (by women and men) to assume.

Connections (p. 542)

1. Smith's speaker offers a different point of view — the woman's — in her critique of women's oppression. Your students may analyze Smith's poem as an example of what the bonsai tree might say, given the chance to speak and the opportunity to recognize its oppression.

2. You may want to ask students to answer this question in an essay, directing their attention to the similarities between the gardener's song in this poem and Helmer's diminutive treatment of his wife in *A Doll's House.* They might note, for example, the implied smallness in the nicknames Helmer gives Nora ("my little songbird," "my little Nora") or his references to her helplessness and his mastery over her. Ask them to pay particular attention to the way Helmer's words encourage Nora to assume a certain role in relation to him and society.

3. Piercy's poem pits the gardener against the bonsai tree, or man against woman, to illustrate the damage that has been done by sexist language and behavior patterns. In "Patriotism," the man and woman join in an act of political and moral determination; their duty to each other is subservient to the lieutenant's duty to his country. In her loyalty to him, the wife performs her own duty to her country. The wife's loyalty and submission to her husband are to some degree the same as the bonsai tree's submission to the gardener. Neither is aware of a way to act independently. Although Piercy's tone is much angrier and more explicit, Mishima quietly points out the wife's servitude as he draws our attention to her submission to her husband's code. In many ways, Mishima admires the wife's submission. The difference in tone between his story and Piercy's poem probably has to do more with culture than with personality; feminism has only begun to be discussed in Far Eastern countries such as Japan, whereas it has been a strong movement in Western countries such as the United Kingdom and the United States for many years.

STEVIE SMITH, *How Cruel Is the Story of Eve* (p. 542)

Before they read this poem, you might ask students to recount the story of Adam and Eve. Once they have offered an account of the "facts," ask them to consider Smith's poem as an interpretation of the biblical myth. Discuss the mythical references in the poem.

Considerations (p. 544)

1. Words such as *history, story, legend, mythology,* and *Nature* are subject to reinterpretation in this poem. For example, "his-story" may be replaced with "her-story." Smith shows the damaging effect of his story when she talks about the cruel treatment of Eve and all women that originates in and results from that story. Words such as *master* and *rule* define women's position as historically inferior to men, subject to them. Men have been responsible for gathering food, governing, and ruling women for centuries: "Bring food and shelter, kill enemies?" (line 31).

2. The questions (18–20, 21–23, 30–31, 39–40, 40–44) present an opportunity for students to discuss the implied reinterpretation of the biblical story in this poem. Smith makes the essential point that Eve's story was written by men, to keep women in their "proper

places." She rewrites the story in her questions. The questions intimate that touching should not include pain, that women are not insufficient, that men are not the only ones able to provide their own food and protect themselves, that stories significantly influence our lives, that women should not be punished or blamed for their gender.

3. Repeated words include *cruel, cruelty, history, story,* and *misery.* The slight changes in the refrain of the first line alter its meaning, from "cruelty" to "misery," for example. The repeated words first establish Eve as a victim, then show how others (women and men) have become miserable as a result of the legend.

4. The speaker's voice laments the tragic influence of the sexist story of Adam and Eve. If students read the poem aloud, they may hear its softness, the way it quietly grieves its victims. This tone is effective in complicating the anger that could be produced in a discussion of this myth. It invites men and women to share in the song.

Connections

1. *Discuss Shakespeare's presentation of a woman in "My mistress' eyes are nothing like the sun" (p. 648). How does he undermine the stereotypical love poem? Can you see any connection between "How Cruel Is the Story of Eve" and Shakespeare's rewriting of the idea of woman?*

2. *Compare this poem's account of the story of Adam and Eve to William Butler Yeats's presentation of the story in "Adam's Curse" (p. 872). How is Yeats's Adam different from Smith's? How are their Eves different? How would Smith's speaker feel about Yeats's "old high way of love". . .?*

Another topic for discussion is the word *nature* in the poem; what does it mean in the final stanza? Has nature, or have human beings, defined gender roles so unequally?

Critical discussions of Stevie Smith include Christopher Ricks's "Stevie Smith: The Art of Sinking in Poetry" (*The Force of Poetry,* Oxford: Clarendon, 1984) and Stephen Wade's "Stevie Smith and the Untruth of Myth" (*Agenda,* 1977).

JANE KENYON, *Thinking of Madame Bovary* (p. 544)

Considerations

1. *Madame Bovary is the title character of Gustave Flaubert's novel of domestic realism published in 1856. Emma Bovary, recently married to her physician-husband, Charles, finds herself afflicted with boredom, the mental torment of the bourgeois class. The couple moves; she has an affair and puts herself deeply in debt. Little by little, her husband discovers the truth but still professes his love for her. She dies by taking arsenic.*

   The poem describes appetencies, relentless needs of the soul and body that will be fulfilled despite all obstacles. Just as Mme. Bovary would risk reputation, financial solvency, and security to fill her particular longing, flies flare up, crocuses blossom through dead leaves, and ants drag out their destiny in nature at its lowest orders, but the poem attains a more human and universal applicability with its title.

2. *In the final stanza, the speaker's thoughts seem to change tack and show the other side of the dialectic. The concluding sentence has an impersonal opening: "It must have been / the Methodist in me. . . ." Such a construction makes it seem as though the person is not the subject and originator of her actions but is moved by some force outside and beyond herself — in this case Methodism and the ideas of struggle and judgment.*

3. *The poem closes with ellipsis marks following a description of the ant's struggle to get over the obstruction of the twig. These marks seem to imply that the struggle itself will go on without any foreseeable end or reward. The struggle with desire is shared by human beings*

and animals, but, because of our rationality, human beings are better able to articulate the terms of the battle. Nonetheless, we cannot end it.

Connections (p. 545)

1. In both Marvell's and Wilbur's poems, the speaker attempts to convince the listener to succumb to the powers of the flesh, to make haste in order to fight the passage of time, which will dull and destroy love. In Kenyon's more contemplative poem, the rhetorical strategy is quite different, as she includes both male and female in the struggle "with its own desire." Kenyon's poem is more about desire than about persuasion, more a celebration of a natural fact than an urgent struggle with another human being. Time dictates an urgency in the other poems, whereas the ellipses at the end of Kenyon's poem reveals its more pensive tone.

2. Millay's playing with desire is double-edged; she urges lovers to make haste in the pursuit of love's momentary pleasures, but she is well aware (in the final lines) of love's short-lived cycle. Kenyon dwells much more on the earthbound, endless struggle of human animals with their desires. She does not meditate, as Millay does, on the end of the struggle; rather, she chooses to capture and sustain the moment of conflict.

3. Unlike Mme. Bovary, Mrs. Mallard does not act on her desire. She accidentally discovers it when she hears that her husband is dead. Were this poem about her, it might concern itself more with the limitations of human desire than with its inevitable outbursts.

Most poems have a fulcrum, a line or perhaps a stanza at which the direction and meaning seem to shift. The fulcrum in this poem is "Everyone longs for love's tense joys and red delights" (8). You might ask the class to write an essay of two to three pages demonstrating how this line points back to the previous stanzas and seems to call for some resolution in the concluding lines.

14. Images

WILLIAM CARLOS WILLIAMS, *Poem* (p. 546)

William Carlos Williams was born and lived most of his life in Rutherford, New Jersey, a town near Paterson, the city that provided the title and much of the subject matter of his "modern epic" poem, *Paterson*. He had a thriving medical practice for fifty years, delivering more than 2,000 babies and writing his poems, novels, short stories, and essays at night and in the moments he could snatch between patient visits during the day.

This poem is an imaged motion, but the verse has a certain slant music too. Notice the *t*-sounds that align themselves in the second tercet, the consonance in "hind" and "down," the repetitions in "pit of," "empty," and "flowerpot." Sound also helps convey the poem's sense of agility and smoothness.

ADELAIDE CRAPSEY, *Triad* (p. 547)

This poem is a *cinquain,* a five-line poem of two, four, six, eight, and two syllables, respectively. Crapsey was an experimentalist in structural and rhythmic forms. Note how the equal, stressed heaviness of "Just dead" ends the poem with an almost palpable silence.

WALT WHITMAN, *Cavalry Crossing a Ford* (p. 548)

Walt Whitman is, with Emily Dickinson, one of the two poetic giants of the American nineteenth century. Born in Huntington, Long Island, he grew up in Brooklyn, leaving school at age eleven for a job as an office boy in a law firm. His poetry grew out of his experiences as a reporter, teacher, laborer, and Civil War nurse. He self-published the first edition of his book — his life's work, really — *Leaves of Grass* in 1855.

Considerations (p. 548)

1. Whitman's descriptive words lend a colorful, paradelike quality to the scene. The flashing arms with their musical clank along with the guidon flags fluttering gaily create an image that suggests liveliness and energy.

2. "Behold" in lines 3 and 4, with its biblical overtones and its arresting sense of absorbing the sight ("be-hold"), is more stately than look or see and, with its long vowels, is almost ministerial.

3. The speaker in this poem (we can assume Whitman himself) seems to be fairly distant from the scene and possibly slightly elevated to see the entire picture. He scans the troops with a panning gaze that is, nonetheless, able to come in for some close-ups as he looks at the brown-faced men, "each group, each person, a picture."

4. "Serpentine" in line 2 seems to hold only benign and matter-of-fact connotations, describing the zigzagging path from one island to the next, although it may be justifiably difficult to disregard completely the "evil connotation" of "serpentine."

THEODORE ROETHKE, *Root Cellar* (p. 548)

The theme of this brief lyric with its powerful images is stated in the penultimate line: "Nothing would give up life." In the darkness of the root cellar, dank with a perpetual humidity, nothing sleeps; the atmosphere is ideal for engendering life. Normally we associate the underground with death and decay, but here decay is shown to be a source of life.

Some of the imagery in this poem is aimed at the olfactory sense, particularly when Roethke summons up the "congress of stinks." "Congress" is an especially appropriate word choice here, for it can mean not only a political body but sexual intercourse as well. Coming together, as all these odoriferous bodies do, brings forth life out of putrefaction, mold, slime, and bulbous decay.

The sense of sight, however, also operates in the poem, and we are asked to use our imaginative powers to see shoots "lolling obscenely" or hanging down "like tropical snakes." Even our sense of touch is called upon to apprehend the "leaf-mold, manure, lime, piled against slippery planks." Note too the consonance of *m*'s and *p*'s in this carefully constructed line. As ugly and odoriferous as some of these images are, the poem ends on a small cry of victory — "Even the dirt kept breathing a small breath" — and this closing line recapitulates the tone of admiration, even wonder, that Roethke seems to feel as he enters the root cellar.

MATTHEW ARNOLD, *Dover Beach* (p. 549)

Matthew Arnold was born in the English village of Laleham, in the Thames valley. His father was a clergyman and a reformist educator, a powerful personality against whom the young Arnold rebelled in a number of ways, including nearly flunking out of Oxford. After several years as private secretary to a nobleman, in 1851 Arnold became an inspector of schools, a post he held for thirty-five years. For the characteristic jauntiness of his prose style, Walt Whitman once referred to him as "one of the dudes of literature."

Many of us have had the experience of looking out on a landscape and registering both its beauty (and possibly its tranquillity) and its undercurrent of something lost or awry. Such is the case for the speaker of "Dover Beach" as he looks out at the shore awash in moonlight. The private moment has its wholeness, for he stands in the "sweetness" of the night air with his beloved. But all the security and peace he could expect to feel are shaken by his concerns beyond the moment and his awareness of the ravages that history brings to bear on the present. We are not fragments of our time alone, the poem seems to say; we are caught in the "turbid ebb and flow / Of human misery" that Sophocles himself heard so long ago.

In the third stanza Arnold goes beyond commenting on the sadness that seems an inevitable part of the human condition, as his thoughts turn to the malaise of his own time. Faith, which once encircled humanity, is now only the overheard roar of its waters withdrawing to the rock-strewn edges of the world. In short, for whatever happens there is no solace, no consolation or reason to hope for any restoration, justice, or change. Humankind is beyond the tragic condition of Sophocles, and in this poem Arnold seems to be tipping the balance toward a modernist existential worldview. The tone of the poem barely improves by the final stanza, for the image Arnold leaves us with is that of "ignorant armies" clashing in the night — the sound and fury once again signifying nothing.

The images of Dover Beach itself or some other imagined seascape work well to evoke the tone that Arnold is trying to convey. In discussion, or perhaps as a writing topic, you might ask the class to review the poem for natural details and images (in lines 9–14 or most of the third stanza, for example) that suggest the drear, stark, and ominous portrait Arnold is painting here.

General essays on this poem appear in A. Dwight Culler's *Imaginative Reason: The Poetry of Matthew Arnold* (New Haven: Yale University Press, 1966) and James Dickey's *Babel to Byzantium* (New York: Farrar, Straus & Giroux, 1968).

Connections (p. 550)

1. The crippled soldiers in Owen's poem illustrate the final line of Arnold's, their decrepitude confirming what Arnold only hinted at. The gruesome images — "coughing like hags" (2),

"blood-shod" (6), "choking, drowning" (16) — graphically demonstrate the consequences of those "ignorant armies clash[ing] by night."

2. Hardy speaks of the dying of religious belief in more hopeful, less resolute images than does Arnold, who hears only the receding tide of the sea of Faith.

3. In a conversational style and lighthearted tone, Hecht's speaker refers to the immediate pleasures of a more bawdy reality while defending the implied listener in Arnold's poem. Hecht's images evoke the daily life of the woman, contrasting sharply with Arnold's interest in the more philosophical issues of his day. Although we cannot assume much about the listener in Arnold's poem (is she even real?), we might presume that she would be far more respectful toward the speaker than Hecht's images imply. Indeed, Hecht intimates that the listener is a "loose woman": "I give her a good time" (26).

H. D. [HILDA DOOLITTLE], *Heat* (p. 551)

Hilda Doolittle was born in Bethlehem, Pennsylvania, and educated at private schools in Philadelphia. In 1911 she moved to London, where she married English poet Richard Aldington. Although an American poet and novelist, H. D. was involved with the Bloomsbury group for a time and was an important figure in the Imagist movement as well. Ezra Pound, who encouraged her poetic aspirations and submitted her work to *Poetry* magazine under the name "H. D., Imagiste," was probably the most influential of a group of friends that included T. S. Eliot, William Carlos Williams, and D. H. Lawrence. In 1933, Freud agreed, at the request of the poet, to accept her as a subject of study, and H. D.'s later poems, such as "The Walls Do Not Fall" of 1944, are markedly influenced by her own and her mentor's interests in psychoanalysis, religion, and mythology.

Considerations (p. 551)

1. Heat becomes a living force in these lines, capable of occupying space and offering resistance to seemingly denser objects: "Fruit cannot drop / through this thick air — " (lines 4–5).

2. The ripeness and fullness implied in the images of the fruit in the second stanza are somewhat threatened by the relentless heat. We can almost feel the fruit shriveling in response, deprived of oxygen, unable to participate in the natural cycle that will make them fall to the ground. Heat able to blunt the points of pears and round grapes (8–9) acquires the power of an elemental force.

3. The image of the cutting plow in lines 10 through 13 builds on the personification of the wind in the first line. The wind becomes a creative agent, a matching elemental force called up to cut through the heat and restore order in the natural world. However, the plow is also a domestic tool at the service of human beings. The poet's words conjure and direct the wind. By framing the poem as an invocation, the poet calls attention to her own ability to control this natural scene.

WILLIAM BLAKE, *London* (p. 551)

William Blake's only formal schooling was in art, and he learned engraving as an apprentice to a prominent London engraver. After his seven years' service, Blake made his living as a printer and engraver, writing poetry on the side. The private mythology that came to dominate his poems was worked out in almost total obscurity: at the time of his death Blake had acquired some notice for his art but almost none for his writing.

Considerations (p. 552)

1. The use of "chartered" to describe both streets and the River Thames makes all boundaries seem unnatural and rigid.

2.,3. The cries heard are of pain and sadness. Like the rigidities of the chartered streets, the legislation of the "mind-forged manacles" does nothing to promote civil liberty and happiness. Blake implies here that the "manacles" of religion and government that should protect individuals fail miserably to ensure good lives. Children are sold into near slavery as chimney sweeps, their own dark and stunted faces casting a pall (appall) on the benevolent state and the Christian tradition. Soldiers sent off to war die or kill other soldiers. Sexual restrictions invite prostitution and thus promote disease, which may, in turn, afflict marriages and resulting births. Social regulations ("manacles") thus induce societal ills.

4. The image of the soldier dying for the state (lines 11–12) is described in a very condensed and effective manner that suggests not only his lucklessness (or helplessness) but also the indifference of a government removed from the individual by class (palace), its insularity (walls), and the imperturbable security of law.

5. Denotative and connotative meanings reinforce each other, and in fact merge their levels of meaning as the literal here becomes allegorized and powerful in its iconic suggestiveness.

6. Comparison of the two versions of the final stanza provides an excellent writing topic. Notice, though, how much more endemic the societal failings and wrongdoings appear in the second (revised) version. Instead of "midnight harlot's curse," the phrase becomes the "midnight streets" (evil as pervasive) and "the youthful Harlot's curse" (a blighting of innocence at an early age). By reversing marriage hearse and infant's tear, Blake suggests not a mere (and societally sanctioned) cause-effect relation between marriage and the birth of afflicted infants but the presence of syphilis in even the youngest members of society and the conditions that would sustain its presence.

WILFRED OWEN, *Dulce et Decorum Est* (p. 552)

Considerations (p. 553)

1. This poem is an argument against war, not against a country. So often war is an act surrounded by image-making words of glory and honor and flanked by the nobility of slogan sentiments. Here Owen has presented the actuality of battle and death by a particularly dehumanizing and agonizing weapon: poison gas. He wants his audience to know a little more exactly what war entails.

2. The images are visually striking, especially in the opening lines and in the lines that describe the man who was gassed. But Owen also appeals to the sense of hearing in lines 21–22 and to taste in lines 23–24.

3. Owen seems to want to collar and talk to each individual directly. After the vividness of his description, some of which is in the present tense, Owen's attitude toward the "lie" that his "friend" might tell is disdainful, yet understandably so.

4. Clean-shaven, bright-eyed, purposeful young men neatly posed in their new uniforms are a far cry from these bleeding, fatigue-drunk men who are probably beyond even fear.

ROBERT LOWELL, *Skunk Hour* (p. 533)

This poem is a modern rendering of the dark night of the soul, and Lowell himself in published comments refers readers to the poem by St. John of the Cross. For this observation and several other analyses, turn to *The Contemporary Poet as Artist and Critic: Eight Symposia,* edited by Anthony Ostroff (Boston: Little, Brown, 1964).

Considerations (p. 554)

1.,3. The town appears to the speaker as a kind of off-season hell. The millionaire Mainer decked out in his L. L. Bean array has left — for warmer climates. The heiress buys up eyesores only to let them rot. Love is nothing more than sexual pleasure performed to the ironically accurate pop-tune lyric, which makes the speaker respond with his own sense of sickened despair.

2.,4. "Skunk Hour" encapsulates the spirit of the speaker as he surveys the scene before him. The very life around him reeks of its dying; the skunks, of course, are the one element in the poem that celebrate life with wholesome desire and the will and pluck to survive. The speaker watches them with an admiration and almost audible applause in the heavy three-stressed words "will not scare," which conclude the poem.

This poem is dedicated to Elizabeth Bishop. You might ask students in a two- to three-page essay to compare the theme and conclusion here with those of Bishop's "The Fish" (p. 501).

MARGARET ATWOOD, *Dreams of the Animals* (p. 555)

Considerations (p. 556)

1. The images used for the frog are wet and green, describing both its body and its habitat. The fish's dream of stripes suggests the physical characteristics of fish as well as fish behavior — "meaningful patterns" of "defense, attack" (lines 16–17). The birds' dreams define both their occupation of space and their melodious songs. Each image somehow shows us what it is like to be the animal described.

2. The dreams of these captured animals are influenced by their strange, polluted surroundings. Each animal has been domesticated: the fox in the zoo, the armadillo in the cage, the iguana in the pet shop. The dream images suggest the violation of these animals committed by human beings, who have forced them into artificial environments.

4. Animal dreams, like human dreams, reflect the environment in which the creatures live. Atwood infers that the environment produces the individual's idea of self and his or her relationship to the world: "the iguana . . . dreams of sawdust" (35, 39). The theme of this poem concerns the importance of allowing all beings, human and animal, the right to a natural, interference-free environment.

Connection

1. *Compare the animal images in this poem with those images in Richmond Lattimore's "The Crabs" (p. 557). How do the images reflect the tones of each speaker? Do the poems take a similar stand, or do they seem to be at odds, philosophically?*

MARK STRAND, *Pot Roast* (p. 556)

Considerations (p. 557)

1. The poet is in a decidedly urban environment with tall buildings that block the view. He feels a sense of isolation from anything organic and finds here "little / to love or to praise."

2. Proust had his madeleines and Strand his pot roast. Some writers are especially good at evoking formative memories — Nabokov comes to mind as an example. You might use this poem as an example for a poetry- or prose-writing assignment centered on recalling childhood memories.

3. Could "Pot Roast," a most unpoetic title for a poem, be considered a kind of prayer of thanksgiving or praise for memory and some spot of quintessential, unchanging goodness?

RICHMOND LATTIMORE, *The Crabs* (p. 557)

The words in this poem are chosen, one imagines, to reinforce the crabs' apartness from human beings, who are not "precision made." Lattimore uses a great deal of wordplay here, making "barbarian" in his description of the crabs collide with "civilized," as applied to human beings who kill crabs and eat them. Rhyme is also used to make ironic statements on the barbarian/civilized dichotomy as Lattimore observes that the urbane "chatter" of those about to have dinner accompanies the death-dance "clatter" of the crabs in the boiling can.

You might ask the class whether they share the speaker's attitude toward the crabs. Crabs are fine creatures, boiled, that is, and the phrase "they died for us" may sound too portentous and sentimental in this context.

SALLY CROFT, *Home-Baked Bread* (p. 558)

Considerations (p. 558)

1. "Cunning triumphs," appearing amid the measured dryness of a cookbook text, certainly has the potential to arrest someone's poetic sensibilities. *Cunning* seems more appropriately applied to the feats of Odysseus than to the food in *The Joy of Cooking*. At any rate, "cunning triumphs" rises, as it were, beyond the limits of technical discourse. It shines, it sparkles, it almost titillates the kitchen soul.

2. At first we hear the speaker reading and questioning the cookbook. Then we hear the speaker transformed into a new identity — of Lady Who Works Cunning Triumphs. She is addressing someone she would charm and seduce.

3. *Insinuation* is a pivotal word in the poem. It looks back on the questioning attitude of the opening lines and points toward the wily, winding seductiveness of what will follow.

4. The poem achieves a unity through the repetition of certain images, such as the room that recalls the great-aunt's bedroom as well as the other reiterated images, of honey, sweet seductiveness, warmth, and open air.

JOHN REPP, *Cursing the Hole in the Screen, Wondering at the Romance Some Find in Summer* (p. 559)

John Repp grew up in southern New Jersey, where summers can be murderously hot and humid. Although the speaker of this poem holds no truck with the cult of sun worship, a late-summer overripeness pervades what he says about the season and "its random tiny horrors" (line 6). The announced subject of the poem doesn't even appear until line 6, after an extended metaphor that sets the tone and reverses the conventional celebratory notions to be found in many poems concerning summer. Nature appears alien, malevolent, its fruits overwhelming not just the speaker's desperate need for relief but his disdain for a certain kind of music as well. You might ask students to examine how assonance, off rhyme, alliteration, allusion, personification, and metaphor are used here both to evoke the season and to critique it.

Considerations (p. 559)

1. The invasion of slugs, mosquitoes, and midges makes the speaker's home seem like a scene from *Apocalypse Now*. Note how the images mesh the human and natural worlds, personifying insects ("Wasps lumber," 9) while describing their menacing presence in human homes.

2. Whereas the initial lines grasp at images to describe the physical discomfort of a hot summer, the later lines (16–20) introduce a more intellectual, more cynical, less earthy vocabulary. Comparing the sounds of the frogs to postmodern music, the speaker both betrays his "civilized" tastes and imitates a "hip" tone. In the initial lines his tone is more somber and brooding, producing more concrete images and metaphors.

3. Your students may argue that the title is too long, that it interferes with their experience of the poem by encapsulating the speaker's attitude before the poem begins. On the other hand, they may think the title humorous, befitting the poem's shifting tone.

Images

Connections (p. 560)

1. H. D.'s image of heat is less discursive than these. Her poem attempts to eliminate the human bias, leaving the images to create the natural world on the page. Repp is much more intent on meshing the domestic and natural worlds, particularly in images such as "Night wrings / its filthy washcloth" (21–22).

2. Bogan's poem presents a perfect contrast to Repp's images of summer. Whereas Bogan's summer is expectant and melodious, Repp's intrudes upon the speaker, to his annoyance and frustration. Bogan suggests a fullness in summer and a mysterious allure, whereas Repp's plenty is excessive and oppressive, promising more discomfort in the days ahead.

PERSPECTIVE

T. E. HULME, *On the Difference Between Poetry and Prose* (p. 560)

As a class exercise, you might ask students to bring in examples of prose that contradict Hulme's claims. The prose poems by Carolyn Forché ("The Colonel" p. 671) and George Starbuck ("Japanese Fish" p. 667) might be useful in a comparison between prose and poetry, but students might also want to bring in examples of prose they read earlier in the course (Hemingway's "Soldier's Home" p. 121) or elsewhere.

In another writing assignment, you might ask students to flesh out Hulme's theory with especially vivid examples of poems that "hand over sensations bodily."

15. Figures of Speech

WILLIAM SHAKESPEARE, *From* Macbeth (p. 562)

Discussed in text.

MARGARET ATWOOD, *you fit into me* (p. 563)

Students may need help with the allusions called up by the first two lines of this poem: the hook and eye that fasten a door shut; the buttonhook used to fasten women's shoes in the early twentieth century. You might ask students to compose a poem in which a figure of speech produces first pleasant associations and later unpleasant or, as in Atwood's poem, lurid ones. You might also ask the class in a brief writing assignment to determine how the simile and its expansion work. Would the poem be as successful, for example, if "eye" were not a part of the human anatomy?

EMILY DICKINSON, *Presentiment — is that long Shadow — on the lawn* (p. 563)

Discussed in text.

ANNE BRADSTREET, *The Author to Her Book* (p. 565)

Ask students to trace the extended metaphor in this poem, pointing out the way diction influences tone. What, for example, do the words "ill-formed" and "feeble" (line 1) tell us about the speaker's attitude toward her work? Does this attitude change at all as the poem progresses? Although her initial attitude toward the book is disdain, the speaker's reluctance to part with her creation in the final lines could be the result of both modesty and affection.

Sound patterns and meter are also good topics for discussion of this poem. The meter is iambic pentameter, but there are variations in rhythm that are linked to meaning. Line 15 presents the problem of metrical arrangement, providing an example in line 16: "Yet still thou run'st more hobbling than is meet."

In a writing assignment, you might ask students to discuss the way this poem talks about the writing process. How does Bradstreet suggest a book is written?

Connection

1. Compare the speaker's description in this poem of writing a book with Robert Francis's description of the process in "Glass" (p. 912). What are the differences in the writers' processes of production as they are outlined in these poems? How do you think these differences would affect the work of the two writers? How would you account for their diverse visions?

EDMUND CONTI, *Pragmatist* (p. 566)

As a writing assignment, you might ask the class to discuss whether the mixed tone of this poem is successful. Is, for example, "coming our way" too liltingly conversational for the idea of apocalypse?

DYLAN THOMAS, *The Hand That Signed the Paper* (p. 567)

Discussed in text.

Dylan Thomas's *Eighteen Poems,* published in 1934, when he was twenty, began his career as a poet with a flourish: here, it seemed, was an answer to T.S. Eliot, a return to rhapsody and unembarrassed music. Thomas's poems became more craftsmanlike as he matured, but they never lost their ambition for the grand gesture, the all-embracing, bittersweet melancholy for which the Romantics strove. Thomas himself lived the role of the poet to the hilt: he was an alcoholic, a philanderer, a wonderful storyteller, a boor, and a justly celebrated reader of his own poems and those of others. Although he never learned to speak Welsh, (he was born and grew up in Swansea, Wales), it is said that his poems carry the sounds of that language over into English. He died of alcohol poisoning during his third reading tour of the United States.

JANICE TOWNLEY MOORE, *To a Wasp* (p. 568)

Discussed in text.

MICHAEL CADNUM, *Cat Spy* (p. 569)

Discussed in text.

ERNEST SLYMAN, *Lightning Bugs* (p. 570)

Considerations (p. 570)

1. Without the title, we would think this poem is about people. The title frames the experience by identifying the image to be captured in the lines that follow.

2. The image of the peepholes (in line 2), coming as it does before the snapshots (in line 3), makes us first imagine the bugs as human beings, who require peepholes to see who is outside. When mention of snapshots is added to this image, the bugs become like tourists, waiting for someone to come out of the house so they can take a picture. This is ironic, for it is really the bugs who are the celebrities, fascinating the speaker, who watches them.

SYLVIA PLATH, *Mirror* (p. 570)

Sylvia Plath grew up with an invalid father (he refused to seek treatment for what he thought was cancer but was actually diabetes) who died when she was eight. Her mother was a teacher, who by example and instruction encouraged her daughter's precocious literary ambitions (Plath published her first poem before she was nine). Plath attended Smith College on scholarship, won a Fulbright to study in England, received a number of awards for her writing, and eventually married the English poet Ted Hughes. In the last few harrowing months of her life (which she spent alone because Hughes was having an affair), she wrote most of her finest poems, sometimes at the rate of two or three a day. She killed herself on February 11, 1963.

Considerations (p. 571)

1.,4. Without the use of personification, the poem would simply be another flat statement on a woman watching herself grow old. But that action of watching is enlivened by the mirror taking on some organic attributes. The pink wall it reflects becomes part of its heart, for example; and, despite the truth it gives back to the woman, it feels important and necessary. Without the responsive quality of the mirror, it is unlikely that the last images would be quite so startling. But the personified mirror literally acquires a depth it probably would not have otherwise, and it figures in the poem as lake, a drowning pool, and the source of the "terrible fish."

2. The mirror as lake recalls the Lady of the Lake in Arthurian legend.

3. The light shed by candles or the moon is kind to the appearances of those illumined. Candles and moonlight too are the trappings of romantic evenings, when the best in someone is highlighted and the worst is muted or invisible. At this point the woman seems very much alone, perhaps thinking of a past love and a moonlit night.

4. In the final simile, the image is no longer a mere reflection but a figure of assault coming up out of the depths of self, "like a terrible fish" to frighten her.

EMILY DICKINSON, *The thought beneath so slight a film —* (p. 571)

Just as laces and mists (both light, partial coverings) reveal the wearer or the mountain range, so a veiled expression reveals the inner thought or opinion. Dickinson is here implying that the delicate covering makes the eye work harder to see the form behind the veil; therefore, misted objects appear in sharper outline.

EMILY DICKINSON, *Portraits are to daily faces* (p. 571)

In this poem, as in the preceding one, analogies are being drawn — between the controlled rendering of a portrait and the unposed variations of the daily face and between a sunset, muted and softly golden, and the brilliant, almost too obviously flashy, sunlight of the day.

Connections (p. 572)

1. Dickinson's preference in these two poems is for the muted image. She implies that poets reveal great ideas through a veil of words, that the audience must look carefully at her poems to catch what's really there. To Francis, poetry is a game of catch, or pursuit. The poet works to outwit prose, quickly changing foot, rhyme, and image to capture the moment before it flees: "Anything, everything tricky, risky, nonchalant" (line 7). While each poet insists that poetry is an always-changing, risky business, Francis seems more concerned with shifting form, whereas Dickinson concentrates on the many possible perspectives on a single thought or personality. Francis's poem is "showier"; he wants to make his audience "scramble" (10); Dickinson seems more interested in making her audience muse.

WILLIAM WORDSWORTH, *London, 1802* (p. 572)

William Wordsworth was born in the English Lake District, in Cockermouth, West Cumberland, and grew up roaming the countryside. He completed his undergraduate degree at Cambridge University in 1791 and spent a year in revolutionary France. By the age of 27 he had settled in Somersetshire to be near Samuel Taylor Coleridge, with whom, in 1798, he published one of the most influential volumes in the history of English poetry, *Lyrical Ballads*. Wordsworth enjoyed increasing public reward as a poet (becoming poet laureate in 1843) even as his private life suffered from frequent tragedy and disappointment.

The metonymic nouns following the colon in line 3 of "London, 1802" all point to areas within British culture and civilization that Wordsworth thinks have declined since Milton's day. All things have suffered loss — from the strength of the church, the army, or the accomplishment of writers to the more immediate and individual quality of home life — in particular an "inward happiness," along with a sense of strength and security.

Milton seems to have represented for Wordsworth an epitome of the heroic, a kind of guiding star apart from other human beings, with a voice that was expansive, at one with the sublime in nature, and morally incorruptible.

ROBERT GRAVES, *Down, Wanton, Down!* (p. 572)

If students have already read Cummings's "she being Brand" (p. 527), they will probably quickly perceive the sexual puns in this poem, in which military metaphors, especially those in stanza II or the phrase "staunchness at the post" in line 4, describe the young man's arousal and desire. The poem does, however, have a serious theme. At its midpoint in stanza III is a thematic admonition that love should rise far beyond sexual attraction if we are to distinguish ourselves from the beasts.

WALT WHITMAN, *A Noiseless Patient Spider* (p. 573) and *The Soul, reaching, throwing out for love* (p. 574)

In this poem Whitman participates in a fairly long and distinguished tradition, starting with the homely tropes of Edward Taylor or Anne Bradstreet, that explores analogies between lower forms of natural life and the human condition. In this instance the analogy is effective since both soul and spider are isolated — and are trying to reach across vast space to forge connections between themselves and the rest of the world. The emphasis within the soul seems to be a reflective activity (musing, venturing, throwing, seeking), while the activity of the spider seems more a physical compulsion, especially with the repetition of "filament."

In the revised version, which this reader prefers, the poem is structured by the analogy, which renders the soul's casting of its "ductile anchor" as being as much a natural phenomenon as the spider's web-building. The earlier version is more a personal cry for love, and the spider analogy becomes an incidental metaphor.

DYLAN THOMAS, *Do not go gentle into that good night* (p. 574)

This poem is a villanelle, a French verse form ordinarily treating light topics, whose five tercets and concluding quatrain employ only two end rhymes. The first and third lines of the poem must alternatively conclude the tercets and form a couplet for the quatrain. Despite these formal restrictions, Thomas's poem sounds remarkably unforced and reflects quite adequately the feeling of a man who does not want his father to die.

Just as remarkable is the poem's rich figurative language; this villanelle could be used as a summary example of almost all the points outlined in this chapter. Variety is achieved through the metonymies for death, such as "close of day" (line 2), "dark" (4), "dying of the light" (9). The overall effect is to describe death metaphorically as the end of a day and thus, in some sense, to familiarize death and lessen its threat. Even to describe death as "that good night" (1) reduces it to a gesture of good-bye. Other figures of speech include a pun on "grave" men (13) (both solemn and mortal), an oxymoron in "who see with blinding sight" (13), various similes, such as "blaze like meteors" (14), and the overall form of the apostrophe.

Thomas introduces several examples of people who might be expected to acquiesce to death gently but who, nonetheless, resist it. "Wise men" (philosophers, perhaps) want more time because so far their wisdom has not created any radical change ("forked no lightning"). Men who do good works (theologians, possibly) look back and realize that the sum total of their efforts was "frail" and if they had devoted more time to a fertile field ("green bay"), their deeds might have been more effective. "Wild men" (inspired artists, writers) know their words have caught and held time, but they know too how in various ways — with their relations with others or perhaps with alcohol and drugs — they have "grieved" the sun. Grave men at the end of their lives realize too late that joy is one means of transcending time. All these groups experience some form of knowledge that makes them wish they could prolong life and live it according to their new insights.

As a writing assignment you might ask students to analyze a character or group of people that they have read about in a short story who seem to fit into one of the categories Thomas describes. What advice would he give them? How otherwise could they lead their lives?

Connections (p. 575)

1. Donne personifies death, intimating that it can be beaten, because there is an afterlife. Thomas's emphasis is on life, because he perceives death as an unconquerable finality. Donne demeans death by describing it as friend to vice and evil, whereas Thomas's view

of death is more inevitable and impersonal. Whereas Donne claims that death will be killed by immortal life, Thomas begs his father to "rage" against death until he can no longer fight it. Donne is a far more religious poet than Thomas, for whom death is truly the end of existence.

2. Plath's rage is ostensibly produced by her inability to know and to communicate with her father. But there are other enemies here: Plath herself, the oppression of women by men, the helplessness of the individual in the face of political and social machines. Plath's rage, unlike Thomas's, is motivated by the human will. Had people decided to behave differently toward one another, Plath's poem would not be.

JOHN DONNE, *A Valediction: Forbidding Mourning* (p. 575)

The questions in the text show how richly metaphorical this metaphysical poem in fact is. Virtually every statement here is made through a comparison. The lovers should tolerate their separation with the same grace with which "virtuous men" leave this earth. They are not like the "dull sublunary" lovers who need physical presence to sustain each other; they represent something finer. This sense of refinement is picked up and developed further in the simile in line 24, when the strength of the love between Donne and his wife is compared to gold, which does not shatter when beaten but expands to delicate, fine plate. Donne concludes his poem with the well-known compass metaphor. You might have to explain at this point what sort of compass Donne is describing, since we live in an age of computer graphics and not drafting skills. Because the compass here is used to draw circles, it is a most appropriate simile to describe unity and perfection.

MAY SWENSON, *The Secret in the Cat* (p. 576)

Considerations (p. 577)

1. There is no secret in the cat. The poem tries to find out what its mysterious workings are, but it destroys the cat in the process. Looking for machinery, dials, gears, and mechanical gadgetry, the speaker loses all contact with the "essence" of the cat.

2. The cat is compared to electrical gadgets and machines, clothing, a house. All these images are of containment; they are also artificial. The comparisons make us realize that the life of an animate object cannot be analyzed through dissection. The creature will not reveal its workings and then return to its former state.

Connections (p. 578)

1. Updike's eulogy for his dog treats the dog as one would a human being. It explores its characteristics, its habits, its virtues. The poem celebrates the life of the dog even as it relates its tragic death. Swenson, on the other hand, reduces her pet to a machine, killing it in order to understand it more completely. Whereas Swenson criticizes our desire to possess knowledge the way we might possess machines, Updike lauds the pet as an extension of the family. It is interesting that the dog in Updike's poem is female, while Swenson's cat is male; these poems may tell us more about their speakers than about their subjects.

LINDA PASTAN, *Marks* (p. 578)

In teaching this poem, it would probably be a good idea to discuss the social expectations of motherhood and those of being a student. The latter relationship, in which the person is constantly being judged and is answerable to an authority figure, is not always ego enhancing, a point that Eugène Ionesco carried to absurd limits in *The Lesson*. The situation of the mother in Pastan's poem seems not much better; although anyone in any job or academic setting is frequently under review, is not a mother's "job" more an act of ongoing generosity than a fulfilling of job or course requirements? Class discussion could challenge the appropriateness of the metaphor here.

The speaker's increasingly bitter, ironic tone serves (as irony often does) as a weapon against the "marks" (the hurt and disillusionment) inflicted on her by her family. Can she easily leave school; leave her responsibilities?

As a writing assignment, ask students to analyze how this poem challenges and mocks its central metaphor.

EMILY DICKINSON, *I know that He exists* (p. 578)

Once again, Dickinson here seems to be at the cutting edge of modern sensibility and its dare-seeking fascination with death. She reminds us that the "fun" might "look too expensive" if the death-skirting glee should glaze over into death's stiff stare. The "He" of the first stanza is virtually an Old Testament God, refined, hidden, far removed from the gross affairs of earthly life. In the stanzas that follow, "He" continues to seem aloof in his silence.

Considerations (p. 579)

1.,2. The controlling metaphor of this poem is a game of hide-and-seek — between God ("He that exists") and whomever else will play.

3. The speaker states in the third stanza, however, that finding God, so to speak, can mean finding oneself in God at the moment of death.

4.,5. The lightness of the first two stanzas turns abruptly to a sense of ambush and entrapment. The poem begins on a rather conventional note — "I know that He exists" could easily begin a hymn — but by the final stanza, particularly with the use of "crawled," which summons up the image of the serpent in the Garden of Eden, we feel the ironic barb pierce through the texture of the ordinary language.

This poem receives a brief but adequate discussion in Karl Keller's *The Only Kangaroo among the Beauty* (Baltimore: Johns Hopkins UP, 1979), 63. Keller observes that the "tone of voice moves from mouthed platitude to personal complaint."

ELAINE MAGARRELL, *The Joy of Cooking* (p. 579)

Considerations (p. 580)

1. The tongue and heart are extended metaphors for the siblings. The sister is described as needing spices to make her more interesting. We can imagine that hers is not an effervescent personality. The brother, characterized as a heart, seems heartless. Whereas most hearts feed six, his "barely feeds two" (line 16). He is "rather dry" (line 10), requiring stuffing to make him palatable. Neither sibling is complete enough when left alone to warrant the speaker's unadorning description; she must "doctor them up" to make them palatable to her audience and herself.

2. The speaker is sarcastic and bitter. She compares her siblings to largely unappealing foods, indicating that her relationships with them are far from admiring or intimate.

Connections (p. 580)

1. Croft at first questions *The Joy of Cooking,* wondering why it should treat its subject as one would a human mystery. Carried away by the language, she moves into the role of seductress, luring her listener into the erotic sensuality of her poem. Magarrell's adaptation from the same book takes an entirely different form. Her tone is bitter. Rather than seducing her listeners, she startles and perhaps alienates them through her arresting images.

PERSPECTIVE

JOHN R. SEARLE, *Figuring Out Metaphors* (p. 580)

In a writing assignment, ask students to find two poems in which the metaphors work and two in which they don't. The students' essays should explain their choices, that is, define the metaphors in the poems and explain why they work (or why they don't). If possible, the students should speculate about the characteristics of a successful metaphor based on the evidence of the poems they have chosen.

A class exercise or another writing assignment might involve students finding metaphors in sources other than poems — in the newspaper, for example, or in popular songs or television programs. Once found, these examples could also be analyzed as successful or unsuccessful metaphors.

16. Symbol, Allegory, and Irony

ROBERT FROST, *Acquainted with the Night* (p. 582)

You might ask the students to discuss in a two-page essay the function of the clock in this poem. How does its presence modify the tone of the poem? Do we read it literally, symbolically, or as a mixture of both?

EDGAR ALLAN POE, *The Haunted Palace* (p. 584)

Discussed in text.

Edgar Allan Poe was born in Boston, the son of itinerant actors. He lived an often harrowing life marked by alcoholism, disease, and misfortune, managing to eke out a rather precarious existence primarily as an editor for a number of newspapers and periodicals in Philadelphia, New York, and Baltimore. Although he was renowned in his lifetime as the author of "The Raven," his most abiding ambition was to be a respected critic. He died after collapsing in a Baltimore street. (For additional biographical information see manual p. 46.)

EDWIN ARLINGTON ROBINSON, *Richard Cory* (p. 586)

Edwin Arlington Robinson became a professional poet in the grimmest of circumstances: his father's businesses went bankrupt in 1893, one brother became a drug addict and another an alcoholic, and Robinson could afford to attend Harvard University for just two years. He eked out a livelihood from the contributions of friends and patrons, finally moving to New York City, where his work received more critical attention and public acceptance. He won three Pulitzer Prizes for his gloomy, musical verse narratives.

As a writing assignment, you might ask students to analyze how Robinson achieves the power of the final line of "Richard Cory," paying special attention to the regal language that describes Cory as well as the strong contrasts in the couplets of the final stanza.

KENNETH FEARING, *AD* (p. 587)

Discussed in text.

E. E. CUMMINGS, *next to of course god america i* (p. 588)

As a writing assignment, you might ask students to analyze how Cummings portrays character without employing direct description.

STEPHEN CRANE, *A Man Said to the Universe* (p. 589)

Discussed in text.

CONRAD HILBERRY, *The Frying Pan* (p. 589)

Considerations (p. 590)

1. The "mark" in the first stanza is first the mark of gender, an indelible identity afforded a woman at birth, which she can either resist or accept. The first stanza shows how this mark makes other "marks"; the woman is written into what can become imprisoning roles,

such as those of housewife and mother, roles perhaps characterized by "collar and leash" (line 7). The mark may also be her written word on the page; using language, perhaps she tries to improve her position.

2. When the pan's handle is crossed, transforming it into the mark of the female gender, the woman speaking is herself transformed. She is "Venus / . . . the egg / and the pan it cooks in" (12–14). The symbols refer to the female reproductive system, but they generate in the female-run kitchen, intimating that this woman's freedom is perhaps not as "miraculous" as it seems. The analogy to the sun gives the woman a life-giving power. She is mother earth, to use a well-known representation of women. We must wonder, however, given the analogy to the frying egg, if the woman does not destroy herself in the process of calling attention to her heat-giving powers.

3. The poem's title plays with the cliché "out of the frying pan into the fire," perhaps illustrating by allusion the woman's failed gesture toward freedom. How conscious is the implication of this allusion?

4. In the first stanza, when the symbol for female sexuality is unadorned by the crossbar, the speaker of the poem feels only her ordinariness, even emptiness. As soon as the handle of the frying pan receives its characteristic cross, however, the speaker seems to enter into consciousness of her sexuality. No longer empty, she is "both the egg / and the pan it cooks in." The imagery that follows suggests fire: "the slow heat, the miraculous / sun rising." Thus the speaker, by entering into the fullest possible acceptance of her female sexuality, transcends the suppressed dilemma of the poem and establishes the imagery of fire and warmth as a life-generating power. The final lines of the poem seem filled with wonder at female creativity. This might be a male response. A woman conscious of the way motherhood has at times prevented women from achieving other goals might choose a different strategy to express her feelings about gender roles.

WILLIAM BLAKE, *The Sick Rose* (p. 590)

This seems to be a poem that straddles the fine line between symbol and allegory. Unlike Robert Frost's "Acquainted with the Night" (p. 582), this poem appears to demand an interpretation that will explain "rose" and "worm" so that they assume some importance within human affairs. Typically, whether "rose" is taken as allegorical figure or symbol (and many follow the latter course), it is connected with innocent love that succumbs to the corrupting worm. The worm itself signifies an illicit passion and preys on the rose's repression and vulnerability. Dark times and ill weather (an indicator of societal evil, perhaps) accompany the arrival of the worm. To be sure, this poem is more open-ended in the meanings that can be assigned to it and is therefore symbolically suggestive. The poem tends not to be didactic, as most allegories are, yet we seem to want to know, in the manner of allegory, what "rose" and "worm" mean for us.

A reading suggesting that this poem should be taken literally is in Michael Riffaterr's "The Self-sufficient Text" (*Diacritics,* Fall 1973). See also E. D. Hirsch, Jr.'s *Innocence and Experience* (Chicago: U of Chicago P, 1975), which argues that Blake is satirizing the rose's innocence: "Her ignorance *is* her spiritual disease because in accepting 'dark secret love' she has unknowingly repressed and perverted her instinctive life, her 'bed of crimson joy.'"

W. D. SNODGRASS, *Lobsters in the Window* (p. 590)

Considerations (p. 591)

1. The images used to describe the lobsters initially draw on childhood experiences — "school room clock" (line 5), "run-down toy" (9) — then move back to a glacial period before human beings appeared — "As if, in a glacial thaw" (17). The images set the lobsters in a primeval context, appropriate for their alien form, and they call for an imaginative struggle to understand the lobsters.

2. The images of coldness suggest paralysis and old age, perhaps implying a comparison between lobsters and human beings.

3. The speaker's uncertainty — "I guess" (25) — identifies his position as ambiguous. He uses the word "still" (26) to indicate that no movement has occurred, that all returns to the way it was in the first moment of the poem. Like the lobsters, the speaker stands in the rain: helpless, unwilling to act or even to move.

4. The first line invites us to consider "they" as humans as well as lobsters. The references to human childhood experiences and to our common history link the lobsters' experience to that of human beings. Images of human body parts — "fist . . . . wrist" (21, 24) — also invite symbolic readings.

This poem is about indifference, helplessness, and paralysis; all of these threaten the human being who surrenders to his or her environment, unable or unwilling to act. The artificiality, the human cause of the lobsters' plight, suggests that we might do something to avert this disastrous way of living.

Connection

1. Compare this speaker's tone and use of images with those in T. S. Eliot's "The Love Song of J. Alfred Prufrock" (p. /81). Are the two speakers describing a similar world? How does each poet's choice of images reflect his individual consciousness, as well as suggesting something about the relationship of human beings to the universe?

WILLIAM STAFFORD, *Traveling through the Dark* (p. 591)

Considerations (p. 592)

1. One of the surprising qualities about this poem is just how much time Stafford takes to describe his car. Given this description, with its glowing light, its "warm exhaust," the "steady" engine that "purred," the car acquires a stronger lifelike sense than anything else in this poem, which laments the death of something beautiful in the natural world. The car, "aimed ahead," seems symbolically to foreshadow a darker, more inhuman future, in which mechanization replaces old-fashioned Fate.

2. Providing every physical detail of his encounter with the deer, the speaker sounds like a news reporter, calmly telling his story to his listeners. But the final stanza suggests that he is meditative and brooding, that this incident means much more to him than its details imply, that his thinking involves the fate of the deer as well as that of the human race.

3. The short final stanza emphasizes its contemplative tone, setting it against the previous stanzas, moving the focus away from the deer, toward the speaker and his fellow human beings. It also suggests the finality of his decision.

4.,5. Stafford intends by his title a comment on the dark quality of the future. If anything, the poem is a counterstatement to didacticism, for it seems to argue that the world is moving increasingly beyond intelligible control, and it presents its case through images rather than through statements about ideas.

RICHARD EBERHART, *The Groundhog* (p. 592)

The most lengthy and vigorously described reaction to the groundhog is the first segment of this poem, in which Eberhart presents the groundhog's physical decay. The speaker observes the body with loathing and love, a reasonable mixture of emotions when viewing death so close at hand. On the second visit, the speaker sees only a "bony sodden hulk" — something in direct contrast to the "Vigor" and "immense energy" of before; now the speaker too feels a deadening of emotional response. He returns again to the spot and this time sees only a little hair and whitened bones. The groundhog now is a visual symbol for transcendence and the ideal. Appropriately, the metaphors used to describe the groundhog possess the cool abstraction of architecture and geometry. There is nothing to see on the fourth visit. Everything changes and passes away, no matter how vast, wise, or seemingly perdurable and passion filled.

The groundhog, of course, carries with it the conventional symbolism of a messenger or sign that heralds the end or the continuation of winter. It thus suggests renewal and the transcendence of death.

Connections (p. 594)

1. The deaths of the groundhog and the deer give the speaker in each poem an opportunity to think about his own mortality, the fate of the human race, and the relationship between human beings and the natural world. The speaker in Stafford's poem has a more tragic view than does the speaker in Eberhart's, who is simply pensive. One reason for the tonal difference could be that Eberhart's poem considers a process of decay, whereas Stafford's dwells on a sudden experience of recent death — in which the speaker has to participate by throwing the mother deer and her live, unborn fawn over the edge of the road. The experience of Stafford's speaker reaffirms what might already be his apocalyptic view of the world; Eberhart's leaves more room for positive interpretations.

3. Each of the three poems discusses the relationship between human beings and the natural world as somehow difficult, isolating, and thought provoking. In Stafford's poem the death of a deer confirms the speaker's view of the world as a bleak place. He suggests that human beings have consciously or accidentally killed the natural world; their destruction is evident in the exhaust fumes and the murdered fawn. The contemplation of Eberhart's speaker brings humanity into the natural world, recognizing the inevitability of our own decay. Lawrence's poem reverses the process, moving from the symbolic world of the human being back toward the unadulterated animal, without interpretation. In effect, his poem tries to remove the layers of mythology human beings have imposed on snakes to reveal the "real" biological animal that always lies beyond human consciousness. Whereas Stafford and Lawrence feel loss in their contemplation of the natural world, Eberhart's attitude is more accepting and ambiguous.

D. H. LAWRENCE, *Snake* (p. 594)

D. H. Lawrence grew up in the mining village of Eastwood, Nottinghamshire, located in the Midland region of England. He is best known as the author of the novels *Sons and Lovers, The Rainbow,* and *Women in Love,* among others. Lawrence struggled for most of his life to find a community where he could feel at home, but he never really succeeded, largely because of his alienation from conventional mores. He died of tuberculosis in the south of France. (For additional biographical information see manual p. 43.)

Students will no doubt quickly recognize that the snake in this poem is a symbol of vitality, lordliness, and the life force itself. Although its color indicates that it is poisonous, Lawrence describes the snake lushly and reverently — two words, by the way, that would not ordinarily be paired according to Lawrence's past education, which he evaluates in this poem. The snake is "earth-brown, earth-golden from the burning bowels of the earth / On the day of Sicilian July, with Etna smoking." Its warmth, connection to the earth, right of place are established here, as is its likeness to a god later in the poem.

Yet the snake is richly ambiguous as a symbol. Literally, it is dangerous, and therefore it is a challenge to the speaker's manliness to take courage, attack, and kill it. The snake's presence, on one level, is a satanic taunt, mocking a more liberal, humane course of conduct and impiously upholding the conservative, institution-ridden code of behavior and value.

Meanly, the speaker falls in with his education and does what he thinks he is supposed to do, despite his own recognition of the snake's majestic presence. Now, like Samuel Taylor Coleridge's mariner, who killed an albatross, the speaker has a crime he must expiate. He longs for the return of the snake, as if it could reappear, like a transformed and rejuvenated Fisher King, to restore the sources of vitality within life itself.

As a writing assignment, you might ask students to draw examples from two of the three preceding poems and discuss the degree to which their writers feel that the modern world is alienated from the natural world. What sort of loss do the poets imply that humankind may be suffering?

LOUISE BOGAN, *The Dragonfly* (p. 596)

Considerations (p. 596)

2. In the first stanza, the speaker begins a celebration of the dragonfly; the third begins the journey toward its death and toward the end of the poem.

3. Bogan could be referring to human beings as well as dragonflies, particularly if we consider "grappling love" (line 7), which seems to signal a human predicament more than an insect's struggle. The verbs "dart" (15), "rocket" (17), and "fall" (20) all suggest human subjects as well, because they have particular reference to human technology, mythology, and activity.

4. The final stanza moves the single dragonfly into the collective "husks of summer" (21), returning the once-isolated image to its environment. The word "husks" emphasizes the finality of the dragonfly's life, transforming a once-beautiful image into a leftover on the ground. Without the final stanza, this poem would be about a dragonfly; with it, the applications to human experience are invited.

Connections (p. 538)

1. Compare the speaker's attitude toward love in Millay's "Never May the Fruit Be Plucked" (p. 538) with Bogan's speaker's description of the dragonfly as "grappling love" (7). Do the poems have a similar message?

HENRY REED, *Naming of Parts* (p. 597)

The irony of this poem is situational. The instructor (no doubt an army sergeant addressing a group of raw recruits) is filled with self-importance as he drones on about naming the rifle parts, wholly oblivious to the silent beauty of the spring day. The season, though, arouses in the young recruit's thoughts reminders of a world far more vibrant than that of weaponry. Students should be able to distinguish between sergeant and recruit in the exchange of voices. The recruit's musings begin in the second half of the fourth line of each stanza, and the final line works to deflect the authoritative tone of the earlier part of the stanza. Discussion of rifle parts summons up with ironic aptness physical allusions, which the young recruit inevitably thinks of as he looks at the beautiful gardens in spring, assaulted by the vigorous bees.

ROBERT BROWNING, *Soliloquy of the Spanish Cloister* (p. 598)

Robert Browning lived with his parents in a London suburb until he married Elizabeth Barrett at age 34; he had previously left home only to attend boarding school and for short trips abroad. He and his wife lived in Italy for fifteen years, a period in which he produced some of his first memorable poems. *Men and Women,* published in 1855, gained Browning the initial intimations of his later fame. The poet returned to England after his wife died in 1861. His work continued to elicit increasing public (if not always critical) acclaim.

Probably no one is better than Browning at portraying maniacal hatred through the dramatic monologue. Here this hatred rages in a monastery, where the speaker (not at all to be identified with Browning) complains bitterly about the genteel Brother Lawrence, who enjoys gardening. The speaker charges his fellow brother with sins of pride (cf. the monogrammed ware in stanza III), lust in stanza IV, and gluttony, stanza VI. In addition Brother

Lawrence is faulted for being a bore and for failing to observe the niceties of token symbolism while eating.

The speaker is behaving wholly inappropriately for one who has joined an order that extols self-abnegation, love, charity, and good works. The raging hatred probably aroused by the sight of goodness — which this prideful, plotting, and sanctimonious speaker himself lacks — is in ironic defiance of the appearances of one who is a monk. If there is someone in your class with thespian inclinations, this poem, particularly its opening lines, can profit by an oral reading.

WILLIAM BLAKE, *The Chimney Sweeper* (p. 600)

There is an ironic distance in this poem between the speaker, who seems to be too young to make judgments, and Blake himself, who through his ironic perspective underscores the harm that comes from too meekly doing one's duty, not to mention the evil of a society indifferent to the plight of "thousands of sweepers" whose only pleasure is in dreams. Needless to say, sacrificing one's hair for the sake of on-the-job cleanliness is not a principle Blake would endorse.

On the surface the poem could be interpreted as a dream of desire for some beneficent angel to release the boys from their "coffins of black" (the chimneys). More likely, the dream expresses a desire for release through death from the tortuous and life-threatening trials of sweeping soot from chimneys. Here again, irony operates in that a dream of death makes it easier for the boy to face his life the next morning.

EMILY DICKINSON, *Lightly stepped a yellow star* (p. 600)

Students should enjoy the dry, thin-lipped commentary the speaker in this poem springs on the reader after her sweetly pleasant and mockingly conventional portrait of fairyland.

As a writing assignment of one or two pages, you might ask students to explore how Dickinson "sets up" the reader for the jar of the final word. Explore too whether there is a measure of superiority of relationship claimed by a supposed underling who would take note of the punctuality (like workers punching a time clock) of another.

Connections (p. 601)

2. In "Lightly stepped a yellow star," the speaker's tone is playful and possibly ironic. God is a timekeeper, supervising the universe so that everything works properly. Dickinson may have a tongue-in-cheek attitude toward traditional notions of a God who watches over our every move, influencing our daily lives favorably when we do good and punishing us for misbehavior. In "I know that He exists," Dickinson begins with another traditional picture of God, only to undercut it in later stanzas. In both poems, the feminine pronouns work against the masculine depiction of God, suggesting that the poems may also concern the complexities of male-female relationships.

17. Sounds

LEONARD COHEN, *Suzanne* (p. 603)

In this lyric (which Cohen sings) the three stanzas that speak of Suzanne, Jesus, and the "you" as listener drawn into the song inscribe a circle that marks out an exchange of trust and eventual oneness among the three. Like Jesus, who was not believed, especially when he laid claim on the miraculous, Suzanne, this "lady of the harbour," is considered by some to be "half crazy." Nevertheless, she bestows blessings, gives and receives love, and especially in stanza III accomplishes the miraculous. The repetition, rhythm, and symmetry of the three stanzas, which imply a unity beyond themselves, all reflect the characteristics of poetry.

JOHN UPDIKE, *Player Piano* (p. 604)

This poem is a listening exercise in how to translate the sounds poetry can produce to musical analogues we have already heard. From light ditties through more somber 1920s chase-scene music, perhaps, to a medley of chords and light cadences, this poem explores a player piano's repertoire.

MAY SWENSON, *A Nosty Fright* (p. 605)

Discussed in text.

EMILY DICKINSON, *A Bird came down the Walk* — (p. 606)

Discussed in text.

GALWAY KINNELL, *Blackberry Eating* (p. 608)

Some poems are memorable for their themes, while others are enjoyed not for what they say but for how they say it. This poem seems to fall into this second category, as Kinnell tries in lieu of the blackberries themselves to offer us a blackberry language. It would probably be a good idea to read this poem aloud in class. Kinnell here plays with the kinesthesia of the sound in words such as *strengths* or *squinched,* which by their compacted consonance physically suggest to him the pressure of the tongue bursting open the berry's mysterious ("black art") icy sweetness. What other words are there (you might ask) that seem to touch the inside of the body before they are spoken? Look at some of the heavily consonantal words in lines 12 and 13, marking especially words like *splurge* and *language.* Lines 4–6, besides containing good examples of consonance patterns, also express a pathetic fallacy, with Kinnell's imaginative supposition that blackberry bushes are punished with nettles for knowing the art of blackberry making. You might ask what, if anything, this image adds to the poem. Probably it underscores Kinnell's whimsical sense of the black artistry of blackberry making.

Attempting to write a poem can be as much a learning experience about poetry as attempting to write about a poem. Perhaps some members of the class would like to try writing their own lyric beginning with the words *I love to.*

Considerations (p. 609)

1.   Alliteration (*black, blackberries, breakfast,* 2–3; *prickly, penalty,* 4; *strengths, squinched,* 10; *squeeze, squinch,* 12) is the structuring element of this imagistic poem. The sound

moves from the hard *b* of *blackberry* to the softer *s*'s of the final lines. Many assonant *o*'s occur in the first lines, *e*'s and *a*'s in the middle of the poem. The sounds attempt to capture the delectable berries, making the experience of reading the poem as sensuous as eating a berry.

2. Providing an opposition to the overwhelmingly appealing aspects of the berries, their prickles make them even more of a prize to those who dare to pick them. Blackberry picking is a black art for Kinnell's speaker, as is the art of the poet who describes it.

3. More than providing a message of "truth" for its reader, this poem invites us into an experience of sound and image. The poem is about language in that it considers the difficulty of capturing an idea in words and communicating it effectively.

RICHARD ARMOUR, *Going to Extremes* (p. 609)

Discussed in text.

ROBERT SOUTHEY, *The Cataract of Lodore* (p. 610)

Discussed in text.

PERSPECTIVE

DAVID LENSON, *On the Contemporary Use of Rhyme* (p. 614)

You might ask students to find contemporary poems that make subtle use of rhyme. Philip Larkin's poems are good examples of the effective use of slant rhyme and enjambment to camouflage the rhymes in a poem. Conversely, you might ask students to look for songs that don't use rhyme. Tracy Chapman's "Fast Car" (p. 513) uses some rhyme, but not in every line. What is the effect of the sporadic rhyme in her song?

Students might be interested in speculating on why writers are returning to rhyme. Is more formal poetry appropriate for our time and culture? Or is it simply a question of rebelling against the norm (in our time, unrhymed poetry)?

GERARD MANLEY HOPKINS, *God's Grandeur* (p. 614)

Discussed in text.

Gerard Manley Hopkins was a deeply religious man, a Jesuit ordained in 1877. He had previously graduated from Oxford University and joined the Roman Catholic Church in 1866. He served a number of parishes before being appointed a professor of Classics at University College, Dublin. Although he tried to keep his poetic vocation from interfering with his spiritual one, he wasn't successful, and he suffered greatly because of this conflict, once burning all his finished work and another time forsaking poetry for seven years.

LEWIS CARROLL [CHARLES LUDWIDGE DODGSON], *Jabberwocky* (p. 616)

"'Jabberwocky' is no mere piece of sound experimentation but a serious short narrative poem describing a young man's coming of age as he seeks out and kills the tribal terror." Test that description on your students, and they will, one hopes, turn around and tell you that the fun of this poem and the justification for its being reside in its sound and word creations.

Carroll had his own glossary for some of the words in this poem, which Alice read through her looking glass. The glossary entries and copious notes about the poem are provided by Martin Gardner in *The Annotated Alice* (New York: Bramhall House, 1960), pp. 191–197. The notes are too extensive to include here — but as a sampling here is the first stanza "translated":

Twas time for making dinner (bryllyg — to broil)
    and the "smooth and active" (slimy + lithe) badgers

> Did scratch like a dog (gyre — giaour)
> and drill holes (gimble) in the side of the hill:
>
> All unhappy were the Parrots (now extinct; they lived on veal and
> under sundials)
>
> And the grave turtles (who lived on swallows and oysters) squeaked.

Reality bores its head through the hills and holes of "Jabberwocky," and certain words in the poem have their place in the *OED*. These include *rath,* an Irish word for a circular earthen wall; *Manx,* a Celtic name for the Isle of Man; *whiffling,* smoking, drinking, or blowing short puffs; *Caloo,* the sound and name of an arctic duck; *beamish,* old form of beaming; *chortled,* Carroll's own coinage, meaning "laughing"; and *gallumphing,* another of Carroll's creations, which according to him is a cross between *gallop* and *triumphant* and means "to march on exultantly with irregular bounding movements."

Connections (p. 617)

1. Whereas Swenson transposes letters to create amusing sound patterns and effects, Carroll combines and alters words to invent a new language for his speaker. Carroll's technique is harder to translate word for word; it requires more of his audience's imaginative effort.

2. Francis's speaker presents a somewhat traditional attitude toward effective language; it should not draw attention to itself. Carroll holds an opposing view. He seems to think that the best poem compels its audience to struggle to make it mean something; this is how to "make it new," to draw the audience into the experience.

3. This poem narrates the well-known tale of the pursuit and slaying of the dragon. It fits Marcus's description of an initiation tale in that the speaker encounters a ritual struggle that should make him ready for adulthood. Because he does slay the dragon, the young man can be said to have had a decisive initiation in Marcus's terms, although it is difficult to determine the extent to which the young man realizes the importance of his feat. Our decision about his initiation into adulthood depends upon how we choose to interpret the event of the poem; does slaying a dragon constitute an "adult" experience? We must also consider that the father narrates his son's experience, inferring perhaps that the boy is not yet ready to tell his own story. If we emphasize that point, the tale is not an initiation but rather an adventure story.

JEAN TOOMER, *Reapers* (p. 617)

"Reapers" is taken from Toomer's experimentalist novel *Cain* (1923), which combines poetry and prose and was one of the works that helped launch the Harlem Renaissance. The poem is ominous and grim in tone. Long before it was fashionable to call his people blacks, Toomer here stressed the dire nature of the scene by talking about black reapers and black horses. Scythes and mowers call to mind the image of death as a grim reaper, sometimes cutting down people in their prime. That symbolic association is enhanced by the death of the field rat, which seems to indicate also the vulnerability of the reapers themselves to being cut down by some impersonal, indifferent force.

The sound of the rasping blade being honed to sharpness is suggested in lines 1 and 2 by the many *s*-sounds. In question 4's version of line 6, certain alliterative and assonantal sounds are linked by echoing sounds, as in "*field* rat," "squ*eal*ing," "b*leed*s." A cause-effect relation is underscored by Toomer's version, which places "squealing" and "bleeds" together. Finally, the caesura provides rhythmic reinforcement of the action described.

JOHN DONNE, *Song* (p. 618)

Considerations (p. 618)

1. Donne manages to mix cynicism and lightheartedness here as he verbally throws up his hands at the possibility of finding an honest mind or a woman who is both true and fair. You might spend some time in class discussion exploring how he holds at bay the darker tones of his cynicism. Can we identify with Donne's dilemma today, or have attitudes toward women changed too much? What does the humor in the poem tell us about his fundamental attitude toward women? Students will probably appreciate the hyperbole in the poem. It is as though Donne were saying, "You might as well get with child a mandrake root, as find an honest mind."

2. The last stanza is especially humorous. Donne claims he would not even go next door to see this reputedly loyal woman. Her reputation for loyalty might hold long enough for his friend to write a letter describing her, but by the time the speaker has arrived, she would have been false to two or three other lovers.

3. Feminine rhymes occur with "singing" and "stinging," "met her" and "letter." Slant rhymes appear with "find," "wind," "mind."

As a writing assignment you might ask the students to discuss the humor in this song, humor that would definitely include Donne's use of hyperbole. The students should then try to anticipate a listener's reaction to the speaker and decide whether the speaker is perfectly "straight" in his observations.

JUDY GRAHN, *She Who bears it* (p. 619)

Considerations (p. 619)

1. The hard, alliterative *b*'s push the poem toward its completion, while the assonant *o*'s seem to resist that push, calling our attention to the woman's struggle and pain.

2. The repetitions of *bear* and *breathe* become almost an incantation accompanying the experience of the woman in labor, which consists of contractions that repeat and become more severe until the baby is born. Then the lines become longer, more expansive, as the poem projects a release.

3. The reference to "the first labor" (line 7) may indicate both the first labor pain and the woman's first experience of giving birth. In lines 12 and 13 the expression is redefined; the woman's job in the home is, according to the speaker, the most important, primary job. She speaks in challenge to those who would belittle the work of a housewife and mother.

Connections

1. *In what ways might this poem respond to Hilberry's "The Frying Pan" (p. 589)?*

2. *Discuss this speaker's view of motherhood compared with the narrator's view in Olsen's story "I Stand Here Ironing" (p. 239). Are their concerns different? What might account for the similarities or differences you notice?*

THOMAS HARDY, *The Oxen* (p. 619)

So often a poem's source is childhood memory or belief, as though childhood were a period in our lives that made poetry possible. You might ask the class if they already knew of the belief about animals on which this poem rests. There is a kind of pathos about the poem, in which Hardy recalls his own readiness to believe that the oxen knelt in reverence on Christmas Eve. The feeling is of a wistful longing for a belief that probably never can be reinstated in this (even for Hardy) more mechanistic and rationalistic age. It is not so much a loss of childhood, but rather the loss of belief itself that is mourned. In the final stanza the doubled *o*-sounds suggest the tones of lament and mourning.

ALEXANDER POPE, From *An Essay on Criticism* (p. 620)

Alexander Pope was born in London and, after age twelve, grew up in Windsor Forest. Because his family was Catholic, and because he had been afflicted with tuberculosis of the spine, most of his education was completed at home. Catholics couldn't attend university or hold office, chief routes to patronage in those days, so Pope became by necessity as well as by desire and talent the first writer to show that literature could be one's sole support. His work, beginning with translations of the *Iliad* and the *Odyssey*, was both critically approved and financially profitable.

You might begin discussion of this selection by reminding students that the debate over which should take precedence, sound or sense, has been of greater concern to poets than many of us realize or recall.

Considerations (p. 621)

1. Pope enjoys a little self-reflective mockery in these lines. Like the bumper sticker that reads "Eschew Obfuscation," the problem is in the line itself. The iambs march with strict, tuneful regularity in line 4. The word *do* in line 10 is an expletive or meter filler. Line 11 presents a parade of monosyllables. "Chimes" in line 12 sets up the anticipated "rhymes" in line 13, and line 21 exceeds its bounds, albeit slowly, with the long alexandrine.

2. Expected rhymes are predictable and therefore boring. Pope varies his pattern and upsets our expectations by giving us slant rhyme in lines 24 and 25 and by offering some good thoughts in lines 28 and 29: " ' Tis not enough no harshness gives offense, / The sound must seem an echo to the sense."

3. Line 23 uses assonance and some alliteration to suggest what it means; line 24 is a fine example of "easy vigor," straightforward and brief enough; lines 32 and 33 imitate the thought through the manipulation of sounds, in particular the sibilance of the *s*-sound, the growling of the *r*'s, and the forcefulness of the blocks of heavy-stressed words, as in "when loud surges lash."

    In line 34 the sounds get stuck in one's throat ("rock's vast weight") and reflect this resisting struggle. Accents in line 35 on "líne tóo lábors," and on "wórds móve slów" create an almost plodding rhythm that imitates the sense of the words. These lines contrast with lines 36 and 37, which contain far more light-stressed words and employ a much more direct and smooth syntax.

4. Even though inverted word order has long been out of fashion and an overfastidious attention to sound and rhyme can pull words out of their customary order, careful reading of much contemporary poetry will reveal the continuing validity of Pope's observation. In any case, the power of words fashioned into lines with close attention to sound can be amply demonstrated by observing the structure of popular songs and advertisements.

RICHARD WILBUR, *The Death of a Toad* (p. 621)

Considerations (p. 622)

1. The cineraria, with its heart-shaped leaves covered with an ashlike down, is etymologically related to *cinerarium*, a container for the ashes of the dead.

2. Toads are not usually thought of as admirable or likable creatures. See, for example, Philip Larkin's symbolic use of them in his poem "Toads" (p. 809). But Wilbur here pays homage to his toad. With language that is elevated and honorific, even at times on the verge of being archaic as though in deference to the toad's antique origins, Wilbur eulogizes this

creature. Notice some fine word choices: the use of "sanctuaried" in line 3 or "rare original heartsblood" to mark the toad's dying (7).

3. In line 2 Wilbur speaks of the "hobbling hop" of the injured toad. With the repetition of the *h*-sound, we almost sense the effort the toad is expending. The *p* at the end of *hop* also echoes the sound of *clipped* earlier in the line. In line 15 the repeated *d*'s sound out the dying of the frog and the *n*'s find their rest in the word *gone*.

4. Most of the end rhymes in this poem reinforce each other in terms of sense. Review especially stanza II in this connection.

JONATHAN GALASSI, *Our Wives* (p. 622)

Considerations (p. 622)

1. The speaker is suddenly struck by the limits of his life. In a bemused tone he realizes that he is happy enough but that he is not creating "history" in the sense of heroic events and actions. He recognizes his life as the somewhat mundane present. He might be disappointed with this present, but he shows great tact in noting that it contains "these lovely women," their wives.

2. The three "leaves" in the final three stanzas illustrate the speaker's relationship to time, calling attention both to the turning of the seasons and to the role of memory in our sense of what time means. Initially thinking of his life in the future, the speaker moves toward a clearer understanding of the past and the present. The mirror provides the medium for his experience, suggesting that our sense of time is refracted and distorted at best. Stating that "time deceives" (line 4), the speaker points out that looking toward the future is finally looking toward death; only in appreciating the present and remembering the past can we stop racing with time.

3. Many lines end in either *wives* or *lives,* with the terms alternating until they finally come together in the last stanza. This movement follows that of the poem, in which the speaker alternates his focus between his own experiences and his wife in the mirror, finally discovering that the two are one subject: "our wives. . . became our lives" (18–19).

PAUL HUMPHREY, *Blow* (p. 623)

The class may not be familiar with the term *luffed*, which is a nautical word meaning "to turn the head of the ship into the wind." The woman here is metaphorically transformed into a sailing ship — appropriately enough since both would be addressed as "she." The marvelous final line gives a blow to the gesture of the speaker trying to quell the woman's wind-filled skirt. Here the alliteration creates a kind of humor, and the quick end-stopped monosyllables with their *t*-sounds emphasize the deftness that marks the woman's movements. Point out to the class how these short, light sounds are used, almost as a verbal photograph, to capture the moment.

ROBERT FRANCIS, *The Pitcher* (p. 623)

Considerations (p. 623)

1,2. If a pitcher is too obvious, the batter will easily figure out how to hit the balls he throws. The pitcher and batter play a cat-and-mouse game, in which the pitcher must stay within the boundaries but not pitch directly to the hitter. While the other players throw directly to one another, he must seem to throw a fast ball only to throw a curve and vice versa. But he cannot throw wildly, or he has failed to do his job.

In a similar way, the poet's play with language must "avoid the obvious" and "vary the avoidance." Line 4, almost (but not quite) a repetition of line 3, does what it says by avoiding the repetition.

3. Like the pitcher's task of avoidance within bounds, the rhymes in the poem are not quite but almost there. We have the sense of a potential never actualized. The final lines illustrate the perfect rhyme that is avoided in the previous lines, indicating the completed pitch and the finished poem.

4. In writing poetry as in pitching, the actors work in a dangerous relationship to the receivers of the action. If a poet is too obvious, he or she lapses into sentimentality. Too abstract, the poet loses the audience altogether. Language being deceptive and imperfect, the poet must work to communicate effectively to the reader, using indirection, imagery, and cunning rhymes, as does this poet when he describes his art. Like the pitcher, who holds both the ball and the strength to throw it as he decides, the poet chooses his words and delivers them as he feels he must, making the reader wait patiently. Ironically, the pitcher is on the defensive side, although he appears to be on the offensive as he aims at his target. This fact may lead us to question the real relationship between poet and audience suggested in this analogy.

Connection (p. 624)

1. Wallace's analogy discusses the importance of agility and skill in the writing of poetry, whereas Francis's concentration on the pitcher reveals his belief that poetry is more involved with moderate deception than with speed or skillful movement.

HELEN CHASIN, *The Word* Plum (p. 624)

Considerations (p. 624)

1,2. The alliteration and assonance make our lips move the way they might when eating a plum. They also call attention to the sound of the poem, so that it is also about writing poetry.

3. The title suggests that the poem is about words. The relationship of the word *plum* to the object plum will generate an interesting discussion of the nature of language. Do words correspond to objects? Does poetry do more than point dimly to the sensuous realm?

4. Each poet uses the fruit to develop an appealing description of writing poetry. Chasin's view of the art centers on "pleasure" and "self-love." Kinnell suggests that these are also his concerns, that poetry is an individual experience of self-expression. Both poems emphasize and celebrate the difficulty, the near impossibility, of conveying an experience in language.

18. Patterns of Rhythm

WALT WHITMAN, From *Song of the Open Road* (p. 626)

Discussed in text.

WILLIAM WORDSWORTH, *My Heart Leaps Up* (p. 629)

Discussed in text.

WILLIAM BUTLER YEATS, *That the Night Come* (p. 630)

Discussed in text.

William Butler Yeats was born in Dublin and spent his youth in Dublin, London, and Sligo (his mother's family's home) in the west of Ireland. After graduating from high school, Yeats decided to attend art school (his father, J. B. Yeats, was a painter) and made poetry an avocation. He dropped out soon after and published his first poems at age twenty in the *Dublin University Review*. His poetic influences include Spenser, Shelley, Blake, and the Pre-Raphaelite poets of 1890s London, but a perhaps equally important shaping force was his religious temperament. Never satisfied with Christian doctrine, he invented, piecemeal, a mythology that informs his poetry in often obscure ways. For range and power, no twentieth-century poet equals Yeats.

A. E. HOUSMAN, *When I was one-and-twenty* (p. 631)

The basic metrical pattern here is iambic trimeter. The first stanza is tightly rhymed, with only two rhyming sounds. The second stanza picks up on the first rhyming word of stanza I (*twenty*), but Housman in this stanza uses more rhyming words (four sounds in the eight lines), as though he were opening up to experience. Appropriately, given his unhappy romance, "rue," "two," and "true" echo one another in rhyme. Love in both stanzas is metaphorically treated with marketplace terminology. In the first stanza the wise man advises the speaker to keep his fancy free. In the second stanza the wise man observes that the heart "was never given in vain" and, moreover, the cost of buying or selling this seat of affection is immeasurable. The repetition of " 'tis true" is like a shaking of the head, of one in a state of endless "rue."

ROBERT FRANCIS, *Excellence* (p. 632)

Considerations (p. 632)

1. Alliteration in the first line links the three most important words and calls attention to the units of measurements Francis is contrasting.

2. The meter here is iambic hexameter, probably to recall the metrical line used by Roman poets such as Virgil to record heroic deeds.

3. The caesura in line 2 allows the first statement to "settle," so that it can be comprehended and appreciated. Again alliteration ties "good" to "great." The second half of the line, exactly parallel in syntax, has the effect of an echo, a much more softly intoned statement.

4. Francis's version of the line has seven stressed beats (iambic heptameter) and by its extended length reflects "that split-second longer."

You might as a writing assignment ask the class to paraphrase the poem and discuss its title. What frequent connotations of the word *excellence* does the poem try to counter?

ROBERT HERRICK, *Delight in Disorder* (p. 632)

Considerations (p. 633)

1. You might begin discussion of this poem by asking students what connotations the word *neat* holds for them. Then explore Herrick's use of *disorder*, as contrasted with our word *disorderly*, along with *wantonness*. Clearly, disorder and wantonness arouse in the speaker here a "fine distraction" and exercise a certain appeal that would not be present if the person addressed were prim and proper.

2. Herrick subtly illustrates his theme by working changes on the basic iambic tetrameter rhythm. Iambs change to trochees (cf. lines 2 and 4, for example), and in line 10 dactyls appear.

3. The speaker here is bewitched but not bothered by his lady's "sweet disorder." Words are chosen to indicate a tantalizing of the passions by "erring" lace, "tempestuous" petticoats, and shoestrings tied with a "wild civility."

Ask students to turn back to the second question in the text and in a writing assignment analyze how patterns of rhyme and consonance work to create a subtle and pleasing artistic order.

BEN JONSON, *Still to Be Neat* (p. 633)

Stepson of a bricklayer, Jonson was one of the first English writers to make his living by his pen. Admired for his lyrical poetry and literary criticism, Jonson is perhaps best known for his satiric comedies — including *Volpone* (1605), *The Alchemist* (1610), and *Bartholomew Fair* (1614) — and for the elaborate masques he created with designer Inigo Jones for the court of James I.

Considerations (p. 633)

1. The speaker dislikes the artful manners and dress of the woman. "Sweet" refers both to her smell, which is sweet, and their relationship, which presumably has some difficulties, perhaps because of her preoccupation with her own appearance. The speaker is suspicious about the reason for this preoccupation.

2. The speaker asks the woman to be more sincere in her attentions to him, to pay less attention to her appearance. Neglecting herself is "sweet" to him because it is more natural, less deceptive. Words such as "adulteries" (line 11) and "face" play with the relationship between art and nature, intimating that the woman's efforts to make herself into a beautiful object only mar her natural beauty.

3. The disruptions in the rhythms reinforce Jonson's point until the final line. In line 6 the rhythm and the caesura in the middle of the line force the reader to slow down, emphasizing the speaker's insistence that the woman stop her artful motion and remove the mask. In the final line, the iambic tetrameter brings the speaker's point home in a succinct statement of his case.

Connections (p. 634)

1. Herrick's speaker asks for a similar absence of artistry and emphasis on irregularity. But the poems seem to treat the art-nature dichotomy differently. For Herrick, a "sweet disorder" may be part of the art, whereas for Jonson the relationship between art and nature is more troubled. Jonson's speaker does not want his beloved to be artful; Herrick's simply asks that the art not be "too precise in every part."

2. With trochees interrupting the iambic rhythm throughout, Jonson's poem is more insistent than Herrick's. The speaker in "Still to Be Neat" is calling an end to false art. Herrick's smoother rhythm and more easily flowing syllables suggest the speaker's delight in observing the disorder of his lady's dress. The differences in meter are in keeping with the different relationship between art and nature in the two poems.

WILLIAM BLAKE, *The Lamb* (p. 634) and *The Tyger* (p. 635)

These two poems when paired make excellent examples of diction, rhythm, and sound and how these elements enhance tone. Ostensibly, each poem employs a four-stress pattern of trochaic feet, but the gliding *l*-sounds of the opening of "The Lamb" make the first stress on "Little" seem much lighter than the emphasis "Tyger" receives. The rhyme in the opening two lines of "The Lamb" is feminine, again unlike the stressed rhyme in "The Tyger." Only one question ("Who made Thee?") is asked of the lamb, and that question is repeated several times, giving the poem a sense of childlike simplicity and innocence. In this poem, moreover, there is a figural pattern of exchangeable identities between Lamb and Creator (Lamb of God), and speaker as child and Christ as God's child. Unlike the fearful symmetry of "The Tyger," this poem reflects a wholeness and innocence by the cohesiveness of these identities.

"The Tyger" poses far more questions about the creation of this powerful, regal beast, including the question in line 20: "Did he who made the Lamb make thee?" Ways of reading that question include the debate over the presence of evil in a God-created universe and the possibility of a second creator from whom darkness, evil, and fierce energy emanate. Could not the tiger stand for positive expressions of power? By and large, though, the questions in "The Tyger" go unanswered. Notice, for example, the substitution of *dare* in the final line for *could* in line 4.

As a writing assignment, you might ask students to examine several elements in each poem, including rhythm, patterns of consonance and assonance, pace, tone, even levels of ambiguity so that they are able on a fairly sophisticated level to articulate the differences between the two lyrics.

DOROTHY PARKER, *One Perfect Rose* (p. 636)

Considerations (p. 636)

1. The tone of the first two stanzas is dreamy and romantic. The speaker builds a sense of adulation for the rose as a symbol of love and beauty. The *abab* rhyme scheme and the iambic pentameter rhythm are in keeping with the poem's seemingly traditional theme.

2. The meaning of the rose flip-flops in the third stanza. In the first two instances, we read the rose as a beautiful symbol of love for the speaker. In line 12 it becomes a material object like any other, only far less valuable than "one perfect limousine."

3. The speaker is sophisticated and witty. She plays on our traditional (and somewhat sentimental) associations of love with fragile flowers and purely idealistic emotion. Then in a deft stroke she unmasks herself to reveal a materialistic strain — one that may exist in all of us.

ALFRED, LORD TENNYSON, *Break, Break, Break* (p. 636)

Alfred, Lord Tennyson, was one of twelve children of a reluctant and eventually alcoholic clergyman. He attended Cambridge University, there beginning, at the urging of a group of undergraduate writers known as the Apostles, his lifelong devotion to poetry. The publication of *In Memoriam* in 1850 and his appointment as poet laureate in the same year brought him out of poverty, allowing him to marry and move to the country.

The repetition of the word *break* in this poem gives a sense of relentless beating, as though the speaker were trying to break emotionally through something but could not. The anapestic trimeter (with some iambic substitution) can be read as wavelike, and lines 1 and 13 (metrically lame, since each preserves the trimeter but without the unaccented syllables) seen as instances of the occasional asymmetry in any natural wave rhythm. The lines create a tone of agony and frustration, of the broken heart trying willfully to heal itself.

THEODORE ROETHKE, *My Papa's Waltz* (p. 637)

From the perspective of a man looking back at his childhood the speaker recollects the drunken lurchings of his working-class father as he waltzed around the room. The remembrance is one of those strong early memories that, years later, one sifts through. The rhythm of the poem reflects well those moments the speaker recalls with some pain. Notice the spondees, for example, in "My right ear scraped a buckle" (line 12) or in "You beat time on my head / With a palm caked hard by dirt" (13–14). The title with its use of *Papa*, seems to indicate a memory from early childhood — as does line 12. It also connotes a certain gentle affection for "Papa," despite all the other memories.

ROBERT BROWNING, *My Last Duchess* (p. 637)

Students may have already read this dramatic monologue in high school. The second time around they should appreciate the irony even more as the duke reveals so much of his own character while ostensibly controlling the situation.

Considerations (p. 639)

1. Ironically, the speaker is talking about the portrait of his last duchess (how many went before?) to the marriage broker, who is handling the current arrangement between the duke and the broker's "master," father of the bride-to-be.

2. The last wife's principal fault was that she was too democratic in her smiles; she did not reserve them for the duke alone. The duke holds no regard for kindness and thoughtfulness; he thinks only of money, rank, and name. He treats women as objects and possessions.

3. The visitor seems to want to leave early, perhaps to warn his master of the unfeeling tyrant who would marry the master's daughter at a cut rate (cf. lines 47–54).

4. Breaks in rhythm help to indicate natural speech patterns, and the caesuras often pull attention away from the rhyme word at the end of a line and thus reduce the possibility of a singsong intonation or a too-obvious line. Note, for example, the natural music in lines 19–24. The searching for words in "how shall I say?" opens pauses in line 22. "Joy" and "say" in midline find slant echoes, while the rhyme of "had" and "glad" is muted by the pauses and the enjambment.

EMILY DICKINSON, *Because I could not stop for Death* (p. 639)

Considerations (p. 640)

1. The speaker could not stop for death because she does not want to; doing so means ending her life.

2. Death is personified as a courtier. The speaker willingly joins him on the journey, amazed by what she finds and sees. The accompanying Immortality indicates the speaker's belief in an afterlife.

3. They pass the three stages of a person's earthly existence in stanza III: childhood, maturity, and old age.

4. The house is the speaker's grave.

5. In line 14 "Dews drew," two long syllables whose length is emphasized by the internal rhyme, help to intensify by contrast the sensation of "quivering." Dickinson expertly exploits the possibilities of the basic iambic rhythm in this line and throughout the poem.

The turning point of the poem — aptly figured as the chill felt the instant the sun goes down — is signaled by a reversal of the basic pattern in lines 13 and 14 of a four-foot line alternating with a three-foot line. Without departing from the iambic rhythm, Dickinson introduces a caesura after "Or rather" in line 13 that emphasizes the speaker's double take.

Connections (p. 640)

1. Whereas this poem concerns itself with images of the afterlife, making death into a panoramic journey, "I heard a Fly buzz — when I died — " is much more centered in the physical images of the moment of death.

2. The speaker in "If I shouldn't be alive" concerns herself with life on earth after she has died. The appalling detail of the "Granite lip" suggests her refusal to let go of this life. In contrast, "Because I could not stop for Death" is a poem of release. The hold on earth is relaxed, and the speaker moves through death as if it were an adventure in increasingly unfamiliar territory.

RICHARD LOVELACE, *To Lucasta, Going to the Wars* (p. 640)

In this poem the sharp contrast between love and war is made to seem less distinct through the vocabularies of romance and religion that are applied to each. The woman is nunlike in her quietness, and she will come to "adore" (a word that could be drawn from either altar) the speaker's inconstancy, for it betrays his code of honor and duty to his country. Lovelace, by the way, fought in the service of King Charles I in the Puritan Revolution of 1642–1645. As for war itself, it is described as a "mistress," and Lovelace promises to "embrace" this new undertaking with a "stronger faith."

In this poem lines of iambic tetrameter and iambic trimeter alternate, though there are several variations, as, for example, the opening protest.

EDWARD HIRSCH, *Fast Break* (p. 641)

Considerations (p. 642)

1. Run-ons make us feel that we are watching the basketball game as we read the poem. The one long sentence is an appropriate choice because the poem describes a few seconds of activity on a basketball court; we feel both the urgency and the rapidity of the play. In keeping with the spirit of the game, in which quick moves, sudden reversals, and surges of power are of the essence, the meter is irregular.

2. The tribute to the dead friend attempts to sing the praises of a short but successful life. The image of the power forward exploding past other players in a fury (lines 25, 26) suggests someone burning through life radiant with energy and resolve. The player scores the point in the final lines. We sense both a resolution to the play and a resolution to the life.

3. In its attempt to capture a single moment on the court, to encircle the actions of all of the players in that moment, and to make the audience feel as if they are a part of it, this poem can be called "a momentary stay against confusion." The poem freezes a moment in time, seeming to simplify a life's journey in a single play. The poem shows us the player's life making sense.

PERSPECTIVE

LOUISE BOGAN, *On Formal Poetry* (p. 642)

You might ask students to compare Bogan's questions about form as repression with Whitman's assertion that "The rhyme and uniformity of perfect poems show the free growth of metrical laws and bud from them as unerringly and loosely as lilacs or roses on a bush, and take shapes as compact as the shapes of chestnuts and oranges and melons and pears, and shed the perfume impalpable to form" (p. 666). Students could write an essay about these perspectives on "form" in poetry, using two or three examples from the collection of poems in Chapter 22.

19. Poetic Forms

A. E. HOUSMAN, *Loveliest of trees, the cherry now* (p. 644)

Considerations (p. 644)

1. The speaker greets life with a warmhearted *joie de vivre*. Although he is young, he already has a sense of life's limits. He means to enjoy the beauty of life every minute he is alive. Even then, he claims, he could not absorb all the beauties of life.

2. Spring is a season of purity and rebirth. The connotations of spring are reinforced by the mention of Eastertide in line 4.

3. The poem is almost a syllogism: the world is beautiful; life is short; therefore, I will enjoy the world while I can. If "twenty" won't come again, then he will enjoy what is left over — an additional fifty years.

4. Behind the gaiety and cheerful resolve is an awareness of the imminence of death. You might explore either in class discussion or as a writing assignment the question of whether this could be considered a *carpe diem* poem.

ROBERT HERRICK, *Upon Julia's Clothes* (p. 645)

Herrick uses so many of the elements of poetry — rhyme, rhythm, the sound and choice of words — so well in this brief lyric that it is worth taking some class time to analyze. The first tercet of iambic tetrameter is absolutely regular and thus suggests the sweet*ly* flowing *li*quefaction of Ju*li*a's *clo*thes. In the second tercet, trochees interrupt the established pattern to capture in rhythmic terms "that brave vibration." *Brave* is used here in the sense of "making a fine show or display," as in a banner waving.

WILLIAM WORDSWORTH, *The World Is Too Much with Us* (p. 646)

Like Hopkins in "God's Grandeur" (p. 614), Wordsworth is protesting here the preoccupation with worldliness — banking, buying, getting, spending — that makes it increasingly difficult to feel the mystery and power in the natural world. Proteus (a god of the sea) and Triton (another sea god, who stirred up storms) lie dormant, their power to kindle in the human soul a spirit of awe suppressed in the commercialized world, where people have bartered their hearts away. "Great God!" is the speaker's spontaneous and ironic response to the decline of spirituality, for it appears that the pagan world possessed a stronger sense of godliness.

Connections (p. 647)

1. Both Wordsworth's sonnet and "God's Grandeur" draw from the social and industrial worlds to discuss the greatness of creation and the human threat to that greatness. The speaker in Hopkins's sonnet places his faith in the creator, who can overcome the destructive actions of human beings. Wordsworth's sonnet returns to pagan myths for comfort, although the speaker has little hope of overcoming the bleakness of the world that is "too much with us." Hopkins dwells on bleak images of all "seared with trade," but he is convinced that nature is still available to us and that even humanity can be redeemed.

2. Clampitt's poem, a response to Wordsworth, reverses his sonnet's movement. Wordsworth's speaker looks around him, blames humanity for its own destruction, then turns to the past for hope for a better future. Clampitt's speaker celebrates the excesses around her — the fruit and flowers from all over the world that human technology makes available to her, a city dweller. The past she invokes is the domestic past of her childhood, not the mythic past of Wordsworth. She wonders at and finally accepts the continuous motion of the world in which nothing stays put, not exotic fruit from the tropics nor the wild plum of her childhood. Wordsworth's speaker seems to want to stop the motion of the world for a moment's peace of mind.

WILLIAM SHAKESPEARE, *Shall I compare thee to a summer's day?* (p. 647)

The speaker in this sonnet praises his beloved not only for her loveliness but also for her temperateness of manner. Unlike nature, which is forever changing, she shows a steady devotion. Moreover, the speaker tells us that this love will extend well into the future, even beyond the grave. Such love, like the art that celebrates it, confers a measure of immortality on the lovers and, self-reflexively, on the sonnet. Notice, for example, how the stressed words in the couplet reinforce this idea. *Long* is stressed in both lines of the couplet, along with other significant words that link continued "life" with "this," the sonnet that confers immortality, and "thee," the object the sonnet addresses.

WILLIAM SHAKESPEARE, *My mistress' eyes are nothing like the sun* (p. 648)

Students may have read this sonnet in high school, and you might begin by asking them what they think the mistress looks like. Some clarification of Shakespeare's use of the term *mistress* (beloved or chosen one) may be in order. This sonnet plays with the conventions and clichés of the Petrarchan sonnet, which elaborated on the extraordinary qualities of the maiden's eyes to the splendor of the sun. But Shakespeare refuses to do this and thus argues for a poetry that avoids cliché and the excess metaphor that tries to outdo reality. He is, in fact, asserting the beauty of his beloved in the last line. She is as attractive as any other woman who has been "belied" (made to seem more beautiful) by false comparison.

VILLANELLE

THEODORE ROETHKE, *The Waking* (p. 649)

You might want to compare this villanelle with Thomas's "Do not go gentle into that good night." Most critics find Thomas's poem the stronger, with Roethke's repeated lines sounding a little forced in places. The problem with "The Waking" is that it resists sense more than a poem should; for poetry, like the speaker in the poem, blesses the ground and needs that common point of communication.

Roughly paraphrased, this villanelle seems to say, "Take each day as it comes without fear and enjoy it, for Nature has decreed that someday we all shall die." But meaning problems abound, from the opening line to the poem's close with the paradoxical "What falls away is always. And is near." Is this a case of Nothing lost, nothing gained in its most cosmic sense?

Connections (p. 650)

1. The refrain in Thomas's poem is easier to understand than that in Roethke's. Roethke's poem as a whole is more ambiguous than "Do not go gentle into that good night," in which the speaker expresses his feeling in vivid and precise images.

2. There is a greater distinction between thought and feeling in Cummings's poem than in Roethke's. Cummings's looser form suggests a giving in to more spontaneous feeling. The speaker urges his listener to seize the moment and the feeling. In Roethke's poem thinking and feeling come together in a living that learns "by going." The strict rules of the villanelle result in the repetition of lines that by accumulation seem to evoke being as luminous and

mysterious. Roethke is contemplating final things and a movement that blurs distinctions between thought and feeling, waking and sleeping, life and death.

SESTINA

ELIZABETH BISHOP, *Sestina* (p. 650)

This poem strikes the ear as particularly sad because it portrays unexpressed emotion in an intimate domestic setting. There seems to be no shared awareness between grandmother and child, although one suspects they are sad for similar reasons. To make matters even worse, that sadness seems as foreordained as the rain showers that the almanac predicts. Here the almanac functions for the grandmother as a soothsayer, foretelling sadness and loss. For the child, the Marvel Stove operates in the same way (cf. line 25), its cast-iron blackness serving as a kind of mute doom sayer. Note, for example, the repetition of "tears" and "rain" in stanzas II and III and how they are connected with "grandmother," almanac," "child," and "stove."

Bishop's father died of Bright's disease at age thirty-nine, when the poet was only eight months old. Her mother subsequently suffered several nervous breakdowns, and Bishop was sent from her home in Worcester, Massachusetts, to live with her maternal grandmother in Nova Scotia. The grandmother had lost her own father in a sailing accident when she was a child. A good summary of Bishop's childhood is offered by Robert Giroux in his introduction to *Elizabeth Bishop: The Collected Prose* (New York: Farrar, Straus & Giroux, 1984). If your students enjoy Bishop's poetry, they might also enjoy the fiction and descriptive pieces offered in this collection.

EPIGRAM

SAMUEL TAYLOR COLERIDGE, *What Is an Epigram?* (p. 652)

A. R. AMMONS, *Coward* (p. 652)

DAVID MCCORD, *Epitaph on a Waiter* (p. 652)

PAUL RAMSEY, *On Industrialism* (p. 652)

EMILY DICKINSON, *"Faith" is a fine invention* (p. 652)

Coleridge's epigram is definitional; Ramsey's and Dickinson's sharply pierce the notion of industrialism as progress and faith as the final source of knowledge and salvation. Much is said in little space in these works, and brevity itself, particularly in Ramsey's poem, is a source of wit.

LIMERICK

ANONYMOUS, *There was a young lady named Bright* (p. 653)

Discussed in text.

LAURENCE PERRINE, *The limerick's never averse* (p. 653)

Perrine's poem departs from traditional metrics in the first, fourth, and fifth lines.

CLERIHEW

EDMUND CLERIHEW BENTLEY, *John Stuart Mill* (p. 654)

Discussed in text.

HAIKU

MATSUO BASHŌ, *Under cherry trees* (p. 654)

RICHARD WILBUR, *Sleepless at Crown Point* (p. 654)

ETHERIDGE KNIGHT, *Eastern Guard Tower* (p. 655)

Bashō is usually considered the greatest of the haiku poets. He was born near Kyoto, growing up as the companion of a local nobleman's son. He moved to Edo (now called Tokyo) when he was twenty-three and eventually became a recluse, living outside the city in a hut. He made several long journeys, always relying for food and shelter on the generosity of local Buddhist temples and on other poets. *The Narrow Road to the Deep North,* a collection of interlocked prose and haiku chronicling one of these journeys, is perhaps his best-known work in the West.

Often, as in Knight's "Eastern Guard Tower," a contemporary poet will use the haiku form to make a point about the relationship of humanity and nature. Note how the convicts are compared to lizards here.

Considerations

1. The first haiku images a moment of restfulness, quietude, and delicate sensual pleasure. The second depends for its effect on the reader's ability to relate the title to the scene described. It portrays a moment of anguished aloneness.

2. Epigrams tend to be witty, terse observations made at a distance. They often pass judgments on concepts (industrialism), qualities (cowardice), or, sometimes, persons.

   Haiku are more likely to evoke landscape, atmosphere, or another person close or meaningful to the poet. Haiku tend to be more imagistic than intellectual, more suggestive than pointed. Having the class write haiku can teach much concerning image, connotation, and sound.

ELEGY

SEAMUS HEANEY, *Mid-term Break* (p. 655)

Considerations (p. 656)

1. The starkness of the images in this poem tells us a lot about the speaker. He observes the scenes as if from a distance, trying to control his own reactions to the tragedy. The simple details of the baby coming and laughing (unaware of the tragedy) and the old men greeting the speaker awkwardly make the young boy's death even more somber and haunting.

2. The last line tells us more about the boy than we know until this point. He is four years old. Standing apart, the line suggests that the poem is another kind of vessel for the young boy's life. As the coffin holds his body, the poem remembers him long after death.

3. Using the alternative form for its assonant *a* to accompany "bandaged," Heaney emphasizes the meaning of the word *stanched.* The nurses stopped the flow of blood in the boy's body to no avail.

4. We would normally think of a midterm break as a vacation for a schoolboy. This break is for grieving.

Connections (p. 656)

1. The rhymes and regular meter in "To an Athlete Dying Young" give that poem a more formal, more public tone than the stark, conversational tone of Heaney's elegy. Heaney's

little brother is not mythologized the way Housman's hero is. The athlete is an older boy who has presumably accomplished more than the young child. Heaney's poem reads as both elegy and catharsis for the speaker, whereas Housman's speaker is at some distance from the dead boy he commemorates.

ODE

PERCY BYSSHE SHELLEY, *Ode to the West Wind* (p. 656)

Percy Bysshe Shelley was born to wealth in Horsham, Sussex. Educated in conventional privileges, he was taunted by his schoolmates for his unconventionality and lack of physical prowess. His rebellion against this environment helped make him both a nonconformist and a democrat. He was expelled from Oxford in 1811 for coauthoring a pamphlet called *The Necessity of Atheism*. He eventually married Mary Wollstonecraft Godwin and in 1818 settled in Italy, where he wrote his most highly regarded work, including "Prometheus Unbound" and "Ode to the West Wind." Shelley drowned while sailing with a friend, and his ashes were buried in a cemetery in Rome near the graves of his son, William Shelley, and John Keats.

The west wind in England is hailed as the harbinger of spring. As an introduction to this ode, you might have the students read the anonymous "Western Wind" (p. 506).

The tercets and couplets that form each section of this ode should hold no problems; basically, the tercets interweave (*aba, bcb, cdc, ded, ee*). Since Shelley is describing wind, the ethereal element, it is appropriate that the sounds of the couplet (*ee*), which appear at the end of every twelfth line in the first three sections, should have an airy, wind-rushed quality, as in "hear," "atmosphere," "fear."

The first three sections describe the powers the wind has in nature — on land in autumn, in the clouds in "the dying year" (winter), and on the bay (a mixture of land and sea) in the summer. When Shelley turns to his own problems, including his sense of despair and his need for inspiration (sections IV and V), the rhyme of the couplet (*ee*) is changed and a more mournful, weighted sound ("bowed," "proud") is substituted. The rhyme scheme almost makes the poem generalize in the final section, when "Wind" and the promises of spring are bestowed upon "mankind."

For a close reading of this ode, see S. C. Wilcox, "Imagery, Ideas, and Design in Shelley's 'Ode to the West Wind,'" *Studies in Philosophy* 47 (October 1950): 634–649.

As a three-page writing assignment, ask students to analyze the symbolic meaning of the west wind.

PICTURE POEM

GEORGE HERBERT, *Easter Wings* (p. 659)

George Herbert was brought up by his widowed mother, the matron of an old Welsh family and a friend of John Donne's. After graduating from Cambridge, he served as its public orator, which meant he declaimed, in Latin, on the university's position on matters of public concern. He began serving the Church of England in 1626, entered the ministry in 1630 and died of tuberculosis three years later. His single book of poems, *The Temple*, was published shortly after his death.

Considerations (p. 659)

1. If the poem is turned on its side so that the words are right side up, the poem resembles a baptismal or holy water font. As printed, the poem suggests open wings. Either way, the visual imagery suggests resurrection or renewal of life and spirit within the community of Christ.

2. The lines are shortest at the speaker's ebb and separation from the Lord, and they are longest when he is praising or acting in concert with God.

3. The rise and fall of the lark's song and flight are a parallel image to humanity's relation with God and the Adamic breach of trust in the Fall. The Fall, though, occasioned the possibility of resurrection.

MICHAEL MCFEE, In Medias Res (p. 660)

Students will probably have fun identifying the puns in this portly poem. A handful for consideration: "His waist / like the plot / thickens" (lines 1–3) — just as in a murder mystery, his increasing girth is out to get him, as the darker tone of the second half of this poem implies. "Wedding / pants" (3–4) — do we read this as the pants from the suit he wore at his wedding, no doubt a smaller size, or as the waist "wedding," or uniting, with the waistband of the pants? "Breathtaking" (4) no longer means spellbinding but rather a kind of choking. The "cinch" (5) can be read either as a girth or belt, or a snap, an easy thing to do.

PARODY

ANDREA PATERSON, *Because I Could Not Dump* (p. 661)

Considerations (p. 661)

1. Paterson's version uses many of the same words and phrases, as well as the same form, as Dickinson's poem.

2. Paterson's use of the very same words Dickinson uses makes her parody funny because we see these words employed to such different effect. Dickinson's poem is about death, Paterson's concerns a garbage truck; this is a wry comparison of the immortal and the everyday.

PETER DEVRIES, *To His Importunate Mistress* (p. 662)

Money is at the root of the distress in this work. In contrast, Marvell's main complaint was lack of time (see p. 534). "Picaresque" (line 7) is used in the sense of "our roguish affair." DeVries imitates Marvell's idiom quite closely. He picks up on the middle to high level of diction, the long sentences with verbs separated from their objects, and Marvell's rather Latinate style with the verbs coming at the ends of the sentences.

PERSPECTIVE

ROBERT MORGAN, *On the Shape of a Poem* (p. 663)

Students might enjoy analyzing Morgan's own "Mountain Graveyard" (p. 504) in light of his idea that "All language is both mental and sacramental, is not 'real' but is the working of lip and tongue to subvert the 'real.'" How does his anagrammatic spore prose "subvert the 'real'"?

Elizabeth Bishop's "Sestina" in this chapter (p. 650) and her villanelle, "One Art" (p. 757), or Dylan Thomas's villanelle "Do not go gentle into that good night" (p. 574) are good examples to use when discussing Morgan's statement that "Poems empearl irritating facts until they become opalescent spheres of moment, not so much résumés of history as of human faculties working with pain."

Ask students to think about form in other aspects of their lives — the formal behavior at a funeral, for example, as a way of dealing with painful emotion.

20. Open Form

E. E. CUMMINGS, *in Just-* (p. 664)

Exactly how poems operate as a graphic medium on our visual sense is not well understood by critics. The very open-endedness of the question therefore provides a good occasion for students to make their own guesses. Notice, for example, that the most important thematic word in this poem, *spring,* either is set off from the line (as in line 2) or appears by itself, as in lines 9 and 18. In fact, the placement of *spring* at approximately the beginning, middle, and end of the poem is almost an organizational motif. Another repeated phrase, *whistles far and wee,* also is placed first on one line (5) with *whistles* receiving separational emphasis, later over two lines (12 and 13) with *far and wee* receiving space — like long pulses on the whistle — and, at the close of the poem, on separate lines, as though the sound of the whistle were still present but moving away.

The whistle is, of course, united with spring as a modern rendition of Pan's pipes drawing Persephone from the underworld and awakening the calls of birds and the sounds of wildlife. In response to the "goat-footed" (Pan) balloon man's pipes, "bettyandisbel" come running — the elision of their names mimicking the pronunciation, the swift movement, even the perception patterns of children.

Many other word patterns offer themselves for discussion in this poem. These comments are only a beginning, and an enthusiastic class can discover much more.

WALT WHITMAN, From *I Sing the Body Electric* (p. 665)

Considerations (p. 666)

1. In a word, Whitman offers here an anatomy of wonder.

2. The rhythm of this portion of the poem is striking. Notice how many of the lines begin with a trochee or a spondee. The initial heavy stresses lend a kind of relentless thoroughness to Whitman's catalog of the human body. You might have the class scan a portion of the poem, say from line 25 to line 30. The lines change from heavily accented to a lighter, roughly iambic rhythm that suggests "the continual changes of the flex of the mouth."

PERSPECTIVE

WALT WHITMAN, *On Rhyme and Meter* (p. 666)

In addition to assigning Consideration 3 as a writing topic, you might ask students to write a few paragraphs about Whitman's use of catalogs or lists as an element of the organic form he espouses. From *I Sing the Body Electric* (p. 665) is especially useful for this exercise. Why is Whitman's tactic of listing appropriate to his subject?

GEORGE STARBUCK, *Japanese Fish* (p. 667)

Probably a certain measure of sophistication — familiarity with the idiom of Craig Claiborne if not the ambience of sushi bars — is helpful in the enjoyment of this poem. Another aid to its appreciation is an oral reading. Then it will become quite apparent that "We who are about to dice a luchu" rhymes perfectly with *Nos morituri salutamus te,* when translated. The prose has its own internal rhyme and structure, of course, in the repetition of *You.*

WILLIAM CARLOS WILLIAMS, *The Red Wheelbarrow* (p. 668)

This poem has a syllabically structured form, like a haiku, of four and two, three and two, three and two, and four and two syllables in each couplet. Also, like a haiku, this poem is imagistic and suggestive rather than directly representational. Each couplet contains two stresses in its first line and one in its second.

X. J. Kennedy, in a footnote to the poem that appears in his *Introduction to Poetry,* Sixth Edition, notes that according to a librarian's account, Williams was "gazing from the window of the house where one of his patients, a small girl, lay suspended between life and death" (Boston: Little, Brown, 1986, 32). This information does enrich the first phrase, "so much depends," which seems to speak of a sympathetic vitality exchanged between ourselves and the objects of our landscape. Without this biographical detail, the poem is usually described as an example of imagism, in which the image is made to speak for itself.

Does the poem "improve" with the librarian's recollection? This question might be taken up in a writing assignment.

ALLEN GINSBERG, *A Supermarket in California* (p. 668)

Probably the most widely known contemporary poet, Allen Ginsberg was the son of schoolteacher-poet Louis Ginsberg and his wife, Naomi. His mother's eventual descent into madness would inspire one of her son's most powerful works, the long elegy "Kaddish." Ginsberg has associated with some of the most talented and notorious figures in contemporary letters: William Burroughs, Jack Kerouac, Gary Snyder, Gregory Corso. His long poem "Howl" did much to usher in what came to be known as the Beat movement. His *Collected Poems* were published in 1984.

In "A Supermarket in California" Ginsberg uses elements of Whitman's style, especially his "enumerations" or catalog style, which so richly informs *I Sing the Body Electric* (see the excerpt on p. 665). Ginsberg makes a survey of the supermarket: "What peaches and what penumbras!"

Robert K. Martin remarks that "the California supermarket is the world of beautiful young men, which Ginsberg imagines himself sampling" *(The Homosexual Tradition in American Poetry* [Austin: U of Texas P, 1979], 167). The supermarket functions symbolically, as Martin also acknowledges, as a locus for kaleidoscopic variety, where "penumbras" might very well emerge from the peaches, and a delicious mélange of sexuality and spirituality shine through the marketplace.

The poem both gives homage to Whitman and laments a lost America that can never again know the physical and spiritual dynamism as well as the innocence and open-ended possibility that Whitman celebrated in poems such as "Song of the Open Road" (see the excerpt on p. 626).

Connections (p. 669)

1. (See the opening discussion.) Ginsberg here recalls elements of Whitman's style, especially his "enumerations" or catalog style.

2. The speaker of Ginsberg's poem searches for an example to follow, "shopping for images," whereas Whitman's speaker knows his way and invites his listener to come with him. Ginsberg's supermarket appeals to the senses in its images, but Whitman trusts that the only image he requires is that of his beloved.

3. Ginsberg imitates Whitman's use of parallel syntax as a way of structuring verse. This device appears in "Song of the Open Road," with its repetitions in the last section, for

example, of sentences that begin with "Let the." Like Whitman, too, Ginsberg at the end of the poem turns to his listener and asks some direct questions.

SYLVIA PLATH, *Elm* (p. 669)

Considerations (p. 670)

1. Like the elm, beaten and ravaged by the environment and housing birds without choice, the speaker feels she is controlled by external and internal forces: "I have suffered the atrocity of sunsets." The tree seems to be inhabited by the poet's bad dreams, verging on madness. There is an anguished search for the right image to capture this state of mind — as if the image might exorcise the state of mind.

2. The title of the poem evokes an image of a large, peaceful, shady tree. This tree is anything but peaceful, though it speaks to a listener in line 1 but seems to become the listener later on. The tree, with its many branches, can sustain these metaphoric personalities.

3. The poem's tone is restless and forbidding. The speaker becomes more and more morbid, ending with a desperate cry.

4. The repetition in the final stanza brings the poem to an ominous, obsessive halt. The external world — moon and clouds caught in the tangle of branches — becomes a claustrophobic reflection of the speaker's unease.

DENISE LEVERTOV, *O Taste and See* (p. 671)

Levertov wants us to use our senses and our imaginations to "[pluck] the fruit" of the world. The sense she invokes most frequently is that of taste, as the many verbs in lines 10 and 11 indicate. The idea is an interesting one, for we usually speak of "seeing" with the imagination's "eye." The *See* in the title can also be read in the sense of "come to know."

At any rate, the words here are arranged almost in breath units; they cluster themselves according to meaning. The first three lines act as a preface or introduction. The second group of four lines seems to indicate that the imagination is the foundation of all meaning, even of spiritual truth. The third stanza lists the fruit and food of the imagination and describes how we actively assimilate these items. The final two lines, set off, seem to underscore a desire as strong as hunger to bring the world's richness back into our lives.

In a writing assignment you might ask the class to compare the metaphor of tasting over seeing as an effective vehicle for expressing what Levertov says here.

CAROLYN FORCHÉ, *The Colonel* (p. 671)

It may be true ("What you have heard is true"), but is it poetry? Students will probably be surprised to find this paragraph of ostensible prose in the poetry section of the anthology, and you may want to bring in other examples of prose poetry by Charles Baudelaire or W. S. Merwin to illustrate the idea that this form is a continuing tradition.

In "The Colonel" the apocryphal (what you have heard to be true) becomes realized as apocalypse. Reality here knows a variegated texture in which the daily papers and pet dogs are conjoined offhandedly with the omnipresent pistol on the couch. As in poetry (and not prose), the real world and the fictional world, the natural and the fantastic, are placed alongside each other without the pointers of transition, causality, or connection. The effect is to merge the real and the surreal in an amalgam of potent horror that blurs the line between the two. An example of this merging occurs between the introduction of the "cop show" in sentence 7 and the reference to the broken bottles (used to scoop out kneecaps) in sentence 9. The arenas of violence shift back and forth between the TV screen and the living room itself, with the moon (cf. sentence 6) arcing its ominous pendulum over the house like a swinging hangman's rope or the glare of the inquisitor-torturer's lamp.

121

This discussion is intended as an illustration of the suggestive power of prose poetry. Words, images, even patterns of speech and silence ricochet off one another to create meanings beyond themselves. The poem comes to an end when the forces of its own energy collide and cannot break apart again. The horrifying evidence of the actual killings (the bags of ears) metamorphoses into a surreal horror show as the ears ("like dried peach halves") become alive in water. Likewise, language as both damnation ("go fuck themselves") and salvation (poetry) meet head on in the colonel's taunt and the fact of the poem itself.

You might explore the close of the poem with students or ask them to describe in a brief essay the import and tone of the final two sentences. Is Forché intimating here that both poetry and a voice beyond the colonel's might someday be heard?

SHARON OLDS, *The Elder Sister* (p. 672)

Considerations (p. 673)

1. Images of imprisonment and war ("prison," line 10; "shield," 25) contrast with images of release ("swans on a pond," 13; "threads of water out of the ground," 17), portraying the girls' lives as both embattled and mysterious.

2. The younger sister now realizes that part of her older sister's harshness and coldness resulted from her position in the family. She realizes that her sister shielded her from "the blows that did not reach me" (25).

3. Lines 25–30 imagine the older sister as a hostage — she is forced by time to go ahead of the younger sister, protecting her by living through everything first. The younger sister finally appreciates this role, seeing her sister as a shield behind which she can make her escape. In a sense, the one who experiences things first suffers them more.

4. The lines read almost as if we are following the two sisters down the birth canal, with the speaker the last to emerge, in the final word of the poem.

DONALD JUSTICE, *Order in the Streets* (p. 673)

Considerations (p. 674)

1. The poem outlines a process, with each step in a separate stanza. As we read the poem, we observe the process with the speaker. The word "jeep," without an article, is repeated at the beginnings of three stanzas, lending an air of impersonality to its actions, as if there were no driver. The poem is itself impersonal, reducing "Order in the Streets" to a series of mechanized steps, devoid of human presence.

21. A Study of Two Poets:
John Keats and Robert Frost

JOHN KEATS

On First Looking into Chapman's Homer (p. 678)

Discussed in text.

On the Grasshopper and the Cricket (p. 679)

By "the poetry of earth," Keats seems to mean the pulse of utterance within nature itself. In summer, when the heat stills (in the sense of both movement and sound) all birds, the grasshopper sustains the poetry of earth. Out of the cold of winter, the cricket interrupts the chill silence with its hearth-side song. Nature here seems a perpetual vital echo of itself.

To One Who Has Been Long in City Pent (p. 680)

Considerations (p. 680)

1. From the sonnet's title we may derive the speaker's attitude toward the city — it is prisonlike.

2. The country is personified as a friendly, welcoming host. This poem makes a good contrast to "On the Grasshopper and the Cricket," which says that nature must be tempered in its spots of silence and harsh heat and cold by the songs of the grasshopper and cricket. Nature is a more variable and extreme environment in this sonnet, whereas "To One Who Has Been Long in City Pent" describes it as stable and loving.

3. From the emphasis of the final lines, we might infer that this sonnet is more an expression of loss than a celebration of nature.

On Seeing the Elgin Marbles (p. 680)

Considerations (p. 681)

1. The speaker's pain is caused by a recognition of his own mortality; the remains of once grand figures, the Elgin marbles, remind him that he "must die." His physical weakness contrasts with the power invoked by the marble monuments.

2. Art, in the example of the Elgin marbles, is for Keats the result of human effort to create something that will outlive us. The species of the natural world, including in this sonnet eagles and human beings, are doomed to die. Works of art last longer, but they are still subject to the "rude/Wasting of old Time." Looking at the magnificent ruins reminds the speaker of his mortality and stimulates his own art, "dim-conceived glories of the brain" — gestures against death.

When I have fears that I may cease to be (p. 681)

The fears described in this sonnet are increasingly human, mortal, and intimate. Keats fears first that death may cut short the writing of his imagined "high-piled books"; then that he may never trace the "shadows" of "huge cloudy symbols of a high romance"; and, finally, that he might not see his beloved again. In the couplet love and fame sink to nothingness, but Keats confronts his fear and is deepened by the experience.

There is a subtle order to the presentation of Keats's objects of regret. In a writing assignment you might ask the class to comment on how one item seems to lead to the next and how their arrangement lends form and substance to this sonnet.

The Eve of St. Agnes (p. 682)

The essential event in this narrative poem is the elopement of Porphyro with Madeline on the Eve of St. Agnes, a night, as legend has it, that promises to maidens who observe the proper rituals a glimpse of their beloved upon waking. Both Madeline and Porphyro are stock types of romance, yet they have their distinguishing features, which lend a touch of humor to the poem. Porphyro, for example, is dismayed to think of his "Madeline asleep in lap of legends old." A true romantic would hold those legends sacred. Madeline, as it turns out, would, like Poe's feminine prototype, far prefer a living lover to a dead one. One feels keenly here that Keats enjoys toying with romantic convention even while he fulfills it. Consider, for example, the almost Byronic line as Keats describes Madeline's St. Agnes observance: "Full of this whim was thoughtful Madeline" (line 55).

The chosen pair are connected in the poem with images of sumptuous elegance (cf. the description of setting and of Madeline's appearance in stanzas XXIV–XXVI), elaborate dining (note Porphyro's "picnic" in stanzas XXX and XXXI), warmth — Porphyro is on fire for Madeline (stanza IX), while she is enraptured (stanza VII), and the tumultuous music Porphyro plays (stanza XXXIII). All this description is in direct contrast to the frigid and silvery pale night, the aged Beadsman about to die, the haggard Angela, who will die "palsy-twitched," and the drunken, bloated revelers (stanza XXXIX). Keats is clearly on the side of love, life, and the miracles that can be achieved between two mortals.

"The Eve of St. Agnes" calls for a close reading if it is to be taught well. For studies of this poem you might turn to Bernice Slote's *Keats and the Dramatic Principle* (Lincoln: University of Nebraska Press, 1958) and Judith Little's *Keats as a Narrative Poet* (Lincoln: University of Nebraska Press, 1975). See also Jack Stillinger's Perspective on this poem (p. 707).

Bright star! would I were steadfast as thou art (p. 691)

For all intents and purposes, this sonnet is composed of one long sentence with the dash at the close of line 8 signaling a follows a Shakespearean rhyme scheme with a Petrarchan division of thought. In the first eight lines Keats reflects on the star, which is "steadfast" but alone. In the sestet he claims that he would like to be steadfast and unchangeable, like the star, but "pillowed upon [his] fair love's ripening breast," and, therefore, hardly alone.

There is a kind of nighttime serenity to this poem. Notice the use of assonance in lines 5 and 6 to describe the shoreline. "To feel forever its soft fall and swell" (11) is a fine example of consonance used to suggest the gentle, perdurable pleasure Keats hopes might be his. Keats varies the iambic pattern so that words that have especial importance to the meaning receive heavy stress, such as "Bright star," "not," the "no" of line 9 when he differentiates himself from the star's state, and the "still" in line 13, which signals his wished-for suspension of time. See Harold Bloom's perspective on this poem (p. 705).

Why did I laugh to-night? (p. 692)

Considerations (p. 692)

1. The speaker pursues an answer to his question, only to find that the answer to any question of cause is a recognition of his own mortality.

2. The sonnet moves from questioning to frustration and despair to a kind of grim contentment. The speaker's tone is anxious until the end, when he reaches a resigned resolution.

La Belle Dame sans Merci (p. 692)

You might read this ballad in connection with other ballads in this book ("Sir Patrick Spens," p. 517, for example). How is it that ballads have stood the test of time and continued to appeal to many generations of listeners and readers? Is this ballad any different from medieval ballads? Is it more suggestive, perhaps, of a state of mind?

The opening three stanzas hold a descriptive value for the reader, for they present the knight as pale, ill, possibly aging and dying. The stanzas possess a rhetorical value as well, for they whet our curiosity. Just why is the knight trapped in this withered landscape?

The femme fatale figure goes back at least to Homeric legend and the wiles of Circe. Note how the "belle dame" appeals here to several senses — with her appearance, her voice, the foods she offers, the physical comforts of sleep. Above all else, though, she seems otherworldly, and Keats here seems to insist on her elfin qualities, her wild eyes and her strange language.

Words change meaning and grow in and out of popularity over generations (even decades). Contrast the way we might use *enthrall* today (with what subjects) and what Keats intends by "La Belle Dame sans Merci / Hath thee in Thrall!" (lines 39–40). Note how the shortened line of each quatrain gives both a sense of closure and the chill of an inescapable doom.

In his well-known essay on the poem, Earl R. Wasserman begins by remarking, "It would be difficult in any reading of Keats's ballad not to be enthralled by the haunting power of its rhythm, by its delicate intermingling of the fragile and the grotesque, the tender and the weird, and by the perfect economy with which these effects are achieved" (from "La Belle Dame sans Merci," in his *The Finer Tone: Keats's Major Poems* [Baltimore: Johns Hopkins UP, 1953, 1967], pp. 65–83, and reprinted in *English Romantic Poets: Modern Essays in Criticism,* edited by M. H. Abrams [New York: Oxford UP, 1960], pp. 365–380). In a writing assignment you might ask students to select any one of these elements and discuss it with several examples to show how it shapes the tone and mood of the poem.

Other studies of this poem include Jane Cohen's "Keats's Humor in 'La Belle Dame sans Merci,'" *Keats-Shelley Journal* 17 (1968): 10–13, and Bernice Slote's "The Climate of Keats's 'La Belle Dame sans Merci,'" *Modern Language Quarterly* 21 (1960): 195–207.

Ode to Psyche (p. 694)

Before the class begins to address the questions for consideration on this ode, it would be a good idea to establish clearly the offices and nature of Cupid and Psyche and what their union might portend for Keats.

In some ways the union of Psyche with Cupid — held in suspended animation like the figures on the Grecian urn — seems about as Keatsian an occasion as one could hope to find. Cupid, of course, represents love. Psyche completes the union with the soulful essence of eternal forms and the suggestion of the intellect. The amalgam of soul and love produces the poetic imagination or the ability to see with feeling or "sensation," Keats's preferred term. The union is even more inviting to the creative spirit, for Psyche has not been defined and celebrated by centuries of singers. As a newcomer to the pantheon of mythic forms (born too late to be celebrated by the "antique lyre"), Psyche calls forth Keats's informing powers of poetic imagination. For that reason Keats constructs his "bower" as fit setting for this union.

Helen Vendler in "Tuneless Numbers: The 'Ode to Psyche,'" from her *Odes of John Keats* (Cambridge: Harvard UP/Belknap Press, 1983), pp. 41–74, treats this ode at some length. She claims, "The ode declares, by its words and by its shape, that the creation of art requires the complete replacement of all memory and sense-experience by an entire duplication of the external world within the artist's brain. . . . *Psyche* asserts that by the constructive activity of the mind we can assert a victory, complete and permanent, over loss" (49).

Ode to a Nightingale (p. 696)

Earl R. Wasserman in *The Finer Tone: Keats's Major Poems* (Baltimore: Johns Hopkins UP, 1953, 1967) discusses this ode at length and places it in context with other Keats poems, including "Ode on a Grecian Urn" and "La Belle Dame sans Merci." He finds here a set of impossible contradictions, for it appears that happiness or ecstasy can be achieved only by an annihilation of self. As Wasserman writes, "By attempting to gain 'happiness,' one is brought beyond his proper bound, and yet, being mortal, he is still confined to the earthly; and thus he is left with no standards to which to refer, or rather, with two conflicting sets of standards" (183).

As a result of his complete empathic entrance into the bird's state, the poet finds himself "too happy in thine happiness." The poet has exceeded his own mortal bounds. In stanza II he longs for escape from this world — through an inebriation from the waters of poetic inspiration. Such a fading or leave-taking would be a means of fleeing from the strain of mortality (stanza III). The bird, which at first had signified beauty and oneness with nature, is now becoming identified with immortality and the ability to transcend the mortal state. The speaker admits his fascination with "easeful Death," but at the close of stanza VI, he realizes the ultimate dilemma: if he did die, the bird would go on singing but the speaker would be as responsive as "sod."

The introduction of Ruth is interesting, because she symbolizes life, family, and generational continuity. Having lost her husband, she stayed with her mother-in-law in an alien land, remarried, and bore a son.

The word *forlorn* recalls the speaker to his senses in stanza VIII, for he realizes that in this world of death, spirit, and the imagination — this ethereal world of transcendent essences — he is as nothing, and the word *forlorn,* like a bell, not only recalls him to himself but could also serve as his death summons. Note how many of the attractive sensuous details in the poem exalt physical, mortal life. At the close of stanza V, for example, Keats rescues even the flies for our poetic appreciation.

Ode on a Grecian Urn (p. 698)

The speaker's attitude toward this object of beauty is a rapt expression of awe at its evocative and truth-bearing power and presence. Life portrayed on the urn is forever in suspended animation: no one gets old; the "wild ecstasy" goes undiminished; the love, never consummated, is yet never consumed and wearied of. Keats seems to admire this portrait of the sensuous ideal, which exists unmarred by mortality or the vagrancy of human passion.

The significant question about this ode (beyond the meaning of the closing two lines and whether the speaker or the urn pronounces all or a part of them) appears to rest with "Cold Pastoral!" and the ambivalence these words seem to imply. Earlier, in stanza III, Keats had admired the love "for ever warm and still to be enjoyed" that was portrayed on the urn. Has the temperature of the urn changed by stanza V? Has the speaker discovered, in essence, that even though the urn portrays a sensuous ideal of courtship and pursuit, it is still merely a cold form that, because it is deathless, can never feel the warmth of human life?

Still one of the best studies on this ode is the essay (bearing the same title as the ode) by Earl R. Wasserman in *The Finer Tone: Keats's Major Poems* (Baltimore: Johns Hopkins UP, 1953, 1967, pp. 11–63). For the record, Wasserman argues that the closing lines are spoken by the poet to the reader; as Wasserman explains, the ode is *on* a Grecian Urn, not *to* the urn. Hence, "it is Keats who must make the commentary on the drama" (p. 59). Refer students to Brook Thomas's "A New Historical Approach to Keats' 'Ode on a Grecian Urn'" (p. 1806) for a contemporary perspective on the poem.

Connections (p. 699)

1. In Keats's ode time wastes human beings but does not affect art. Art provides hope, friendliness, and beauty to human beings, making their misery more understandable in its "truth." Marvell's poem, which dwells much more in the physicality of human experience, the speaker urges his listener to "make [the sun] run," because time will destroy her anyway. The difference in the poems' treatments of time results from their very different subjects. Whereas Keats's ode discusses art *vs.* human existence, Marvell's work claims that human existence is all we have.

2. Keats presents the moment before the kiss as the peak of a relationship because this moment is full of anticipation and ripeness, but Wilbur makes the very earthly lovers into heavenly angels. The value of anticipation over experience in Keats's mind is ambiguous, however. After all, he describes his vision as a "Cold Pastoral" in stanza V. Perhaps he thinks that loving is more important than art, but it is hard to tell. Unlike Keats's speaker, the speaker in Wilbur's poem traces the moment after the epiphany, when souls descend from fresh laundry into the living bodies of lovers waking to ordinary day.

3. In "To Autumn" Keats celebrates a moment at the end of fall, asking us to appreciate the passage of time in his timeless work of art. In a sense the Grecian urn, a celebration of timeless beauty in art, competes with the ephemeral season of autumn. The poems are perfectly juxtaposed; one celebrates finitude, the other immortality. "To Autumn" appeals directly to the senses, whereas in "Ode on a Grecian Urn" the urn stands between the speaker and his audience, and between the audience and the ephemeral experience frozen forever on the urn. "Ode on a Grecian Urn" creates a sense of aesthetic distance and self-consciously questions the meaning and value of art in a way that "To Autumn" does not.

Ode on Melancholy (p. 700)

This ode shows a hyperextension of Keats's tendencies. The first stanza, if paraphrased, states that it is far more noble to suffer the "wakeful anguish of the soul" than to deaden (the body) with any of the lethal substances mentioned. Suffering hurts more than dying, and, one infers, pain is poetry, poetry pain.

Stanza II talks about coping. When melancholy pours down like rain that "fosters the droop-headed flowers all," that is the hour to hold your mistress's eyes in thrall.

The third stanza warns that the "Beauty" of the beloved is evanescent. Keats also capitalizes, and thus allegorizes, Joy, Pleasure, Poison, Delight, and Melancholy and warns the reader that there is nothing untouched by sorrow. The capacity to feel this sorrow is raised to the level of refined taste and tempered emotional capability. You might explore with students whether they find this poem sentimental. What, despite the cloudy concealings, is "Veiled Melancholy" really all about? Is "wakeful anguish" (line 10) a reasonable correlate to Melancholy? Why does Keats want to sustain that anguish? Why can only the strong suffer from melancholy? Finally, you might explore with the class whether our emphasis on the control of our emotions is not at odds with the value Keats accords to feeling.

Helen Vendler's reading of this ode is very useful. In her book *The Odes of John Keats* (Cambridge: Harvard UP/Belknap Press, 1983), she observes, "The *Ode on Melancholy* offers a therapeutic theory of aesthetic experience. In *Nightingale,* aesthetic response is finally judged useless, a cheat. *Melancholy* sees it as a recourse against depression, an alternate to opiates" (p. 187).

To Autumn (p. 701)

"To Autumn" was the last major lyric Keats wrote. But despite its tone and imagery, particularly in the last stanza, there is no indication that Keats had an exact foreknowledge of his impending death.

Personification is a major device in this poem. In stanza I, which suggests the early part of the day, autumn is the "bosom-friend" of the sun and a ripener of growing things. In stanza II, which has a midday cast, autumn is a storekeeper and a harvester or gleaner. In the final stanza, which reflects "the soft-dying day," the image of autumn is less directly named, but the idea of the contemplative is suggested. One sees things ripening in the opening stanza; in stanza II autumn feels the wind and drowses in the "fume" of poppies; in the final stanza autumn and the reader both are invited to listen to the special music of the close of the day and of the year. You might compare in class the effect of the closing line in this poem, "And gathering swallows twitter in the skies," with the "extended wings" imagery that concludes Wallace Stevens's "Sunday Morning" (p. 853). How does Stevens develop or abandon the themes and images of Keats?

In his brief poetic career, Keats seems to have grown into a more serene acceptance of death, preferring the organic ebb and flow of life over the cool, unchanging fixity of the artifact.

Connections (p. 702)

1. More metaphoric, perhaps, than literal, the apple picker's description of the recent harvest in "After Apple-Picking" could be a summary of his life. Already drowsy, he allows the time of day and the season to ease him into a reverie. The harvest he contemplates is a personal one — the apples he picked or let fall. This musing might occasion more brooding than is found in "To Autumn," in which the poet surveys more impersonally the season's reign and the year's end. "To Autumn" captures the last moments before winter, preserving them in all their ripeness and sensuality. Although both poems imply that death is near, Keats's speaker is far less willing to yield to it before appreciating the last moments of life as fully as he can.

2. The images in "To Autumn" provide a sharp contrast to those in "Root Cellar." The root cellar is "a congress of stinks," a place where ripeness is dank and almost obscene. Keats's images of fruitfulness are, in his word, "mellow." One reason for the difference could be that Keats describes the end of a harvest, the cessation of growth, whereas Roethke traces the undying process that will begin growth all over again.

PERSPECTIVES ON KEATS

Keats on the Truth of the Imagination (p. 702)

Considerations (p. 703)

1. It is important to point out that Keats here is uttering a desire for himself and that he recognizes in others a need for both sensation and thought.

2. Sensation, apparently, was for Keats the direct way into the creative imagination, poetry's source. You might contrast Keats with Wordsworth, for example, who had a more reflective temperament.

3. Keats's famous chiasmus offers to the intellect a dilemma: if you need an explanation, you will never understand; once you have had the experience, however, you will never need to ask.

For comments on the general subject of ideas and on this letter specifically, you might want to look at Douglas Bush's essay "Keats and His Ideas" in *English Romantic Poets: Modern Essays in Criticism,* edited by M. H. Abrams (New York: Oxford UP, 1960). Bush observes, "If we put the letter beside the just completed *Endymion,* it is perhaps not too much to say that the brief piece of prose is, as a statement of ideas, more arresting than the diffuse and wayward poem" (330).

Keats on Unobtrusive Poetry (p. 703)

Keats does have a "palpable design" upon us, if we take the word *palpable* literally, for his is a poetry of feeling. Didactic poetry is definitely not Keats's mode, not only because he prefers sensation but also because he seems to delight in the anguish of choices, say, for example, between the still, unchanging world of the "Cold Pastoral" and the charged, uncontrollable world of living passion.

Keats on His Poetic Principles (p. 704)

Considerations (p. 704)

1. He resolves the contradiction in his second axiom by stating that one should not falter by halves in rendering beauty.

2. Poetic history seems to bear out the idea that those who espouse organic form and the spontaneous overflow of their emotions seem to work hardest at grooming their poetic techniques and devising forms that accommodate this expression.

Keats on the Vale of Soul-Making (p. 704)

According to Keats's notion of the earth as the vale of soul-making, one is fashioning identity and salvation (or damnation) now. The enterprise is in the individual's hands and is not the province of a judgment-making deity in the afterlife. Pain informs (gives shape to) the person in the process of acquiring identity or soul. Keats seems at times to want to flee from these trials and rest with the carved forms. His stronger, more ambiguous, and more self-wrought "Ode to a Nightingale," however, demonstrates a willingness to confront pain, confusion, and death.

PERSPECTIVE

HAROLD BLOOM, *On "Bright star! would I were steadfast as thou art — "* (p. 705)

Bloom seems to question the biographical criticism that would use the facts of a poet's life to explain his poetry. He also casts a skeptical glance at psychological reductions (as he puts it) of human desire. He would reverse the common practice and have a Keats poem explain the poet's life and psychological theories about desire. You might ask students what Bloom is implying about the use and value of poetry by these reversals.

The allusions to Milton and Blake might be difficult for students if they haven't read as much of these poets. But Bloom more or less explains the associations in the essay. The Miltonic bright star is the distant light hung far off in "lone splendor." Blake represents an opposite impulse in Bloom's view of Keats. It seems his is the humanizing principle. The contrast between the star and the waters, brought into sharp focus by Bloom, helps us see the contrast between the octet and the sestet of the poem, in which Keats transforms the meaning of the star's steadfastness to fit his own vision of desire.

PERSPECTIVE

JACK STILLINGER, *On "The Eve of St. Agnes"* (p. 707)

To continue Stillinger's argument that "The Eve of St. Agnes" is no mere fairy tale, you might ask students to concentrate on the way Keats builds up then subverts conventional romance expectations in the poem. The portraits of Porphyro and Madeline are especially enriched and deepened by this strategy.

As a writing assignment you might ask students to begin with the contrasts Stillinger cites — youth and vitality vs. old age and death, warmth and security vs. hostility and storm, and so forth — and write about the poem as a series of contrasts structuring the narrative. Is there a resolution of contrasts at the end?

ROBERT FROST

The Road Not Taken (p. 711)

Discussed in text.

The Pasture (p. 713)

Discussed in text.

Mending Wall (p. 713)

Students may already be familiar with this work from their high-school reading. Although the poem is often considered an indictment of walls and barriers of any sort, Frost probably did not have such a liberal point of view in mind. After all, the speaker initiates the mending, and he repeats the line "Something there is that doesn't love a wall." For him, mending the wall is a spring ritual — a kind of counteraction to spirits or elves or the nameless "Something" that tears down walls over the winter. It is gesture, ritual, and a reestablishment of old lines, this business of mending walls. The speaker teases his neighbor with the idea that the apple trees won't invade the pines, but to some measure he grants his conservative neighbor his due.

Connections (p. 714)

1. The neighbor in "Mending Wall" might accuse the speaker in Dickinson's poem of being foolish and impractical. Dickinson's speaker does not seem to think that boundaries make people happier, but the neighbor's experience has proved to him that "Good fences make good neighbors." The speaker in Frost's poem, more open to the kind of imagination Dickinson celebrates, wants his neighbor to imagine that elves have brought the wall down — but the neighbor probably won't.

2. In both poems Frost presents people who seem to be content with a single point of view, resisting new or even alternative views of the world. The neighbor, "like an old-stone savage armed," appears to be part of some primeval mystery that fascinates the speaker in "Mending Wall." In contrast, the people themselves in "Neither Out Far nor In Deep" are the ones transfixed by a mystery — that of the vast ocean.

Home Burial (p. 715)

Biographical criticism is beginning to come back into fashion, and you might remind the class of some of the introductory notes on Frost in this chapter before discussing the poem. Clearly the speaker is more matter-of-fact than his wife, and there is decidedly a communication problem between them. Note how Frost splits their dialogue in the interrupted iambic lines. But doesn't the husband deserve some special commendation for possessing the courage and integrity to initiate a confrontation with his wife? Discussion of the poem might also consider the value that ancients and moderns alike ascribe to a catharsis of emotions.

You might, if the class seems at all responsive, examine the speaker's claim that "a man must partly give up being a man / With women-folk" (lines 52–53). What does this statement mean? Has feminism done anything to challenge what are uniquely man's and uniquely woman's provinces of concern?

After Apple-Picking (p. 718)

The sense of things undone and the approach of "winter sleep" seem to betoken a symbolic use of apple picking in this poem. Moreover, the speaker has already had an experience this day — seeing the world through a skim of ice — that predisposes him to view things strangely or aslant. At any rate, he dreams, appropriately enough, of apple harvesting. Apples take on connotations of golden opportunity, and inspire fear, lest one should fall. As harvest, they represent a rich, fruitful life, but, as the speaker admits, "I am overtired / Of the great harvest I myself desired" (lines 28–29).

Apples are symbolically rich, suggesting everything from temptation in the garden of Eden, with overtones of knowledge and desire, to the idea of a prize difficult to attain, as in the golden apples of Hesperides that Hercules had to obtain as his eleventh labor. Here they can be read as representing the fruit of experience.

Refer students to Donald J. Greiner's "An Analysis of 'After Apple-Picking'" (p. 739) for a critical perspective on this poem.

Birches (p. 719)

This poem is a meditative recollection of being a boyhood swinger of birches. In the last third of the poem, the speaker thinks about reliving that experience as a way of escaping from his life, which sometimes seems "weary of considerations." Swinging on birches represents a limber freedom, the elation of conquest, and the physical pleasure of the free-fall swish groundward. Note, in contrast, Frost's description of what ice storms do to birches. Words like "shattering and avalanching on the snow-crust" suggest a harsh brittleness. The speaker in the end opts for Earth over Heaven, because he (like Keats, to some extent) has learned that "Earth's the right place for love."

Frost's blank verse lends a conversational ease to this piece, with its digressions for observation or for memory. A more rigid form, such as rhymed couplets, would work against this ease.

In a writing assignment students might analyze the different forms of knowing in "Birches," contrasting Truth's matter-of-factness (lines 21–22) and the pull of life's "considerations" (43) with boyhood assurance and the continuing powers of dream and imagination.

Out, Out — (p. 720)

So often when disaster strikes, we tend to notice the timing of events. Frost implies here that "they" might have given the boy an extra half hour and thereby averted the disaster. This perspective, coupled with the final line, in which the family seems to go on with life and ordinary tasks, can appear callous. But compare the wife's chastisement of her husband in "Home Burial" or the sentiment expressed in "The Need of Being Versed. . ." (p. 723). Is the attitude callousness, or is it, rather, the impulse of an earth-rooted sensibility that refuses pain its custom of breaking the routine of life-sustaining chores and rituals? Very little in this poem seems to be a criticism of the survivors; rather, like *Macbeth* and the famous speech that proclaims life's shadowy nature, it seems to acknowledge the tenuous hold we have on life.

Connections (p. 721)

1. In this poem and in "The Need of Being Versed. . ." the speakers present a tragic experience involving human beings or property and then set it in the larger context of the natural world. In each case the reader is urged to sympathize with the bereaved but also to recognize that such suffering is part of our ordinary lives. We must turn our attention toward the living even while mourning the lost and the dead.

2. Grief separates the couple in "Home Burial," as the wife accuses the husband of being unfeeling while the husband suggests that they must go on living despite their child's death. Miscommunication lingers in the split lines, as well as in the situation of the couple,

separated by the length of a staircase. In "Out, Out —" the bereaved "turned to their affairs," choosing the response of the man in "Home Burial." Death unites them in that it reaffirms their commitment to the duty of living.

3. "Out, Out —" and Crane's poem share a moral view that there is little ground on which humanity and the universe might meet. Crane's tone is slightly humorous, whereas Frost's approach is more poignant, but both rely heavily on dialogue to make their opinions known. Frost's borrowing from *Macbeth,* as well as the subject of the dead boy, gives his poem a more tragic quality than is present in Crane's sobering message.

Fire and Ice (p. 722)

With a kind of diabolic irony, the theories for the way the world might end grow as our knowledge and technology increase. Students can probably supply a number of earth-ending disaster theories: an overheated earth because we are moving sunward; the greenhouse effect with the chemical destruction of the ozone layer; war, apocalypse, or "nuclear winter"; a change in the earth's orbit away from the sun; the return of the ice age; and so on. Frost here also speaks of the metaphoric powers of hatred (ice) and desire (fire) as destroyers of the earth. To say that ice would "suffice" to end the world is a prime example of understatement.

Dust of Snow (p. 722)

There is a lightness in this poem, as though the "dust of snow" were some kind of chance blessing or, at the very least, a light slap that commanded a change of mood. The experience happens quickly, and the one sentence elides act and mood and reinforces the sense of cause and effect that associates the two stanzas.

As an essay topic, you might ask students to demonstrate to what ends both Frost (especially in this poem) and Thomas Hardy in "The Darkling Thrush" (p. 791) use nature to explore and make bearable the situation of being human.

Stopping by Woods on a Snowy Evening (p. 723)

With very few words, Frost here creates a sense of brooding mystery as the speaker stops his horse in a desolate landscape between woods and frozen lake. The attraction of the woods is their darkness, the intimation they offer of losing oneself in them. The speaker gazes into them with a kind of wishfulness, while his horse shakes his bells, a reminder to get on with the business of living. The repetition in the last lines denotes a literal recognition that the speaker must move on and connotes that there is much to be done before life ends.

You might use the final question in the text as a brief writing assignment to show how rhyme relates and interlocks the stanzas and offers in the final stanza (*dddd*) a strong sense of closure.

The Need of Being Versed in Country Things (p. 723)

The title of this poem refers to the idea of a down-to-earth sensibility that affirms that life can and does go on, no matter what magnitude of disaster befalls one. Consider, for example, the close of "Out, Out —" where the unnamed "they" go back to their affairs. Students might find this poem sentimental, despite its coolheaded theme. The use of personification ("the dry pump flung up an awkward arm," line 19) contributes to the sentimental overtones, yet also (as in the final two lines) reasserts the knowing sadness of "being versed in country things."

Once by the Pacific (p. 724)

In this description the night, waves, and storm clouds take on qualities of human malevolence and create a scene that is anything but "pacific" or placid. The poem is apocalyptic, and the final line lends a sense of foreordained doom.

Desert Places (p. 725)

As with so many of Frost's poems, the physical setting and its realistic details here become transmuted into a symbolic landscape before we know what is happening. The speaker watches the woods once again fill up with snow, but, rather than feeling attraction and repose, he now experiences a kind of terror and, at the very least, a strong sense of loneliness. Students will quickly pick up on the cosmic implications of "they." What the speaker fears "nearer home," though, may require some discussion. Haunting the poem is the empty silence of the landscape — its "blanker whiteness" almost reminiscent of the close of Edgar Allan Poe's "The Narrative of Arthur Gordon Pym of Nantucket." Perhaps, too, the speaker fears that there is "nothing to express" in his own heart, which is, needless to say, a profound fear for a poet.

As a writing assignment, ask students to compare the tone in this poem with that in "Stopping by Woods on a Snowy Evening" (p. 723).

Design (p. 725)

The opening octave of this sonnet is highly descriptive and imagistic in its presentation of spider, flower, and moth, all white. The sestet asks the question of design: who assembled all these elements in just such a way as to ensure that the moth would end up where the spider was — inside a "heal-all" (ironic name for this flower), its "dead wings carried like a paper kite." Frost has in mind the old argument of design to prove the existence of God. There must be a prime mover and creator; otherwise, the world would not be as magnificent as it is. But what of the existence of evil in this design? Frost asks. The final two lines posit choices: either there is a malevolent mover (the "design of darkness to appall") or on this small scale of moth and spider, evil occurs merely by chance ("If design govern. . ."). The rhyme scheme is *abba, abba, acaa, cc,* and its control provides a tight interlocking of ideas and the strong closure of the couplet.

Randall Jarrell's remarks on the imagery and ideas here are superb; he appreciates this poem with a poet's admiration (see his *Poetry and the Age,* [New York: Farrar, Straus & Giroux, 1953, 1972] 45–49). He notes, for example, the babylike qualities of "dimpled . . . fat and white" (not pink) as applied to the spider. Note, too, how appropriate the word *appall* is since it indicates both the terror and the funereal darkness in this malevolently white trinity of images.

A comparison with the original version of this poem, "In White" (p. 730), should prove that "Design" is much stronger. The title of the revised version, the closing two lines, and several changes in image and diction make for a more effective and thematically focused poem.

As a writing assignment, you might ask students either to compare this poem with its original version or to analyze the use of whiteness in "Design" and show how the associations with the idea of whiteness contrast with the usual suggestions of innocence and purity.

Connections (p. 726)

1. The speakers in this poem and in "The Need of Being Versed. . ." observe destruction from an impersonal distance. Neither seems to want speculation on the meaning of the events to go too far. In "Design" pondering the larger significance of the moth's death leads to troubling conclusions about the nature of divinity. Feeling too much about the loss of a house and human presence in "The Need of Being Versed" prevents one from recognizing nature's regenerative powers. In both poems Frost seems to honor nature's right to exist without the shaping force of human interpretation.

2. Hathaway's "Oh, Oh" has a far less serious tone than Frost's poem, as the poet plays a joke on his audience, beginning the poem in a slaphappy, conversational tone, only to change it to a note of impending doom. To be more like Frost's poem, "Oh, Oh" would have to make its audience aware of the entire situation from the beginning.

3. In "Design" the speaker questions the existence of God by suggesting that only a malevolent deity could preside over the relentless mechanisms of nature whereby one

species destroys another to survive. In "I know that He exists," Dickinson's speaker speculates not on the nature of God, but just on the hiddenness — the absence against which she must assert her belief. Frost is less comfortable with a God who must be malevolent than with no God at all. God's absence is what troubles Dickinson.

Neither Out Far nor In Deep (p. 726)

This poem, particularly in its last stanza, comments on humanity's limitations in comprehending the infinite, the unknown, the inhuman and vast. Again, Randall Jarrell's comment is useful. He writes, "It would be hard to find anything more unpleasant to say about people than that last stanza; but Frost doesn't say it unpleasantly — he says it with flat ease" (*Poetry and the Age*, 42–43). You might organize a writing assignment around the tone of this poem.

Provide, Provide (p. 727)

The tercets here, each rhymed with the same sound repeated three times over, lend a tight-lipped tone to the words of the advice giver. Is this poem straight or satiric? That question will no doubt stir some discussion in class. The speaker sounds a little too terse and clipped, even allowing for a New England twang, in his directive to "die early and avoid the fate," and the poem becomes rather hyperbolic, especially with the recommendation to buy out the stock market.

As a writing assignment, you might ask students whether they agree or disagree with the advice in the poem and how, depending on their point of view, the poem itself makes this advice more or less effective.

Departmental (p. 727)

This allegory "couldn't be called ungentle," yet it's certainly not as lighthearted as it may seem on first reading. With very little prodding, students will discern the poem's commentary on the antlike behavior human beings often exhibit: everything will be all right if everyone does her job and reports anything out of the ordinary to the proper authorities. "Ants are a curious race" (line 13) indeed — only morticians handle the dead, only members of the clergy consider "the nature of time and space," and only storekeepers distribute food. Carried in large part by the end rhyme (especially "any/antennae" and "Formic/McCormic"), the poem's humor, dry though it is, prevents a reading that would wholly damn the species, at the same time emphasizing the absurdity of a completely departmentalized life.

An examination of the poem's metrical structure will show just the sort of orderly variety it figuratively argues. With the exception of line 18 (in which the eagerness to "report" requires a little extra time), the poem is written in trimeter using various feet. A careful study of the prosody of "Departmental" would, in fact, go far toward demonstrating how meter works. Note, for instance, how the two anapests in line 7 make the line "run"; how the effort of "seizing" and "heaving" can be felt in the dactyls in lines 37 and 38; how unaccented syllables clog up the final line just as a rage for order clogs up the need for reflection and compassion.

Having students look up *sepal* and *ichor* could open rich discussion (or writing) concerning how Frost's diction operates throughout. "Petal/nettle" (lines 30–31), for example, embodies the poem's dialectic in small.

The Silken Tent (p. 729)

This Shakespearean sonnet uses an extended conceit to compare one woman's equipoise to the silken tent that remains erect on a summer's day. The center-positioned cedar pole, we are told, points "heavenward," and this detail, as well as the silken substance of the tent, suggests the spiritual centeredness of the person. She seems serenely balanced but not aloof from human affairs, since the ties that connect her soul to their groundward stakes are those of "love and thought." Only by slight changes ("the capriciousness of summer air") is she made to feel these ties, which are more connection than bondage. Overall, the tone of the poem, enhanced by the sounds of the words, suggests serenity.

The sonnet was originally titled "In Praise of Your Poise" and was written for Frost's secretary, Kay Morrison.

The Gift Outright (p. 729)

This poem was read at the inauguration of President John F. Kennedy in 1961. The history described here is largely that of the colonial period and the American Revolution. The period of exploration and westward expansion is alluded to as well. Frost's theme seems to be organized around a pun in line 13, which suggests that land can be lawfully secured (deeded) only through many deeds of war. The notion that possession often entails suppression of others' rights (consider, for example, the Civil War, the Indian wars, and the war with Mexico) seems to go unnoticed. In lines 6 and 7 Frost plays on "possessed," first to indicate colonial enchantment in a land not yet the colonists' to own, then to acknowledge English control, which was daily being loosened or denied.

Connections (p. 730)

1. Cummings's speaker has a very different attitude toward his country than does Frost's, whose respect for his ancestors resounds in his attention to their struggles for possession of themselves and "their" land. Cummings's speaker uses rapid-fire clichés to undermine the solemnity of his words, and to insult those who, like Frost's speaker, revere their country and the wars by which it defines and asserts itself.

2. Frost's discussion of America is largely devoted to its history, whereas both McKay and Ginsberg develop a sense of their speakers' relationships to their country, and the attitudes that frame those bonds. McKay is far less cynical than Ginsberg, whose complaints about the corruption and injustices in America in the middle of this century verge on the solipsistic toward the end of the poem. McKay takes a more ambiguous stance, alluding to the problems of the nation but admitting that he loves "this cultured hell that tests my youth!"

PERSPECTIVES ON FROST

"In White": Frost's Early Version of "Design" (p. 730)

See discussion of "Design" (p. 730).

Frost on the Living Part of a Poem (p. 731)

Intonation in musicians' parlance refers to pitch and the idea of playing in tune. Does Frost use the word in that sense here? If not, what does he mean later on by the "accent of sense" and how the word *come* can appear in different passages as a third, fourth, fifth, and sixth note?

In introducing this prose passage, you might point out that poets construct poetry out of fairly near-at-hand vocabularies, words we have already tasted on our tongues. One of the appeals of poetry is the physical way we intone its sounds, even when we read silently, so that we become in a sense a resonating chamber for the poem. It might be well to recall too that poetry originally was a spoken, not a written medium, and those things that were regarded as important enough to be remembered were put in verse.

Frost makes several unqualified statements here. Students, by and large, receive as part of their first-year college training the advice to be chary of the committed word. You might spend some of the class discussion exploring when and where rhetoric must be unequivocating.

PERSPECTIVE

AMY LOWELL, *On Frost's Realistic Technique* (p. 731)

Elsewhere in her review, Lowell describes Frost's vision as "grimly ironic." She goes on: "Mr. Frost's book reveals a disease which is eating into the vitals of our New England life, at least in its rural communities." In discussing the characters in Frost's poems she calls them "the leftovers of old stock, morbid, pursued by phantoms, slowly sinking to insanity." You might ask students to find evidence for Lowell's observations in the Frost poems in Chapter 21 or elsewhere in the book (check the index). Are there opposite tendencies in these characters that save them from what Lowell describes as a disease eating into the vitals?

Frost on the Figure a Poem Makes (p. 732)

Considerations (p. 734)

1. Almost any Frost poem would suit this assignment, for different reasons. More conversational poems, such as "Home Burial," provide insight into individual characters through an imitation of their speech patterns. The contemplative poem, exemplified by "Birches" or "After Apple-Picking" can be analyzed both for the speaker's character as it is revealed in his diction and for the way sounds both reaffirm and undermine the speaker's point.

2. According to Frost, poems are spontaneous in that they are derived from the poet's imagination as it interacts with his surroundings. But the imagination is not groundless, because poets take many of their ideas from what they've read, often unconsciously: "They stick to nothing deliberately, but let what will stick to them like burrs where they walk in the fields." Frost's belief in the predestination of poetry involves the idea that the poem is an act of belief, of faith: "It must be a revelation, or a series of revelations, as much for the poet as for the reader." Not entirely the product of either spontaneity or predestination, the poem takes on a life of its own: "Like a piece of ice on a hot stove the poem must ride on its own melting."

3. In giving up claims to democracy and political freedom, Frost resists the process of naming something that supposedly is without limitation. Once defined as "free," whatever we call free ceases to be just that. Frost uses as an example our "free" school system, which forces students to remain in it until a certain age; it is, therefore, not free. Resisting confining labels, Frost as an artist is more able to reach a world audience; once he states a political bias, his art is one of exclusion. You might ask students to compare Frost's attitude toward democracy and politics in relation to poetry with Doctorow's statement that "Fiction is democratic" in "The Importance of Fiction" (p. 486). You might also ask students to examine Frost's statements in the context of the more political poems in the Album of World Literature, for example, Czeslaw Milosz's "A Poor Christian Looks at the Ghetto" (p. 884).

5. This question gives students an opportunity to experiment wildly with Frost's rather ambiguous statement. You might even ask them to conclude this prose assignment by writing a short poem, following Frost's advice.

Frost on the Way to Read a Poem (p. 734)

Experience with one or two poems by an author often eases the way for reading other poems by him or her. But will reading "Birches," for example, prepare the way for understanding "Provide, Provide"? Not necessarily. Beyond our literary experience, some of our "life learning" enters into the reading of poems as well.

The image of reader as "revolving dog" also seems a little discomforting, no matter what one's feelings about dogs. Poetry reading requires a certain point of stability, like the cedar pole in "The Silken Tent." Without it, one might be at a loss to distinguish sentiment from the sentimental, the power of the image from the fascination of the ornament.

You might ask students to try Frost's advice with two or three of his own poems. They can read one in the light of another and then write about the experience.

LIONEL TRILLING, *On Frost as a Terrifying Poet* (p. 735)

Considerations (p. 736)

1. Trilling objects to the Frost of readers who use the poet to promote their causes: Frost as simple American, Frost as simple poet, Frost as modernist with a twist. He argues, using D. H. Lawrence's conception of the American writer, for Frost as a truly radical poet, in a tradition of radical American thinkers whose poetic work "is carried out by the representation of the terrible actualities of life in a new way."

2. You might refer students to Lawrance Thompson's 3-volume biography of Frost: *Robert Frost: The Early Years, 1874–1915; Robert Frost: The Years of Triumph, 1915–1938,* and Lawrance Thompson and R. H. Winnick, *Robert Frost: The Later Years, 1938–1963* (New York: Holt, 1966, 1970, 1976). For a more contemporary and controversial biography, consult William H. Pritchard, *Frost: A Literary Life Reconsidered* (New York: Oxford UP, 1984).

GALWAY KINNELL, From *For Robert Frost* (p. 737)

Presidential inaugurations, coming infrequently as they do, are among the high holy days of American patriotic fervor. They operate too as a barometer of American attitudes and values. Americans, ever since the Frenchman Alexis de Tocqueville observed them in 1835, have been known more as doers than as philosophers, more as artisans and mechanics than as artists and poets. The occasion of this poem offers a forum on the national mind. Frost was the United States's virtual poet laureate during his later years, and his passing would represent the loss of a poet who was at once regional and universal, conservative in values and poetic techniques yet innovative in fostering the development of both.

The presidents merely tolerate Frost's presence. The managers do not want the show ruined; Frost's death might upstage the "real" event. Kinnell, on the other hand, realizes the magnitude of Frost's great gift (both as talent and as his special offering). Writing poetry, Kinnell acknowledges as a fellow poet, is an act of love and supreme generosity.

HERBERT R. COURSEN, JR., *A Reading of "Stopping by Woods on a Snowy Evening"* (p. 738)

This critical spoof offers a fine opportunity to articulate just what we seek from literary criticism and why we accept one writer's word and reject another's. One important factor in the Frost poem that is not considered here is tone and the speaker's own fascination with the woods, which are "lovely, dark, and deep."

If we were to isolate factors that mark good literary criticism, we might speak of (1) completeness (are there any significant details omitted?); (2) coherence (Coursen advertises the simplicity of his theory but then talks at length about veiled allusions and obfuscation); and (3) fidelity to experience (No, Virginia, a horse is never a reindeer, not even on Christmas Eve). Good criticism avoids the overly ingenious.

This spoof also lends itself to a review of principles of good writing, which students have probably already acquired in a composition course. You might ask, too, what it was that inspired Coursen to write this essay. What, in other words, is he objecting to in the practice of literary criticism?

PERSPECTIVE

DONALD J. GREINER, *An Analysis of "After Apple-Picking"* (p. 739)

Students might be encouraged to use Greiner's analysis as a model for their own analysis of another Frost poem — "Birches" (p. 719), for example, or "Mending Wall" (p. 713) — a poem they would nominate as great. You might point out to them the way Greiner moves effortlessly between comments about Frost's technical brilliance (demonstrated in Frost's use of rhyme, varied line lengths, and meter) and speculations about the poem's final implications. Greiner links the technical concerns with the poem's meaning, as when he notes that "the meter invariably returns to the predominant rhythm of iambic pentameter as the meditator struggles to keep his balance in uncertainty as he has kept it on the ladder of his life."

BLANCHE FARLEY, *The Lover Not Taken* (p. 740)

The fun of parodies derives in part from recognition of their sources — in this instance "The Road Not Taken." In Farley's parody we see again the distressed speaker who wants to have it both ways. As is usually the case with Frost's deliberators, the woman in this poem seems to have many hours to devote to "mulling." Farley mimics Frost's faint archaisms with the line (present in both poems) "Somewhere ages and ages hence." She also plays with and lightly satirizes the rigors of Frost's blank-verse line. Notice, for example, how she carries over the key word that would round out the sense of the line between lines 8 and 9, only to accommodate the pentameter scansion. At the close of her poem, Farley plays down the need for choosing and asserts that there was no difference between the lovers. Appropriately, for this parody, she closes with a heroic couplet.

22. A Collection of Poems

LEONARD ADAME, *Black and White* (p. 743)

Not often does a title so summarily and incisively make ironic comment on a political and moral judgment while serving as a stark rubric for the imagery of a poem. Either in class discussion or as a writing assignment, you might ask students to work out the imagery of the poem in terms of "black and white." Think, for example, of Africa as the dark continent and Rhodesia as the "sweaty/[dark] flank of the world." Note that the bodies of the guerrillas (native blacks) are imaged as fish ("catch") and are counted by the whites in power. Note too that the rifles over the dead men's heads are described as a "keyboard" (black and white), and that the photographs themselves are black and white. Likewise, the black-and-white newspaper account is supposed to present the unbiased truth, but such an accounting seems the most remote of possibilities.

You might also spend some time discussing the tone of this poem. It has a black-and-white evenness of delivery, almost as though this flat narrative of what took place were a lie that lacked the truth of moral outrage.

A. R. AMMONS, *Winter Saint* (p. 744)

This poem's title is provocative enough to elicit some discussion. One interesting question of typography, Ammons's use of the colon, might profitably be raised. Its effect seems to be a continuous patterned flow between one set of observed details and the next. Is the device overworked in the second-to-last stanza? Clearly, Ammons has a sharp eye and a fine ability to transmute images into sounds. In the third stanza, for example, we hear and feel the clenched-throat silence of someone who is appalled.

You might ask students in a writing assignment of two to three pages to compare and contrast the attitude of the speaker in this poem and in Frost's "Mending Wall" (p. 713) toward their neighbors. What does each dislike about his neighbor? Does either poet demonstrate a sense of humor? Which speaker seems the more tolerant?

MAYA ANGELOU, *Africa* (p. 744)

It would be difficult to miss the pronounced rhythm in these lines: two strong beats in each, the initial accent typically falling on a line's first syllable. Read this poem aloud, and the sound of rage and bitterness becomes unmistakable, as does the "striding" mentioned in line 24. The contrasting imagery in the first two stanzas, as well as the pattern of rhyme, helps build the poem's stark effect. Note, too, that important rhymes are accented — *cold/bold/sold* and *white/rime white/icicle* in stanza II, for instance.

A NOTE ON BALLADS (p. 745–750)

Ballads can provide a good introduction to poetry, for they demonstrate many devices of other poetic forms — such as rhyme, meter, and image — within a narrative framework. Ballads, however, often begin abruptly, and the reader must infer the details that preceded their action. They employ simple language, tell their stories through narrated events and dialogue, and often use refrains. The folk ballad was at its height in England and Scotland in the sixteenth and seventeenth centuries. These ballads were not written down but were passed along through an oral tradition, with the original author remaining anonymous. Literary ballads are derivatives of the folk ballad tradition. Keats's "La Belle Dame sans Merci" (p. 692) is an example.

Despite their ostensible narrative directness, ballads can be highly suggestive (rather than straightforward) in their presentation. Psychological motivation is often implied rather than spelled out. To explore this point, you might request, for example, that students in a two- to three-page essay examine and compare the reasons for and effects of the vengeful acts of Barbara Allan and Frankie. Or you might, again in an essay assignment, ask students to explore the implied psychological relationship between mother and son in "Edward."

All these ballads contain central characters whose awareness (and, hence, voice) comes into full power near the moment of their death. Again, this observation seems to support the psychological realism and suggestive truth that ballads can convey.

ANONYMOUS, *Scottsboro* (p. 749)

Ballads often speak the concerns of a culture, giving voice and hope to an oppressed people by encouraging them to keep their spirit alive in harsh circumstances. The black American folk tradition contains many examples of this kind of ballad. Written long after the Civil War, "Scottsboro" addresses a particular political situation, the Scottsboro case. The poet draws on the tradition of black folk ballads, finding a way to speak in a context where his words are not welcome.

JOHN ASHBERY, *Crazy Weather* (p. 750)

Anyone looking for an easily paraphrased narrative or theme in an Ashbery poem will find nothing but frustration. It may help to inform students that Ashbery typically writes to classical music and intends his poems to embody musical themes, movements, and phrases. That's not to say he's writing poetic versions of particular pieces of music — his poems simply operate on principles different from those of many other poets.

Ashbery's work has been described as surreal, a quality "Crazy Weather" exhibits most obviously in line 9, which is also where the poem ceases being a report, however odd, of various weather facts and becomes a sort of meditation on memory, poetry, childhood, the "literature" the speaker wants and needs. Live in this poem enough and imagining the weather as a restless, invisible animal or a garment in the making becomes less and less absurd. The poem can even be seen as an enactment of the recovery of "the then woods" and the "simple unconscious dignity we can never hope to/Approximate now except . . ."

MARGARET ATWOOD, *Spelling* (p. 750)

One could hardly ask for a more pointed refutation of W. H. Auden's statement "Poetry makes nothing happen." You might assign an essay comparing the definition of metaphor given on page 563 with Atwood's in lines 26–36, suggesting that students try to apply the two definitions to poems you've already discussed in class. It's also worth pointing out the fact that for feminists, and not only feminist writers, poetry has been a vital means of articulating worldview and has been used in important respects as it was in ancient times: to tell compelling stories, to embody values, to sing the essential news. Before allusions to feminist politics, contemporary social realities, witchcraft, or seventeenth-century witch burnings are explained, you might let students grapple with "Spelling" on whatever basis they're able.

W. H. AUDEN, *As I Walked Out One Evening* (p. 751)

W. H. Auden was born in York and took a degree at Oxford, after which he taught school for five years. His early poetry, collected in *Poems* (1930) and *On the Island* (1937), reflects leftist political views and shows the strong influence of Freud and Marx. Auden eventually developed a style capable of incorporating colloquial diction and everyday subject matter along with technical facility and an often formal tone. He became an American citizen in 1946.

Relate "As I Walked Out One Evening" to the ballad tradition and review it for its rhythmic devices which both give a sense of the vastness and enduring quality of the love and — in the final line — suggest closure. The claims of the lover are an example of hyperbole. You might compare notes with the class to see if love songs today still use this device.

In the sixth quatrain, however, the poem turns away from the form of the traditional love ballad, and we hear the clock's ominous song on the passing of life. A class that is alert to fine shades of meaning and tone might want to contrast this poem with a more or less traditional *carpe diem* work. Love here is not a defense against time's inevitable work. The critical notion for students to grasp is that this poem treats the erosion and failing of life, not its sudden and tragic demise. Note that life "vaguely. . . leaks away" (line 29) and "the crack in the teacup opens/A lane to the land of the dead" (43–44). Review why someone cannot bless life, even though it is a blessing. What is the difference in tone signified by the clock's chiming and the deep river flowing in the final stanza?

W. H. AUDEN, *Lay Your Sleeping Head, My Love* (p. 753)

You might find it productive to compare this poem and the other aubades in the text. Auden's speaker comes down unambiguously on the mortality side of the love-as-transcendence question, even though he says in stanza III that "Soul and body have no bounds." That's true, in this poem, only when the lovers are in the grip of love's "ordinary swoon" (line 14). Despite the fact that everything dies, the speaker finds, and hopes his lover finds, "the mortal world enough" (36), not just because that's all we have but because that's where love confers its blessings, one of which is the night of bliss chronicled in this poem.

W. H. AUDEN, *Musée des Beaux Arts* (p. 754)

The Musée Royaux des Beaux Arts is the museum in Brussels that houses Pieter Brueghel the Elder's *Landscape with the Fall of Icarus*. The feature that seems to impel Auden to write this poem is the placid banality of life that continues despite startling disasters and history-making events. In the second half of the poem, the speaker notes "how everything turns away/Quite leisurely from the disaster." His remark is, of course, an aesthetic observation, but the year of its coining, 1938, seems to demand an application beyond the art gallery. Other Brueghel paintings alluded to in the poem are "The Census" ("The Numbering at Bethlehem"), lines 5–8, and "The Massacre of the Innocents," lines 9–12.

You might ask students to compare this poem with William Carlos Williams's "The Dance" (p. 867) and Frost's "Out, Out —" (p. 720).

W. H. AUDEN, *The Unknown Citizen* (p. 755)

Clearly, the speaker of this poem is not Auden himself, and the distance between what the speaker says and what we assume Auden feels makes for a sharply satiric poem about this "unknown" yet statistically well-documented citizen. The important question for the class is at what point and in what way do they realize they are reading satire. Focus first on the epitaph, its impersonal numbers and precise rhymes. In the opening lines, consider how to reconcile "sainthood" with "One against whom there was no official complaint." Students familiar with George Orwell's fiction will probably enjoy this caricature of bureaucracy. You may want to explore the fine line that separates duty and regard for civic law from blind obedience.

JOHN BERRYMAN, *Dream Song 14* (p. 755)

This poem forms part of a lyric sequence (Berryman finished 385 dream songs and drafted others) in which the speaker takes on several personae, sometimes in the same song. The protagonist of the sequence is Henry, considered by most critics to be Berryman's alter ego.

The mixture of colloquial and formal diction that characterizes *The Dream Songs* appears here, helping to create an ironic tone (immediately felt in the first two lines, where conventional verbs attach to sea and sky, but only after the startling initial assertion) and helping us imagine a speaker eager to pour out his heart. It may be useful to tell students that, as he does here, Henry frequently refers to himself in the third person during the sequence. You might discuss whether we feel compassion for Henry or whether his insistent self-concern prevents our feeling anything but pity.

ELIZABETH BISHOP, *Five Flights Up* (p. 756)

This poem treats the simultaneous gift and burden of consciousness. You might begin by asking students to imagine the poem without its last line. Would the effect be any different? The dog and bird in this poem seem to be waking as inevitably and gradually as the new morning, which Bishop describes as "enormous," "ponderous," and — almost sardonically — "meticulous." A difference in levels of awareness between human, bird, and beast is posited first by the half denials of any real meaning to be attached to the bird's question (line 7) and by its yawn (14). Later the concept of "shame" clearly misses the mark with the dog, and the last stanza seems to celebrate the unmindful nonchalance of bird and dog, who slip through time as dawn skips through the tree branches. The speaker, though, remains conscious only of time passing and its burdens.

You might ask students in a writing assignment to compare this poem with any other "aubade" in the text.

ELIZABETH BISHOP, *One Art* (p. 757)

Until the final stanza, this villanelle seems a skillful exercise in hyperbole. It seems to change entirely once the final stanza ends: Perhaps the speaker *did* lose "two cities, lovely ones" (line 13), in the sense of being forced to leave. Perhaps beloved rivers, an entire continent, "three loved houses went." The understated tone appears not just part of a wry commentary on human nature but a way of bearing up under the weight of loss, a way of continuing to speak in the face of pains that constantly grow. The most massive pain is the loss of "you" and the "joking voice" heartbreakingly echoed in these lines. The struggle rises completely to the surface with the parenthetical exclamation at poem's end; the canny variations of the "disaster" lines (strict adherence to the form demands that lines 3, 9, 15, and 19 be identical) reveal themselves as ways of denying what even at the last the speaker can admit may only "look like . . . like disaster."

WILLIAM BLAKE, *The Garden of Love* (p. 757)

This brief lyric poses in customary Blakean fashion the natural, free-flowing, and childlike expression of love against the restrictive and repressive adult structures of organized religion. The dialogue between the two is effectively demonstrated in the closing two lines, with their internal rhyme patterns, in particular the rhyming of "briars" (of the priests) and "desires" (of the young boy). The process of growing into adulthood is costly, according to Blake; it requires the exchange of simple pleasures for conventional morality.

WILLIAM BLAKE, *The Little Black Boy* (p. 758)

This poem is from the "Songs of Innocence," unlike the other two given here, which are from the "Songs of Experience." As is usually the case with the "Innocence" figures, the boy in this poem must wait until the afterlife for moral justice and gratification of his wishes. You might ask the class to interpret some of the lines — line 4, for example, and line 17. Is "heat" here somehow tied in with the "beams of love" in line 14, or does it refer to some vulcanizing of moral strength?

WILLIAM BLAKE, *A Poison Tree* (p. 758)

Once again the eating of an apple (here the apple of deceit) occasions a fall. Is Blake inverting Christian symbolism here? If so, in what way? You might ask the class whether they find the first stanza of this poem a true enough portrait of human behavior. For discussion purposes, you might also raise the question of whether the foe is implicated in his demise.

In a writing assignment of two to three pages, ask students to discuss whether Blake seems to identify with the attitude of the speaker in this poem. Does he share in the speaker's happiness over the death of the foe? Would Blake find the speaker's behavior admirable?

ROBERT BLY, *Snowfall in the Afternoon* (p. 759)

This poem provides students with good experience in reading for tone and mood. You might try reading it with Wallace Stevens's "Thirteen Ways of Looking at a Blackbird" (p. 856). Both poems explore interrelationships between the landscape and the perceiver. In this poem, though, the continuity between numbered sections seems more organic and the poem as a whole more lyrical. In fact, the poem seems to break down into two parts, with the darkness of section II finding an ominous parallel in the blackness of the lost sailors at the end of section IV. Explore with the class the emotional connotations the darkness arouses. It seems to be an imaginatively fertile element that shrinks the landscape into a tighter communal bond. The final line of this poem, which stands in contrast to all that has gone before, carries a certain shock. You might want to spend some time talking about reactions to this line, the connotations it holds, and how it reflects back on the earlier sections of the poem.

LOUISE BOGAN, *Dark Summer* (p. 759)

The images in the first stanza of this poem draw our attention to the mystery of the natural world. We immediately notice the repetition of *the,* suggesting the speaker's inventory of the natural world. Ask students to describe the tone of the stanza. How does the speaker build our anticipation? Do "found" and "resound" intimate something lost, or inaccessible? Why are they rhymed? The repetition of "not yet" suspends our experience and builds expectation for possible interpretations in stanza II. The verbs "mounts" (line 2) and "wait" (3), as well as the initial preposition "under" (1), build a sense of mystery and suspense.

Ask students to identify the shift in images in the second stanza. The speaker moves from natural to human images here, but the tone remains mysterious and uninterpretable: "not for our word." How is a poem, made of words, able to describe an experience that seems to be beyond language? How do "spell" and "rite", words evoking human beliefs, relate to the natural images in the first stanza?

A writing assignment might ask students to examine the shift in images from the first to the second stanza. How does the speaker arrive at the last line?

ANNE BRADSTREET, *Before the Birth of One of Her Children* (p. 759)

Until Anne Bradstreet's brother-in-law took a collection of her poems to London and had it published in 1650, no resident of the New World had published a book of poetry. Bradstreet's work enjoyed popularity in England and America. She was born and grew up on the estate of the earl of Lincoln, whose affairs her father managed. Bradstreet's father was eager to provide his daughter with the best possible education. When she was seventeen she and her new husband, Simon Bradstreet, sailed for Massachusetts, where she lived the rest of her life.

As a child Bradstreet contracted rheumatic fever, and its lifelong effects compounded the dangers attending seventeenth-century childbirth. What may seem at first an overdramatized farewell to a loved one can be viewed in this context as a sober reflection on life's capriciousness and an understandable wish to maintain some influence on the living. Perhaps the most striking moment in the poem occurs in line 16, when the only inexact end rhyme ("grave") coincides with a crucial change in tone and purpose. What had been a summary of Puritan attitudes (deeply felt, to be sure) toward life and death and a gently serious offering of "best wishes" to the speaker's husband becomes, with that crack in the voice, a plea to be remembered well.

RUPERT BROOKE, *The Soldier* (p. 760)

Students may not at first realize that this is a Petrarchan or Italian sonnet, so gracefully do the rhymes fall within the flow of the enjambed expression. The sonnet is remarkable for its sincerity and directness, reciting a compounding of riches in the midst of inevitable and terrible loss. Appropriately, as in a wish or prayer, the poet ends on a supposition of peace to be experienced in an "English heaven." What is there in this poem that makes those references to England seem fitting and not blindly nationalistic?

GWENDOLYN BROOKS, *The Bean Eaters* (p. 761)

Take some time to review with the class the pattern of rhyme in this poem. The flatness of "pair" with "affair" and "flatware" in the first stanza, for example, almost echoes the spare flatness of the lives of this aged couple, so limited by poverty. The second stanza characterizes their conduct in the reductive pattern of borrowed and anticipated phrases. Note how "wood" summons the sound of "Mostly Good." The third stanza seems to bring us closer to the couple's perspective on the lives they have led. With remarkable economy (and the pleasures of consonance and assonance), Brooks views their lives as a summation of "twinklings and twinges" (joys and pains). The itemization of the contents of their rented back room illustrates the strength of showing details over telling what to make of them. We begin to be able to share in the poverty. The final line illustrates the power of free verse to break out of a standard line length in order to make a point.

GWENDOLYN BROOKS, *The Mother* (p. 761)

This poem discusses a controversial issue in very contradictory images. The difference between the title and the first word points out this contradiction immediately. Isn't an abortion about *not* being a mother? Students may tend to simplify this poem because abortion is a heated moral and ethical issue. Urge them to consider the way the poem talks about the experience. They might begin by noting the matter-of-factness of the first stanza: the perfect rhymed couplets, the direct statements. This directness breaks down in the second stanza, as "You" shifts to "I."

Ask students to compare the first and second stanzas. How, for example, does "sweet," a word that appears in both stanzas, mean something different each time? The rhyme scheme changes in the second stanza. How does this change affect the speaker's attitude toward her experience? She speaks of "I" and "you" in the second stanza. Is this poem directed to her unborn children, or to herself? Why does she list the events of her children's lost lives in lines 15–20? How does this listing affect the reader? Does the speaker effectively separate herself from her lost children, or is she somewhat confused about their loss? She returns to the direct statement at the end of the stanza, perhaps trying to regain control over herself. In the third stanza the speaker admits that she is unsure of how to describe her experience in order to say "the truth" (28). Ask students to identify possible meanings for this truth. Is it definable? Finally, you might consider why the last stanza is separated from the rest.

A writing assignment might ask students to discuss at length the form of the poem. How does the structure illustrate the speaker's feelings or change of feeling?

ROBERT BROWNING, *Meeting at Night* and *Parting at Morning* (p. 762)

The titles of these two lyrics ask that they be taught together. Have students summarize in a writing assignment the poems' themes and suggest their complementarity. Here are portrayed the coexisting desires in human beings for the bonds of love and the freedom of adventure. Discuss with the class the use of natural imagery in each poem and the relative displacement of the sense of a speaker.

You might also ask students if we can still read these poems with the unhesitating acceptance of the divisions that Browning seems to take for granted, namely, that Eros and the night world are linked in the acceptance of the feminine, but that the day world of action and adventure is the exclusive realm of man.

ROBERT BURNS, *John Anderson My Jo* (p. 762)

This is a sincere lyric with little distance between the speaker and Burns himself. It expresses the importance to him of companionship and looks back on a friendship that has lasted into old age.

GEORGE GORDON, LORD BYRON, *She Walks in Beauty* (p. 763)

In the nineteenth century, George Gordon, Lord Byron, was commonly considered the greatest of the Romantic poets. He spent his childhood with his mother in Aberdeen, Scotland, in deprived circumstances despite an aristocratic heritage. In *Childe Harold, Don Juan,* and much of his other work, Byron chronicled the adventures of one or another example of what came to be known as the "Byronic hero," a gloomy, lusty, guilt-ridden individualist. The poet died of fever while participating in the Greek fight for independence from Turkey.

The title and first line of "She Walks in Beauty" can be an excellent entrance to the poem's explication. Students might puzzle over what it means to walk *in* beauty: is the beauty like a wrap or a cloud? The simile "like the night" hinges on that image. You might ask students if the speaker makes nature subservient to the woman, or the reverse. You might point out "gaudy" (line 6), a strange adjective for describing the day, to draw attention to the speaker's attitude toward nature.

Note the mood of timeless adoration in the second stanza. There is really no movement, only an exclamation of wonder. The exclamation is even more direct in the final stanza, where the woman's visage becomes a reflection of her spotless character. Students might explore the images in all three stanzas, looking for shifts from natural to social. How does the speaker move from "like the night" (1) to "a mind" (17) and "a heart" (18)? Why would he want to describe a woman in these terms? What effect does this description have on our idea of her? Do we really know her by the end of the poem?

For discussions of Byron's poetry, consult Alan Bold, ed., *Byron: Wrath and Rhyme* (London: Vision, 1983); Frederick Garber, *Self, Text and Romantic Irony: The Example of Byron* (Princeton: Princeton UP, 1988), and Peter Mannings, *Byron and His Fictions* (Detroit: Wayne State UP, 1978).

Connection

1. Compare the natural images in this poem with those in William Wordsworth's "She Dwelt among the Untrodden Ways" (p. 869). What is each speaker's relationship to the natural world?

THOMAS CAMPION, *There is a garden in her face* (p. 764)

There is something exquisitely perfect about this love lyric, and its perfection may stem from its ability to tease near clichés into successful verse. All too often, sixteenth- and seventeenth-century conventional verse describes a woman's beauty in terms of lilies or roses. Perhaps these same metaphors work here because of the evasiveness of the refrain. Ask the class to paraphrase the refrain and compose a character sketch of the lady.

LUCILLE CLIFTON, *For de Lawd* (p. 764)

This poem provides an opportunity to explore delicacies of tone. Ask students to describe the speaker's attitude toward those people who "say they have a hard time/understanding." Does she defend her world against their definitions in order to incriminate them? The various repeated words in the poem ("grief," "pushing," "inner city," "home") explore the relationship between the speaker's world and "uptown." After students have noted the pale, lifeless images describing uptown, ask them to return to the earlier lines to seek contrasts or comparisons. Note, for example, the way "houses straight as/dead men" (lines 27–28) subtly contrasts with the lively "playing my Ray Charles" (4) and the curly "Afro" (6).

In a writing assignment, students might explore the way the speaker works to rename things in this poem, the way she subverts the stereotypes implied by the term *inner city*. The speaker admits that violence exists in her world, but she shows herself and her friends working against it. You might draw students' attention to the grammatical ambiguity of the word *grief* in lines 12 and 16; this word is both subject and object, painting the mothers as both victims and survivors.

Connection

1. *Giovanni's "Nikki-Rosa" (p. 520) also provides an "insider's" view of the ghetto. What do the speakers of both these poems think is ignored or misunderstood about their homes? Pay particular attention to the tension in the poems.*

SAMUEL TAYLOR COLERIDGE, *Kubla Khan: or, a Vision in a Dream* (p. 765)

Samuel Taylor Coleridge was born in Ottery St. Mary, Devonshire, but was sent to school in London, where he impressed his teachers and classmates (among whom was Charles Lamb) as an extremely precocious child. He attended Cambridge without taking a degree, enlisted for a short tour of duty in the Light Dragoons (a cavalry unit), planned a utopian community in America with Robert Southey, and married Southey's sister-in-law. He met William Wordsworth in 1795 and published *Lyrical Ballads* with him three years later. Coleridge became an opium addict in 1800–1801 because of the heavy doses of laudanum he'd taken to relieve the pain of several ailments, principally rheumatism. For the last eighteen years of his life he was under the care (and under the roof) of Dr. James Gillman, writing steadily but never able to sustain the concentration needed to complete the large projects he kept planning.

Reputedly, "Kubla Khan" came to Coleridge "as in a vision" after he took a prescribed anodyne and fell into a deep sleep. What Coleridge was able to write down upon waking is only a fragment of what he dreamed. Figures here, such as the "pleasure-dome" and "the sacred river," take on an allegorical cast and suggest the power that inspires the writing of poetry. Although phrases such as "sunless sea" and "lifeless ocean" appear gloomy, they could also suggest mystery and the atmosphere conducive to bringing forth poems.

For a reading of this poem, consult Humphrey House, "Kubla Khan, Christabel and Dejection," in *Coleridge* (London: Hart-Davis, 1953), also reprinted in *Romanticism and Consciousness*, edited by Harold Bloom (New York: Norton, 1970). Another good essay to turn to is by Charles Patterson in *PMLA* 89 (Oct. 1984): 1033–42. Patterson points out, for example, that the river in the poem is "sacred" because it seems to be possessed by a god who infuses in the poet a vision of beauty. Likewise, he identifies the "deep delight" mentioned in line 44 as "a daemonic inspiration." In a writing assignment you might ask students to explore imagery and sound patterns in order to demonstrate how Coleridge uses words to embody and suggest the idea that poetry is truly a "pleasure-dome," visionary and demonically inspired.

COUNTEE CULLEN, *For a Lady I Know* (p. 766)

Cullen was raised by his grandmother until age eleven, then adopted by a Methodist minister in Harlem. He was a leading poet of the Harlem Renaissance and was highly regarded until the 1960s, when black critics found his poetry too lacking in the spirit of social protest. Cullen certainly shows a sense of humor here, though, especially with his mock outrage, signaled by "even" in line 1.

COUNTEE CULLEN, *Saturday's Child* (p. 767)

The title of this poem alludes to the following nursery rhyme:

Monday's child is fair of face,
Tuesday's child is full of grace,
Wednesday's child is full of woe,
Thursday's child has far to go,
Friday's child is loving and giving,
Saturday's child works hard for his living,
And the child that is born on the Sabbath day
Is bonny and blithe and good and gay.

Students usually enjoy this poem, especially if they have some sense of the nursery rhyme it recalls. Here, in an almost balladlike song, certain abstractions (Sorrow, Pain, Poverty) are allegorized. The first three stanzas present a balanced expression of what some have received and what the speaker has received. Houston A. Baker has described this poem as an "ironical protest . . . against economic oppression" in his book on Cullen, *A Many Colored Coat of Dreams* (Detroit: Broadside, 1974).

E. E. CUMMINGS, *anyone lived in a pretty how town* (p. 767)

In the dislodged syntax of this poem, seeming nonsense makes narrative sense and tells its own story. You might begin a discussion of the poem by playing with the opening two lines until the words fall into a more customary sequence (How pretty a town anyone lived in with bells floating up and down). The story in the poem is like an Everyman play in miniature: youth and age, love and marriage, and the death of the principal figures, "anyone" and "noone," are enacted within the mutable constants of the four seasons.

Anyone and noone seem to be exceptions to the rest of the community, who "slept their dream." They seem to be its aberrational romantics, true to ideals and to each other. R. C. Walsh, however, sees their death as only a figurative way of saying that they too succumbed to the deadening rites of convention (*Explicator* 22:9 [1964]: item 72).

E. E. CUMMINGS, *Buffalo Bill 's* (p. 768)

An interesting few moments of class discussion could address whether Cummings is singing the praises of Buffalo Bill in this poem. How does the word *defunct* strike our ears, especially in the second line of the poem? What is the speaker's tone as he asks the concluding question? Is he sincere or contemptuous?

E. E. CUMMINGS, *my sweet old etcetera* (p. 769)

This poem has a bittersweet quality that ends in a smile as the "etcetera" is used to chide the garrulous and duty-seeking aunt and sister as well as the parents, who cling to their high-flown rhetoric and the myth of valor. The use of "etcetera" changes, of course, when it is applied to the soldier dreaming while on the front — of "Etcetera." This is a good illustration of how words modulate in context. You might also explore why the "etcetera" is humorous. Not only does it obligingly change meaning to suit all speakers in all contexts but it caps off all rhetorical fireworks with a pop-gun fizzle.

E. E. CUMMINGS, *since feeling is first* (p. 769)

Once again in the head-heart debate, the heart comes out the winner in this poem. The eliding of the syntax supports the value of feeling over rational thought. Students will probably enjoy the syntactical turn of line 3, which can either complete line 2 or be the subject of line 4. Considering the mention of death and its prominent position in the poem, you might explore with the class — or use as a writing assignment — a defense of this as a *carpe diem* poem.

JAMES DICKEY, *Cherrylog Road* (p. 770)

How to obtain bliss in a junkyard like this is the question facing the young man as he slides in and out of the jammed-in cars, driver side to passenger side, making his lateral journey to the hub of his emotional universe to meet his own true love, Doris Holbrook. Doris arrives, lips atremble and wrench in hand, to lift parts from the wrecks as appeasement to her gun-toting, strap-wielding father. Love among the kudzu triumphs, and even the natural world gets a restorative boost with renewed activity among beetles, mice, and one somewhat geriatric blacksnake.

Poetry is serious business, and it is tough to encourage students to be comfortable enough with the genre to observe and enjoy its potential for humor. Try to make students see the setting here for what it is and appreciate some of the disparities in romantic convention between, for example, the image of the beloved and Doris's arrival with her wrench. Examine too the speaker and his fantasies. Beyond the humor, though (or perhaps at its center), is the pathos of being human — and young, when the slim ties of our sexual passion and our solitary imaginings help keep us from the dead calm that would engulf us.

EMILY DICKINSON, *The Brain — is wider than the Sky* — (p. 772)

This poem composes a theology in twelve lines and does so with scientific precision while using homely metaphors. OK, Dickinson says, do you know that the sky is the sky? Are you aware of yourself and the sky at the same time? All right, then. Are you aware that the sea is the sea? Can you see it, smell it, imagine it, absorb its sea-ness? All right, then. If you can apprehend the sky and sea just so, aren't you like God? Even if we don't go that far, God makes sound and the brain makes sound language. What a difference!

Of course, Dickinson fashions her poem with incomparable economy and the finest craft. Notice that the first and third lines of each stanza have four beats, the second and fourth lines three. The dashes enforce telling pauses, once in each stanza, for example, to exhort experiment ["put them side by side" (line 2), "hold them" (6), "Heft them" (10)]. The scheme of end rhymes mirrors the experiment-result rhetoric. Ask students, Is she right? and a lively discussion is almost sure to follow.

EMILY DICKINSON, *I heard a Fly buzz — when I died —* (p. 773)

This poem is typical of Dickinson's work as a willed act of imagination fathoming life after death and realizing the dark void and limitation of mortal knowledge. David Porter in *Dickinson: The Modern Idiom* (Cambridge, MA: Harvard UP, 1981) observes:

> At a stroke, Dickinson brilliantly extracted the apt metonymical emblem of the essential modern condition: her intrusive housefly. . . . The fly takes the place of the savior; irreverence and doubt have taken the place of revelation. Her fly, then, "With Blue — uncertain stumbling Buzz" is uncomprehension, derangement itself. It is noise breaking the silence, not the world's true speech but, externalized, the buzz of ceaseless consciousness (239).

You might introduce this idea, and then either in discussion or in a writing assignment, ask the class to explore the tone of this poem and its accordance with Porter's comment.

EMILY DICKINSON, *It dropped so low — in my Regard* — (p. 773)

This poem describes an experience of disillusionment. Disillusionment is literally the breaking up of how something is perceived. As is so often the case, the speaker here feels chagrin at not having realized the truth earlier.

Review with the class the images of fragility and obdurate resistance here. The object of Dickinson's disillusionment is as breakable (and, by the poem's standards, as worthy of protection) as cheap tableware. She had thought it was made of more precious and durable metal — as the final two stanzas imply.

Ultimately, the poet's mind — a "Ground" covered with "Stones" — is the hardest element here. And, by the poem's inner logic, it is the element that is to be most exalted. If anything is now to remain in high regard, it is the self. Authority, as it were, has turned inward.

You might explore with the class what specifically "It" could be. Biographies of Dickinson often recount her "failure" to become one of the elect saved by God's grace. Perhaps she is reevaluating the promises and perceived shortcomings of her Christian training. That suggestion, though, does not exhaust the possibilities of "It" for this poet, who lived out her years in New England spinsterhood. More could be said of this topic, perhaps in an essay assignment.

EMILY DICKINSON, *Much Madness is divinest Sense* (p. 774)

This poem could be the epigram of the radical or the artist. For all its endorsement of "madness," however, its structure is extremely controlled — from the mirror-imaged paradoxes that open the poem to the balancing of "Assent" and "Demur" and the consonance of "Demur" and "dangerous." Try to explore with the class some applications of the paradoxes. One might think, for example, of the "divine sense" shown by the Shakespearean fool.

EMILY DICKINSON, *Success is counted sweetest* (p. 774)

The power of this poem is, to some degree, its intangibility. We puzzle over how desire enables those who will never succeed to know success better than those who actually achieve it. Ask students to talk about the comparison of success to "a nectar" (line 3). It is odd that the verb "comprehend" should be paired with nectar; what does it mean to comprehend? When they begin to talk about the pairing of understanding and physical images, ask students to think about "need" (4) as both a physical and an intellectual desire for success. You might also have students discuss the word "burst" in the final line. Are the failures the true achievers? If so, what is it they achieve?

EMILY DICKINSON, *Wild Nights — Wild Nights!* (p. 774)

This is a poem of romantic ecstasy. The subject and even the pace may be a surprise to some students, who have in mind a fixed image of Dickinson's poetry. Technically, the poem is a good example of a sustained metaphor, with Eden and the Sea implying an unbounded paradise.

JOHN DONNE, *Batter My Heart* (p. 775)

Christian and Romance traditions come together in this sonnet. Employing Christian tradition, Donne here portrays the soul as a maiden with Christ as her bridegroom. Borrowing from Petrarchan materials, Donne images the reluctant woman as castle and her lover as the invading army. Without alluding to any particular tradition, we can also observe in this poem two modes of male aggression, namely, the waging of war and the pursuit of romantic conquest, again blended into a strong and brilliantly rendered metaphysical conceit. Donne is imploring his "three-personed" God to take strong measures against the enemy, Satan. In typical metaphysical paradox, Donne moreover asks God to save him from Satan by imprisoning him within God's grace.

Rhythm and sound work remarkably in this sonnet to enforce its meaning. Review the heavy-stressed opening line — which sounds like the pounding of a relentless fist and is followed by the strong reiterated plosives of "break, blow, burn."

JOHN DONNE, *Death Be Not Proud* (p. 775)

Many students will have read this sonnet in high school. It should serve as a reminder that the logic of a poem can be as tightly constructed as any other form of rhetorical argument. In the frame of Donne's religious belief, which promises life after death, death is a very brief moment and is, furthermore, slave to the darker dealings of fate. As usual Donne has a sense of the rhythmic force of words. Notice the quartet of heavy-stressed beats in his opening injunction; the sonnet concludes with another group of four stressed syllables.

Ask students to compare in a brief essay the attitude toward death taken by Donne in this poem and by Dickinson in "Because I could not stop for Death" (p. 639).

JOHN DONNE, *The Flea* (p. 775)

An interesting discussion or writing topic could be organized around the tradition of the *carpe diem* poem and how this poem both accommodates and alters that tradition.

The wit here is ingenious, and after the individual sections of the poem are explained, more time might be needed to review the parts and give the class a sense of the total effect of the poem's operations.

The reason the speaker even bothers to comment on the flea stems from his belief that a commingling of blood during intercourse (here, admittedly, by the agency of the flea) may result in conception. Hence his belief that the lovers must be "yea more than" united and that the flea's body has become a kind of "marriage temple." For the woman to crush the flea (which she does) is a multiple crime because in so doing she commits murder, suicide, and sacrilege (of the temple) and figuratively destroys the possible progeny. The flea in its death, though, also stands as logical emblem for why this courtship should be consummated. The reasoning is that little if any innocence or honor is spent in killing the flea, and, likewise, neither of those commodities would be spent "when thou yield'st to me."

JOHN DONNE, *The Good-Morrow* (p. 776)

Unlike in other love lyrics, the lovers here do not need each other for completion. They can together find such natural harmony as to make one world, but they are each possessed of a world. What does Donne mean when he says each of the lovers "is one" world?

JOHN DONNE, *Hymn to God, My God, in My Sickness* (p. 777)

This is a good example of a poem that can give delight despite great seriousness of subject. Convinced he's dying, the speaker devotes himself to preparing for the end by singing this hymn, his way of tuning the "instrument" of his soul so he will join the "choir of saints for evermore." The pleasure for the reader comes in tracing how Donne works the extended metaphor (which could also be seen as an extended pun) of geographical straits–spiritual straits, and how the navigation of any difficult passage (or poem) can lead to the sort of insight that appears in the poem's final line.

H. D. (HILDA DOOLITTLE), *Leda* (p. 778)

H. D. was for many years considered the prototype Imagist poet despite writing and publishing poems that, like "Leda," hardly fit the Imagist mold. Feminist literary criticism has had a great deal to do with the much more significant place H. D.'s work now claims in the poetic firmament and with dispelling the shadows cast by some of the men with whom she had significant relationships: Ezra Pound, Richard Aldington, D. H. Lawrence, Sigmund Freud.

"Leda" will likely present problems for students, especially since the woman of the title is never mentioned directly in the poem. Examining the suggestiveness of the poem's diction may be useful. Purple can be considered the color of royalty (Zeus is the father of the gods), red the color of blood, yellow-gold the color, of course, of riches. The repetition of the meeting of river and tide evokes the act of intercourse, especially since the tide depends on the moon, traditionally associated with the feminine. Many words suggest rest and ease, very odd, at least on initial reading, in a poem that concerns rape. Students could be asked to speculate on how the poem would read without the allusion to mythology. Suppose it were called "The Tide and the River"?

Connections

1. *William Butler Yeats's "Leda and the Swan" (p. 874) retells the same myth as H. D.'s "Leda." How can the violence in Yeats's version be reconciled with the lack of violence in H. D.'s?*

2. *Zeus's impregnation of Leda leads to the Trojan War. What attitudes do the two poems betray toward this eventuality?*

MICHAEL DRAYTON, *Since there's no help* (p. 779)

Students will probably enjoy this sonnet for its bittersweet plea for love renewed in the face of supreme obstacles. They may also recognize and perhaps approve the bravado expressed in the first eight lines. It's worth noting that in its rhyme scheme this sonnet conforms to the Shakespearean pattern, while the octave-sestet structure of its argument conforms to the Petrarchan pattern.

T. S. ELIOT, *Journey of the Magi* (p. 779)

T. S. Eliot grew up in St. Louis, received an undergraduate degree from (and did graduate work at) Harvard, and attended the Sorbonne and Oxford for a year each. He wrote several of the definitive poems of the twentieth century, including "The Waste Land" and "The Love Song of J. Alfred Prufrock," (included here), and is considered by some the most important literary critic since Matthew Arnold.

"Journey of the Magi" considers the residue of memory that collects after one has witnessed a miracle. The speaker is an old man, and in his memory the unfathomable mystery of the Nativity is superseded by the pain and hardship of the journey. That there was a miracle, a baby born as the Son of God to save the world from sin, is lost on him. He can perceive the event on only its most literal level, and he misses entirely the idea of personal salvation. He is left, in fact, with feelings of disenchantment and alienation, as he observes the people over whom he rules worship gods that now appear to him as worthless dolls. Is this magus figure symbolic of the modern existential condition of faith?

In a writing assignment, you might ask the class to compare the tone of this poem with that of William Butler Yeats's "The Second Coming" (p. 876).

T. S. ELIOT, *The Love Song of J. Alfred Prufrock* (p. 781)

This dramatic monologue is difficult but well worth the time spent analyzing the speaker, imagery, tone, and setting. Begin with the title — is the poem actually a love song? Is Eliot undercutting the promise of a love song with the name *J. Alfred Prufrock*? Names themselves carry connotations and images; what does this name project?

The epigraph from Dante seems to assure both the culpability and the sincerity of the speaker. After reading the poem, are we too to be counted among those who will never reveal what we know?

The organization of this monologue is easy enough to describe. Up until line 83, Prufrock tries to ask the overwhelming question. In lines 84–86, we learn that he has been afraid to ask it. From line 87 to the end, Prufrock tries to explain his failure by the likelihood that he would be misunderstood or by the disclaimer that he is a minor character, certainly no Prince Hamlet. Notice how the idea of "dare" charts Prufrock's growing submissiveness in the poem from "Do I dare/Disturb the universe?" to "Have I the strength to force the moment to its crisis?" (which rhymes lamely with "tea and cakes and ices"), and, finally, "Do I dare to eat a peach?"

You might ask students to select images they enjoy. Consider, for example, Prufrock's assertion that he has measured out his life in "coffee spoons." You may have to introduce the notion of a demitasse spoon.

Notice how finely Eliot tunes the language: he even employs doggerel to good effect. Aside from the "ices-crisis" lines already mentioned, notice how in a stroke Eliot indicates the shallowness of the ladies Prufrock associates with: "In the room the women come and go/Talking of Michelangelo" (13–14). The poem offers many opportunities to explore the nuances of language and the suggestive power of image as a means of drawing a character portrait and suggesting something about a particular social milieu at a particular time in modern history.

Grover Smith, in his *T. S. Eliot's Poetry and Plays* (Chicago: U of Chicago P, 1960), provides extensive background and critical comment on this poem.

As a writing assignment you might ask the class to explore a pattern of images in the poem — those of crustaceans near the end, for example — and how that pattern adds to the theme. You might also ask the class to give a close reading of a particular passage — the final three lines come to mind — for explication.

LAWRENCE FERLINGHETTI, *Constantly risking absurdity* (p. 784)

Metaphors for a poet's craft are often action filled, as this poem illustrates. Ferlinghetti is one of the San Francisco Beat poets who turned to free verse as a way of more closely imitating natural speech patterns. The groupings of words here give emphasis to certain patterns and also reflect the tightrope walker's back-and-forth juggle.

You might ask the class the following questions: Is the image of a tightrope walker a good metaphor for the poet, and if so, why? Is there a pun on *absurdity*, which means in terms of its Latinate origins, "away from the norm or plane"? Why did Ferlinghetti make his poem so open ended, without any end-stopped lines? What is the poet's relationship to his audience? (He seems to be above them and closer to the standards of being measured by beauty.) Why is the poet a superrealist? (The poet, like the tightrope walker, cannot afford a misstep or an inaccuracy.)

ALLEN GINSBERG, *America* (p. 785)

This poem follows in the Whitman tradition of free verse that seems to reflect the spontaneity of thought. Do any of the passages here seem a little self-indulgent — possibly the latter portion of the poem? You might remind students that they already know another lyric called "America." In what ways does Ginsberg's poem defy the "sweet land of liberty" theme? You might look too at Claude McKay's poem by the same title (p. 814) and at "Scottsboro" (p. 749).

In his poem Ginsberg alludes to historic incidents that mark the legal system itself as culpable in promoting social injustice, in particular, the Sacco-Vanzetti and Scottsboro cases. Sacco and Vanzetti were accused of murdering a Boston area paymaster and his guard. Despite shaky evidence they were executed in 1927, and many believed the sentence had been carried out because of their anarchist leanings. The Scottsboro case concerned the alleged rape of two women in Alabama by nine black youths. The incident occurred in 1931, and, despite the fact that the Supreme Court overturned the charges of the state court twice, pardon was not granted to the last of the "Scottsboro boys" until 1976. Ask the class if they can recall incidents in recent U.S. history that would make this poem continue to be relevant.

NIKKI GIOVANNI, *Poetry* (p. 787)

Considerations

1. *Why is there no (or almost no) punctuation and capitalization in this poem? How does the poem's typography relate to the statement "a poem is pure energy/horizontally contained" (lines 27–28)?*

2. *What does Giovanni have to say about the personality of the poet and his or her working conditions? How is the poet like, yet unlike, others?*

3. *A Renaissance theory of poetry that lasted well beyond Elizabethan times said that the purpose of poetry is to instruct and delight. What is Giovanni's opinion of this theory?*

Connection

1. *Compare Francis's attitude in "The Pitcher" (p. 623) about the poet and his or her relationship to society with Giovanni's, especially on the subject of "controversy" (line 24).*

DONALD HALL, *My Son, My Executioner* (p. 788)

You might discuss the title of this short rhymed lyric. Is *Executioner* too strong and somehow too long a word to be applied to an infant? Hall explores a paradox that comes through with metaphysical clarity in this tightly controlled verse. The son is both a way of sustaining the family name, hence conferring "immortality," and a sign of his parents' aging.

DONALD HALL, *To a Waterfowl* (p. 789)

Obviously this poem does not address a waterfowl. Why then the title? It is, of course, a borrowing from William Cullen Bryant's poem of the same title. Hall uses the title to set up a fairly clichéd set of expectations about poetry and poets. You might explore with the class their assumptions about the life-styles of poets. What notions about "poetic" behavior get turned upside down here?

In another sense, though, Hall does address a waterfowl, especially since he characterizes his audience's hand clapping as "the approbation of feathers." Bryant apparently fared better with his fowl.

If neither the wives who attend the readings nor their husbands can appreciate Hall's poetry, who can be his audience, and what is a poet to do without fit readers and listeners? Does Hall indicate much hope for the next generation? What attitude or emotion is betrayed by the repetition of "not you" that closes the poem? You might introduce to the class the idea that Hall's dilemma here is faced by every American poet, although poetry is experiencing something of a renascence. We are not, by nature, a country of poetry readers.

THOMAS HARDY, *Channel Firing* (p. 790)

This is an interesting poem to discuss, for it invites different interpretations of its tone and conclusion and stands as a kind of monument — in a way that Camelot and Stonehenge do not — to modernism and the transformation of idealism into irony. A good way to structure a discussion of the poem might be first to identify the speakers and then to describe the tone and attitude they project. Surprisingly, for such a compact lyric, there are three speakers — a spokesman for the disturbed dead, who responds to the sounds of the guns in the first three stanzas and frames the observations of his fellow dead in stanzas VII and VIII; the voice of God, who comments on humanity's customary habit of waging war; and, finally, the voice in the last stanza, more distant, which we may assume to be Hardy's own.

Hearing the sound of the guns, the dead man suggests that Judgment Day might be at hand. A reasonable assumption — but note how domestically pedantic are the images of Judgment Day in the second stanza, summed up in the third with "The glebe cow drooled." This speaker then frames God's lengthy disclaimer of Judgment Day. One critic, J. O. Bailey in *The Poetry of Thomas Hardy* (Chapel Hill: U of North Carolina P, 1970), finds God here to be compassionate, for this God withholds the final judgment, lest the dead should miss the sleep they need. Review with students, though, the tone projected through God's words and laughter (stanza VI). This is not the stern, unyielding God of the Puritan tradition but some smugly superior patriarch. At this point, the poem turns toward a mode of light irony, as the (presumably) most God-fearing one among the dead, the Parson, claims he wished he "had stuck to pipes and beer" (stanza VIII).

153

Finally, the poem concludes with what we may take to be Hardy's voice. Of these last lines, John Crowe Ransom in his introduction to Hardy's *Selected Poems* (New York: Macmillan, 1960) has written that by their very lyricism they indicate that the finest contents of civilization, embodied in these places, will prevail over war. Your students may want to argue differently, for the sense of the lines indicates a continuance of war's madness and the sounds of the final two lines, with their persistent repetition of the hard *st*- and *t*-sounds (*St*our*t*on *T*ower, Camelo*t*, and *st*arli*t St*onehenge), are anything but lyrically assuaging. The dead have already implied that the world is even less sane than it was in their "indifferent century," and one senses in this poem Hardy's lost idealism in the face of this civilization, whose decline can be countered only by the staccato laughter of irony.

THOMAS HARDY, *The Darkling Thrush* (p. 791)

Begin by observing the date of composition of this poem. "December 31, 1900" lends to the setting a kind of millennial significance. Explore with the class the power of the setting; a grimmer natural landscape has rarely been portrayed. In stanza III the tone changes and some prospect of hope is offered by the voice of the old thrush. The song is described as "a full-throated evensong/Of joy illimited." Are we to understand that this joy is without bounds, or is there a possible pun here that suggests the joy is poorly limited? Discuss with the class how the darkling thrush functions in the poem in both a natural and a symbolic way as harbinger of better tidings.

THOMAS HARDY, *Hap* (p. 792)

Bad luck, pain, and sorrow seem so happenstance, Hardy says in this sonnet. Does the attitude of the speaker ring true? He claims that it would be easier to bear ill chance if some vengeful god would openly proclaim his malevolent designs. Discuss with the class why even the machinations of some divinity appear preferable to the silent, indeterminate (and inhuman) operations of caprice.

As an essay assignment you might ask the class to compare this poem with Hardy's "Channel Firing," to assess his attitude toward God.

THOMAS HARDY, *The Man He Killed* (p. 792)

This poem about one man killing another just because their meeting happens to be on a battlefield explores the cruel ironies of human relationships. You might point out that some of the speaker's awkwardness and uncertainty is reflected even in the title, which insists on the distance of the third-person *he*, instead of *I*, which might have admitted disgust or moral culpability for the killing. Probably that *he* also reflects the impersonal force of the social structures urging the pursuit of war. Even in so brief a poem, Hardy alludes to the economic issues that impel soldiers to enlist; the idea of war as valor and glory is deliberately bypassed.

The poem is structured fairly tightly, with each quatrain following an *abab* rhyme scheme. Singsong rhymes, like "foe"/"Just so"/"although" (lines 10–12) emphasize — and ironically undercut — the simple, and simplistic, reasoning for the speaker's actions. The language, though, is not so regular and formal. Most interesting in its choice and arrangement of words is the third stanza, where the speaker, resorting to slang and his own conventional speech patterns, tries to come to terms with the fact that he has killed a man. What do the repetitions of words, internal rhyme patterns, and word order inversions tell us about his state of mind?

This poem provides an excellent occasion to illustrate the separation that can exist between speaker and poet. The poet's rejection of war and the forces that cause people to kill each other is clear — but the speaker, in his attempt to understand, can only come up with the idea that "quaint and curious war is." You might ask the class to read this poem together with "Channel Firing" and discuss Hardy's attitude toward war and the way it influences lives.

SEAMUS HEANEY, *Digging* (p. 793)

The speaker of this poem seeks to honor the labor of his forebears even as he breaks with it, honoring his own labor as of equal value. Yet this is somehow not an entirely peaceful poem, perhaps not peaceful at all, given the startling image in line 2. You might ask the class in a short paper to trace the effect of that early image on the others in the poem. What is the speaker doing or trying to do with his pen-gun? How is a pen like both a gun and a spade? What does the spade-work in the poem uncover? What does the pen-work uncover?

Reading Heaney's work aloud is a pleasure. This poem richly repays careful oral reading as well as scrupulous mapping of its interlocking patterns of sound.

ANTHONY HECHT, *The Dover Bitch* (p. 794)

The subtitle of this poem is "A Criticism of Life," and Hecht indirectly makes his criticism by having as a backdrop Arnold's "Dover Beach" (p. 549). That poem too was a criticism of society, of declining religious values and the disappearance of a moral center. The tone of this poem is initially amusing; the young woman is not going to be treated "as a sort of mournful cosmic last resort." She desires a relationship more carnal than platonic. The speaker obliges her, and now, in what seems to be a continuing casual relationship, he occasionally brings her perfume, called *Nuit d'Amour*. At the edges of this poem we still hear the sound of Arnold's armies of the night, a reminiscence that doesn't make the current times seem so much worse but does make our moral comprehension of them so much more slight and haphazard.

GEORGE HERBERT, *The Collar* (p. 794)

Herbert's poems were published after his death. Many of them deal with the hesitancy of commitment he felt before becoming an Anglican priest.

The title "The Collar" echoes *choler* (anger) and suggests the work collar that binds horses in their traces as well as the clerical collar. Explore with the class how the speaker's situation the stress he feels, and his particular argument gradually emerge. In his meditation he tries to argue himself out of his position of submission. His life is free; he deserves more than thorns. He would like to have some of the world's secular awards. The speaker then admonishes himself to forget the feeble restrictions — his "rope of sands." But when all is said and done, he capitulates. You might observe how this poem demonstrates a strong measure of psychological insight.

As a writing assignment you might ask the class to explore in a two- to three-page paper how rhythm reinforces the meaning in this poem.

GEORGE HERBERT, *The Pulley* (p. 795)

Traditionally Sunday was set aside as a day of rest — so that rest was not only available but ordained. Happily, the blessing called "rest" appears at the close of the second stanza and obtains an almost allegorical presence. All other forms of *rest* as verb or noun, including restlessness, appear later.

For a challenging and thorough discussion of this poem, turn to Helen Vendler's *The Poetry of George Herbert* (Cambridge, MA: Harvard UP, 1975). Vendler also sees a pun in *repining*, as "to wither" or "to yearn." Although God appears here as the most strict of patriarchs, Vendler also points out that he is willing to accept those who come to him out of restlessness as well as out of goodness.

M. CARL HOLMAN, *Mr. Z* (p. 796)

Students will readily perceive the irony of this poem: the man who lived so that his racial identity was all but obliterated earned as his summary obituary the reductive, faint, and defaming praise "One of the most distinguished members of his race." His loss is a double loss, to be sure; not only did he fail finally to be judged according to white standards (those he aspired to) but in the process of living up to those standards he "flourish[ed] without [the] roots" of his own racial identity. Review the poem for its ironic phrases. You may have to explain that racial, religious, and ethnic differences were often suppressed in favor of assimilation, and that the celebration of and return to these differences is a relatively recent tendency.

Ask students to compare (in a writing assignment, perhaps) the attitudes toward black experience held by "Nikki-Rosa" in the poem by Giovanni (p. 520) and by Mr. Z in this poem.

GERARD MANLEY HOPKINS, *Pied Beauty* (p. 797), *Spring and Fall* (p. 797), *The Windhover* (p. 798)

Fortunately, a number of glosses and extended critical interpretations of the works of this difficult poet are available. Among these are Graham Storey's *A Preface to Hopkins* (London and New York: Longman, 1981); Paul Mariani's *A Commentary on the Complete Poems of Gerard Manley Hopkins* (Ithaca: Cornell UP, 1969); *Hopkins: A Collection of Critical Essays,* ed. Geoffrey Hartman (Englewood Cliffs: Twentieth-Century Views, Prentice-Hall, 1966); and J. Hillis Miller's *The Disappearance of God* (Cambridge, MA: Harvard UP, 1963).

A. E. HOUSMAN, *Eight O'Clock* (p. 798)

You might consider whether this poem would be as effective if it were titled "The Hanging." Probably not, for some of the surprise would be lost, and the poem would no longer have its temporal frame of wholesome normality.

A. E. HOUSMAN, *Is my team ploughing?* (p. 798)

This poem is in a ballad form with a typical question-response exchange between the Shropshire lad who has died and a supposedly impersonal voice that answers his queries. The surprise comes, of course, with the introduction of the second "I," who has a decidedly vested interest in the earthly life of the deceased.

A. E. HOUSMAN, *Terence, this is stupid stuff* (p. 799)

Terence is a dyspeptic poet who eats (and drinks) well but still writes verse that strikes his reader as "moping melancholy mad." The first section of the poem is in quotation marks because Terence is being addressed by someone else.

Combining Miltonic sobriety (lines 21–22) with fraternity-row sloganism (lines 23–24), "Terence" defends in the second portion of the poem the role of ale in Western civilization. He claims that it eases one's anxieties and gives pleasure — until the next morning.

In the third section Terence proposes poetry as a surer easement for life's "dark and cloudy days." In the final section of the poem he tells the story of Mithridates, who built up an immunity to poison by taking it in small doses. Just so, the lesson of the verse here claims, poetry (rather than poison) in small doses can help build up an immunity to these grim times ("the embittered hour").

You might encourage the class to write a description of the relation between the poem's third and fourth sections. You might also talk about the aptness of couplets to record conversational speech. What challenges do they pose to the naturalness of dialogue?

A. E. HOUSMAN, *To an Athlete Dying Young* (p. 801)

You might discuss this poem in relation to the *carpe diem* tradition. Is it perverse to imagine such a connection in a poem that treats youth and death? Many students will have read this poem in high school. They might enjoy picking out recurrent words and themes — such as "shoulder-high" in stanzas I and II, "shady" in stanza IV, and "shade" in stanza VI; the various thresholds and sills or doorways in the poem; and the image of both the laurel and the rose as evanescent tokens of glory and youth — and exploring their function in the poem.

LANGSTON HUGHES, *Ballad of the Landlord* (p. 802)

Langston Hughes is the best-known writer of the Harlem Renaissance. Born in Joplin, Missouri, he grew up with his grandmother, although he did live from time to time with one or the other of his parents, who had separated early in his life. After attending Columbia University for a year, Hughes wrote and published poetry while working as a seaman in the merchant marine, as a busboy in Washington, DC, and in a Paris nightclub. He wrote in many forms besides poetry: plays, newspaper articles and columns, screenplays, novels, and essays.

In his poetry Hughes was often concerned with incorporating the rhythms and feeling of blues and jazz. It's not difficult to imagine "Ballad of the Landlord" as a slow blues. Whereas the results of the protagonist's rebellion are anything but unfamiliar, his willingness to fight for what little is his — and the verve with which he speaks of that struggle — affords him a certain nobility even though the landlord undeniably "wins." The poem also shows in derisive terms the idiocy of the landlord's and authorities' overreaction to reasonable and modest concerns about safety (even the landlord's) and comfort.

LANGSTON HUGHES, *Harlem (A Dream Deferred)* (p. 803)

Poems should end with a bang rather than a whimper. Test that statement by eliminating the last line of this poem. This experiment is one way to begin talking about poetic closure (cf. Barbara Hernstein Smith's *Poetic Closure* [Chicago: U of Chicago P, 1968]). Consider also the speaker's tone here. Does the final line just occur as another possibility for the fate of dreams, or does the poem mark a crescendo from a sneer to an outraged threat?

TED HUGHES, *The Thought-Fox* (p. 803)

Ted Hughes (who was married to Sylvia Plath at the time of her suicide) wishes in many of his poems to evoke what one might call an "animal consciousness" not unlike what can be found in the work of Robert Bly, James Wright, and Spanish-language poets such as Octavio Paz and Pablo Neruda, in short any poet seeking to represent the non- (or sub- or ir-) rational. In "The Thought-Fox" the speaker imagines his thoughts as foxes; or, read another way, shows how imagination can enable a thinking with the animal mind. In any case, the speaker boldly asserts that each moment is a forest, that measured time is lonely yet hardly alone, that "this blank page" (line 4) will remain so until the ego relinquishes control and the fox can set "neat prints into the snow" (13) of the page. Note how the imprecise adjectives ("dark," "near," "lame," "widening," "deepening"), pronouns ("something," "it"), and nouns ("darkness," "shadow," "a body," "an eye") go a long way toward creating a mood of mystery. You might ask students to what extent they think this poem represents the way poetry gets written.

RANDALL JARRELL, *The Woman at the Washington Zoo* (p. 804)

The woman here, who has evidently been in the employ of the government for years, feels effaced and negated as a person. In the opening portion of the poem, the exotic Indian saris and the patterned leopard create a disquieting contrast to her "dull null/Navy" dress, which seems even to her to define her identity. This woman's real dilemma should gradually emerge from class discussion. It is not the dullness of her job but rather her imaginative capabilities to see beyond her situation as well as her sensitivity to others and how they see (or do not see) her that creates the crisis in this poem. Like the animal, she too is caged, but no one comes to see her.

The close of the poem shows the imagination in extremis willfully crossing the lines between human and animal kingdoms for contact with the mystery, power, and dark beauty the woman can intuit but not attain.

As an essay assignment you might ask the class to write an extended analysis of the speaker's character through observing both the sounds of the words and the imagery used to develop the poem. Ask them to describe the speaker's progress from her workaday world to her final plea for change and release from this world.

BEN JONSON, *Come, My Celia* (p. 805)

The argument here revolves around the *carpe diem* theme. "Time will not be ours forever," the poet tells his beloved; therefore, let us play at the "sports of love." If this light expression for their relationship were not enough, Jonson also advises that whatever social or moral improprieties the lovers may commit do not matter unless they are caught in the act ("taken" or "seen").

X. J. KENNEDY, *In a Prominent Bar in Secaucus One Day* (p. 805)

This poem is a reminder that the ballad form, complete with music and guitar-chord cues, is still very much with us. Taught in conjunction with other ballads, this can be a good introduction to a poetry unit. The tune is familiar, the theme and situation easily apprehensible, and the language sufficiently bawdy in places to short-circuit any fixed notions about decorum in poetry. Unlike many ballads, this one presents a moral. The lady knows only too well that youth does not last forever, and she advises other women who might hear her song to "keep your bottoms off barstools and marry you young." Here we have a latter-day version of the *carpe diem* theme. This theme is dramatized even more vividly by the allegorizing of time as a young suitor (lines 33–35) who, as the vernacular would have it, is one who goes "too far," with the end result in this instance reflecting aging and the prospect of Thanatos, rather than Eros.

Review this poem for the use of hyperbole. The lady "in skunk" is a kind of Pecos Bill of the Smart Set whose limousine set speed records but, nonetheless, required ten minutes to see it pass by (24). You might ask the class to locate and comment on the turning point in the poem, when the humor of the hyperbole begins to slip into a more somber and moralizing tone. Appropriately, that turn occurs with the word *lose* in line 26. At this point you might want to make some comment on the literary quality of this ballad, observing in passing the distance and perhaps even the ironic superiority of the singer as he immortalizes this particular "prominent bar in Secaucus, N.J."

ETHERIDGE KNIGHT, *A Watts Mother Mourns While Boiling Beans* (p. 807)

One of the most striking aspects of this poem is its sound patterns. Alliteration ("blooming," "born," "bold," "blood,") and assonance ("blooming," "blood") project the mother's (speaker's) anxiety and apprehension. She cannot just grieve, for she must worry about her husband's dinner. Ask students to think about how the sound patterns influence their reading of this poem, both literally and figuratively. Does the poem *demand* to be read a certain way? How does this reading affect its meaning?

Connection

1. How does Knight's discussion of a troubled inner-city mother in this poem compare with Clifton's in "For de Lawd" (p. 764)? Are the mothers grieving about the same thing? Compare the images and sound patterns of the two poems, looking for the impact of sound on tone and theme.

PHILIP LARKIN, *Church Going* (p. 807)

You might begin a discussion of this poem by looking at the title. Appropriately for a meditation on a theme, it employs the participle form — but what sort of churchgoer is this bicyclist who comes in to look at "some brass and stuff" and examine the newness of the roof? Apparently, he is not the most devout sort. Moreover, given the poem's speculation on the decay and disuse of churches, surely the title can be taken as a dark comment on the health of the churchgoing tradition.

The speaker is distant enough to be a fair-minded observer, yet he is touched sufficiently by a recalled reverence to enter this setting with a ready sensitivity. After he leaves he begins speculating on the use of churches, especially when they have fallen into disuse. Stanza IV offers a glimpse at the darkest permutation of belief: faith that falls into superstition and superstition that falls into disbelief. The images that follow suggest erosion, decay, Christianity turned into an "olde curiosity shoppe." The sacramental immanence of truth and the sacred mysteries of being are now secularized so that society seems to know value only through what it has lost.

Yet it continues to please the speaker to stand in the stillness of the church. What draws him and holds him there is what theologians and psychologists call an "inner need." When Larkin writes "that much never can be obsolete," he is stating that the human desire to touch and be touched by the "serious" is something that will never go out of fashion.

PHILIP LARKIN, *Toads* (p. 809)

Here the speaker is waging an internal argument. One side of him advocates the throwing off of traces ("toad work") and says, in effect, if others get by without working too hard, so can you. The second voice in the poem appears only in the final three stanzas; nonetheless, it exerts its silent "toad" presence throughout.

What really does Larkin feel about those who don't work every day? The liquid *l*'s of the third stanza are a smooth contrast to the breathtaking *b*-sounds in line 27, but the connotations of the words beginning with *l* are far from appealing. The images that follow of families limping by, barely skirting starvation, are also an unpropitious endorsement for the work-free regimen. It seems, then, that the toads, as warty and unattractive as they might be, carry the day. By the close of the poem, the speaker acknowledges that he is glad to have both the security and the sense of honor and worth conferred on him by work.

You might conclude discussion of the poem by reading aloud Larkin's sequel, "Toads Revisited."

DENISE LEVERTOV, *The Ache of Marriage* (p. 810)

The speaker does not reject the idea of marriage; she does, though, seem to impel both people in the poem to look for "some joy/not to be known outside it." Yet this marriage is not a fulfilling experience and brings both physical ache ("thigh") and the emotional ache of failed communication ("tongue"). The repetition of the word *beloved* seems like a throbbing reminder of this pain.

Two allusions might need some comment in class. The marriage is a "leviathan," a large sea monster, and the couple, like Jonah of the Old Testament, is trapped inside it, feeling the need for some deliverance or at least some pleasure within these confines. At the close of the poem, the couple again feels trapped, this time in a situation reminiscent of the animals in Noah's ark. Seeking again a kind of deliverance, they find their security turning into a burden. Recognizing the emotional constraints of a marriage that no longer brings joy and satisfaction, they are trapped in the "ark of/the ache of it," and they feel desolation. Observe with the class the sound of the end words in this free-verse poem (as in the example just quoted), which makes a subtle music.

AUDRE LORDE, *Hanging Fire* (p. 810)

This poem should be accessible enough to your students, who probably remember all too clearly what life felt like at age fourteen. You might either as a writing assignment or in class discussion ask students to supply and talk about lines from this poem that seem to ring especially true to their own memories of adolescence. Consider, for example, the opening five lines, expressing a bewilderment over a physical body that seems no longer one's own, accompanied by the awakenings and trials of first love directed toward someone whose own maturing processes seem at a standstill. Students might also want to comment on the range of emotional pitches the speaker feels, including the adolescent anxiety and imaginative investment in death.

The three stanzas share a refrain — made up of the most rhythmic lines in the poem: "and momma's in the bedroom/with the door closed." You may want to touch lightly on the similarities this poem shares with the ballad tradition and comment on how this refrain effects a sense of closure in a poem that composes itself primarily according to the cadences of speech rhythms and fairly spontaneous thought patterns. The repetition of this line also lends a certain poignance to the speaker's voice. By the end of the poem we have a clear sense that she will not receive much help from the person who could be expected to help her while she is "hanging fire." You might ask how long one goes through life "hanging fire."

RICHARD LOVELACE, *To Amarantha, That She Would Dishevel Her Hair* (p. 811)

The plea of the poet is clear enough, almost from the title. You might ask whether the aesthetic of feminine attractiveness has changed any since Lovelace's time. Some students may have difficulty with the poem's syntax. In stanza II, Lovelace asks that his lover's hair fall as freely as the wind — which is characterized as a "calm ravisher" — thereby metonymically describing the young woman. "At the best" in stanza III means "at most." "See, 'tis broke!" in stanza V refers back to "day," and again by a process of association connotes the idea that Amarantha with her unbraided locks brings forth daylight and bliss.

ROBERT LOWELL, *Mr. Edwards and the Spider* (p. 812)

Lowell, himself of old New England stock (he was a distant relative of James Russell and Amy Lowell, although he rarely cared to admit it), here turns toward, or upon, the stern Calvinistic author of "Sinners in the Hands of an Angry God" (see the reference in line 10) and upbraids him for his harsh morality. An acidic irony introduced by "It's well" in line 24 informs Lowell's attitude toward Edwards's punitive faith. The same attitude is echoed in the last stanza, where the focus is upon the eternal punishment of Josiah Hawley. Here Lowell uses Edwards's rhetorical tactics and beats him at his own game. Implicit in the poem is the idea that one should find death easeful and untroubled, as do the spiders "urgently beating east to sunrise and the sea."

ARCHIBALD MACLEISH, *You, Andrew Marvell* (p. 813)

The underside of every *carpe diem* poem is an awareness of death, for it is the fading of youth and the possibility of death that motivate one to seize the day. The speaker of this poem is in a prone position, already feeling "the earthly chill of dusk." Yet, at least mentally, he travels to far-off and exotic places — in lines that might be compared with the first stanza of Marvell's "To His Coy Mistress" (p. 534). Discuss with the class the tone in the last stanza. Perhaps the speaker is more accepting of death's approach than was Marvell, for he has gone full circle and is part of a circular, not linear and terminal, movement. You might observe how the open-ended punctuation also enhances this theme.

CLAUDE McKAY, *America* (p. 814)

Compare this poem in terms of theme with Langston Hughes's "Harlem (A Dream Deferred)" (p. 803) and Percy Bysshe Shelley's "Ozymandias" (p. 848). You might also discuss with the class the inverted word order and why it strikes our ears now as forced and archaic. Still, some of the language difficulty could be explained by the fact that this is a Shakespearean sonnet that divides into two parts. The first half expresses McKay's "love" for "this cultured hell," despite the fact that he receives from it only the "bread of bitterness." In the second half McKay describes himself as a kind of mute rebel who foresees his country's decline and decay, even though he felt infused by its "vigor" only a few lines earlier. You might explore here the problem of coherence in poetry, and in class discussion try to work toward some resolution of the two parts of the sonnet.

CHRISTOPHER MARLOWE, *The Passionate Shepherd to His Love* (p. 814)

Marlowe was the first English dramatist to use blank verse in his plays. He completed a master of arts at Cambridge in 1587 and was stabbed to death six years later, having lived an eventful, though to some extent mysterious, life.

Anyone with an ounce of romance will respond favorably to this pastoral lyric, whose speaker pledges to do the impossible (yet how inviting to entertain the vision of "a thousand fragrant posies" on demand!) if only his beloved will be his love. What lovers have not believed, for a time at least, that they could "all the pleasures prove," that all the pleasure the world offered was there for the taking?

It's significant, of course, that his song is sung in May, the month when spring takes firm hold (in England, at least) and when the end of winter was (and still is) celebrated with great exuberance.

The nymph in Sir Walter Raleigh's "The Nymph's Reply to the Shepherd" (p. 834) calls Marlowe's shepherd's bluff. Considered the best of numerous replies to Marlowe's poem, Raleigh's lyric introduces us to a decidedly realistic nymph who mocks the shepherd's patently ludicrous promises, each of them, "in folly ripe, in reason rotten." She reminds her suitor that just as in nature winter always comes, so for life death always comes.

ANDREW MARVELL, *The Definition of Love* (p. 815)

This poem owes a debt to the elaborate conceits of Metaphysical poets such as John Donne, who established a tradition of enigmatic, often scientific, metaphors to describe difficult love relationships. Marvell's geometric images are clearly in this tradition. Draw students' attention to these images and to the terminology borrowed from geometry: "Angle, . . . Parallel" (lines 26–27), asking them what these terms tell us about the speaker and his notion of love. Relating the terms to the final stanza is difficult. You might ask the class how the first stanza prepares us for this final resolving opposition.

In a writing assignment, you might ask students to explore the images of "Conjunction" (31) and "Opposition" (32) in the poem. Before writing the essay, students should look these words up in the *Oxford English Dictionary,* determining how they relate to each other.

Connections

1. *Compare the speaker's images in this poem with those in Donne's "The Flea" (p. 775). How does the speaker's choice of comparisons for his love influence the tone of each poem? Do the poems share a similar view of love relationships?*

2. *Discuss Jonson's "Come, My Celia" as an alternative attempt to define love. How does Jonson's rhetorical technique in that poem compare with Marvell's here? Which poem is more persuasive? Why?*

EDNA ST. VINCENT MILLAY, *I Too beneath Your Moon, Almighty Sex* (p. 816)

One way to approach the complex development of this poem is to divide it into sentences. Ask students to talk about the first half of sentence 1 (lines 1–5), to decide to whom the speaker addresses her remarks. Is she talking about sexual desire or the female gender? You might note that she refers to the mythical symbol of woman, the moon, in her first line, and that her catcalls are symbols of sexual desire. In the second half of the first sentence (5–8), the speaker calls attention to herself as an object of others' attentions. What are they looking for? What do they find? What is the speaker's attitude toward them? She seems to fight them off in the definitive lines 9–10: "this tower; it is my own."

The most puzzling image in the poem is the tower, which the speaker leaves "for birds to foul and boys and girls to vex/with tittering chalk" (4–5), only to return to the image as if she had never abandoned it in line 10. The tower may be her own body, the home of her personality: "honest bone/Is there" (12–13), but it may also represent her poetic craft: "reared To Beauty" (11). Ask students if the tower in the first sentence is the same as this tower. The speaker seems to convince herself that the opinions of others are not as important as she once thought, leaving her work to be criticized or accepted by the end of the poem. The last line suggests a communion, perhaps with both her readers and her lovers. The tower may be simultaneously the poet's work and the poet.

Connections

1. Compare the implied "truth" in this poem with the idea of "truth" in Sharon Olds's "Sex without Love" (p. 902). Are these poems using sexual imagery with the same "truth" in mind?

2. Compare Millay's definition of love in this poem with Andrew Marvell's in "The Definition of Love" (p. 815).

EDNA ST. VINCENT MILLAY, *What Lips My Lips Have Kissed* (p. 816)

This poem is a lament for lost love and the passing of love and is quite perfect in its cadenced and rhymed expression. The long, stressed vowel sounds that end the lines reinforce the idea of pain. In lines 10–12 Millay introduces the image of a tree in winter, which will, we imagine, bud again in spring. Is this image to be a token of the future course of her love? Probably not, but the question should provoke some worthwhile discussion on the information-bearing function of metaphor in a poem.

JOHN MILTON, *Lycidas* (p. 817)

Born in London, Milton began writing poetry at the age of fifteen. He had a remarkable aptitude for languages, mastering Latin, Greek, Hebrew, and most modern European languages before he completed his education in 1637. After earning his Master's Degree from Christ's College, Cambridge in 1632, he disappointed expectations that he would become a minister, and embarked instead on a six year period of carefully self-designed study in which he read everything he could. (The eyestrain caused by his voracious study eventually led to his blindness in 1651.)

Milton dedicated his literary talent to the causes of religious and civil freedom during the years 1640 to 1660, writing Puritan propaganda and numerous political and social tracts. Milton argued vociferously on many issues: "Of Reformation Touching Church Discipline in England" (1641) denounced the episcopacy; his troubled relationship with seventeen-year-old Mary Powell, who left him after one month of marriage, inspired him to support the legalization of divorce in "Doctrine and Discipline of Divorce" (1643); "Areopagitica," (1644), one of his most famous polemics, argued the necessity of a free press; and his defense of the murder of King Charles I in "The Tenure of Kings and Magistrates" (1649), although contributing to his appointment as the secretary for foreign languages in Cromwell's government, nearly got him executed when the monarchy was restored in 1660.

He was arrested, but friends and colleagues intervened on his behalf, and he was eventually released. Blind and unemployed, he returned to his poetry and a quiet life with his third wife, Elizabeth Minshull. It was during these last years of his life that Milton produced (by dictating to relatives, friends, and paid assistants) his most famous and substantial works: the epic poems *Paradise Lost* (1667) and *Paradise Regained* (1671), and the verse drama *Samson Agonistes* (1671).

"Lycidas" is difficult and requires at least a full class period, possibly more, to explore its language and theme. Some sources to turn to for background information and critical analysis include J. H. Hanford, "The Pastoral Elegy and Milton's 'Lycidas,'" *PMLA* 24 (1910): 403–447; Rosemund Tuve, *Images and Themes in Five Poems by Milton* (Cambridge, MA: Harvard UP, 1957); John Reesing, *Milton's Poetic Art* (Cambridge, MA: Harvard UP, 1968); Jon S. Lawry,

"'Eager Thought': Dialectic in 'Lycidas,'" in *Milton: Modern Essays in Criticism,* ed. Arthur E. Barker (New York: Oxford UP, 1965).

JOHN MILTON, *On the Late Massacre in Piedmont* (p. 822)

This is a sonnet of accountability — in an almost bookkeeper sense of the term. The basic premise is contractual. The Waldenses have preserved piety and faith in God over four centuries; now God should avenge their massacre. *Even,* as the first word of line 3, is an imperative verb form, as in *Even the score.* Scorekeeping, in fact, matters in this sonnet, and students might find it a good exercise in reading to identify and analyze the numerical images here. Nature, moreover, is shown as sympathetic to the Waldenses, for it redoubles the sound of their lamentations. The passage ends with the elliptical phrase "and they/To heaven." Syntax again provides the verb *redoubled* and says, in effect, that the hills echoed the moans to heaven. Milton expresses the wish that future generations of Waldenses will augment their number "a hundredfold" to offset the Pope's power.

You might ask students to write an analytical and persuasive essay proving that this is either a plea for vengeance or the expression of a hope that the Waldenses will receive God's protection and strength throughout history.

JOHN MILTON, *When I consider how my light is spent* (p. 823)

This sonnet is sometimes mistakenly titled "On His Blindness." You might begin by asking just what the topic of Milton's meditation is. He seems to be at midlife, neither old nor young. If Milton's blindness comes to mind as the subject, does that idea accommodate itself to the description "And that one talent which is death to hide/Lodged with me useless"? It would take some ingenuity to make blindness the equivalent of "talent" here. Far better to let "talent" stand in its old (biblical) and new senses and refer to Milton's poetic capability. At any rate, a discussion of this sonnet should prove useful in developing students' ability to select or discard extraliterary details in connection with a poem.

MARIANNE MOORE, *Poetry* (p. 823)

Moore was editor of *The Dial,* a literary magazine, from 1925 until its demise in 1929, so if this poem at times sounds like a manifesto, it is probably because it shares in the self-consciousness of an American literary scene that was trying to establish its own identity and formulate a modernist aesthetic.

You might pair this poem with MacLeish's "Ars Poetica" (p. 911). Would MacLeish have liked "Poetry," or would he have found it too discursive, too much like prose? What precisely does Moore find objectionable about some poetry — possibly its stilted expressions, its overworked compulsion toward ornamentation, its "prettiness"? What do you suppose she means by "the genuine," and what images does she use to suggest it? The material after a colon usually explains the material preceding it. Is this the case at the beginning of stanza IV? Would Moore endorse the idea that anything can be material for a poem; what, if any, provisos or exceptions would she make?

These questions should help students begin to see not only what Moore is saying but also how similar the process of analysis can be in extracting ideas from either prose or poetry.

OGDEN NASH, *Very Like a Whale* (p. 824)

In order to savor fully Nash's biting wit, read this poem with Byron's "The Destruction of Sennacherib." One of the problems with the Byron poem is the light anapestic rhythm, which jangles with its serious theme. Nash most obviously spoofs metaphor here, in particular metaphors that are clichéd or inappropriate. More subtly, though hardly less humorously, he mocks other poetic shortcomings, such as meandering rhythm and rhymes that take forever to form and are repetitious ("many things/anythings") or are outrageously comic, such as the rhyme of "Tennyson" with "venison." This work also offers some occasion to talk about the persona that comes across in a poem. Despite the rhymed couplets and the control they exert over natural speech patterns, we suspect that on ordinary occasions the speaker of this poem might well rhyme "dimly" with "simile."

HOWARD NEMEROV, *Life Cycle of Common Man* (p. 825)

Ask the class to describe the associations summoned up by the title of this poem — a biology or sociology textbook, perhaps. The poem throughout invites a study of the language. Is the language at odds with Nemerov's attitude toward humankind, or is it complementary and supportive? Probably the latter. The poem divides into two parts. The first section portrays "man" as a being who can be and is "roughly figured" (both as a statistical analysis and as a representative of rude design). The poem turns on its heels in the final seven lines, where the diction is drawn from a more religious and spiritual realm. The energy for this about-face comes, apparently, from the earlier section on man's aptitude for uttering words — the quality, after all, that distinguishes him from the beasts.

Man, however comic he may at times seem, is still the bearer of the Word, and for that special ability, Nemerov ends his poem on a tone of muted grandeur. Although the Word (his language) may force him to eat "the world his apple," in so doing he partakes of consciousness and a Miltonic reinvestment in the Fall.

FRANK O'HARA, *Ave Maria* (p. 826)

This poem reads like an advertisement that advocates sex and violence for children. Once they have identified the playful, ironic tone of the speaker, students should be able to consider the issues the poem presents. O'Hara intimates that the soul grows in conditions like those of a movie theater: "in darkness, embossed by silvery images," but the tone of the poem becomes bitter and mocking when it discusses the results of leaving children to be parented by film stars.

Ask students to consider the way the speaker talks about the child whose identity is formed in the theater. Slang expressions such as "sheer gravy" (line 24), and the clichés such as "truly entertained" (25) give the poem its sales pitch tone, but they also incriminate the life represented by such language and visual images. In an essay, students might identify and explore the conversational elements here, which most effectively carry the poem's irony.

SIMON J. ORTIZ, *When It Was Taking Place* (p. 827)

The shifting notions of time in this poem produce the perfect mood for communicating an old man's alternately muddled and clear thinking. Amado's confusion does not undermine for us the man's intellect or value, rather, it illuminates our impatience with the elderly, and our failure to see their wisdom. But the poem is not just about old age; it shows how our notions of time are intensely personal, as when Amado "wonders/why the weather has changed so early (lines 13–14).

Notice that the poem slowly moves into the present, when, in stanza V, the old man's past becomes his present. Indeed, the man becomes as a child when he explains his childhood to his young grandson; the past takes place again and again in his memory. This is an opportunity for students to discuss the value of memory, and the details that bring memories alive in our writing. Ask them to think about what "was taking place" in this poem. Why would the poet spend so many lines to describe a seemingly obscure encounter?

WILFRED OWEN, *Anthem for Doomed Youth* (p. 829)

Owen was killed fighting in November 1918, just one month before the Armistice ended World War I. This poem treats with proleptic exactness his own doomed state. The sonnet states more or less that war as it is being waged creates its own death ceremony. In developing this idea, Owen skillfully blends sounds so that they onomatopoetically enhance image.

Consider, for example, "the stuttering rifles' rapid rattle" or the wailing shells that find an echo in "sad shires."

But Owen with his sharp, sarcastic edge (cf. his "Dulce et Decorum Est," p. 552) was not merely creating a pattern of sound and image here. He tips his hand with the word *mockeries* in line 5. Explore with the class what he may have had in mind when he used that word. Perhaps he was thinking of the rhetoric of nationalism and idealism encouraging people to enter into and sustain war or the clean-handed and distant pieties of the Church.

SYLVIA PLATH, *Daddy* (p. 830)

Read this poem aloud before you begin teaching it. That way the class will hear some of the insistent and bizarre nursery-rhyme repetitions of sound that hammer their way through it. The critic A. Alvarez describes "Daddy" as a love poem. That idea, given the tone and imagery, might surprise some students, but it can be related to Plath's own comment on her father's early death and her attempt to cut through the entanglements of a relationship that never had a chance to mature.

The person we need most to love but are unable to is the one most likely to be projected in an effigy of hatred. One wants to exorcise what one cannot embrace. The most memorable feature of this poem is the string of transformations Plath projects on the father. From the inorganic statue to the mythical vampire (killed by a stake "in" the heart), the transforming range could not be wider. In this imaginative process Plath begins to think that she is a Jew and that her father is with the German Luftwaffe and then with the armored tank division ("panzer-man"). She eventually connects him with Fascism and the sadomasochism of male aggression on women. The real picture of Otto Plath as teacher is suddenly rendered in Plath's mind as surreal — father as devil. The crescendo of memories and images reaches its peak when Plath recalls an earlier suicide attempt (one she described, in fact, in her novel *The Bell Jar*). She also seems to implicate her husband, the British poet Ted Hughes, in this memory, as she portrays him in the roles of torturer and vampire.

Plath is often described as a "confessional poet." Despite the highly idiosyncratic nature of this poem, what in it allows for a sharing of this personal experience with a wide and impersonal audience? What, if any, are the universal themes touched on here? You might develop one of these questions into a writing assignment.

SYLVIA PLATH, *Metaphors* (p. 832)

Miraculously, this poem is a self-reflective text with nine lines of nine beats each and a nine-letter title all addressing a nine-month phenomenon.

Riddles that focus on the idea of birth in all likelihood antedate King Oedipus; for birth itself, particularly to the woman carrying the child, is always a riddle — of that which is not me, yet of me; apart from me, and yet within. You might for a moment pause to consider the literary characteristics of riddles, with their paradoxes and the surprise and delight they engender when their answers are discovered.

This poem is useful too in discussing tone. The speaker here is self-jesting in her description and seems to accept with good grace the pregnancy's inexorable progress.

SYLVIA PLATH, *Morning Song* (p. 832)

The song the speaker hears here is her baby crying; yet this "morning song" is also Plath's poem, which seems to be more a meditation on the condition of parenthood than a lyric address to the child.

The poem is clear enough and should be examined for the precision of its images. The most challenging moment is the third tercet. "I'm no more your mother/Than the cloud [is]," Plath writes, and she seems to point to the kind of delicate otherliness and impenetrable independence that infants often project.

Examine the poem for its images and how they project mood and tone. Some class discussion can also be generated on the positive or negative connotations of the word *shadows* in line 6. Is it to be taken as the act of a protective covering, as though the infant sustained the parents, or should it be taken negatively, as a token of the parents' mortality? You might read this poem with Hall's "My Son, My Executioner" (p. 788).

EZRA POUND, *In a Station of the Metro* (p. 833)

Ezra Pound was born in Idaho and grew up outside Philadelphia, eventually attending the University of Pennsylvania. There he befriended William Carlos Williams and H.D. (Hilda Doolittle) and concentrated on his image as a poet (affecting capes, canes, and rakish hats) as well as on his studies. He later attended Hamilton College and returned to Penn for graduate work in languages, completing a master of arts in 1906. Two years later he moved to London, beginning a lifelong voluntary exile during which he worked as secretary to William Butler Yeats; began and abandoned numerous literary movements; started his "epic including history," *The Cantos*; lived in Paris, Venice, and Rapallo (Italy); furthered the literary careers of Hemingway, Joyce, Eliot, Frost, and Marianne Moore, among others; broadcast for Mussolini; and ended up under arrest for treason. Declared insane at his trial, Pound spent twelve years in a Washington, DC, hospital. Freed through the efforts of his writer-friends, Pound spent the rest of his life in Italy. Despite his glaring shortcomings, Pound is seen by many as the most technically accomplished poet and one of the most gifted critics of his generation.

Pound helped articulate the ideas of Imagism, one of his early efforts to "make it new." Although the halves of this poem work as if the second half were describing the first, each of the two lines possesses its own integrity as well as a capacity to make us see those faces.

EZRA POUND, *Portrait d'une Femme* (p. 833)

One issue that might provoke discussion about this poem is the relation of the speaker to his word portrait. How distanced is he from his subject? What is his emotional stance toward her: sympathy, pity, admiration — or perhaps all of these?

The Sargasso Sea with its swirl of currents is the locus of shipwrecks and thus the repository of treasure from past ages. The lady too is a treasure house of riches, with the gossip that she hears and stores as "strange spars of knowledge and dimmed wares of price." The woman's life is the embodiment of paradox: people come to her, yet she is passed over (as wife). The "slow float" of the words she receives is, in fact, "nothing"; yet it persists as her very substance.

It is worth some class time to comment on the sounds of certain lines. Line 26, for example, with its alliterative patterns is reminiscent of an Anglo-Saxon kenning.

EZRA POUND, *The River-Merchant's Wife: A Letter* (p. 834)

Although its title claims that its genre is epistolary, this poem is clearly historical as well. As she describes her childhood, the speaker uses particular verbs: "pulling, playing" (lines 2–4), which depict that period as active and life affirming. Ask students to identify the shift in tone signaled by her formal address to her husband: "My Lord you" (7). How does this indicate their changed relationship?

The second stanza expresses a deeply personal experience in few words. Ask students to describe the tone of the final line of the stanza. The speaker projects her grief on the world around her, and she renders this world in evocative images: "The monkeys make sorrowful noise overhead" (18). Ask students to explain why the speaker does not simply say, "I miss you." Why does this seem to be an inappropriate expression from this wife to her husband? Regardless of cultural custom, why would a metaphor sometimes work better to describe an intense emotional experience?

The images in the final stanza, like the monkeys in the third, express the speaker's grief. Ask students to categorize these images. They are autumnal, Western, dying images, which underline the speaker's reference to the passing of time: "I grow older" (25). What is the speaker's tone in the final lines? Is she hopeful, solemn, sad?

In a writing assignment, students might compare the images in the four stanzas.

Connection

1. *Compare the tone of the speaker in this poem with that of the speaker in Levertov's "The Ache of Marriage" (p. 810). How are the differences accentuated by the poems' forms? What, apart from simple differences in personality, might account for such drastically contrasting presentations of romance?*

SIR WALTER RALEIGH, *The Nymph's Reply to the Shepherd* (p. 834)

This poem is in response to Christopher Marlowe's "The Passionate Shepherd to His Love" (p. 814). The poem can be looked at alone, but students would probably like to know the first part of the conversation, as it were. Essentially, Raleigh mocks the pastoral tradition and its simplicities. Life with its hardships and temporal constraints is a much more difficult affair than the shepherd wants to admit.

The nymph (young maiden) proposes an impossible set of conditions to her love in the last stanza. Is she acting out of cruelty or out of a sense of reality?

In a writing assignment ask students to defend the argument of either the nymph or the shepherd.

DUDLEY RANDALL, *Ballad of Birmingham* (p. 835)

This poem offers a good opportunity to discuss how form can support theme. The simplicity of this ballad told in clear language enhances the stark horror of the bombing of the church where the children were worshiping. The mother's terror fills the penultimate stanza and narrows to the pathos of the single shoe that images her worst fear. If the daughter had gone downtown for the freedom march, she would have escaped the bombing, as the ballad ironically points out.

Fourteen years elapsed before a former Ku Klux Klansman, age seventy-three, was convicted and sentenced to life imprisonment for masterminding this bombing.

JOHN CROWE RANSOM, *Bells for John Whiteside's Daughter* (p. 836)

Robert Penn Warren has written about this poem in *Kenyon Review* 5 (1943): 238–40. Contrasted here are the stillness of death, "lying so primly propped" and the memory of the boundless, life-filled energy of this young girl, which made her seem a part of nature (clouds, pond, grass, geese) when she was alive.

ADRIENNE RICH, *Diving into the Wreck* (p. 837)

For various points of view on this poem, you might turn to essays by Wendy Martin and Erica Jong in the collection *Adrienne Rich's Poetry*, ed. Barbara Charlesworth Gelpi and Albert Gelpi (New York: Norton, 1975). There exists in this poem and in others by Rich a kind of monastic rigor that claims that the way down is the way out toward sexual and spiritual fulfillment. Rich (the speaker, we will assume) begins her descent with two instruments of truth and freedom (camera and knife), after "having read the book of myths" that would forewarn her of typical traps and distortions of belief. She seems to lose consciousness in stanza IV but maintains a relationship with the "deep element," or the sea, which is typically viewed as a feminine and self-generative force. Her journey seems to be propelled by the desire to examine the wreck of self, the elements suppressed or hidden inside her, the remnants still recoverable. As she says, "I came to see the damage that was done/and the treasures that prevail." She appears to discover what she came for by the eighth stanza, where she is mermaid and merman, an androgynous whole. The unity of selves seems secure, so much so that Rich can write, "We are, I am, you are . . . the one who find our way/back to this scene." At this juncture, she also declares her freedom from myths.

This poem is an allegorical journey toward self-identity. In at least one place Rich makes certain distinctions about what she is seeking: "the wreck and not the story of the wreck/the thing itself and not the myth." As a writing assignment, you might ask students to comment on these distinctions as they relate to the theme of the poem. They could be encouraged to comment also on how the nautical imagery enhances the allegory.

ADRIENNE RICH, *Living in Sin* (p. 839)

Levertov's "The Ache of Marriage" (p. 810), Raleigh's "The Nymph's Reply to the Shepherd" (p. 834), and this poem might be read together and mutually commented on. Students will enjoy the title and its ironic reversal in context with the poem. Rich was married at the time she wrote this, but her "sin" was to see through the myth of romantic bliss in a one-room flat to the harsh particulars of daytime reality. Compare the roles of the man and the woman here. What might be some of the "minor demons"?

The images in this poem are worth examining. In lines 4–6, for example, the romantic point of view becomes an artful still life, a painting by Renoir perhaps.

ADRIENNE RICH, *Rape* (p. 839)

This poem implies that when a woman has been raped (violated), she has nowhere to turn for retribution since the law, in both a secular and a religious sense, is the province of male authority. The first crime, committed by a "maniac" who knows no law, is followed by the second crime, wherein the woman is made to feel guilty for having been raped. Students should observe the male figures in the poem: rapist, cop, prowler, father, priest (confessor), even the stallion — and make note of the disquieting community of power and suppression that exists among them. The poem is also effective as a study in imagery and repetition. In terms of both devices "Rape" might be usefully compared with Plath's "Daddy" (p. 830).

EDWIN ARLINGTON ROBINSON, *Mr. Flood's Party* (p. 840)

Robinson published his *Collected Poems* in 1921 and was awarded the Pulitzer Prize that year. "Tilbury Town" is a mythical reimagining of Gardiner, Maine, where Robinson grew up.

In a discussion of this poem, you might ask students to characterize the attitude Robinson takes toward the title character. Consider especially the allusions to heroic figures.

Eben Flood's name is symptomatic of the man (ebb and flood), who is drowning himself in drink and losing his hold on the relationships that help sustain our lives. Flood is an old man when he conducts this dialogue of one (with "two moons listening" — stanza VI) in his town, "where strangers would have shut the many doors/That many friends had opened long ago." Discuss with students their attitude toward Flood and the overall tone of the poem. Do we regard Flood as pathetic and the poem as sentimental, or do we perceive the pathos of Flood's situation and buy into — if only for a moment — the chivalric portrait of the former man, who now, ghostlike, transposes jug into Roland's horn as he stands alone overlooking the town?

The gesture, the dialogue, the bravura show of gentility here are finally the death song of a man who senses his hold on life ebbing away. Robinson writes of the particular case, to be sure, but before concluding discussion of the poem look back with the class for instances where it seems to generalize toward the condition of all humankind, as, for example, in stanza IV's reference to "the uncertain lives of men."

EDWIN ARLINGTON ROBINSON, *New England* (p. 842)

The difference between New England, "here" (line 1), and "elsewhere" (4) is a matter of vitality and passion. New England, to this speaker, kills passion with its attention to religious rules for ideal behavior, signified by "Conscience" (12). Personification may be your focus here. Ask students to identify the non-human words that are given human qualities: "Passion," "Love," "Joy," "Conscience," "Care" (9–14). Contrast these personified virtues (and their effects) with the lively, pagan feast in the first stanza. How do the images there ("lyric yeast," "feast," "chalice," (4–7), compare with the virtues in stanza II? According to the speaker, which life is more socially beneficial? Why is the virtuous life so destructive? Note the cat "killed by Care" (14). What are the dangers of replacing passion with abstract principles such as "Care" and "Conscience"?

In a writing assignment, you might ask students to explore the speaker's point of view. Where does he place himself in relationship to New England? to elsewhere? He claims a simultaneous affinity with the place by calling it "Here," then speaks as if he were away from it in the second stanza: "We're told" (10).

Connections

1. *How does the speaker's description of New England compare with the speaker's description of her home in Clifton's "For De Lawd" (p. 764).*

2. *Compare this poem with Frost's "The Gift Outright" (p. 729). How does Frost's notion of U.S. geography and history differ from Robinson's?*

THEODORE ROETHKE, *I Knew a Woman* (p. 842)

In the first stanza of this poem, Roethke, rather than introducing this woman, cloaks her with veils of literary convention. One convention mocks another (cf. lines 5–7) so that the verse becomes self-parody. The chief attribute of this woman begins to grow clear, her quality of movement.

In stanza II, Roethke describes the courtship and tells what the lovers do when they are together. With the words *Turn, Counterturn,* and *Stand* — terms that are analogous to the strophe, antistrophe, and epode of the Pindaric ode — Roethke achieves the comedic effect of the mock heroic, for, surely, these high-toned literary terms have little to do with the lovers' courtship patterns. Roethke then undercuts his own grandiose use of language by describing the lover as though he were an animal, probably a horse, who could be commanded to turn and stand. The stanza degenerates, if that is the word, into puns of lovemaking.

In the third stanza the woman is stripped of literary convention — and anything else, for that matter. She is an enchantress, and alternately a flautist and flaunter of the lead she knows she can seek in this courtship. Roethke's woman is a radical departure from the demure, chaste, and passive beloved of an earlier day, and in the closing lines of this stanza she becomes movement personified.

You might ask the class in a writing assignment to read this poem with Marvell's "To His Coy Mistress" (p. 534) and describe some of the literary conventions as well as accepted notions about women these poems counter.

CHRISTINA ROSSETTI, *Uphill* (p. 843)

Students will probably be quick to catch the use of "journey" in this poem as a conventional symbol of life's progress toward death. You might speculate on why Rossetti calls this poem "Uphill," since that word implies a struggle rather than a reclining. You might also ask the class to characterize the second speaker. Does the speaker exist on this Earth? Is the speaker's language conversational in tone or ominously allegorical? Some students will probably point out that they have heard some of the phrases in this poem, such as "the very end," or "the slow dark hours," before.

DELMORE SCHWARTZ, *The True-Blue American* (p. 843)

Like America itself, this poem jostles together all categories of experiences and levels of language, so that the choice (between a sundae and a banana split) mocks — heroically — the sophisticated language used to describe that choice. A kind of comedy results, but, as Schwartz tells us, to be an American it is necessary to have a sense of humor.

Using vocabulary that echoes every American decree of ordained supremacy from the Puritan doctrine of souls elected to God's grace ("electing absolute affirmation") to the golden-tongued perorations of Manifest Destiny (the nation as chosen), Schwartz is saying here that America accepts no limits and never honors the implied limitation of choices. That is saying a great deal for the price of a sundae and a banana split.

ANNE SEXTON, *The Kiss* (p. 844)

This is a poem of ecstasy, of one saved by love. It opens with a simile that recalls the power of metaphor to shock metaphysically. You might take a moment in class to review a similarly compelling metaphor in Eliot's ". . . Prufrock" (p. 781), where the evening is described as "a patient etherized upon a table."

Sexton committed suicide in 1974 and had often suffered periods of deep depression. Here she is coming out of one of those periods; "old Mary" was her nickname for her darker self. You might discuss with the class her use of the two religious terms in the poem, *resurrection* and *elected,* both of which ensure an everlasting life. Her "resurrection" sounds a little facile ("Zing"), as though she were making a statement about electroshock therapy and its ability to cure the soul. The boat image in stanza III, though, seems more secure and offers a deeper tribute to the lover's power to heal.

The metaphysical sensibility does not cease with the opening line, and we hear the speaker describe the music her lover awakens in her as instruments "incurably playing." A final metaphysical pun comes as the composer-lover steps into the "fire" (of her passion, one presumes). This poem will be rewarding and highly accessible if students are provided with some insight into its religious vocabulary and metaphysical affinities.

ANNE SEXTON, *Lobster* (p. 845)

Sexton uses words normally associated with human behavior to describe the lobster. Ask students to identify and characterize the words describing the lobster. Why does the speaker compare it to a human being? Once she has humanized the lobster, she proceeds to recount his capture, noting the outside world's passive acceptance of this act in the repetition of "Somewhere far off." What events are happening beyond this one? How are they related (if they are) to the lobster's capture?

In lines 11–14 we get a glimpse of the lobster's point of view. But the intrusion of "they" in the final lines disrupts any peace in the poem, returning us to the harsh reality of the lobster's death. How does the speaker feel about this event? It isn't just an isolated occurrence to her but an example of our mass-produced, artificial society, which cannot comprehend the vantage point of a solitary nonhuman being. Students may best understand Sexton's social criticism by looking at "paint" (line 16). Do we really paint lobsters red? Why would she use this verb to describe what from the lobster's point of view is a violent transformation?

In a writing assignment, ask students to think about lines 11–14. How does this description of the lobster relate to what they see as the poem's "message"?

Connection

1. *Compare this poem with Lattimore's "The Crabs" (p. 557). How does each poet talk about the destruction of the environment for human pleasure? Pay special attention to the human/nonhuman distinctions in the poems.*

WILLIAM SHAKESPEARE (pp. 845–847)

Shakespeare's sonnets have been widely discussed. Some books that may offer useful observations on them include *A Casebook of Shakespeare's Sonnets*, ed. Gerald Willen and Victor B. Reed; Edward Hubler, *The Sense of Shakespeare's Sonnets* (Westport, CT: Greenwood, 1976); and *Shakespeare's Sonnets*, ed. with commentary by Stephen Booth (New Haven: Yale UP, 1977). The two songs given in this section, "Spring" and "Winter," are discussed by Bertrand Bronson in *Modern Language Notes* 63 (1948) and by C. L. Barber in *Shakespeare's Festive Comedy* (Princeton: Princeton UP, 1972).

PERCY BYSSHE SHELLEY, *Ozymandias* (p. 848)

Many students will have read this Petrarchan sonnet in high school. You might begin by asking whether in an unintentionally ironic way Ozymandias may have been right; although he is far from outdistancing the rest of humanity in possessions and power, his statue is a reminder that all things are subject to decay and is thus a source of despair. The sonnet, despite its familiarity, still surprises by the quality of its versification. Observe in line 6 the delayed placement of "well," which underscores the closing cautionary note. The final lines, moreover, with the alliterated "boundless and bare" and "lone and level" do suggest the infinite reaches of both the desert and time.

SIR PHILIP SIDNEY, *Loving in Truth, and Fain in Verse My Love to Show* (p. 848)

This sonnet's irregular meter matches its speaker's labored attempt to write it. Ask students to scan its lines, looking for irregularities. For example, the trochees at the beginnings of lines 1, 3, 4, 13, and so on illustrate the forced style that the speaker is trying to avert, while the irregular meter in line 9 aptly illustrates "words . . . halting forth."

Ask students to think about the images the speaker uses to describe his struggle to find the perfect writing style. His "sunburnt brain" (8) and the pregnancy metaphor ("great with child to speak," 12) evoke an overfull, overcooked speaker, who has worded too hard and gained little. How does the final line affirm our suspicions that there may be an easier way to write? Of course, Sidney has constructed his poem to make us feel this affirmation in the end.

Studies of this sonnet are included in the following discussions of *Astrophel and Stella* ("Loving in Truth" is the first sonnet in that sequence): David Kalsone, *Sidney's Poetry* (New York: Norton, 1970); Richard Lanham, "Pure and Impure Persuasion," and Collin Williamson, "Structure and Syntax in *Astrophel and Stella*" (both in Arthur Kinney, ed., *Essential Articles for the Study of Sir Philip Sidney* [Hamden, CT: Archon, 1986]).

Connection

1. *Discuss voice in this poem and in Herbert's "The Collar" (p. 794). How does the intrusion of another voice help resolve the conflict for each speaker? How do their conflicts compare?*

LESLIE MARMON SILKO, *Deer Song* (p. 849)

Much of the atmosphere of this dying song is created before we know what, exactly, the speaker is talking about. Ask students to categorize the images in the first two stanzas. Note how the initial images of whiteness and silence ("clotted white in silence," line 3) give way to the harsh "red froth tide" (12). The repeated *s*'s in the two stanzas also lend an air of solemnity to the scene. How does "choking" (11) disrupt this scene?

Note how the scenery becomes gloomier as the speaker moves toward the dying deer. The tone becomes more meditative and contemplative. Ask students if they sense a changed tone when the deer begins to speak ("Do not think that I do not love you/if I scream," 21–22). Here the images become simultaneously more violent and obscure: "the struggle is the ritual/shining teeth tangled in/sinew and flesh" (26–28). Is the "you" of the final stanzas the audience? If so, what kind of human-animal relationship is established in these lines?

You might assign an essay that discusses the various "shades" in the poem. How does the interplay of darkness and light develop its concerns?

Connection

1. Compare this poem with Wilbur's "The Death of a Toad" (p. 621). How does each poem discuss something larger than the death of an animal? Why would a poet write about such an event? How do sound patterns establish tone in the early lines of each poem? Is there a shift in either or both in later stanzas?

W. D. SNODGRASS, *April Inventory* (p. 850)

It can be a disquieting experience to bring to class a poem that means something to you, only to find that it does not generate the same response in your students. First- or second-year students might, for example, find the distinction between "solid scholars" (specialists) and any other professors in the field hard to discern. The difference between the speaker of the poem and the specialist seems to depend on choices made and an outwardly controlled image of success. The specialists publish in a narrow field; the true humanist, according to the poem, gives learning to others. As the speaker implies in stanza VII, that learning may also require a relaxing of the code against emotional expression. From here to the end of the poem, the speaker vacillates between the specialist and humanist modes of conduct. He concludes, however, with the observation that "there is a gentleness survives." This poem is a fine example of a meditation in progress, and it illustrates well the passages of development that continue to occur long after we achieve so-called adult status.

You might ask students in a brief essay to make their own inventory of typically "feminine" virtues (gentleness, for example) that appear praiseworthy in this poem.

GARY SNYDER, *After weeks of watching the roof leak* (p. 851)

Because of its brevity this poem is ideal for a discussion of the importance of every word. Ask students to define all the words in the poem and discuss how they are related to one another. They may move to consider the form of the poem; it looks like its subject matter — a board. Direct their attention to the position of "I" (line 2). Why is this pronoun so important to the interpretation of the poem? Note the inverted grammar of the sentence; lines 1 and 3 are prepositional phrases, whereas the main clause is the second line.

A poem of this length provides an excellent opportunity to show students how much they can say about a very short poem. Ask them to free-write, making connections between the words and lines of the poem, trying to figure out what the speaker is attempting to express. Then you might move them into small groups, where they can share their writing with their peers, working on a main topic for a formal essay.

Connection

1. Discuss this poem's similarities to Williams's "The Red Wheelbarrow" (p. 668). Is Williams's speaker less or more abstract than Snyder's? How does point of view establish the tone and theme of each poem?

GARY SNYDER, *Hay for the Horses* (p. 852)

Could this be described as a "found" poem, a scene and a tag end of conversation set down as a poem? Propose this notion to the class, and see what they can tell you about image, rhythm, stress pattern, and the like.

WALLACE STEVENS, *Disillusionment of Ten O'Clock* (p. 852)

Wallace Stevens grew up in Reading, Pennsylvania, attended Harvard (without completing a degree), and eventually earned a law degree. He began a lifelong career with the Hartford Accident and Indemnity Company in 1916. His first book was *Harmonium,* published in 1923. Stevens spent most of his life in virtual isolation from the literary scene, although he kept up an active correspondence with Marianne Moore, William Carlos Williams, and others. His *Collected Poems* appeared in 1954.

French Symbolist poets were well aware of the suggestive potential of color, and this short lyric continues their tradition. The class should begin to see the "white night-gowns" as quiescent banners of cautious living and 10:00 P.M. bedtimes. The inner lives of the people in this poem are so blank they don't even dream; hence they are disillusioned. The only person in the poem whose imaginative and dream life still flourishes is the old sailor, "Drunk and asleep in his boots." The poem is more suggestive than directly symbolic, and its color words ("red weather," for example) should intimate ideas but not be pressed for direct correlatives.

WALLACE STEVENS, *The Emperor of Ice-Cream* (p. 853)

Even more than a parting word to the old woman about to be buried, this poem is a celebration of her mourners, who could still touch imagination's fire despite their impoverished surroundings. By covering the woman in her own embroidered winding sheet ("fantails" here are fantail pigeons), transforming the cigar roller into ice-cream creator, and gathering together like extras in a film extravaganza, they celebrate and affirm the gaudy, bawdy vitality of their lives, together with their creative power to "let be be finale of seem." As a note, "deal" is furniture made of cheap wood, lacquered over to look more expensive.

You may want to ask students why the emperor of ice-cream is an emperor. Is this an indication that he knows how to move people through the pleasure principle, perhaps?

WALLACE STEVENS, *Sunday Morning* (p. 853)

For readings of this poem (and others by Stevens in this text), consult Ronald Sukenick's *Wallace Stevens: Musing the Obscure* (New York: New York UP, 1967) and Helen Vendler's *On Extended Wings* (Cambridge, MA: Harvard UP, 1969).

Briefly stated, this is an elegiac meditation, resonating with the autumnal tones of Keats and progressing by means of dialogue between the somber-voiced narrator, who knows loss, and the narrator's alter ego (a woman), who searches for her secular heaven.

Section I reflects the woman's nostalgia for a principle of faith that reaches beyond her paganlike material comforts. Section II is her attempt to expunge this concern about faith and cherish instead her earthly pleasures and passions. In section III, with the mention of Jove, the speaker entertains the idea of a conflation of earth and heaven. In section IV the woman questions whether the earthly paradise could last. In section V she still maintains her desire for the dream of some imperishable bliss. In section VI the narrator offers the argument that the very transitoriness of this earthly paradise provides it with the pulse to change. "Death is the mother of beauty," the force that makes way for change. Section VII is the pagan counterpart to the pluckings of the "insipid" paradisal lutes in section VI and an acknowledgment of mortality. The final section of the poem, after its elegiac celebration of life, returns to the pagan order of things and effects a response to the natural mortal world unprotected by the promise of everlasting life. The final image, so elegant in its sense of downward glide, analogizes the most harmonious attitude toward death and dying.

As a writing assignment you might ask students to analyze why the speaker turns at the poem's end to the pagan and natural worlds. Why are these more habitable, human realms? How does the poem anticipate and prepare for this final direction?

WALLACE STEVENS, *Thirteen Ways of Looking at a Blackbird* (p. 856)

The idea of this poem is that the blackbird shapes whatever landscape it appears in. Reality is not absolutely measurable but is relative to both the perceiver and the perceived. But even though this poem calls on the power of the mind's eye to shape reality, Stevens in section VII seems to chide those men of Haddam (a town in Connecticut) who would seek only the extraordinary golden birds from some Yeatsian realm and overlook the beauty of reality around them.

It is probably well to keep in mind two ideas when teaching this poem: don't try to overexplicate and constrict the poem's resonance with too many specifics, and don't expect too much or try to do too much with this poem on a first reading. For some students understanding of this poem will grow as their critical and imaginative faculties develop.

ALFRED, LORD TENNYSON, *Crossing the Bar* (p. 858)

The experience of reading a poem through, then rereading it, shows how words change from neutral description to rhetorical persuasion. Line 3 in this poem, for example, can refer to sailing conditions or funeral etiquette. The rhythms and rich assonance here make it possible to retain multiple levels of meaning.

ALFRED, LORD TENNYSON, *Tears, Idle Tears* (p. 858)

This is probably one of Tennyson's best-known lyrics and reflects his usual themes of autumnal despair. You might read it in connection with Shelley's "Ode to the West Wind" (p. 656) or Keats's "To Autumn" (p. 701) for some changes in perspective. The image of approaching death (stanza III) seems to be one of the most effective here.

ALFRED, LORD TENNYSON, *Ulysses* (p. 859)

Tennyson was only twenty-four when he wrote this monologue, magnificently creating the thoughts that must have plagued this hero who had striven with the gods. The poem is written in blank verse and preserves a certain conversational eloquence through its use of parallelism. Consider the infinitives in "How dull it is to pause, to make an end,/To rust unburnished, not to shine in use!" (lines 22–23). Ulysses seems to be passing on his power and authority to his son Telemachus, who will, apparently, have a gentler, less warlike (though no less important) kind of work to do. You might ask the class what they suppose Ulysses has in mind when he says in the final stanza, "Some work of noble note, may yet be done." Could this poem bear some autobiographical reflection on the life of a poet? This question could prompt a brief research paper.

DYLAN THOMAS, *Fern Hill* (p. 861)

Fern Hill is an actual place, a farm in Wales once owned by Ann Jones, Thomas's aunt. It was a childhood haunt, and Thomas speaks of it here in Wordsworthian high style, celebrating this spot of green innocence in his memory. *Grace, Holiness, Loveliness:* Thomas never hesitates to use these words that later generations shy away from in embarrassment, and for that reason alone his work is worth sharing with students.

His picture of this farm is truly Edenic — it is like "the first, spinning place," and it is remembered as a place that held unconscious innocence ("Nothing I cared, in the lamb white days"). But even innocence is no guard against the passage of time, and the speaker, though he sings like the sea, is still caught in the chains of time, could not, in fact, sing otherwise.

ROBERT WALLACE, *The Double-Play* (p. 862)

You might in teaching this poem ask the class the following questions: In the terms of the game, what literally happened? (Outs were made at second, then first base.) For what other reason is this poem called "The Double-Play"? (Words are object, then subject of the sentence or phrase; from their syntactic position, they demonstrate a double play.) For a clear example, examine how "the ball" is used in the second tercet. Does this syntactic double play serve any purpose? (It does, for it suggests the split-second fluidity of motion and the quick redirection of the ball necessary to make the double play.) Overall, the poem suggests analogically the relation of baseball to poetry — another sort of double play.

EDMUND WALLER, *Go, Lovely Rose* (p. 863)

Metaphor can be the subject of a class discussion of this poem. The personified rose is ordered to perform the speaker's duty of convincing his beloved to "come forth" and accept praise. The praise, though, is enclosed in the metaphoric association of her with the rose. You might ask students to consider this poem as a lesson in how metaphor works. How does the speaker direct the rose to act?

In stanza II, the rose and the beloved become interchangeable. Ask students why they think the speaker makes the shift to the desert. What does this tell us about his beloved? Why might she shun praise? Line 15, "And not blush so to be admired," presents a paradox. Students will enjoy figuring out that the woman blushes, looking like a rose, but she is supposed to take her flattery (a comparison of her to a rose!) more easily, which would make her pale, and unlike the rose. The final stanza concludes this persuasion to love, with a warning to the woman. What is the speaker trying to urge her to do? How does the rose figure in the persuasion?

In an essay you might ask students to characterize the tone and diction in the poem. What vocabulary or vocabularies does the speaker draw from to persuade his love to rush into his arms?

Connections

1. *Discuss the similarities between this poem and Herrick's "To the Virgins, to Make Much of Time" (p. 532). Pay particular attention to the image of the rose in each. Does it function in exactly the same way in both poems? How does the function of the rose contribute to the effect of the speaker's appeal?*

2. *Wilbur's "A Late Aubade" (p. 536) is another poem in the* carpe diem *tradition. Read it as a reply to Waller's. How does Wilbur manipulate the conventions Waller uses, bringing a modern tone to an old form?*

WALT WHITMAN, *The Dalliance of the Eagles* (p. 863)

Still the best guide to Whitman's poetry is James E. Miller, Jr.'s *A Critical Guide to Leaves of Grass* (Chicago: Chicago UP, 1957). Miller treats this poem as a precursor to Imagism and discusses its sound patterns as well as its imagery fairly extensively. The eagles, as Miller observes, merge in a moment of union but do not lose their individual identities.

This is a poem that probably ought to be read aloud in class, and some time should be taken to discuss how the sound of words can almost suggest the physical sensation of the meaning they intend to convey. Note, for example, the hard *c-* and *g*-sounds, and the plosive sound of *b* in lines 4 and 5 describing the fierce, aggressive, and wild "dalliance." Later on, after the union described in lines 6 through 8, the line rounds out with long vowel sounds and the echo of more liquid sounds in words such as "falling" and "lull," as well as "motionless still balance" and "talons loosing." The poem is composed of a single sentence. You might discuss with the class why Whitman did not break up his narration of this sight into shorter verse sentences. No doubt the swiftness, the sense of time caught and held, and the release into the upward course of continued flight all would have been compromised by a more fragmented account.

WALT WHITMAN, *One's-self I Sing* (p. 864)

This poem opens *Leaves of Grass* and is a kind of bugle announcement of several of Whitman's fondly held themes: the individual as both separate and a member of the democratic community; the equality of the sexes; the importance of both body and soul; the "divinity" of modern humanity, who were not subject to kingly law. Some students will probably hear echoes of the opening lines of a traditional epic poem. Whitman is inverting epic convention somewhat by not singing of arms and men with the requisite bowings to the gods, but hailing the individual self.

As a writing assignment you might ask the class to describe how and why this brief poem is a good opening for a book of poems. You might also ask students to say what seems particularly American about the poem.

WALT WHITMAN, *There Was a Child Went Forth* (p. 864)

The idea is fairly direct and clear in this poem: we are what we have experienced. The class might like to talk about the validity of Whitman's psychological insight. Do we not also change by our actions and perceptions the world around us? A few aspects of the poem's language may need some clarification. Whitman long admired the Quaker faith — from a distance — and he borrowed the Quaker manner of naming the months ("Third-month" for March, and the like). The poem makes long lists of what the child became, and these lists are an example of Whitman's famous (or infamous) catalogs. Catalogs seem to work in this poem, which tries to scan the making of a life in all its varied elements; moreover, the repetition of certain words (*and, the*) gives the long lines a unifying of biblical rhythm and parallelism.

The growth of the child does not seem to end with the poem's conclusion but goes on as though this were a work in progress. Explore with the class the manner in which the details of the natural landscape reinforce this idea of continuing growth.

RICHARD WILBUR, *Love Calls Us to the Things of This World* (p. 865)

You might begin a discussion of this poem by talking about how a poet controls and convinces us of the truth of metaphors. Wilbur spends some time describing the motions of the wind-tossed laundry in order for us to see the laundry as "angels," and thus offer his prayer (lines 21–23) for a Heaven on Earth.

To live as soul in a mock Heaven would be incomplete, to say the least. The soul, like someone trying to sleep in awhile longer, resists the "punctual rape" of the day, which calls the soul back into the world of business and reality. Only when the sun rises does the soul out of "bitter love" join with the waking body and take down the laundry, an image for Heaven. As it dismantles Heaven, it clothes this daily world, without moral consideration for who wears the laundry — itself an act of graciousness and love. The nuns "keeping their difficult balance" suggest both the literal act of walking and the spiritual act of mediating between things of this world and things of the next.

You might review in class discussion phrases such as "punctual rape" (19), "every blessed day" (19), and "bitter love" (26).

RICHARD WILBUR, *Praise in Summer* (p. 866)

This poem of praise takes a while to get to the point. Ask students to talk about the syntax of the first six lines. Why does the speaker seem to qualify his every statement? Why is he reluctant to speak directly about his subject? Lines 7–8 provide a clue to his hedging. Students may realize that this evaluation comes in the middle of the sonnet. How does "uncreation" (8) develop the theme of nature versus art? Is the poet trying to arrive at his point through negation? How do "wrenching" and "awry" (9) illustrate the speaker's own abstractions and convoluted syntax?

The conversational tone of the poem ("I said," 2, 5) contributes to the distance from its subject by distancing the audience; the speaker tells us of a conversation he has already had with someone else. Ask students to consider this conversation in conjunction with the question in lines 10–11 and 11–14. Does the speaker arrive at a conclusion in these questions? Perhaps he realizes that the simple image, the question instead of the statement, the linking of the human and the natural, give him a more satisfying form of praise than his initial attempt, in the first half of the sonnet.

In a writing assignment, ask students to think about the evolution of a mode of "praise" in the poem. They might begin by looking at the final three lines. What is the speaker asking us to consider? What does the question say about "praise in summer"? Trace the alternative attempt at praise in lines 3–6. Why would the speaker use the word *instead* (7) to describe his first attempt at praise?

Connections

1. *Compare the conversational elements in this poem with those in Frost's "The Pasture" (p. 713). Being careful not to simplify either poem, discuss how each attempts to erase its artifice, to invite its audience to a firsthand experience of nature.*

2. *How does E. E. Cummings's "in Just —" (p. 664) capture the immediacy of the season it describes? Imagine for a moment that Wilbur wrote his poem in response to Cummings's. Is there an "instead" in Cummings's poem? How might Wilbur criticize Cummings's depiction of the season?*

RICHARD WILBUR, *A Simile for Her Smile* (p. 867)

The simile in this poem is rendered with delightful and surprise-filled ingenuity. Comment first on the title and the fortunate pattern of *simile* and *smile.* The situation the poet experiences is exquisite calm in the midst of a highway headache, when suddenly the traffic halts to let the graceful paddleboat slip through the locks. That moment of unanticipated calm is like his lover's smile, or at least the thought of it.

Notice the sound patterns in the later portion of the poem that seem to "smile": *slip, slip, silken, sides, clear bells, paddle wheels.* They do, indeed, contrast with the nasty traffic, which sits "massed and staring."

WILLIAM CARLOS WILLIAMS, *The Dance* (p. 867)

You might ask the class some of the following questions: If you could not see a copy of Breughel's picture *The Kermess,* what could you infer about the people it depicts from a reading of this poem? Why do you suppose Williams describes this picture as "great"? What is there in Williams's diction that shows he shares an affinity with Breughel?

Another suggestion: Tap out the rhythm of some of the lines of the poem in order to hear and feel the dance. Could Williams have been punning on *impound* in line 6?

WILLIAM CARLOS WILLIAMS, *Spring and All* (p. 867)

All sounds a good deal like *fall,* and indeed there is something autumnal about Williams's chill spring, with its "reddish/purplish" bushes and "dead, brown leaves." But these tokens of death actually bespeak a quickening life of the season that connotes rebirth. The images of human birth are not far from Williams's mind in this poem, as he talks about the nameless "they" who come into the world naked. Syntactically "they" (line 16) stands for the vegetation of grass, wild carrot leaf, and the rest (all), but we do not know this until after the pronoun appears. Williams can thus have it both ways and point to both a human and a nonhuman world.

Williams's spring, like so many of his subjects, is earth rooted, literally. No surface change here; this is "profound" change "rooted" far down, so that life springs forth from its depths.

You might ask the class whether there is any significance in the setting of the poem — by the road to the contagious hospital.

WILLIAM CARLOS WILLIAMS, *This Is Just to Say* (p. 868)

Three possible writing assignments can be organized around this poem: (1) An essay talking about line breaks, necessary brevity, and careful word choice that validates this seemingly conversational statement as poetry. (2) A found poem, using a scrap of conversation or some lines from a short story, to make a poem about the length of this one. (3) A parody of this poem.

WILLIAM WORDSWORTH, *I Wandered Lonely as a Cloud* (p. 868)

In his preface to the *Lyrical Ballads,* Wordsworth describes poetry as "the spontaneous overflow of powerful feelings: it takes its origin from emotion recollected in tranquillity." To some extent, this quotation explains the "wealth" that Wordsworth alludes to in line 18, for while reclining on his couch he can recall the heightened sense of pleasure the daffodils first brought him. From his mood of loneliness he moves to a state of gladness. What else characterizes how the daffodils appear to him? Seemingly, they are a token of cosmic splendor in their extensiveness and golden sparkle.

WILLIAM WORDSWORTH, *She Dwelt among the Untrodden Ways* (p. 869)

One of the difficulties and joys of teaching Wordsworth is the starkness of his landscapes and the deceptive simplicity of his characters. To enhance students' appreciation of this poem, encourage them to examine each stanza word by word, determining the connotations of each. They will notice that the natural images become simultaneously more specific and more universal from the first to the second stanza, that the landscape emphasizes the solitude of both Lucy and the speaker. Ask them why a single violet beside a mossy stone relates to Lucy.

The crux of the poem is the word *difference* in the final line. The absence of a single human being makes the speaker's world different, more solitary, more isolated within his own consciousness. Ask students to think about the dichotomy between the unknown and known in line 9. This speaker considers the limits of his own existence as he discusses the death of another human being. Ask the class to look closely at the parameters he establishes for this discussion. What are the limits of his world?

In an essay, have students consider the first and last words of the poem. What is the significance of the movement from *she* to *me*?

Studies of the "Lucy Poems" are included in the following general discussions of Wordsworth's poetry: Frances Ferguson, *Wordsworth: Language as Counter-Spirit* (New Haven and London: Yale UP, 1977); David Ferry, *The Limits of Mortality* (Middleton, CT: Wesleyan UP, 1959); and David Perkins, *Wordsworth and the Poetry of Sincerity* (Cambridge, MA: Belknap, Harvard UP, 1964).

Connection

1. *Compare Wordsworth's treatment of mortality here with Keats's in "When I have fears that I may cease to be" (p. 681). Pay particular attention to the natural images in each poem. What is each speaker's relationship to nature? How does this influence their presentations of mortality?*

WILLIAM WORDSWORTH, *A Slumber Did My Spirit Seal* (p. 870)

This is one of Wordsworth's "Lucy" poems, and the "she" in line 3 alludes to Lucy. Apparently, this poem marks a loss for which the poet was unprepared. He was asleep to the possibilities of aging and death, and Lucy now seems well beyond the province of earthly years and more the spirit of eternal time. Is there a paradox in this poem? Probably so. The speaker's dream, which he had had in a more pleasant period, when he felt that they were both beyond the effects of time, turns out to be for Lucy ironically accurate, for, like the rocks and stones and trees, she is now unaffected by the passage of time.

WILLIAM WORDSWORTH, *The Solitary Reaper* (p. 870)

This poem seems to spill over its limits as fit lyric to become a spontaneous overflow of powerful feeling. Ask the class to note how many boundaries are exceeded here. In stanza I, for example, the song overflows the vales. In the final stanza the song seems without end, and the hearer hears it long after he leaves the singer behind. Implied too in the second and third stanzas is the song's capability to transcend place and history. As with other poetic figures of Wordsworth, this solitary reaper and her song provide a way into perceiving an order of existence beneath the surface. You might ask the class if it matters at all that the singer is female.

JAMES WRIGHT, *Lying in a Hammock at William Duffy's Farm in Pine Island, Minnesota* (p. 871)

For a writing assignment ask students to examine the imagery in this poem and tell how Wright means what he says in the final line.

SIR THOMAS WYATT, *They flee from me* (p. 871)

One of the challenges of this poem is its ambiguous subject matter. Students will want to pin down "they" in stanza I. What is their relationship to "she" in the second stanza? First, ask students what "they" are like. Their comparison to wild animals and their subservience to the speaker ("take bread at my hand," line 6) perhaps tell you more about him than about them. The final line of the stanza describes the subjects of his poem, but in some sense it describes the speaker's tone as well. Ask students how this is the case in the second and third stanzas.

How does the speaker's domination of his subject lapse into subservience to the woman in stanza II? Her question to him ("Dear heart, how like you this?") brings her voice into the poem, muffling the speaker's attempts to control her with his own voice in the first stanza. Ask students what kind of woman he describes. How do her clothes reflect his notion of the ideal woman? Her frailty and filmy attire make her into a sex object rather than a real character in the scene. This view is confirmed by the first line of the third stanza. In what sense is she the proverbial woman of his dreams?

The tone of the third stanza is bitterly ironic. Who does the speaker blame for his desertion? He claims that his "gentleness" turned the woman away. If the woman is indeed a wild animal, as is intimated in the first stanza, then the speaker vindicates himself by painting her as unreceptive to his human softness. The words "strange" (17) and "newfangleness" (19) suggest that the woman will move on to other lovers. The final line judges her actions harshly, blaming her for the speaker's woe. Ask students to look closely at the word "served" (20). Who is serving whom? Is Fortune the enemy here, or is the woman? How does this issue relate to the images of taming and submission earlier in the poem?

In a writing assignment, ask students to categorize the images in the poem. How does the speaker's diction affect his tone? What, for example, does a word like "deserved" (21) tell you about the speaker's attitude toward the woman? toward himself?

Critical discussions of this poem include Ann Berthoff's "The Falconer's Dream of Trust: Wyatt's 'They Flee from Me,'" *Studies in the Renaissance,* (Winter 1962) and Robert Twombly's "Beauty and the (Subverted) Beast: Wyatt's 'They Flee from Me,'" *Texas Studies in Literature and Language* 10:4 [1969]: 489–503. For background information on Wyatt, see Patricia Thomson's *Sir Thomas Wyatt and His Background* (Stanford, CA: Stanford UP, 1964).

Connections

1. *Discuss the relationship of speaker to beloved in this poem and in Sidney's "Loving in Truth, and Fain in Verse My Love to Show" (p. 848). Are the speakers looking for different things in their laments? How do the sound patterns in each affect the meaning?*

2. *Compare the images used to describe the woman in Herrick's "Delight in Disorder" (p. 632) and those in Wyatt's poem. Look for similarities in diction. Write an essay in which you discuss the image of woman developed in each poem.*

WILLIAM BUTLER YEATS, *Adam's Curse* (p. 872)

This poet is addressing Yeats's beloved, Maud Gonne. "That beautiful mild woman" is Gonne's sister, Kathleen. The idea at the poem's center is that with Adam's curse nothing can be achieved except by hard labor. Indeed, all is work, including the making of poems and the nurturing of beauty in women. Natural images reflect the failing of the love between the speaker and his beloved. We hear then the final bitter victory of Adam's curse: the demise of the tradition of the courtier and "the old high way of love." The study of books, the craft of letters, and the demeanor of high courtesy — all have been made to seem trivial, and as a result the grace of this continuing courtship can find no validation for its style.

Maud Gonne married Major MacBride a year after this poem was written.

WILLIAM BUTLER YEATS, *Crazy Jane Talks with the Bishop* (p. 873)

Tradition has it that the fool is the purveyor of truth, and Crazy Jane, whose retort to the Bishop that "fair needs foul," is no exception. The paradoxical mutualities that Crazy Jane endorses find other correspondences in the last stanza, where the romantic ideal of love, we are told, pitches its mansion in "the place of excrement." Puns on *sole* and *whole* also invite a commingling of the platonic with the blatantly physical. According to John Unterecker, the bishop in the poem was a divinity student turned down by Jane for Jack the Journeyman. The bishop banished Jack, but Jane remained true to him (*A Reader's Guide to William Butler Yeats* [New York: Noonday, 1959]).

WILLIAM BUTLER YEATS, *The Lake Isle of Innisfree* (p. 873)

Like Wordsworth, who lived with the recalled sight of daffodils or the reaper's song always with him, Yeats carried with him "in the deep heart's core" the sound of waves at Innisfree. The mention of the bean rows in this poem is in conscious imitation of Thoreau and his experiment in living at Walden Pond. Yeats recounts a most citified occasion for the poem's composition in London, not in Ireland, as follows: "I was going along the Strand and, passing a shop window where there was a little bell kept dancing by a jet of water, I remembered waters about Sligo and was moved to a sudden emotion that shaped itself into 'The Lake Isle of Innisfree'" (*Memoirs* [New York: Macmillan, 1972], 31).

WILLIAM BUTLER YEATS, *Leda and the Swan* (p. 874)

Some references in this poem might require clarification: the offspring of Leda and Zeus (as swan) was Helen, the most beautiful of women, who married Menelaus but was later awarded to Paris. Paris took her to Troy with him, thus occasioning the Trojan War and the death of Agamemnon, the leader of the Greeks. Agamemnon was married to Clytemnestra, Helen's sister.

According to Yeats's view, this rape marks a turning point in history and the downward spiraling of the gyres. The moment is dark and fraught with the onset of much tragedy that Leda cannot possibly know, yet she does seem to take on a measure of Zeus's power and come closer to assuming a consciousness of the divine than is ordinarily possible.

WILLIAM BUTLER YEATS, *Sailing to Byzantium* (p. 875)

Byzantium, in historical terms, was the capital of the Eastern Roman Empire and was the holy city of Greek orthodoxy. Explore with the class what Byzantium symbolically represents, especially in terms of Yeats's career as a poet. In a note to the poem, Yeats commented, "I have read somewhere that in the Emperor's Palace at Byzantium was a tree made of gold and silver and artificial birds that sang" (*The Collected Poems of William Butler Yeats* [New York: Macmillan, 1972], 453). Increasingly in his later poems, Yeats turned to art rather than nature as a means of transcending time.

Ask the class in a writing assignment to compare the speaker in this poem with the speaker in Stevens's "Sunday Morning" (p. 853), who claims, "But in contentment I still feel/The need of some imperishable bliss."

WILLIAM BUTLER YEATS, *The Second Coming* (p. 876)

The pattern here of the falcon circling around the falconer indicates the pattern of the gyre, now tracing its widest circle and thus least subject to the control of the falconer. "Mere anarchy" is loosed on a world troubled by recent wars (World War I and the Russian Revolution of 1917). Yeats himself later claimed he was describing the rise of Fascism in Europe. What kind of order will assume its place over the next two thousand years, if the nature of that world is imaged by a description of the annunciating beast as blank, pitiless, and rough?

You might in a writing assignment ask the class to compare this poem with Hardy's "Channel Firing" (p. 790). Both take a long and apocalyptic view of history. Does one poet hold out more hope than the other for the world's survival?

AN ALBUM OF WORLD LITERATURE

The poems in this section give students an opportunity to experience over one hundred years of world literature written from often contradictory perspectives. The poems range from general comments on modern sensibility to more specific pleas for relief from the political upheaval that has torn apart many of the countries represented. Although it is hardly necessary to teach them chronologically, the poems do present some of the major historic events of the twentieth century, including the two World Wars, the Russian Revolution, the Spanish Civil War, and the revolutions that have racked Central and South American countries in the latter part of the century.

Charles Baudelaire offers a harrowing vision of our time, focusing on the bleakness of our surroundings and on the depravity in ourselves. Sappho presents a contradictory view, from two thousand years earlier, of love as the predominant human problem and joy. Tracing the effects of the Russian Revolution through the perspective of a ghost, Anna Akhmatova suggests that an apparition may be the only way to ground ourselves in such turmoil and change. Federico García Lorca calls on his folk tradition to frame the violence he sees.

In different ways each poet acknowledges that history is not outside us but within us, shaping our sense of reality. Pablo Neruda reminds us that we can enhance life by appreciating one of the simplest and most pleasurable aspects of physical experience: taste. In contrast, Czeslaw Milosz and Shinkichi Takahashi confront the devastation of World War II, particularly the Jewish Holocaust and the bombing of Hiroshima and Nagasaki. Keeping the memory of these incidents alive challenges readers of the poems to act to prevent such devastation in the future, but, perhaps more poignantly, to confront our complicity in the violence as participants in what can be an oppressive Western culture.

Students will read these poems not only for historical and geographical information but for new perspectives on their own lives as well. To answer the challenge of a non-Westerner such as Felix Mnthali, in "The Stranglehold of English Lit.," your class will have to assess the reading they have done in English courses throughout their scholastic careers. How many readings from cultures other than their own have they encountered? What might be the effect of this very limiting education? Muhammad al-Maghut's "Tourist" could quite possibly be one of us. How do we answer the speaker's plea that we see him as he is and not as we have been led to perceive him?

Questioning their own biases will lead students to open up the poems to the extent that they realize that world literature is not simply about some "other"; it is about all of us, living in an ever-contracting world, where we must think as much about our labels and notions of "the Other" as we do about ourselves.

ANNA AKHMATOVA, *Apparition* (p. 876)

A Russian poet, Anna Akhmatova lived during years of struggle and upheaval in her country. She had four husbands, one of whom was shot for anti-Bolshevik activities. She was associated with the Acmeist movement and traveled extensively during her lifetime, but she always returned to her native country, and, although she voiced her political discontent, Russia was her first love.

Love is the most frequent subject of Akhmatova's poetry, although "Apparition" focuses on a political topic, the Russian Revolution. The images of this poem promise excitement and celebration, but there is a decided edge to them. Lanterns "are squeaking," and horses quicken their gait "as if sensing some pursuit." We see the veneer of wealth in "glitter" (line 4) and "gilded" (9); this picture of peace is thinly disguised turmoil. Even the Tsar looks like a great man but is really a hollow shell. In fact, he is a ghost, an "apparition." His "light, empty eyes" intimate that there is nothing behind them; his strange glance looks at a world that is no longer his.

You might ask students to consider tone and perspective in this poem. Presenting the Tsar as a foreigner in the land of his former domain makes us at least slightly sympathetic to his position. Does the speaker lament the loss of the Tsar's power or simply try to capture him in words? Is it possible to determine the speaker's attitude toward revolution from the first two stanzas? Perhaps she laments the loss of power, but her tone is reflective; most probably, she captures a historic moment in this still picture.

For discussion of Akhmatova's poetry, see Leonid I. Strakhovsky's "Anna Akhmatova: Poetess of Tragic Love," *Craftsmen of the Word: Three Poets of Modern Russia* (Westport, CT: Greenwood, 1979): 53–82; Alexander Werth's "Akhmatova: Tragic Queen Anna," *Nation* 203:5 (22 Aug., 1966): 157–60; Mark Slonim, "Anna Akhmatova," *New York Times Book Review* (17 Apr., 1966).

Connections (p. 877)

1. Both Merrill and Akhmatova initially present images from everyday life only to move to the revolutionary and the life threatening in their last lines. In the final stanza of this poem, Akhmatova quietly and gently brings a Czar back from the dead in order to impress upon her audience the changes that have occurred since his murder. Similarly, Merrill chooses a strange tone to deliver a startling message, concentrating on details of clothing to describe a terrorist attack.

2. Dove portrays a lunatic in gentle, green images. She attempts to understand the general from within, describing his habits, his mother, his thoughts. Akhmatova is less graphic in her presentation of the Czar, noting his emptiness, his absence, his almost illusory sense of power. Whereas Dove must make her general present to her audience to shock us with his evil deeds, Akhmatova underlines the absence of the leader in her poem, indicating both the reasons for and the results of his fall from power.

CLARIBEL ALEGRIA, *I Am Mirror* (p. 877)

Born in Estelí, Nicaragua, Alegria moved to El Salvador six months later; she therefore considers herself more Salvadorean than Nicaraguan. She attended George Washington University, graduating in 1948, and is married to the American writer Darwin J. Flakoll. She received the Casa de las Americas prize of Cuba in 1978 for her book *Sobrevivo.* Alegria and her husband have lived in many foreign countries; they now divide their time between Majorca, Spain, and Managua, Nicaragua.

The speaker in this poem describes her attempts to feel again after she has been numbed by violence. She looks for her identity in the mirror, only to see herself as another person; note her use of third-person pronouns to refer to herself: "she also pricks herself" (line 11). In an ironic twist of Descartes's *Cogito ergo sum,* the speaker feels her arm, saying, "I hurt/therefore I exist" (32–33). Her attention continually turns to the horror around her as she alternates between scenes of violence and an attempt to keep her identity amid the turmoil. In a series of negations that begins in line 44, the speaker denies the violence, losing her self in the process. She cannot sustain an identity and survive, so she becomes an object: "I am a blank mirror" (48).

In a writing assignment, you might ask students to trace the two strands of images in this poem: the speaker's images to describe herself and the images of violence. They might construct an argument explaining the relationship between the two, discussing the effect of the images on the poem's tone and theme.

Another writing assignment might ask the class to compare this woman's relation to political upheaval with that of the self-sacrificing woman in Mishima's story "Patriotism" (p. 412). They might consider why the women have such different attitudes toward violence.

Connections (p. 878)

1. Plath's speaker is first mirror, then lake. In a reversal of Alegria's technique, in which the speaker becomes the mirror, Plath shows how the mirror absorbs the woman looking into it. Both poets play with the notion of women as objects, but Alegria does so to reflect the turmoil in war-torn Nicaragua, whereas Plath considers woman's aging process and approaching death.

CHARLES BAUDELAIRE, *To the Reader* (p. 878)

A French poet who was prosecuted and fined for offenses against public morals, Charles Baudelaire was thought by Victor Hugo to possess a modern sensibility that would quicken to beauty only when it had seen all the elements of corruption. It is not surprising that Baudelaire admired Poe and translated many of his works into French. In fact, you might teach this poem alongside Poe's story "The Pit and the Pendulum" (p. 398), asking students to write an essay discussing Poe's influence on Baudelaire's imagery.

In "To the Reader" Baudelaire's speaker accosts his listener with lists of the bleak and disgusting realities of mortal existence. One way to approach the many images in this poem is to categorize them on the blackboard. When they see the words line up, students will be ready to begin to invent their own paper topics, investigating certain strands of images in the poem and tracing their importance to the theme. For example, they will find examples of "avarice" (line 1) in "like the poor lush who cannot satisfy" (17) or "mouthing the rotten orange we suck dry" (20).

The final stanza, aside from playing a key role in T. S. Eliot's *The Waste Land,* introduces a fascinating relationship between the speaking poet and his reader. Once cast into the role of his double, the reader cannot retain any distance from the poem, as he or she is implicated in it as much as the speaker is.

You might ask students to write about the possible implications of the final line. What kind of model for poetry's place in the world does it propose?

Connections (p. 879)

1. Prufrock's language is similar to the images of Baudelaire's poem; each contains grim, bleak, suffocating impressions of life in society. Each speaker attempts to reach out to a listener but fails to hear the listener's response; Prufrock cannot summon the courage to ask the question ("Do I dare/Disturb the universe?"). Baudelaire's speaker cries out at the end but is never answered. Baudelaire is perhaps bleaker even than Eliot, making his message quite appropriate for a world in which environmental ruin and political turmoil are daily realities.

3. The boredom of Baudelaire's speaker has a more pernicious effect than the boredom disturbing the speaker in Berryman's "Dream Song 14." In both poems boredom empties the sensual world of meaning and interest, but Baudelaire's sense of the emptying is more caustic. His boredom drives us toward the guillotine (murder or suicide) as the one remaining experience that can make us feel. The boredom of Berryman's speaker seems more personal — it is not the sickness of a whole generation — but it leaves him isolated and forlorn.

FEDERICO GARCÍA LORCA, *Somnambule Ballad* (p. 880)

Perhaps the most significant Spanish poet and dramatist of the twentieth century, Federico García Lorca was born in Grenada. He learned there the folk tales of his region, which he incorporated often into his later poems. Lorca particularly admired the gypsies and their musical traditions, and in 1928 he published *Romancero Gitano* (The Gypsy Ballads), drawing on those traditions. His most successful dramatic works include three tragedies admired for their rich imagery and forceful women characters: *Blood Wedding* (1933), *Yerma* (1934), and *The House of Bernarda Alba* (1936). Lorca was murdered by agents of General Francisco Franco during the early part of the Spanish Civil War.

The speaker and his subject in "Somnambule Ballad" are both arresting characters. The first stanza sees the speaker longing for green, looking at the gypsy on her balcony. Because the woman does not speak for herself, the speaker invents a voice for her, framed by his own longing. The images of the second stanza reveal Lorca's interest in inventing a mythology for the gypsies; the fish, fig tree, and cat provide a mysterious lore, whose significance the audience can only guess. Ask students what these images say about the gypsy woman. What feeling is the speaker conveying?

Repetitions of green throughout the poem steep the symbolic landscape in a kind of natural mysticism. The wounded man and his ghostlike friend recede into tragic legend as they climb the balustrades, "leaving a trail of blood." The gypsy woman swaying over the cistern seems transformed into a creature of the water with "green flesh, hair of green,/. . . eyes of cold silver."

Note the way Lorca transforms emotion into sensation: "A thousand crystal tambourines/ were piercing the dawn" (lines 59–60) or "The long wind was leaving/ in the mouth a strange taste/ of gall, mint and sweet-basil" (64–66).

In a writing assignment, you might ask students to look at the images in the poem. How do they establish a sense of the woman's world? What is the speaker's relationship to that world? to her?

Critical discussions of Lorca's poetry include M. Duran's *Federico García Lorca: A Collection of Critical Essays* (Englewood Cliffs, NJ: Prentice-Hall, 1962) and Rupert C. Allen's *The Symbolic World of Federico García Lorca* (New York: Library of Social Science, 1972).

Connections (p. 882)

1. Southey's repetitions in "The Cataract of Lodore" are more singsong and childlike than the meditative, sleepy repetitions in Lorca's poem. The different functions of the repetitions in these two poems are the result of their very different subjects. Whereas Southey tries

to capture babbling water, Lorca attempts to draw us into the mysterious and painful world of the gypsies.

2. A comparison of the tone of this poem and that of Keats's "Ode on Melancholy" might begin with a discussion of the role of mythology in each poem. Keats's allusions are classical and controlled, whereas Lorca invents his mythology from the natural materials of the gypsy world. But the speakers have a similar relationship to the woman in each poem; both long to know her mysteries, but neither can sustain a mystical union with her. Lorca's poem, like Keats's, is melancholic, but the forces of fate and death seem to play a greater role in Lorca's work.

LI HO, *A Beautiful Girl Combs Her Hair* (p. 882)

Like his predecessor Li Po (see Ezra Pound's version of Li Po's "The River-Merchant's Wife: A Letter" on p. 834), Li Ho did not serve as a civil servant, an unusual choice for poets of the T'ang dynasty in China. He wrote poems while riding on a donkey and revised them at the end of each day.

Juxtaposition, one of the most important techniques in Chinese poetry, is amply evident in this poem, as is one of Li Ho's characteristic touches: supernatural mystery appearing alongside unvarnished description ("singing jade"; "her mirror/two phoenixes/a pool of autumn light"). The poet deftly brings the senses into play; the girl's "spilling hair" has a precise fragrance; it is not simply black but the "color of raven feathers/shining blue-black stuff"; and it defeats her "jade comb," which in the middle of the poem falls without sound.

You might ask students to think about where the speaker is in relation to this scene and what significance his location might have for his exasperation. Reading the poem without the speaker's outburst in lines 23–26 might lead to a productive discussion of the effects of metaphor and connotation. What sort of girl is this "wild goose" with blackest hair so carefully attended? How much does the speaker know of her? How much does he wish to know?

Connection (p. 883)

1. Song's "The White Porch" has a tone similar to that of this poem, with alluring, almost seductive images of a woman's hair. Both women's hair is thick and unmanageable. Each woman gathers vegetation from the garden, again pointing to her ripe sexuality. In both poems hair serves as a way of knowing the women, an access to their restlessness and self-consciousness. You might ask students to comment on differences in the poems resulting from the difference in speakers. Li Ho's speaker watches the woman dress her hair and is upset by her "slovenly beauty" (line 24). The speaker in Song's poem is the possessor of the hair and of the erotic power it symbolizes and releases.

MUHAMMAD AL-MAGHUT, *Tourist* (p. 883)

Poets from the Arab world are often ignored or misunderstood by Westerners, who have preconceived notions about them. For a collection of Arab poetry and a few articles on this subject, consult *Mundus Artium: A Journal of International Literature and the Arts* 10 (1977).

This poem could be called "Education of a Tourist" because it points out the tendency of tourists to enter an Eastern country (Syria, in this case) and find what they have been told exists there rather than try to understand what it really means to live in the country. The speaker cries for the tourist's attention, asking for "a hand or a handkerchief/In this whole world/Waving at me." He asks the tourist to throw away his guidebooks and impressions of himself in a strange land, and to look at the speaker, "a poet from the East." The 'Atāba folk song will tell the tourist more about the culture than he could ever know otherwise, but the tourist will not hear it unless he asks and listens carefully. Indeed, perhaps because of the language barrier, but more probably because of cultural barriers, it is unlikely that any tourist will ever hear these songs.

You might ask students to write an essay discussing the speaker's quotation in relation to the rest of the poem. What do his words to the tourist tell us about his culture? How does this view of him differ from the picture we get in the early lines: "Crouching in my tatters on the steps of the hotel"?

Connection (p. 884)

1. Unlike al-Maghut's tourist, the "average tourist" in Merrill's "Casual Wear" is not addressed directly. She, like the terrorist who kills her, becomes a statistic, representative of the desperate conflict between cultures. She is not portrayed as an individual capable of meeting an "other" in an authentic way. In al-Maghut's poem the speaker offers such an opportunity to the tourist he addresses. In the second half of each poem, the tourists are shaken from their original blindness — in Merrill's poem by violence and in al-Maghut's, by the promise of an authentic tale of the East.

CZESLAW MILOSZ, *A Poor Christian Looks at the Ghetto* (p. 884)

Born in Lithuania and raised in Poland, Czeslaw Milosz was involved in the underground resistance against Nazism in 1939. He later moved to Paris and then to the United States where he is now a citizen. Milosz's poetry reflects his belief that both Eastern and Western countries lack morality, that life in the twentieth century is life in an abyss. He has said that writing poetry is an act of faith, and that it is the poet's role to write about historic events concerning a whole people. Milosz's particular interest is the history of the Polish people; many of his poems explore the effects on the individual of living in such a scarred country.

"A Poor Christian Looks at the Ghetto" approaches the Nazi extermination of the Jews in World War II from the perspective of a Christian. You might ask students to delineate the images that reveal the poem's background. The destruction of nature's minerals ("copper, nickel, silver") along with human artifacts ("iron sheets, violin strings, trumpets") teaches a lesson about mortality; humans and animals, natural and synthetic materials are all destroyed by the Nazis, who literally turn people into things, making lampshades and soap from their remains.

You might direct students' attention to the relationship of the "Poor Christian" to the Jews. Is he poor, for instance, economically, or does he feel overwhelmed and paralyzed by what he sees? Both are possible. You might ask students to explain the speaker's fear. Already a victim of the insanity ("my broken body will deliver me to his sight"), why is he afraid of being blamed for it? The ambiguous answer to that question is clearest in the reference to the guardian mole in the final stanza: "What will I tell him, I, a Jew of the New Testament?" How does the poem reflect on the long antagonism between Christianity and Judaism?

References to bees and ants associate the activity of social insects with that of human beings as social creatures. But whereas the insects continue building on mortal ruin ("red liver," "black bone," and the "honeycomb of lungs"), the human beings can only count their dead. Order has broken down in human society. What are the implications of the insects' survival in this scene of devastation?

In an essay, you might ask students to determine how the final stanza illuminates the theme of the poem, looking carefully at the images in the first three stanzas to support their arguments.

Critical studies of Milosz's work include G. Goemoeri, *Polish and Hungarian Poetry, 1945–1956* (Oxford: Oxford UP, 1966); Milosz's own *The Captive Mind* (New York: Knopf, 1953); and Adam Gillon and Ludwik Krzyzanowski, *An Introduction to Modern Polish Literature* (New York: Twayne, 1964).

Connections (p. 885)

1. Both Milosz's poem and Harper's respond to particular historic circumstances. One receives from these poems a general sense of the oppression of the blacks in South Africa and of the persecution of the Jews in the Polish ghetto. Enough of the images are legible to readers who do not know the exact circumstances of the uprising in Soweto or of the "night of breaking glass" (*Kristallnacht*, when Nazi agitators initiated a wave of violence against the Jews by smashing the windows of Jewish shops in 1938). But knowing about these incidents and others to which the poems allude provides further insight into the poems and the poets' attitudes. Just as knowledge of history can illuminate these poems, a sensitive reading of the poems can deepen our understanding of the frightening history they reflect.

    Unlike Milosz's speaker, who surveys disaster, Alegria's is in the midst of ongoing devastation. Her transformation into a blank mirror, which nothing can penetrate, is her defense against the violence. Both speakers give a painfully objective description of the destruction around them. Perhaps Alegria's speaker records her experience to preserve the possibility for real feeling that eludes her in the present.

2. Alegria's "I Am Mirror" does not demand the political and moral commitment that Milosz's poem does. Milosz expects readers to consider the plight of the Jews not as an event but as something they were complicit in, as a sin they must atone for, and a possible destiny for themselves if they do not work for social justice. By contrast, Alegria's speaker concerns herself more with the immediate realities of life in a country besieged by violence, whose numbing effects she records.

FELIX MNTHALI, *The Stranglehold of English Lit.* (p. 885)

Born in Zimbabwe, to parents of Northern Malawi origin, Mnthali was educated partly in South Africa, partly in Canada. In 1969 he received a doctorate in literature from the University of Toronto. He rose steadily toward a professorship at the University of Malawi, until the Malawi Congress Party became concerned about the political implications of the Homeland writer's group he belonged to. Mnthali was imprisoned for this affiliation. After his release he taught at the University of Botswana, but he is now back at the University of Malawi.

In "The Stranglehold of English Lit." Mnthali accuses English literature of being the backbone of the European colonial domination of Africa until the second half of this century. The speaker calls Jane Austen's fiction an "elegance of deceit," an imaginary world that crippled those in the real world. What is behind the wealthy world of an Austen novel, Mnthali suggests, is the slaves whose work gives her characters their money: "the victims of branding irons/and sugar-plantations."

Although they may not have read an Austen novel, your students will probably have some sense of British domestic fiction of the eighteenth and nineteenth centuries. You might photocopy a page or two of Austen, asking students to identify what Mnthali is addressing in her work. Do they think more authors are guilty of "strangling" colonial Africa?

In a writing assignment they might discuss the idea of colonial as a direct influence on politics and daily life. How does Mnthali claim it to be so? Is it so in their experience? What might account for the relationship of their answers to Mnthali's accusations?

Connections (p. 886)

1. Dakar in Senegal, Ibadan in Nigeria, and Makerere in Uganda were all major cities of British imperialism that did not become independent until the 1960s. Often the site of conflict between European countries (England versus France, for example) fighting for domination in the region, these cities lost some of their culture while being forced to adhere to the customs of another. This poem is about the silence that is enforced by centuries of enslavement and domination by an outside force. Takahashi's "Explosion"

shows a similar squelching, which occurred in a matter of moments. Takahashi provides a twentieth-century version of the eighteenth- and nineteenth-century oppression Mnthali discusses.

PABLO NERUDA, *Sweetness, Always* (p. 886)

As much as any poet of his time, Chilean-born Pablo Neruda insisted on the connection between poetry and politics. In an essay on "impure poetry," he defended the importance of not-so-nice images and words to the poet's craft. Neruda criticized American poets for ignoring politics to pursue their own, "loftier" pleasures. Art was life for Neruda; he believed that poetry must be kept near the bone, where it originates, and not elevated to irrelevancy. "Sweetness, Always" illustrates this point in delicious, sense-appealing imagery, which contrasts with the dullness of more abstract poetry. The speaker defends the poor, the politically oppressed, the mundane, and the earthy as the truly valuable subjects for poetry.

The poem appeals to the sense of taste, pointing out that even the builders of great monuments have to eat. Talking about the body makes Neruda's appeal appropriate for every man and woman. Poems do indeed feed the world, although clearly the poets Neruda distrusts claim that feeding is not their job: "We are not feeding the world." Working from the extremes of underground and sky, Neruda focuses on the earth — at the level of the people: "and the poor adults' also." He derides the typical monuments of human power in favor of the food that creates living monuments of joy and misery — human beings.

Neruda's poetry has been discussed in Manuel Duran and Margery Safir's *Earth Tones* (Bloomington: Indiana UP, 1980); Rene de Costa's *The Poetry of Pablo Neruda* (Cambridge: Harvard UP, 1979) and "Pablo Neruda, 1904–1973" *Modern Poetry Studies* 5:1 (1974).

Connections (p. 888)

1. The speaker's call for "sweetness, always" in Neruda's poem asks us to avoid vanity and seek "Verses of pastry which melt/into milk and sugar in the mouth (lines 12–13). This call contrasts with the speaker's claim in Frost's "Provide, Provide" that it is "better to go down dignified/With boughten friendship at your side" (19–20). Although both speakers ask us to grab earthly things, Neruda's speaker asks us to return to the sweetness of existence, whereas Frost's urges a clinging to material objects. Of course we must question the sarcasm in Frost's speaker's tone, but taken at face value these two poems offer opposite views of the world. In fact, Neruda's poem may be approached as an answer to Frost's. Neruda's speaker asks us not to forget "the joyous/love-needs of our bodies" (22–23), whereas Frost's tells us to "make the whole stock exchange your own" (10).

2. In Kinnell's "Blackberry-Eating" and Chasin's "The Word *Plum*," the fruits could easily represent the "sweetness" the speaker asks for in Neruda's poem. The plum and the blackberries invite listeners to experience the world through a single, sensuous image, without much concern for "deep, philosophical" issues.

OCTAVIO PAZ, *The Street* (p. 888)

A Mexican poet of metamorphic surrealism, Octavio Paz has influenced many writers, including William Carlos Williams, Denise Levertov, and Muriel Rukeyser, each of whom has translated him. He has served the Mexican diplomatic service in Paris, New Delhi, and New York.

Students may let this poem too easily defeat them or too easily collapse into platitudes: "OK, a guy becomes his own shadow or he can't tell whether he's real or not." The poem's simple diction, pleasing (and very frequent) rhymes, and skillful alliteration work in opposition to its mournful tone and shadowy imagery, a tension that mirrors the speaker's situation: the everyday world of streets, leaves, stones, and people is not at all everyday. Nothing has definition on "The Street" (note the references to night, blindness, and awkwardness, and to the unstated reasons for the pursuit), yet the urgent certainty of the "narrative" is almost palpable.

You might ask students to change all the verbs in the poem to the past tense and comment on the resulting differences in tone. Other questions that would yield productive discussion or writing include How would the poem's effect be altered if it ended with line 11? How does the speaker know the street is "long" if he walks "in blackness"? How can stones be anything but "silent"? To what extent could the poem's logic be considered dream logic?

Connections (p. 888)

1. Frost's speaker in "Acquainted with the Night" vacillates between himself and the outside world, alternating between images of light and darkness, good and evil. Paz's speaker begins and ends in darkness, in the solipsistic prison of his own mind. Whereas Frost's speaker seems indecisive and brooding, Paz's is forever fixed in darkness, without hope. Frost's speaker feels himself alone in a realistic night setting where he sees "one luminary clock against the sky." His poem conveys loneliness rather than anxiety. Paz's scene, in contrast, is the landscape of persecution and nightmare.

2. In Wright's poem, a pleasant array of images from the natural world is quashed with a simple statement: "I have wasted my life." The final line undercuts the peaceful, soothing images of the rest of the poem. In fact, the poet may be speaking of his own activity, writing down his experiences instead of simply living in the experience. Paz's speaker does not leave any room for hope or escape from his own consciousness; thus, his tone is far more dismal than Wright's.

RAINER MARIA RILKE, *The Panther* (p. 888)

Born in Austria-Hungary (now Czechoslovakia), Rainer Maria Rilke was educated in Catholic schools but later rebelled against his faith. He migrated to Munich after studying philosophy at Prague. In 1909 he went to Paris, where there were many artists at the time. Rilke's images have been described as having classical plasticity, being precise, chiseled, and visual. His mixture of squalor and art may have come from the time he spent in Paris.

The images of containment versus freedom in this poem provide excellent material for discussion and writing assignments. Ask students to identify the negative images: "cramped" (line 5), "paralyzed" (8), "tensed" (11), "arrested" (11). These images depict physical restriction, contrasting with the spiritual images, which relate to the panther's vision. The panther's vision is restricted by his prison bars, making even a single image a painful experience. The animal's body is confined, so the will is restricted and the vision almost completely annihilated.

In a writing assignment you might ask students to discuss how this poem relates to human experience. Are human beings ever "caged in" like this? How do prisons of our birthplaces (our history, our gender, our race, our class, and so on) limit our vision and restrict our ability to move beyond ourselves? They might compare this poem with Piercy's "The Secretary Chant" (p. 493) or Clifton's "For de Lawd" (p. 764), looking for similarities in diction, theme, and mood.

Connections (p. 889)

1. Like the panther, the animals in the late stanzas of Atwood's poem are restricted by their confinement, their dreams becoming a reflection of their cramped reality.

2. The movement of Rilke's poem is circular and somewhat lethargic, in keeping with the "ritual dance" of the panther's confinement. Dickinson's poem is far more musical and linear; the bird is jittery when on the ground because it is unused to that environment. The bird and the speaker have a sense of adventure, newness, and nervousness in Dickinson's poem, which contrast with the repressed movement and expression in Rilke's. The contrasting senses of movement in the poems derive from their very different subjects.

SAPPHO, *With his venom* (p. 889)

Born on the Greek island of Lesbos, Sappho was forced at an early age to seek political exile in Sicily. Later, she returned to her home, where she lived with a group honoring Aphrodite and the Muses. The group offered Sappho an opportunity to write poems praising the women around her and celebrating their marriages. She wrote personal poetry, almost always in the vernacular of Lesbos, and occasionally translated poems from folk songs.

In "With his venom" Sappho writes of one of her favorite themes: love. Her attitude toward it can be discussed using the second stanza's description of love's venom as "irresistible/and bittersweet." Students might discuss the reasons for talking about love as a snakebite, paying particular attention to the alliterative *l* in the third stanza.

You might assign a short essay about the words that frame the poem: "with" and "down." How do these words set the mood of what's in between?

Because of its structure, this poem could be favorably compared with imagistic poems such as Williams's "Poem" (p. 546) or H.D.'s "Heat" (p. 551).

Connections (p. 889)

1. The description of the speaker's hair in Song's "The White Porch" may be compared with the idea of love as a "loosener/of limbs" in Sappho's poem. Both poems present love as a dangerous, exciting business. If they examine the final line of each, students will see that whereas Song's speaker invites love in, Sappho's is struck down by love's force.

2. Millay's poem presents love as more of a chosen occupation than does Sappho's shorter poem, with its emphasis on the momentary experience of love's power. Millay also introduces the relationship between physical love and thought, linking the two with beauty, and, more abstractly perhaps, poetry. Sappho does not develop any aspect of love but the physical. The image in "With his venom" is from the natural world, whereas Millay's images mix the human and the natural to describe lust as an essential part of being a person and an artist.

SHINKICHI TAKAHASHI, *Explosion* (p. 889)

Born on the island of Shikoku, Japan, Shinkichi Takahashi was largely self-educated. In 1921 he published a book of Dadaist poems that shocked his audience. One critic called him the Japanese Rimbaud. His life changed drastically when, at twenty-seven years of age, he fell and hit his head. Thought to have brain damage, he was sent to an asylum, where it was believed he would never write poetry again. But he continued to recover and to write. He became a Zen Buddhist in 1932, and many of his poems, including this one, are influenced by that tradition.

Alluding to the U.S. nuclear bombing of Hiroshima and Nagasaki, this poem traces both the attitude of those who decided to drop the bomb and that of those who were affected by it. In the first stanza the speaker compares himself to a cat, a dog, fog, and rain, pointing out not only that those who dropped the bomb failed to think of the people it would affect but also that their attitude toward their targets was cold. In the second stanza the bomb's long-term biological and environmental effects are evident; in the third stanza the speaker claims to want to outrace its destruction: *"reduced to emptiness by nuclear/fission, I'm running very fast."*

In a writing assignment, you might ask students to discuss the relationship between the first and third stanzas. How does the dropping of the bomb change the speaker's diction and tone?

You might also ask students to compare this poem with Czeslaw Milosz's "A Poor Christian Looks at the Ghetto" (p. 884), paying close attention to how both speakers react to similar scenes of destruction.

For information on and an interesting interview with the poet, consult Lucien Stryk, *Triumph of the Sparrow: Zen Poems of Shinkichi Takahashi* (Urbana and Chicago: U of Illinois P, 1986).

Connections (p. 890)

1. In both "Running on Empty" and "Explosion" the speakers run away from their fears toward death. But their fears are very different. In "Running on Empty" the speaker runs away from himself and, more subtly, the society that has produced him. The enemy is more tangible and probably more terrifying in "Explosion," and the runner's journey is shorter.

2. Takahashi's speaker "whoop[s] at what/remains," whereas Neruda's urges us to linger over the sweetness of our lives. Neruda's emphasis on the pleasure of the body contrasts sharply with Takahashi's concern with its inevitable and imminent destruction. The very different tones of the speakers result from the contrast between the tragic subject of "Explosion" and the more meditative subject of "Sweetness, Always."

AN ALBUM OF CONTEMPORARY POEMS

Both the difficulties and the rewards of contemporary poetry derive from the same characteristics; namely, there are no set principles for the construction of contemporary poetry or the range of its style. It can be structured in stanzas, or in open free-verse paragraphs, or even as an uninterrupted block of prose. Contemporary poetry by practitioners such as James Merrill is as likely to be rhymed as unrhymed. The level of diction can be lofty and elegant or it can be spiced with slang, as in Peter Meinke's "The ABC of Aerobics." In short, the idea of decorum, if it exists at all in contemporary poetry writing, is open ended.

Thematically, the field for discovering material for poems is also more extensive than ever before. Some of the poems here, for example, Michael Harper's "The Militance of a Photograph in the Passbook of a Bantu under Detention," take as their motive an area of public concern relevant not only to the country of the poet but to an area other than or far more inclusive than a specific national concern. We are living in an age that has given new meaning to the word *global,* and North American poetry especially seems to reflect this broadened interest. Other poems, like Robert Phillips's "Running on Empty," embody a more private concern and voice the particular anxieties and observations of the individual. One point, though, that students should grasp is that our age does not dictate either an introspective poetry bound to extol and explore nature and the human mind or a public poetry pitched for a celebration of reason, country, and the famous. We can, and do, address both public and private issues, and in certain poems, such as Denise Levertov's "Gathered at the River," we manage to merge the dialectic of *polis* and *poesis.*

Without question, contemporary poets write about the age-old issues of love and death and the pain of growing up, but these themes, seemingly so essential and enduring, are changed by recent history, technology, and our systems of belief and values. Knowledge of the casualness of death and one's consequent vulnerability, as well as the prospect of mass extinction, also influences the way poets today think and write about death. Rita Dove's "Parsley" examines the consciousness of a murderous general in Haiti, illustrating in a mixture of tranquil and horrific images the irrational bases for his slaughtering innocent people who cannot pronounce their *r*'s. The world of the contemporary poet is violent and nonsensical, but it is also diverse and, in Amy Clampitt's "Nothing Stays Put," "exotic."

The poetry included here exhibits a wide range of techniques and levels of diction. The tools for reading poetry learned in earlier chapters will find their fullest application here. On the whole, though, the poems are highly accessible and offer a fine occasion for you and your students to observe the events, vocabulary, and concerns of the day worked into a poetic context. Perhaps that context will enable all of us to articulate more clearly what we desire, value, and wish to protect in this world.

AMY CLAMPITT, *Nothing Stays Put* (p. 890)

Amy Clampitt's debt to Gerard Manley Hopkins is evident in many of her poems. In fact, her first collection of poetry, *The Kingfisher,* takes its title from one of his poems: "As Kingfishers Catch Fire, Dragonflies Draw Flames." Clampitt also admires the work of Dylan Thomas, whom she mentions in her poem "The Kingfisher." Critical discussions of Clampitt's work that might be helpful to you and your students include Richard Howard's "The Hazardous Definition of Structures," *Parnassus* 11:1 (Spring, Summer 1983): 27–75; Richard Tilinghast's "Nature, Fantasy, Art," *New York Times Book Review* (7 Aug. 1983); and Helen Vendler's "On the Thread of Language," *New York Review of Books* (3 Mar. 1983).

Connection (p. 891)

1. Wordsworth's "The World Is Too Much with Us" has inspired many modern poets' imitations. This interpretation reverses the tone of the earlier poem. Instead of dwelling on the evils of the modern sensibility, Clampitt prefers to sing the praises of our plenty, our diversity. Cultural diversity is one of her favorite topics; the fruit of the tropics, "The exotic is everywhere." If she has a complaint, Clampitt's speaker mourns the overwhelming plenty of our society; this is what goes unappreciated. Wordsworth's speaker, in contrast, bemoans our inattention to nature, our increasing concentration on exclusively human concerns.

As you discuss this poem, ask students to note the transitions. The *But*'s in lines 23 and 37 halt the spilling-over quality of these lines; with this word the speaker reevaluates, takes stock of where she's been, and defines the progress of her thoughts.

In a writing assignment, you might ask students to categorize the "lists" of images in the poem. How do these groupings reflect the speaker's attitude toward her subject? In a separate, perhaps shorter, essay, they might examine the last three lines. Are they celebratory or disenchanted? How do they inform our reading of the first three stanzas of the poem?

ROBERT CREELEY, *Fathers* (p. 891)

Born in Massachusetts, Robert Creeley attended Harvard University, which he left in 1944 to serve as an ambulance driver in India and Burma during World War II. After living in France and Spain in the early 1950s, he returned to the United States and taught at Black Mountain College in North Carolina and at various colleges and universities throughout the U.S. and Canada. From 1954 to 1957 he published *The Black Mountain Review.* Critics have associated Creeley with a group they label the "Black Mountain Poets" including Charles Olson, Robert Duncan, and Denise Levertov, among others. Creeley was awarded a Guggenheim Fellowship for poetry in 1964.

"Fathers," an account of the speaker's attendance at his father's funeral, illustrates a "column" of mourners in a column of run-together observations and memories. Ask students to talk about what the speaker notices. How do the details reflect his thoughts on this occasion? He notices the height, surface, and dimensions of the graveyard and the surrounding area, but he seems to find it hard to penetrate to his innermost feelings. Ask students to identify the source of the speaker's reticence. Does it have something to do with his relationship with his father?

When he does refer to his father's life, the speaker characterizes him by looking at his life through his death. His "curious/reticence" (lines 22–23), "his dead state" (23), "his emptiness" (24), "his acerbic/edge" (24–25) can describe both a hard-to-reach living being and a dead man.

In a writing assignment, you might ask students to examine the speaker through his language. What does his diction tell you he thinks is important in life? What would his relationship with his father have been like? Is this poem a form of grief or a recognition of his own mortality — or both? Ask students to note the repetitions of *his, hold,* and *wants* in the final lines. How do these words illustrate what is happening?

For discussions of Creeley's poetry, consult Cynthia Edelberg's *Robert Creeley's Poetry: A Critical Introduction;* (Albequerque, NM: Univ. of New Mexico Press, 1978); Albert L. Ford's *Robert Creeley* (Boston, MA: Twayne Publishers, 1978); and Ann Mandel's *Measures: Robert Creeley's Poetry* (Toronto: Coach House P, 1974).

Connection (p. 892)

1. Hall's "My Son, My Executioner" presents a speaker in a position opposite to that of Creeley's speaker here. Whereas Creeley's speaker watches his father being buried, Hall cradles a newborn son. Each poet thinks about mortality, but their very different perspectives produce diverse tones. For Creeley's speaker, the poem is a form of mourning, a grim acceptance of a loss. Hall's speaker knows when he looks at his son that his own death will come, but it seems far off and he believes it will be preceded by many happy and difficult times with his child. Hall's tone is meditative, Creeley's, sobering.

RITA DOVE, *Parsley* (p. 892)

Born in Ohio in 1952, Rita Dove graduated from Miami University (Ohio) and earned an M.F.A. from the Writer's Workshop at the University of Iowa. In 1987 she was awarded the Pulitzer Prize for poetry for *Thomas and Beulah.*

In "Parsley" Dove gives voice to the inner life of the murderous general, whose meditation on killing is the only remedy — a temporary one — for "the little knot of screams" that threatens to overwhelm him. The voices of the general's victims rise up out of the sugar cane swamp to which they are condemned by poverty and oppression. Their work songs rise up, a sign of life, perhaps, even in terrible adversity. The general exacts revenge for that life, ongoing while his beloved mother lies dead. To him, her death calls out for the mindless sacrifice of thousands.

Connections (p. 894)

1. Forché's colonel is power hungry, vain, and temperamental. His mannerisms, his house, his wife all tell us that he is used to getting what he wants through force. For him, politics is merely a matter of physical superiority. Like him, Dove's general is eccentric and violent, killing people because they cannot pronounce the letter *r.* Whereas Forché's colonel rationally conceives of human rights as inconsequential, Dove's general seems to have made up his own mystical code of behavior, to which his people must conform. You might ask students to discuss the role of the parrots in each of these poems. Perhaps, the parrot signifies the role of the people, who must imitate their ludicrous leaders to survive. Dove's general is entirely idiosyncratic; Forché's colonel has much more control over his behavior. The colonel's plan is frightening because it is so coolly murderous; the general's behavior terrifies us because of its arbitrariness.

2. In Thomas's poem the destruction wrought by the stroke of the ruler's pen seems abstract compared with the slaughter in "Parsley," perhaps because the voices of the victims, as well as the voice of the ruler, are present in Dove's poem. Both poets focus on the weaknesses of the rulers causing terrible havoc. Thomas's ruler has a sloping shoulder and finger joints cramped with chalk. Dove's general seems demented by his mother's death. In both poems the callousness of rulers who have power over so many lives appalls the poets. But they record the deeds and thoughts of these rulers with a seemingly dispassionate objectivity to allow the reader to experience the horror of the situation.

RUTH FAINLIGHT, *Flower Feet* (p. 894)

Born in New York City, Ruth Fainlight now lives in England, where she writes many poems about women and their relationships with their families, children, pets, and others. Her interest in non-Western cultures is clear from her travel sketches of India, as well as this poem.

The terrible price of "beauty" is one consideration of this poem. Ask students to talk about the custom of binding feet. How do the speaker's descriptions of the process reveal the mentality of those who invented and sustained this custom? Notice how the speaker talks about the shoes as artifacts in the first stanza, painting their appearance in complimentary images, then, in the second stanza, undercuts their appealing exteriors by examining what they produced.

In a writing assignment, you might ask students to consider the speaker's attitude toward women. How does she feel about "nurse and mother" (line 15)? What are the larger implications of her perspective on sex discrimination sanctioned by cultural custom?

Connections (p. 895)

1. In "Mending Wall" Frost's speaker subtly disdains the custom of keeping other people at a distance. The neighbor's statement "Good fences make good neighbors" does not convince the speaker that they need a fence, but he cannot end the tradition by arguing with his neighbor. Similarly, Fainlight feels helpless when confronted with the cruelty of a cultural custom that caused pain to many women. Fainlight examines a tradition that no longer continues; Frost points out a problem that many Americans consider a fact of existence. Comparing the poems, students might examine the similarities between these very different cultural customs.

2. The final line of the poem is startling because we would ordinarily blame men for these women's torture, whereas Fainlight's speaker wonders at how women could torture their own daughters out of custom. Merrill's "Casual wear" attacks its listeners similarly, using the familiar topic of women's apparel to explore the possible causes and effects of a terrorist attack. Just as Fainlight challenges our notions of sex discrimination, Merrill asks us to consider terrorism from a less glossy position than the news presents; the implication of the rich in the act is undeniable and fascinating to discuss.

3. Clampitt's poem celebrates motion and modernity, whereas Fainlight looks at change as freedom from physical pain.

MICHAEL HARPER, *The Militance of a Photograph in the Passbook of a Bantu under Detention* (p. 895)

Born in Brooklyn, Harper cultivates interests that include music, nature, history, and myth. He looks to Africa for the roots of the black experience in America, believing it is important not to dislocate oneself from the continuum of history. Before reading this poem, students might need to talk a bit about the history of South Africa and to define the words that are unfamiliar to them.

The many layers of this poem might best be approached through the photograph versus the reality. Ask students to paraphrase the poem, to try to figure out who is who, and to identify where it takes place. In their efforts to pin down the sense, they will notice that the images mingle one passbook with another, one body with another, articles of clothing with bodies, lives with deaths, politics with the ordinary. How, for example, do the images of covering, dust, and concealment open up the issues of the poem? How do the references to silence, to what cannot be translated or expressed, affect the tone of the poem? The speaker subtly illustrates the way white people have covered black skins in South Africa with shame, changing people's identities as one might change clothes.

You might ask students to write an essay discussing the way the italicized epigraph frames the poem. How does this poem illustrate justice or its absence? What is justice, according to this speaker?

Connections (p. 897)

1. In both Dove's poem and Harper's, the images work as metaphoric equivalents of the political situations. In Dove's poem parsley becomes the death sentence of all who pronounce its name without an *r*. In Harper's poem the photograph embodies an ongoing struggle, freezing its monstrosity. Parsley, an innocuous word, with no reasonable connection to politics, becomes a sign of the destructive and arbitrary rule of the oppressor.

3. Adame's title would not work for Harper's poem because Harper's issues are hardly black and white. Harper explores the places where these margins overlap, indicating that skin color has far less to do with justice than we might infer from looking at the racial division in countries like South Africa. Far more puzzling to Harper's speaker is the difficulty of telling issues and individuals apart when the real issue is justice — the right of human beings to live their own lives as they would, not as they would be told.

GALWAY KINNELL, *After Making Love We Hear Footsteps* (p. 898)

Kinnell's poetry is known for its directness, precision, and carefully controlled idiom. In his *Book of Nightmares,* from which this poem is taken, he explores the difficult project of explaining human mortality to our children. Love is his answer in many of the poems, but it requires confronting physical as well as emotional aspects.

This is a popular poem with students because it vividly presents a scene that is familiar to many of them. Ask them to describe the speaker. What does his language tell us about his character?

In an essay, you might ask students to explore the poem's auditory appeal. How do the various sounds create a mood for the speaker's discussion of his relationship to his child and his wife?

Connections (p. 898)

1. The tone of the speaker in Plath's poem is more self-absorbed and less celebratory than Kinnell's. Plath works at defining her relationship to her child by experimenting with different, vivid images to describe the infant. She makes no mention of her spouse, whereas Kinnell's speaker sees the child as the gift of love between himself and his wife. Kinnell's child seems less enigmatic and more a miracle, a cause for belief rather than a symbol of struggle to come.

2. In concrete images such as the baseball pajamas and the expression "loving and snuggling," Kinnell's speaker establishes a sense of what his child is like. The boy's presence fills the poem as it fills the space between the speaker and his wife. Frost's poem explores what it would be like to have this space suddenly emptied, how he would talk to his wife about their loss, how it would affect their relationship. Frost's speaker's relationship to his wife is painfully awkward, just the opposite of Kinnell's. As Kinnell's poem overflows with affection and love, Frost's echoes in emptiness, silence, grief, and loss.

DENISE LEVERTOV, *Gathered at the River* (p. 898)

Levertov is a fine example of a poet who has used her energies and gifts to speak her views on human rights and political issues, including U.S. presence in Vietnam, oppression in Nicaragua and El Salvador, and the manufacture of nuclear weapons and power plants. In this poem she catches the image of a strikingly contemporary gesture, the launching of small candle boats, in a communal act of witness against the atrocities of the past and what might occur in the future.

You might begin by commenting on how the poem opens with a fragment — "As if the trees were not indifferent. . . ." Why is this a good opening in terms of the rest of the poem? The reference to trees introduces the central image of the poem, one that will obtain symbolic import by the close. Another obvious question to ask is how the events of Hiroshima and Nagasaki are different from other military events of the past and how the trees illustrate that difference. In lines 12–16 the difference is spelled out with an underscoring of the idea that war is no longer just a "human war" but a war against nature, with the trees as a kind of natural synecdoche. At the close of the poem the trees become a symbol for what could be lost if people are unsuccessful in arresting the possibility of nuclear war. The trees, in their "slow and innocent wisdom," seem to stand for growth (bole/branch), protection (shade), and continuing life (pollen). Although pollen is the most evanescent of the trees' properties, it assures the continuance of the life cycle and therefore serves as an appropriate close to the poem.

By all means, teach this poem in conjunction with Levertov's own remarks on it (p. 920). Writing assignments could be organized around the tone of the poem, the appropriateness of the trees as symbol, or the need to revive the idea of heroes and heroines in the contemporary world.

Connections (p. 900)

1. Levertov's notion of a "great design, a potential harmony" struggles against the selfish intervention of human desires in this poem. Were it not for our "war against earth,/against nature," we might hope for the actualization of the potential she describes. In Frost's poem the malevolent images are natural, indicating that Frost's view of nature's design may be darker than Levertov's. Unlike Levertov's speaker, the speaker in "Design" finds a "darkness to appall" in a natural setting.

2. In their comparison of one of the Hopkins poems with Levertov's, ask students to pay particular attention to the poet's relationship to his or her subject. They will notice that Hopkins has much more cause for celebration than does Levertov, perhaps because of their different eras. Levertov has clearly seen more horror than Hopkins has, thus she is less celebratory and more foreboding.

PETER MEINKE, *The ABC of Aerobics* (p. 900)

Born in Brooklyn, Peter Meinke experiments often with form, preferring to let the poem dictate its own form. Works whose titles begin "The ABC of. . ." usually are primers designed to teach the basic elements of a subject. You might start discussion of this poem by asking whether it fulfills the expectations its title sets up. In a kind of playful, semisatiric thumbing of the nose at cholesterol-level and heart-rate calculators, the poem at least acknowledges the obligations of its title. The speaker, apparently, has tried to ward off the effects of aging by jogging, but he expends all this effort with a despairing sense of his past sins and the dark forebodings of his genetic history manifested in the portrait of Uncle George. Small wonder, then, that his thoughts turn to Shirley Clark, and the poem concludes with the speaker "breathing hard" and gasping for his lost flame at his own "maximal heart rate."

At least two aspects of this poem merit some consideration. One is the carefully controlled use of consonance and alliteration, often for humorous effect. Notice, for example, the alternating *l*- and *b*-sounds in line 12 followed by the nasal hiss of "my/ medical history noxious marsh." Later, in a spoofing of health and fitness fads, Meinke shows the direction of his true inclinations by exchanging "zen and zucchini" for "drinking and dreaming."

The second aspect of this poem that students should feel comfortable enough to enjoy is the humor, which derives in part from the poem's dip into the vernacular. "Probably I shall keel off the john like/queer Uncle George," Meinke unabashedly tells us in line 16, while he describes the lucky lover who married the fabled Shirley as a "turkey" who lacks all aesthetic appreciation for her wondrous earlobes. We are inclined to like the speaker in this poem, and both his personality and the radiated humor act as rhetorical devices, helping us to feel the way he feels about "the ABC of aerobics," which, by the way, takes us to the end of the alphabet with "zen and zucchini."

Critical studies of Meinke's work include Philip Jason's "Speaking to Us All" in *Poet Lore* (Boston: 1982), and Eric Nelson's "Trying to Surprize God" in *Mickle Street Review* (Philadelphia: 1983).

Connections (p. 901)

1. Olds's subject is really not exercise and its obsessions but sex. Her analogy to exercise explores the absence of mutual experience or feeling in sex without love. Meinke's concern *is* exercise. Like Olds, he sees exercise as a desperate attempt to fight off the inevitable process of aging. The difference in the poems' attitudes toward exercise is a matter of diction and theme. Whereas Olds thinks that exercise involves a competition with oneself, Meinke reveals that it is really a struggle against "death and fatty tissue." Meinke's images of exercise are darker and more colloquial.

2. Kinnell's poem celebrates a child as a sign of life and love, whereas Meinke's criticizes our culture's inability to accept death. Kinnell's poem will probably appeal to your more optimistic students; the more cynical will be comfortable with Meinke's view.

JAMES MERRILL, *Casual Wear* (p. 901)

Merrill has been called a conversational poet. His familiarity with the lives of American aristocrats may result from his wealthy background, which especially influenced his earlier poetry.

Jeans, of course, are "casual wear," and by implication this act of random terrorism appears to be a casual flourish of some unseen hand. That relation in sum seems to be the import of this poem. Because of the enjambment of lines between stanzas, students may not at first observe that the stanzas rhyme with an *abba* pattern — except the middle two lines of the first stanza. But then, what would rhyme with "Ferdi Plinthbower"? Rhyme, however, along with lengthy, odd names, precise statistics, and descriptions of human beings as proper demographic models, detracts from our ability to feel the weight of this crime against humankind and our intuitive understanding of the moral workings of the universe. The inverse parallels between "tourist" and "terrorist" seem just too chillingly neat.

So what might Merrill actually be saying in this poem? Perhaps he is not so much speaking out against terrorist activity as talking about the media, with its formulaic scenarios, and the number-plotting social scientists, who surround such an event with their own dehumanizing mist of facts and figures. In the final irony of the poem, we know the name of the clothing designer but not that of the terrorist's victim.

You might ask the students in a two- to three-page essay to compare this poem with Nemerov's "Life Cycle of Common Man" (p. 825) and discuss each poet's use of statistics and "facts." Which poem is more successful, and why?

Comments on Merrill's poetry include David Lehman and Charles Berger, ed., *James Merrill: Essays in Criticism* (Ithaca: Cornell UP, 1983), and Judith Moffet's *James Merrill: An Introduction to the Poetry* (New York: Columbia UP, 1984).

Connections (p. 901)

1. Meinke's satire directs itself at the frantic health-conscious exercising that has become a part of our culture. Merrill's addresses a different aspect of the same culture, the materialism and media hype that eradicate the individual, leaving us with facts, figures, and wardrobe reports. Merrill's poem has a sobering life-and-death message, whereas Meinke's seems to have more hope for immediate change. Merrill's speaker is bitter; Meinke's satire is comical.

SHARON OLDS, *Sex without Love* (p. 902)

The word *beautiful,* which begins the second sentence of this poem, may puzzle students at first. Coupled with the ambiguity of the initial question (which may indicate either the speaker's envy or her disdain), the appeal of the lovers as performing artists may signal a positive view of them. But students will soon recognize that the beautiful images of the poem are surface images only; they are also empty and somewhat violent. The textural imagery — "ice," "hooked," and even "red as steak" suggests an undertone of danger in this act. As an artist, the poet must show the lovers as beautiful forms, but as an artist with a social consciousness, she must also explore the vacuum beneath the forms.

A discussion of the poem's imagery may begin with an exploration of all the possible meanings of its initial question. The speaker examines not only the moral implications of this self-centered experience but also the mechanics of the physical act: *how* as well as *why* they do it. Discuss the shift in tone from the portrayal of the lovers as ice skaters and dancers in the initial lines to their likeness to great runners. This last metaphor solidifies the coldness of the speaker's assessment. Like great runners, the lovers concentrate only on the movement of their bodies, surrendering their mental and emotional health to the physical act. Students will see that the energy and concentration of runners are essential to a track event but not to an act of mutual communication. It is essential for the couple to think of themselves as athletes in order to escape the negative moral and potentially painful emotional implications of their act.

The religious images of the poem contrast with its athletic metaphors. Beginning with "God" (line 9) and moving into "light/rising slowly as steam off their joined/skin" (11–13), the speaker subtly distinguishes between the false, body-bound vision of the lovers and the "true religion" that is implied through their negation. Ask students to identify the speaker's tone in these lines: is she really talking about a religious experience, or is she pointing out the lovers' self-absorption? The mathematical language with which the speaker imagines her subjects talking about themselves, "just factors" (21), is undercut by her derogatory tone. Although *they* may act as if they are God, if we are searching for truth, we know that we can never really be single bodies alone in the universe . The implied "truth" here is a communal one, just the opposite of what is described.

In a writing assignment, you might ask students to explore what is not said in the poem. What is the alternative? Why would the speaker not state her idea of truth directly?

Connections (p. 902)

1. Cummings and Olds do not share a similar notion of sex in these poems. Cummings's speaker is flippant, implying in his language that having sex is like driving a new car. Olds also talks about sex as mechanistic, but her disdain for that attitude is obvious. Cummings's speaker is less interested in the "truth" of the sexual relationship than he is in making the experience live on the page. Olds's speaker implies with regret that "truth" and love are ignored by those who have sex without love. One of the ways to reveal the different attitudes of these speakers is to compare their poems' very different images and sounds.

2. The lovers in Wilbur's poem may well fall under Olds's definition of sex without love. The speaker in "A Late Aubade" clearly cares for their physical relationship, urging his beloved to forget worldly business and get them some wine and cheese. However, Wilbur's speaker's deliberate persuasive appeal to his lover establishes verbal communication, which is not even present in Olds's poem.

ROBERT PHILLIPS, *Running on Empty* (p. 902)

From the beginning to the end of this poem, the title phrase goes through a number of modulations. You might begin discussion of the poem by exploring the changing connotations of the phrase *running on empty.* At first it holds only its literal content. Then, as the pace quickens and the couplets enjamb themselves, the phrase signals a release from a world bounded by measurements into extremities where the laws of reality do not operate. A final change in direction and pace takes place in the ninth couplet. Fantasy itself becomes displaced, and this journey from mundane reality to a mythical order becomes more interior as the self is momentarily "stalled" and forced to draw on its resources.

Explore with the class the tone of the phrase *running on empty* in the final line. What does it usually mean in common parlance? If we read the poem as autobiography, the speaker was forty-three at the time of the poem's publication. What is the significance then of his once again addressing his father?

Contemporary poetry, if not openly confessional in the manner, say, of Robert Lowell or Sylvia Plath, is often highly autobiographical in content. You might ask students to explore in a two- to three-page essay the pattern of relationship between himself and his father that Phillips directly and indirectly reveals.

Connection (p. 903)

1. In both of Chapman's and Phillips's poems, a car promises escape from a disliked environment. But Chapman's speaker's economic situation places her in a physically unbearable living situation. Phillips's speaker looks selfish by comparison: he has access to a car for leisure and deliberately disobeys his father's simple request that he keep gas in the tank. Apart from the surface, however, we might say that Phillips's speaker is as unstable as the speaker in "Fast Car." Neither can escape turmoil without help, and help doesn't seem real in either poem. Phillips's poem does not seem suited to song; it has no regular rhyme scheme, and its dialogue makes it sound closer to spoken speech than sung verse.

ALBERTO RÍOS, *Seniors* (p. 903)

You might begin your discussion of this poem by asking students to talk about its use of slang, particularly in the first stanza. The slang establishes the speaker's environment, as well as his conversational tone. As the poem progresses, it focuses on the speaker, and the tone becomes more meditative. Although they modify his relationship to other people, the images of cavities, flat walls, and water (particularly in stanza III) distance the speaker from the social realm, until he is left "on the desert" in the last stanza.

Students might write an essay on these images. How does their evocation of sexual experience prepare us for the last line of the poem? What is the speaker trying to say about sex, about life? How does the language of the final stanza compare with that of the first stanza? What might this changed diction indicate in the speaker's attitude toward himself and the world?

Connections (p. 904)

1. Olds talks about sex as a sport, noting how lovers who have sex without love treat their bodies as separate from "truth." The images Olds uses to make her point are unlike Ríos's imagery. Ríos talks about bodies as continually fading away. His speaker calls the body of the woman he first kissed almost "nonexistent" (line 18), comparing sexual experiences to "a flagstone wall" (22), vacationing in Bermuda, swimming ("all water," 27). For Ríos's speaker, sex provides a vehicle for capturing the past; for Olds's speaker, sex is the subject for a lesson about love.

2. J. Alfred Prufrock's voice bespeaks an empty culture, characterized by "sawdust restaurants" and "yellow smoke," as well as by empty conversations and rituals. "Prufrock" is a love poem that never comes to be, because the speaker is too fearful to act: "Do I dare/Disturb the universe?" Ríos's speaker also describes a lost culture, particularly in his use of slang and his references to materialism in the first two stanzas. In fact, many of the images in "Seniors" are complemented by similar, though starker, images in "Prufrock." In each poem love symbolizes both the speaker's individual feelings of loss and the collective emptiness of the culture.

CATHY SONG, *The White Porch* (p. 904)

The speaker in this poem establishes a conversation with her listener in the first stanza: "your," "think." She projects her listener into the future even as she captures the present moment through the description of her newly washed hair. The second stanza moves the conversation toward sexual innuendo, comparing the speaker's arousal to a flower, a flock of birds, and a sponge cake with peaches. Ask students to determine how these images give us a sense of what the speaker is like. What is her relationship to the listener? The final stanza returns us to the initial image of hair, but whereas the first stanza moves toward the future, the third plunges us back into the past. Students will enjoy comparing the images describing the mother to those describing the lover in the final lines. Like the rope ladder (an allusion to Rapunzel?), the poem is column-shaped, inviting its listener into the experience of reading it as it talks about a sexual relationship.

In a writing assignment, ask students to examine the concrete nouns and participial verbs in the poem. How do they evoke the speaker's message? How do images of domestic life summon the speaker's more "philosophical" side?

Connection (p. 906)

1. Croft also uses domestic images to talk about sexual intimacy and poetry writing. Both "Home Baked Bread" and "The White Porch" invite the listener into the experience, promising food and warmth; each poem, for example, uses peaches to seduce its listener. The imagery is full of anticipation and ripeness. There is an element of danger, too, in each poem, enticing the audiences into delicious but forbidden experiences.

23. Perspectives on Poetry

Prose statements on poetry (especially those written by poets themselves) are useful and important for students if only to show them how consciously articulate the creative process can be. In this chapter there are seventeen entries (both poetry and prose). The subjects include the special temperament of the poet, the use and value of poetry, the creative process, and the organic unity of poems themselves.

When assigning these Perspectives, you might take into account how some form a chorus of consent on a particular point. Consider, for example, pieces that speak of the uniqueness of the poet's temperament. Writers such as Wordsworth (p. 907), Shelley (p. 909), Cummings (p. 912), and Shapiro (p. 913), all remark on the poem-making impulse that some gifted persons seem to possess. For Wordsworth, it is a quality of spirit, the response of "a man pleased with his own passions and volitions, and who rejoices more than other men in the spirit of life that is in him." For Shelley, it is a "comprehensive and all-penetrating spirit." For Cummings, the poet responds to what is, simply a "calling."

In class discussion you might also want to explore the different emphases and nuances the poets suggest in their comments on the poetic psyche. Do these statements modify or reinforce certain preconceptions about the poet as visionary, or as the one who sees almost too deeply into the heart of the current social order? Moreover, do they suggest that the poet transmits, almost without design or even volition, the pulse of the imagination's flow? Can these voices finally be read as a dialogue, with one poet supporting or countering another so that students begin to realize that the idea of poetry and the standards that shape its actual writing are as dynamic as the social and political conditions that help form the context of the poems?

The pieces that self-reflexively describe poetry here point for the most part to an organic theory. Ask the class to try to place each poet along some imaginary scale, with insistence on form and regularized meter at one end and open form at the other. How exacting does Pound (p. 910) seem when compared with Whitman, "On Rhyme and Meter" in Chapter 20, or Frost (Ch. 21) perhaps? Would Whitman agree with the lines in the Francis poem "Glass" (p. 912) that read "A glass spun for itself is empty,/Brittle, at best Venetian trinket"? In considering some of these comments on poetry, you might also want to look back on other poems that treat the writing of poetry, including Francis's "The Pitcher" (p. 623), Ferlinghetti's "Constantly risking absurdity" (p. 784), and Giovanni's "Poetry" (p. 787).

Another theme treated in these Perspectives is that of shared obligation between poet and reader or poet and society. Shelley (p. 909) recognizes the poet's special role as "legislator" or value giver. Arnold (p. 910) reverses the direction of the responsibility and sees society as obligated to encourage the development of a sensibility that could appreciate poetry. Whether this aim fails or succeeds, however, poetry will endure, Arnold feels, because it celebrates and is itself derived from instincts for self-preservation. You might in discussion of these pieces direct the students' attention to some poems that treat social, historic, and political conditions. Consider, for example, Milton's "On the Late Massacre in Piedmont" (p. 882), the poems by Owen (pp. 552, 829), or, more recently, Brooks's "The Bean Eaters" (p. 761), Forché's "The Colonel" (p. 671), Levertov's "Gathered at the River" (898), and Dove's "Parsley" (p. 892). You might also glance again at Giovanni's "Poetry" (p. 787), which places the blame for failed communication of values not on the poet but on the people who should be receiving the meaning of the poem. Despite their differences in time and temperament, Arnold and Giovanni seem to agree on many points.

DRAMA

24. Reading Drama

SUSAN GLASPELL, *Trifles* (p. 932)

A discussion of the elements of drama in *Trifles* appears on pages 942–946 in the text; this discussion alludes to most of the questions that follow the play.

The stark, gloomy setting (discussed on p. 943) evokes the hard life Mr. Wright imposed on his wife. Within this cold environment the relationship between the Wrights is immediately and subtly recapitulated in the opening scene by Glaspell's having the men dominate the room as they stand by the stove while the two women remain timidly near the door. The sympathy that we increasingly feel for Mrs. Peters and Mrs. Hale will eventually be extended to Mrs. Wright, despite the fact that she murdered her husband.

Exposition (discussed on pp. 943–944) is used throughout to characterize Mr. and Mrs. Wright; Glaspell makes us feel as if we know the essential qualities of this couple even though we never actually see them. Just as the dialogue reveals their characters, it displays the insensitivity of the men, whose self-importance blinds them to the clues woven into the domestic setting, which they dismiss as mere "trifles." The women understand what these details reveal, for example, that the bird cage and dead bird offer evidence concerning Mrs. Wright's motive for murdering her husband. The cage (now broken) symbolizes the lifeless, joyless, confining marriage Mrs. Wright had to endure and the bird (strangled) suggests both the husband and the wife, Minnie Foster, who used to sing in the choir. Although the women recognize the significance of these objects as well as of the identical knots Mrs. Wright used on her husband and on her sewing, they will not give this evidence to the men because, as women, they empathize with Mrs. Wright's circumstances.

Trifles is packed with irony. On a second reading the dialogue takes on a strong ironic flavor, for example, when the sheriff says there's "Nothing here but kitchen things" (p. 934) or when the county attorney sarcastically asks, "What would we do without the ladies?" (934) and expresses mild surprise to Mrs. Hale about her being "loyal to her sex" (935).

The play's title comments on the kind of evidence that *could* be used to convict Mrs. Wright if the men were not so smugly certain of their powers of observation. What appear unimportant in the play — the domestic details and the two women — turn out to be powerfully significant. In the final line Mrs. Hale answers the county attorney's condescending question about Mrs. Wright's sewing. She is standing center stage, he by the door so that their positions are the reverse of what they were in the opening scene. She has the dead canary in her pocket and Mrs. Wright's fate on her lips, but she chooses to exonerate her.

Mrs. Wright is tried by "A Jury of Her Peers" (the short story title); Mrs. Hale and Mrs. Peters penetrate the meaning of what appears only trifling to the men and go beyond conventional shallow perceptions to discover and empathize with Mrs. Wright's reasons for killing her husband. *Trifles*, although written in 1916, has a distinct contemporary quality, because its feminist perspectives make a convincing case for women stepping outside general attitudes and oppressive values to be true to their own experience. This play is well worth comparing with Henrik Ibsen's *A Doll's House* (p. 1321), especially in terms of characterization and theme.

BARBARA AVEDON, BARBARA CORDAY, AND BARNEY ROSENZWEIG, *From*
Cagney & Lacey, *"You Call This Plainclothes?"* (p. 948)

Discussed in text.

25. A Study of Sophocles

SOPHOCLES, *Oedipus the King* (p. 964)

Student discussions of this play are likely to center on Oedipus's powerful character and the fate that has been prophesied for him. The two compete for our attention, and the ironies associated with each raise intriguing questions about human freedom and fate. For a broad range of critical responses to the play see Berkowitz, Luci, and Theodore F. Brunner, eds., *Oedipus Tyrannus* (New York: Norton, 1970).

Considerations (p. 1006)

1. The opening scene presents Oedipus as a powerful king who has defeated the Sphinx and ruled successfully for many years. The priest's speech (lines 16–68) offers this exposition and characterizes Oedipus as the "first of men" (41) and the "best of men" (57). The city turns to heroic Oedipus to save it once again.

2–4. Oedipus's fury at Tiresias for initially refusing to tell his "dreadful secrets" (374) establishes Oedipus's fierce determination to discover the truth. It also reveals him to be quick tempered and unreasonable when he accuses Tiresias of conspiring with Creon to usurp the throne (414–459). Oedipus's rage renders him, in a sense, blind (the ironies abound) to the information Tiresias directly tells him: "I say you are the murderer you hunt" (413).

When Oedipus also accuses Creon of treason, Creon correctly assesses a significant element — an error or frailty — of Oedipus's personality as a "crude, mindless stubbornness" that has caused Oedipus to lose his "sense of balance" (615–616). Oedipus's absolute insistence on learning who murdered Laius shows him to be a decisive leader while simultaneously exposing him to the consequences of making public the message from Delphi and his cursing of the murderer of Laius.

Oedipus's self-confidence, determination, and disregard for consequences propel him toward both his goal and his destruction. His downfall is not brought about solely by the gods or fate but by the nature of his own remarkable character. The gods may know what will inevitably happen, but it is Oedipus's personality — especially his proud temper — that causes it to happen. As much as he is responsible for the suffering in the play, he is the victim of it. His virtues as well as his vices contribute to his horror and shame.

5. Irony is pervasive in the play, but the greatest irony is that the murderer Oedipus seeks is himself. He sets out to save the city, to appease the gods, and to see that justice is done, but all his altruistic efforts bring ruin on himself. Ignorant of the truth, Oedipus is consistently used as a vehicle for dramatic irony because we know more than he does; this strategy allows Sophocles to charge Oedipus's speeches with additional meanings that the protagonist only gradually comes to perceive. A review of Oedipus's early speeches will yield numerous instances of dramatic irony, as when he declares that if anyone knows about the murder of Laius that person must report to Oedipus "even if he must denounce himself" (257). His curse on the murderer (280–314) is especially rich in ironic foreshadowings.

6. The Chorus voices community values of reason, order, and moderation. It knows better than to defy the gods, and it firmly condemns human pride (for instance, in lines 963–980). It reacts and comments on the action and also links scenes. In contrast to Jocasta's rejection of the oracles, the Chorus worries about the irreverence it observes. Its final words confirm the unpredictable ironies that we must endure: "count no man happy till he dies, free of pain at last."

7. Tiresias's blindness does not prevent him from seeing the truth of Oedipus's past. His insight is in ironic contrast to Oedipus, who sees physically but is blind to the pattern of events that defines his life. Once Oedipus does see the truth, he blinds himself, a fitting punishment that will not allow him to escape his suffering. Oedipus does not choose suicide because to live is even more painful; he takes complete responsibility for what has happened and accepts his suffering as his destiny.

8. The answer to all the questions Oedipus has is not only "man" but more specifically himself. The ultimate riddle is posed by Oedipus when he sets out to learn about his father's murderer as well as his own beginnings. When he is able to answer that riddle he destroys himself rather than the Sphinx.

9., 10.   Students should be encouraged to examine both Oedipus's irrational willfulness — which his behavior demonstrates and the Chorus comments on — and prophecies, coincidences, and actions that transform a powerful, bold man into a tragic figure whose only remaining dignity is in complete suffering. What happens to Oedipus raises questions concerning human guilt, innocence, and cosmic justice. Students are likely to recognize that though Oedipus's circumstances are specific to himself, the larger issues he encounters are relevant to them too.

11. In *The Interpretation of Dreams*, Sigmund Freud reads the play as a manifestation of men's unconscious desire to replace their fathers and have sexual relations with their mothers. In healthy personalities this jealousy and sexual impulse are overcome and suppressed. Jocasta urges Oedipus not to worry that this has happened to him (1074–77). Certainly Oedipus has no conscious design to marry his mother; he is appalled by the possibility. But Freud would argue that a significant part of our fascination with this play is our identification with Oedipus's fears. Students with some background in psychology will probably be eager to pursue the question; others are likely to be wary and skeptical.

SOPHOCLES, *Antigone* (p. 1008)

The conflict in this play derives from two powerful characters — Antigone and Creon — and the two principles they represent. Antigone's loyalty is to her family, individual conscience, and religious law. Creon, however, defines his duty as the enforcement of civil law to maintain order. This produces tensions between human laws and religious law, and between the individual and the state. Sophocles complicates the moral choices each character makes by revealing their personalities so that their choices are not merely abstract sets of principles. Therein lies the drama.

Considerations (p. 1044)

1. Creon forbids Polynices' burial to punish Antigone's rebellious brother. Antigone, however, refuses to abide by this decree because she pledges her allegiance to religious law over civil law. The central conflict of the play revolves around whether one should obey the law of the land or follow one's conscience. Students will probably be divided in their loyalties to Creon's (lines 210–214) or Antigone's (409–524) position. Sophocles does not make the choice easy.

2. The Chorus, rejecting extremes, makes a plea for moderation and reasonableness; "the laws of the land" must be combined with "the justice of the gods" if the city is to prosper (409–412). "Reckless daring" (415) of any kind jeopardizes both individuals and the state. Although the Chorus celebrates the power and genius of humankind, it also emphasizes the importance of subordinating human will to the gods (377–416).

3. Creon is the protagonist despite the play's title. Most readers find that the play endorses fidelity to higher law, but Antigone, who holds that position, remains essentially static from beginning to end. Creon, however, changes; he retreats from the accusations of treason he has hurled at the sentry, Antigone, Haemon, and Tiresias, even if it is too late to avert the tragic consequences of his insecurities and misperceptions.

4. Ismene serves as a foil to Antigone because she urges her sister to be "sensible," to remember that women cannot resist the strength of men and that they must "submit" to "the ones who stand in power" (60–81). Ismene recognizes her sister's passions and sees her as a quixotic romantic "in love with impossibility" (104) and "off on a hopeless quest" (107). Students may find Ismene's position weak and overly cautious, but they are also likely to find Antigone's rejection of Ismene's attempts to martyr herself along with her sister coldly extreme. Perhaps the fairest assessment of each sister's values and sensibilities is voiced by Antigone when she tells Ismene that "your wisdom appealed to one world — mine, another" (628). Both sisters can lay claim to truth, but neither's position is wholly adequate to live in both worlds.

5. With great self-control Haemon calmly pleads for Antigone's life by informing his father that public opinion is against her execution. Haemon is deferential and loving when he urges Creon not to "be quite so single-minded, self-involved / or assume the world is wrong and you are right." He pleads with Creon "not to be too rigid" (789–796). Haemon's demeanor changes abruptly and radically when he realizes that his father will not pardon Antigone. Haemon's despair and suicide are plausible because he has lost his father and his lover. Indeed, his rashness identifies him both as his father's son and as a sympathetic mate for Antigone.

6. Creon's angry reaction to Antigone's disobedience is informed, in part, by what he perceives to be a threat not only to his authority but to his manhood: "I am not the man, no now: she is the man / if this victory goes to her and she goes free" (541–542). He insists that "no woman is going to lord it over me" (593). He tells Haemon to "never lose your sense of judgment over a woman" (723) and "never be rated / inferior to a woman, never" (760–761). For additional moments when Creon expresses contempt for women see lines 836–837 and 848.

7. Both Creon and Antigone must share responsibility for what happens. If neither had acted so rigidly and precipitously, the outcome might have been different. However, Creon must assume more responsibility for the tragedy because he has the power and authority to change things. Both appear guilty of the "stubbornness" that Tiresias says "brands you for stupidity — pride is a crime" (1136–37). Antigone loses her life, but Creon's suffering is finally greater, because he must accept the guilt for his son's and wife's deaths.

8. Creon, like Oedipus, responds to advice he does not wish to hear as if it were a betrayal. He mistakenly equates dissent with disloyalty and reacts with blind rage to anyone who challenges him. Ironically, Creon was the object of similar anger in *Oedipus the King*.

9., 10. Like her father, Antigone "hasn't learned to bend before adversity" (527). Of all the major characters in both plays, only Ismene seems capable of moderation, although she might be regarded as having initially bent too far in obeying Creon's decree.

PERSPECTIVES ON SOPHOCLES

ARISTOTLE, *On Tragic Character* (p. 1045)
Considerations (p. 1047)

1. The tragic figure, according to Aristotle, "does not fall into misfortune through vice or depravity" but through "some mistake." Neither extreme virtue nor vice is appropriate because these characteristics do not produce in the audience the emotional intensity of "pity and fear."

2. Aristotle's objection to a woman being "manly or formidable" should produce considerable class debate, since "in the way I mean" doesn't explain very much in this context. Perhaps a discussion of Creon's attitude toward women in *Antigone* can be related to Aristotle's comments.

3. No, this is not a contradiction. A character's qualities on the stage have to be perceived by an audience at a distance.

SOPHOCLES, *Another Translation of a Scene from* Oedipus the King (p. 1047)

Fagles' more modern diction and tone (lines 1433–1549) are less poetically embellished than Sheppard's. Consider, for example, these lines spoken by the Chorus:

Unhappy in thy fortune and the wit
That shows it thee. Would thou hadst never known. (Sheppard)

Pitiful, you suffer so, you understand so much . . .
I wish you'd never known. (Fagles)

Fagles' version is considerably more direct and less mannered than the many O's and *Alases* that punctuate Sheppard's translation. Although there are no significant differences that affect our interpretation of the scene, it is fair to say that in Fagle's translation Oedipus sounds to the modern ear more like a man who is truly suffering rather than declaiming.

MURIEL RUKEYSER, *On* Oedipus the King (p. 1050)

The "myth" of the title does not merely indicate a mythical allusion; it also refers to the mistaken notion that "when you say man . . . you include women." Although Sophocles' play does not address the issue of equality of the sexes, Rukeyser indicates — with good humor — that the unresolved issue is the cause of great unhappiness and even catastrophe. Her colloquial rendering of Oedipus's second encounter with the Sphinx gives the episode just the right updated tone to establish its relevance to the reader.

JEAN ANOUILH, *A Scene from* Antigone (p. 1051)

Creon refuses to bury Polynices because he believes that refusal will help preserve "peace and order" in Thebes. Unlike Sophocles' Creon, who refuses to be bested by a woman, Anouilh's acts out of a firmer sense of duty and responsibility. He is not a tyrant (being too "fastidious"); instead, he is trapped by circumstances that, he thinks, make his actions necessary to save the ship of state. Anouilh seems more sympathetic to Creon than Sophocles does. Antigone's position is surely morally purer, but she makes her choice in an abstract, absolute context, while Creon is finally anchored in historic circumstances, conditions that Anouilh found parallel to the German occupation of France. There is plenty of room for support of both positions.

MAURICE SAGOFF, *A Humorous Distillation of* Antigone (p. 1053)

Sagoff actually manages to tuck a significant portion of the play into the poem, particularly in lines 8–9, where he alludes to the theme. Creon and Antigone are given short shrift but that, of course, is the nature of a shrinklit and part of its breezy fun.

26. A Study of William Shakespeare

WILLIAM SHAKESPEARE, *Hamlet, Prince of Denmark* (p. 1065)

Two standard sources for the study of *Hamlet* are A. C. Bradley's *Shakespearean Tragedy* (1904; rpt. New York: St. Martin's, 1965) and Harley Granville-Barker's "Preface to *Hamlet*," in his *Prefaces to Shakespeare,* vol. I (Princeton: Princeton University Press, 1946). Both discuss character and motivation in detail. A useful study of the relation of imagery to character is Maynard Mack's "The World of *Hamlet*," *Yale Review* 41 (1952): 502–523, reprinted in Leonard F. Dean, ed., *Shakespeare: Modern Essays in Criticism,* rev. ed. (New York: Oxford University Press, 1967) 242–262. Useful too is Harold Jenkins's introduction in the 1982 Arden edition. He sorts through the criticism and offers a sensible, adaptable reading.

Considerations (p. 1164)

1. Insofar as Claudius's advice generalizes from the traditional Boethian consolation, it is sensible. But if we look back at this advice after we hear of Claudius's crime, its sensibility is undercut by his lurking suspicion of Hamlet. Hamlet cannot heed the advice because it does not address his particular grief, deeply felt because he remembers his father as "Hyperion" (see his first soliloquy, p. 1074). Nor can the advice smooth over other complications in Hamlet's mood arising from his hatred of the "satyr" Claudius and his revulsion at his mother's incestuous "frailty."

2. Polonius's advice to Laertes is sound, albeit in its political content rather than its moral or ethical content. It thus reflects Polonius's political role in court as well as the delicate, sometimes finicky care with which a courtier must conduct himself. Plonius's political view of life is asserted more clearly when he sends Reynaldo to spy on Laertes (pp. 1089–1091).

3. When Horatio first tells him of the ghost's appearance, Hamlet immediately offers an interpretation that hints at prophecy: "I doubt some foul play" (p. 1077), and later, when the ghost beckons him, he says, "My fate cries out" (p. 1083). So there is evidence of Hamlet's foreboding early on. And the fact that the ghost's revelation of the crime (p. 1085) nearly repeats Hamlet's first soliloquy makes the suggestion of prophetic insight more plausible. The ghost's principal demand is that Hamlet "revenge his foul and most unnatural murder" (p. 1084); three secondary demands are

   Let not the royal bed of Denmark be
   A couch for . . . damned incest. . . .
   Taint not thy mind, nor let thy soul contrive
   Against thy mother aught. (p. 1086)

   Hamlet has difficulty fulfilling all of these.

4. What we know of Hamlet before his father's death comes in snippets from other characters. Claudius identifies him as a student (p. 1073). Laertes and Ophelia (and Hamlet himself) speak of his love for Ophelia (pp. 1078, 1109–10, 1152–53). Laertes and Ophelia remark on his greatness as a prince (pp. 1078, 1110). Claudius too recognizes and fears his popularity (pp. 1131–1132) and power (p. 1111). And Fortinbras says, in the end, that Hamlet would have "proved most royal" (pp. 1163–64). We also see him actively fearless in pursuing the ghost (pp. 1083–84); we hear him speak knowledgeably on the theater (pp. 1102–04, 1111–12); and he proves himself an expert swordsman. In addition we are given subtler indications of his former character. Hamlet's friendship with Horatio is evidence of

his gentle nature. His language is richly imaginative. Even the stability he shows after his return from sea and his "readiness" to face his task and his death bespeak a personality that was the "rose of the fair state" (p. 1110).

The initial change in Hamlet occurs before the play begins: with his father's death and his mother's hasty remarriage, the ideas upon which he based his life and his view of the world have been severely shaken. His references to his father as Hyperion and to his mother's doting love for his father, coupled with his pained speech to Rosencrantz and Guildenstern about the earth, the heavens, and humanity all gone to corruption (p. 1099), suggest what his image of the world had been — it is almost romantic in its nobility and beauty. That Hamlet has been robbed of the crown, that the world is now rank, humanity a "quintessence of dust," the king a satyr, and the queen an incestuous beast point to the utter destruction of Hamlet's ideological basis for living. With this sudden demolition comes near madness. Upon receiving news of the murder, Hamlet barely avoids total distraction (p. 1086), but he never, apparently, falls into true madness. His verbal antics are usually contrived, for example, those that fend off Polonius. When his verbal violence is aimed at Ophelia, particularly in III.i, or at Gertrude in the closet scene (III. iv), he seems closer to madness. But uncontrolled passion is probably a better way to describe these expressions of Hamlet's mental condition. In general we might say that in exchanges with the women in the play Hamlet tends toward passionate distraction.

But intermingled with these shifts between feigned madness and violent passion are the soliloquies. While each contains the conflict between reason and passion, between action and inaction, and each ends with a determination to act that remains unfulfilled, there is also from the first soliloquy to the last a traceable development toward logical and rhetorical control. The first (p. 1074) shifts topics frantically, apparently by rapid associations. The second major soliloquy (p. 1105) progresses emotionally, but each topic is more clearly separated, as if Hamlet were becoming aware of and beginning to control his distraction. The third (pp. 1108–09), following hard upon the second, flows smoothly but maintains a delicate tension, only seemingly resolved, between the personal fear of death and the general fear. Its conclusive "Thus conscience does make cowards of us all" is a statement both individual and communal. The last major soliloquy (p.1134) is clearly logical, moving from controlled personal reflection to the contrary example to the particular application of the contrary to Hamlet himself.

This various, sometimes contradictory mental activity creates for us a character unlike any other. Our sense of Hamlet as a tragic hero depends largely on his (and our) endurance through this chaotic progress toward the courageous stability we see in Acts IV and V.

5. (See also question 4.) Hamlet's attempts to define his own character in a corrupt world, his fear of death apparently resulting from his new view of the world's corruption, the fact that death is an inevitable consequence of revenge, the fact that his image of the world is so wrapped up in his now-horrible image of his mother, even his legitimate desire (at least in a revenge-play world) to send Claudius to Hell — all cause delay.

6. The dramatic purpose of the play within the play is to verify the ghost's story and to trap Claudius into revealing his guilt. Its themes refer to Gertrude's inconstancy in love. (She, however, as the closet scene will show, is deaf to all this.) One other interesting feature is the player king's speech (pp. 1115–1116) on the changeability of human affection; its tone suggests acceptance of human frailty.

7. Ophelia is only indirectly connected with the crime. Because the world, including Hamlet, has become sinfully corrupt (see his soliloquy and the nunnery scene, pp. 1108–10) and because women are in two ways the source of corruption — as lusting beasts and as bearers of children — Ophelia must necessarily be corrupt. In III.i Hamlet's vehemence comes from this view of the world and Ophelia's place in it. (In III.ii, however, Hamlet's crudities are aimed through Ophelia at Gertrude and Claudius.) Ophelia's fall into madness mirrors Hamlet's. Having lived, it seems, solely according to the guidance of Polonius, Laertes, and

perhaps Hamlet, she has no strength to bear up when her supports collapse. With Polonius dead, Hamlet, whom she loved, a murderer and madman, and Laertes absent, she crumbles.

8. Hamlet's words to Gertrude after she calls the killing of Polonius "a rash and bloody deed" — "almost as bad, good mother / As kill a king and marry with his brother" (p. 1124) — are a slip that reveals Hamlet's belief that she is deeply, conspiratorially guilty. Her crime, however, seems to be one of omission as well as commission. In setting up a "glass" wherein she will see her soul, Hamlet hits on an image appropriate to his mother's failure to perceive what has occurred. In presenting the pictures of his father and Claudius and returning to an analogy to the gods in describing his father, Hamlet indicates that he feels compelled to reveal to his mother what he has seen and learned. His words must call up the same torment in her that he has felt.

9. Both questions will probably give rise to opposing responses. The likelihood of sympathy for Claudius depends to a great extent on the reader, because Claudius expresses both remorse for his crime and unwillingness to make reparation. One particular source of sympathy will be the speech's closeness logically, rhetorically, and thematically to Hamlet's soliloquies. But sympathy in whatever degree survives only as long as Claudius is on his knees. The safest answer to why Hamlet does not kill Claudius is Hamlet's own: perfect revenge requires that Claudius suffer as much as or more than Hamlet's father did. Perhaps, too, Hamlet wishes Claudius to feel torment equal to his own — the idea of infernal or purgatorial punishment has been strong in Hamlet since the ghost's revelation.

10. This question addresses one of the central complexities of the play — Hamlet finds himself bound by external command to act on a situation that is, in one sense, outside himself and, in another, deeply personal. Because of his complex emotional involvements, he is slow to act. His various perceptions of corruption combine to retard the fulfillment of a seemingly simple command. From the closet scene on, we watch Hamlet come to terms with these ideas of corruption. Cathartic images occupy his mind — the dead Polonius (Hamlet is now an active agent in dealing death), the stricken mother, the ghost again, the planned destruction of Rosencrantz and Guildenstern, Fortinbras's army marching to death for an "eggshell," the graveyard, Yorick's skull, foul-smelling, and Ophelia's corpse.

    Through this process of images and actions Hamlet also comes to terms with corruption and death, including his own, and reaches a spiritual stability, a conception of humanity and the universe, that frees him to act and die. Because we share with him this movement and conclude with him, however unconsciously, that there has been some "special providence" at work, we can have little or no sense of his moral culpability.

11. Fortinbras is the foil toward which Hamlet seems to move. In structural terms, he is Hamlet's most important foil. His situation as described by Horatio (pp. 1068–69) parallels Hamlet's before we met Hamlet, and Fortinbras's action serves twice as a contrast to Hamlet's inaction (p. 1071, 1134–35). His appearance in the final scene concludes the play on a note of order and stability. His armor (he is the only living character to be seen prepared for battle) finally opens the play to a world of action beyond the confines of Denmark.

12. The humor of the play is remarkable for its poignant commentary on the central themes. Hamlet's joke about the "funeral baked meats" (p. 1075), his satiric assaults on Polonius (1096–97), his initial quips with Rosencrantz and Guildenstern (1097–98), his bitter sexual jibes at Ophelia's expense (pp. 1113–14), his dark humor regarding Polonius's body and death (1129, 1131–33), the grave digger's callous joking, and Hamlet's thoughts on the deaths of ladies and great men (pp. 1147–51) — all reflect on the many forms of corruption that Hamlet contemplates. Often the humor reveals the pain inherent in his thoughts and a desire to be released from them. In the grave digger scene there is a nice shift toward a more pathetic although resolved opinion of death and corruption. Such humor, one of the many mirrors of Hamlet's evolution, differs from the humor in the comedies because of its dark tones and its tragic import.

WILLIAM SHAKESPEARE, *Othello the Moor of Venice* (p. 1166)

Alvin Hernan's essay, "*Othello:* An Introduction," in *Shakespeare, The Tragedies: A Collection of Critical Essays* (Ed. Alfred Harbage, Englewood Cliffs, NJ: Prentice-Hall, 1964) provides a useful overall assessment of this play, as do the essays following the play in the Signet edition. For an interesting treatment of the black/white theme in *Othello,* see Doris Adler, "The Rhetoric of Black and White in *Othello,*" *Shakespeare Quarterly* 25 (Spring 1974): 248–57.

Considerations (p. 1249)

1. Shakespeare presents Othello as a soldier renowned for his prowess in battle. He is the choice of the Venetians to defend Cyprus, even though the Duke acknowledges that his viceroy there is competent. Although he is an "outsider" in Venice, Othello claims a lineage of rank equal to Desdemona, and is proud of himself and his accomplishments (I. ii. 18–24). Additionally, he shows himself to be a reasonable man and a proponent of order when he stops the fight between Cassio and Montano in II, iii. However, it is in this same scene that Othello reveals one of his weaknesses. When neither Cassio nor Montano will sufficiently answer his questions about their quarrel, he begins to lose his temper, and indicates that his reason can be overtaken by passion (II. iii. 180–188). Further, Othello's own honesty betrays him, for he expects to find in others a corresponding honesty. It does not occur to him to suspect Iago of duplicity, for he himself is not duplicitous. This ultimately makes Othello gullible, but the gullibility and its consequences are believable, for Shakespeare has prepared the audience for Othello's responses by the earlier characterization.

2. Iago presents himself as the occasion demands, in whatever way will endear him to the persons whom he is trying to manipulate. To Roderigo and Brabantio, he is Othello's enemy; to the other characters, he is Othello's devoted under-officer. He hates the Moor for choosing Cassio over him as his first officer. One reason he so easily stirs up Othello's jealousy is that he is so jealous himself; he is much like Milton's Satan, unhappy in an inferior position and determined to control from the position he occupies.

   Iago is an effective manipulator because he perceives the other characters' weaknesses and plays on them. He uses his knowledge of Cassio's drinking problem to stir up trouble between Cassio and Othello. He exploits his knowledge of Othello's straightforwardness, pride, and the Moor's struggle with his passions to manipulate him. Part of this duplicity is his talent for seeming. He appears to be in complete control of the image he projects for other characters; none of them suspect him of being more than "honest Iago" until nearly the end of the play.

3. From the way all the other characters respond to Iago, it is no surprise that Othello is taken in by him as well. Even his own wife does not recognize Iago's true motivation. The only way Othello can protect himself is to stay in his own military world, in which he is competent. Once he lets passion rule him, by falling in love with Desdemona, he opens himself to other influences, including Iago's malignancy.

4. Shakespeare calls attention to Othello's race in the title of the play, an immediate indication of its importance. Iago plays on Brabantio's racism to upset him about Desdemona's marriage ("an old black ram / Is tupping your ewe," I. i. 88–89), and it is Brabantio's attitudes which eventually result in Desdemona going to Cyprus with Othello.

   Iago plays on Othello's consciousness of race in convincing him of Desdemona's infidelity; Iago persuades him that Desdemona's love for someone of his "complexion" is unnatural. Given her tendencies, it would be easily possible for her to commit another unnatural act, adultery.

5. The two settings of the play have their counterparts in the types of characters and in the overall theme of reason and passion. Venice is ruled by reason and by law; the Duke and the Senate maintain civic order and are able to recognize deception. For instance, they are able to see through the Turks' deceptions to determine the real thrust of the attack. Also, when Iago tries to get Brabantio out of bed, the old man responds, "This is Venice; / My

house is not a grange" (I. i. 108). But when Brabantio does get upset, the civil force of the Duke intervenes to keep order. Finally, in Venice Othello controls his passions, even though he is disturbed on his wedding night.

Cyprus is the frontier, the outpost between the civilized world and the barbarism represented by the Turks. It is not governed by the Duke, but by his substitute, the viceroy. Othello himself terms it "a town of war / Yet wild, the people's hearts brimful of fear (II, iii, 189–190). On Cyprus, Iago is uncontrolled and Othello is in a constant battle to keep his passions in check.

6. The changes in Othello closely parallel the changes in setting. In Venice, Othello is in control of his passions and his destiny; when the scene shifts to Cyprus, Othello finds it increasingly difficult to remain reasonable. Besides the previously mentioned struggle with himself while breaking up the fight between Cassio and Montano, Othello also indicates his wavering control in III. iii, when he calls Desdemona a "wretch," but then follows it with "when I love thee not, Chaos is come again" (90–92), and also in IV. i, when he expresses "pity" for Desdemona, despite his fury. Although in general Othello becomes less sympathetic a character as he becomes more unreasonable, the honesty and perception displayed in his final speech restore some sympathy. He admits both his strengths and his weaknesses, and responds to the crime he has committed against civilization in the only way he can: He executes himself for committing it.

7. Desdemona, Emilia, and Bianca, though all are similarly devoted to their men, are not alike. They represent successively lower social classes; Desdemona is an officer's wife, Emilia a lesser officer's wife, and Bianca is essentially Cassio's prostitute. Bianca is ruled by passion, as seen in her jealous response to the handkerchief Cassio gives her. Emilia responds more with cold reason, declaring she would do anything for her husband for the right price, and also indicating that women should repay their husbands in kind for any ills they suffer at their husbands' hands (IV. iii). In this same scene, Desdemona indicates her true character, as one whose reason is tempered by her love for Othello. She declares she would never betray him, and even if ill-used herself, she would not try to avenge herself, but would seek to "mend the rift."

8. The Clown, or Fool, appears for some humorous moments in III. i, and in III. iv. In both cases, the humorous scene serves to set off, by contrast, the serious nature of the scenes surrounding it. Even in the humor, Shakespeare reinforces the major issues being dealt with in the play. In III. i, the clown parries with Cassio about his "honest friend," and his exit is quickly followed by Iago's entrance. In III. ii, the Clown puns with Desdemona on the word "lies," in a scene which falls between Iago's seductive lies to Othello and Othello's first accusations of infidelity to Desdemona.

10. Chance often comes into play in *Othello*. For instance, the Turks' plans come to light at the same time Othello's wedding is discovered; more significantly, Desdemona accidentally drops her handkerchief after Iago has been trying to get Emilia to steal it for some time. Shakespeare indicates by these events that part of life is simply fate, beyond human control. However, he also notes that people can use chance events to their advantage. The Turkish invasion provides the Duke with a convenient way to get Othello away from Brabantio's wrath, and the dropped handkerchief provides Iago with a way to carry out his plan. Thus fate is not controllable, but sometimes it is "usable."

11. Othello wishes to kill Desdemona immediately because he is convinced that it is a "just" act, but realizes that if he allows himself to let his feelings for her sway him, they might "almost persuade / Justice to break her sword" (V. ii. 16–17). Ironically, he wants the act of killing her to be one of reason, not passion. This becomes even more evident when he says her protests, which have enraged him, have changed his act from sacrifice — something which has to be done and can be performed dispassionately — to murder, an act of passion. This has the dual effect of making the audience realize how much he cares for Desdemona, in spite of himself, and also how completely Iago has perverted his mind.

12. In comparison to the language of prose, the language of poetry is more lofty, more suited to important subject matter, and more controlled. Thus, in *Othello,* characters often revert to prose when they are either discussing base matters, or when they are out of control. For instance, in IV. i, Iago and Othello enact a kind of "joint" blank verse until Othello loses control and goes into a prose tirade which ends with his trance. In IV. ii, Iago uses blank verse in trying to soothe Desdemona (165–67) but switches immediately to the less fanciful, more pragmatic prose when trying to manipulate the pragmatic and increasingly impatient Roderigo. The changes may indicate a shift in subject matter, audience, purpose, or tone.

Even within the blank verse, there are changes to a more controlled poetry, rhymed couplets, at the end of II. i, and in both Emilia's and Desdemona's speeches at the end of IV. iii. These shifts tend to call special attention to lines which are especially important in clarifying themes and characters. The language of poetry is such that it conveys ideas more powerfully in a few words than prose can convey in many more words.

PERSPECTIVES ON SHAKESPEARE

Objections to the Elizabethan Theater by the Mayor of London (p. 1250)

Considerations (p. 1250)

1–3. Plays, says the mayor, are bad influences on bad people and on the young, who may be inclined to a variety of "lewd & ungodly practizes." They are an occasion to diseases of body, mind, and soul. Examples of similar or related late-twentieth-century opinions are readily discoverable. Complaints about violence or sexual immorality in books, movies, and to a lesser extent plays are heard with regularity from religious organizations, some feminist groups, and the government as well. Those in favor of restrictions might argue that art affects perceptions of the world and therefore actions, a position that may well be reasonable, as the mayor's probably was, in some instances. Those in favor of unrestricted expression might argue that art forms, including plays, especially of Shakespeare's kind, do not incite action because they resolve through a cathartic process that expurgates whatever emotional tensions arise.

SAMUEL JOHNSON, *On Shakespeare's Characters* (p. 1251)

As an additional writing assignment, you might ask students to consider Iago in light of Johnson's assessment that in the writing of Shakespeare a character is "commonly a species." Ask students to discuss the attributes of the species of Iago. What else in the world of the play suggests that Iago's malignancy is not simply idiosyncratic or confined to one uniquely demonic figure?

SIGMUND FREUD, *On Repression in* Hamlet (p. 1251)

As a development of Consideration 1, ask students to write an essay supporting or refuting Freud's analysis of Hamlet by citing additional evidence from the play.

JAN KOTT, *On Producing* Hamlet (p. 1253)

Considerations (p. 1254)

1. Because of its variety of themes — military, Christian, sexual, psychological, and so on — the play opens itself to interpretation from all sides. Research into productions will show a wide diversity of treatment.

2. A reasonable argument for truth to Elizabethan theatrical practices can be found in Harley Granville-Barker's "Preface to *Hamlet*"(see entry on *Hamlet*). The problem with interpretations based too closely on current ideas or events is that they tend to disguise the play behind an apparently "really meaningful" significance.

3. Again, students' opinions will vary. Discussions of all four topics should lead to a better understanding of situation, character psychology as expressed in dress, interpretation of character, and reading of the play as a whole. Showing a film or videotape production will help get such discussions started.

KAREN S. HENRY, *The Play Within the Play in* Hamlet (p. 1254)

Henry cites Lionel Abel's discussion of *Hamlet* as metatheater. In Abel's interpretation, the Ghost, Claudius, Polonius, and Hamlet himself are seen as playwright/directors with conflicting ideas of theater. Claudius is a writer of melodrama, as is the Ghost, who writes typically Elizabethan melodrama. Polonius is an amateur playwright. Hamlet has a most excellent sense of theater, according to Abel; he must rewrite the melodrama, but he can't turn it into a tragedy because the Ghost has forbidden him to kill his mother. Abel suggests that death is the dramatist that Hamlet finally accepts (see *Metatheatre* 49–51).

As an additional writing assignment, you might ask students to discuss the theme of spying in the play.

HELEN GARDNER, *On Freedom in* Hamlet *and* Othello, (p. 1255)

The freedom of Othello is constrained by other characters, in particular, Iago. Students might discuss the relationship between Iago and Othello in light of Gardner's assertion that "*Othello* is particularly concerned with that deep, instinctive level where we feel ourselves to be free" (p. 1256).

A. C. BRADLEY, *On Iago's Intellect and Will* (p. 1257)

As a development of Consideration 2, ask students to write an essay discussing Othello's greatness in relation to Iago's. The essay can explore Shakespeare's play as a contrast between these two different kinds of "greatness." One question students might consider is whether these types of greatness are necessarily inimical to each other.

JANE ADAMSON, *On Desdemona's Role in* Othello (p. 1257)

As a followup to Adamson's remarks, ask students to write an essay exploring what Desdemona, Emilia, and Bianca represent in the world of *Othello*.

27. Neoclassical Drama

MOLIÈRE, *Tartuffe* (p. 1263)

Although *Tartuffe* was banished from the stage from 1664 to 1669 because it was perceived to be an attack on religion, Molière's specific target is not religion in general but religious hypocrisy and blind zealotry. (For Molière's defense of the play see p. 1314 of the text.) Students will probably recognize Tartuffe as an ancestor of some contemporary examples of assumed piety, such as certain television evangelists. Molière's treatment of Tartuffe's unctuousness is neither foreign nor dated. The playwright is also concerned with Orgon's extreme piety. Unlike Tartuffe, Orgon is sincere, but he is equally dangerous and destructive. What Molière satirizes in both characters are their excesses, their departures from common sense and reason, whether motivated by selfishness or selflessness. If students can see that the driving force behind the play's witty dialogue is healthy irreverence coupled with vigilant skepticism, they should enjoy its humor and find its implicit values (made explicit by Cléante) to be a celebration of humanity rather than a cynical view of it.

Considerations (p. 1313)

1. Orgon is obviously his mother's son. Madame Pernelle's defense in the first scene of Tartuffe's alleged efforts to save the souls of the family helps explain Orgon's own inability to see clearly. Neither of them understands what true virtue and piety consist of; instead, they are self-righteous prigs who have fallen under what Dorine describes as Tartuffe's "infatuating spell" (I.ii.14). Ironically, Orgon experiences the same frustrations his family has felt about him when his mother refuses to believe his condemnation of Tartuffe.

2. Unlike Madame Pernelle and Orgon, who are convinced of Tartuffe's "great goodness" (I.i.74), the other characters recognize that he is not what he claims to be. To Damis he is a "carping hypocrite" (I.i.46), to Dorine "a fraud" (I.i.70), and to Cléante he represents "humbug and pretense" (I.v.63). Although we don't meet Tartuffe until Act III, his critics are more convincing than his apologists, because Molière casts the apologists in a comic light to discredit their views. Like Cléante, we are inclined to respond to Orgon and his mother with "Oh . . . really" (I. i. 33).

3. Orgon's infatuation with Tartuffe has caused him to turn away from his family; this proves the love and peace he thinks he's found to be an illusion. True piety reinforces "every human tie" (I.v.19) instead of breaking them.

4. True piety, according to Cléante, does not "make a flashy show of being holy" (I.v.72) nor does it behave unreasonably and immoderately. Cléante understands hypocrites: "Their private spleen and malice being made / To seem a high and virtuous crusade" (I.v.119–120). This entire speech is a keen analysis of Tartuffe's personality and its flaws.

5., 6. Dorine, unlike the dutiful and obedient Mariane, is given to irony and refuses to suffer fools gladly. She argues that Mariane should not marry Tartuffe (a lovely complication in the plot) because she would be unhappy with a fraud whom she cannot love, and this unhappiness would result in Mariane's infidelity. A forced marriage would lead her into sin, precisely what Orgon believes Tartuffe can save everyone from. Dorine, as a lady's maid, speaks directly and forcefully. She makes not a romantic case for Mariane marrying Valère but a practical one.

7. Tartuffe's first words are both comic and revealing ("Hang up my hair-shirt, put my scourge in place" [III.ii.l]). They fulfill our expectations of him as an affected, pompous fraud. He is, nevertheless, engaging because Molière makes him cleverly ruthless and an accomplished actor.

8. Tartuffe stays in Orgon's favor by accusing himself of being the "greatest villain that has ever existed" (III.vi.4). Orgon is taken in by this false humility and even thinks of punishing his son. His anger is aimed at his family for their attempts to discredit Tartuffe.

9. The dramatic irony in Tartuffe's assertion to Elmire that "there's no evil till the act be known" (IV.v.118) is, of course, produced by Orgon's presence. In a sense Tartuffe is correct. His evil nature does not exist for Orgon until his victim has firsthand knowledge of it.

10. Cléante rebukes Orgon for his "absurd extremes" (V.i.38) and urges him not to conclude mistakenly that because he was deceived by one man all are deceitful. Once again, Cléante is the voice of "sober moderation" (52).

11. The tables are ironically turned on Orgon when his mother refuses to believe his negative view of Tartuffe.

12. Cléante's eminently reasonable views represent, in effect, Molière's own position: he observes life carefully and is not taken in by appearances. He is not treated comically because his values represent a norm by which to measure others' behavior.

13. Some readers have seen the play's ending as mere flattery for Louis XIV; at the other extreme, some have read it as an ironic attack on the king's powers to set things right. In any case, the *deus ex machina* prevents the play from turning into a tragedy. Without the king's officer Tartuffe wins. Perhaps Molière is implicitly arguing through this device that it isn't enough just to know about evil; there must also be sufficient power to overcome it. These issues warrant class discussion.

14. See the general paragraph at the beginning of this commentary.

15. Surely a prime candidate for such a scene is IV.v, when Tartuffe expresses his determination "to conquer scruple" and Elmire.

MOLIÈRE, *Defense of* Tartuffe (p. 1314)

As Molière points out, there can be no doubt in the play that Tartuffe is a "scoundrel" rather than a "truly devout man." A student report on its initial reception will, however, provide ample evidence that the play offended many associated with the church. This information can lead to a discussion of censorship as it relates to Molière and, by extension, to us today, when the issue continues to affect considerations of plays, novels, films, music, and magazines.

28. Modern Drama

HENRIK IBSEN, *A Doll's House* (p. 1321)

In the final scene of this play, just before Nora walks out on Helmer, he instructs her that she is "first and foremost . . . a wife and mother." Ever since the play was first performed in 1879, Nora's reply has inspired feminists: "I don't believe that any longer. I believe that I am first and foremost a human being, like you — or anyway, that I must try to become one" (p. 1369). As a social problem play, *A Doll's House* dramatizes Nora's growth from Helmer's little pet and doll to an autonomous adult who refuses to obey rules imposed on her by a male-dominated society (see Ibsen's notes on *A Doll's House* [p. 1373] for his comments on "masculine society").

Ibsen himself, however, preferred to see Nora's decision in a larger context. In a speech before a Norwegian women's rights group that honored him in 1898, he insisted that

> I have been more of a poet and less of a social philosopher than most people have been inclined to think. I am grateful for your toast, but I can't claim the honor of ever having worked consciously for women's rights. I'm not even sure what women's rights are. To me it has seemed a matter of human rights.

Ibsen is being more than simply coy here. He conceives Nora's problems in broad human terms, not in polemical reformist ones. The play invites both readings, and students should be encouraged to keep each in focus.

Considerations (p. 1372)

1. Nora lies about trivial matters such as the macaroons, and she deceives her husband about the source of the money that helped restore him to health, but these lies are not to be seen as moral lapses because the trivial lies are inconsequential and her deception about the money is selfless. What is significant is that Nora's *life* is a lie because Helmer has no real idea who she is as a human being.

2. Helmer expects Nora to be a submissive helpmate who leaves all the important matters to the man of the house. He treats her more like a child than a wife. His affectionate terms for her are condescending, perhaps even dehumanizing.

3. The confident expectations for security and happiness that Nora expresses to Mrs. Linde are miserably deflated by the end of Act I. Nora worries that Helmer will regard her with the same contempt he heaps on Krogstad; and, worse, she fears that her husband will judge her to be a destructive influence on their children. The Christmas tree — a symbol of domestic well-being and happiness in Act I — is stripped and ragged at the beginning of Act II, when Nora's world is threatened by both Krogstad's possible betrayal and Helmer's possible harsh judgment. Other symbols include Nora's desperately wild dance, Dr. Rank's fatal illness (the sins of the fathers), and Nora's removal of her masquerade costume as she moves closer to the truth of her circumstances.

4. Although Dr. Rank's characterization has been criticized as unimportant because he is not directly related to advancing the plot — neither Krogstad's blackmailing scheme nor the failure of the Helmers' marriage — his charm and interest in talking with and knowing Nora make him a contrast with Helmer. Moreover, like Nora, Dr. Rank is caused pain (and ultimately death) by his father's corruption.

5. Krogstad and Mrs. Linde are reunited in what appears to be an honest, lasting relationship just as the Helmers are splitting up.

6. Krogstad's decision not to expose Nora's secret is motivated by his love for Mrs. Linde. Many readers find this abrupt romantic reconstruction of his character unconvincing.

7. Nora rejects Helmer's attempts to start over because she realizes that she's never been truly happy as his "doll-wife." Helmer's character is to some degree sympathetic if only because he is thoroughly bewildered and incapable of understanding the transformation his little "squirrel" has undergone.

8. The title points to the Helmers' unreal domestic arrangement. Nora chooses to stop this game when she realizes that she can no longer play her assigned role.

9. We don't know what will become of Nora after she leaves her husband. Although she arrives at a mature understanding of herself as an adult woman, that recognition shatters the pattern of her life and forces her to confront her new freedom on her own. Even if we imagine her as fulfilled and happy in the future (the ending for a comedy), her life at the close of the play takes on tragic proportions — albeit in a modern context — because she is thrown completely back on herself. A discussion of this topic will help bring students to the heart of the play.

10. This alternate ending is a "barbaric outrage" because it undercuts the seriousness of Nora's plight and the significance of her discovery about her life. Moreover, it represents a calculated sentimentalization of the issues raised in the play.

11. Ibsen proposes no solutions to the problems he depicts concerning Nora's individualism and the repressive social conventions and responsibilities she rejects. If we imagine the inclusion of solutions, we can also imagine the play turning oppressively didactic. Ibsen knew what he was doing by leaving the solutions to his audience.

12. The play certainly reflects the kinds of problems we might encounter in our everyday lives. The characters look and sound real. Less true to life are Krogstad's transformation from villain to generous lover, the two forgeries, and the fairly obvious use of symbols, such as the Christmas tree and Nora's dance.

13. Like the protagonist in Godwin's "A Sorrowful Woman," Nora rejects the family circle because it is consuming her. Unlike those of Godwin's mother and wife, however, Nora's reasons for withdrawal are made explicit. Ibsen develops the issues while Godwin works up a mystery that forces the reader to scrutinize the meaning of her protagonist's marriage.

HENRIK IBSEN, *Notes for* A Doll's House (p. 1373)

Considerations (p. 1373)

1. Nora is "altogether bewildered" because she's not sure where she is going or what will happen next. What she is certain of, though, is that she cannot go on living a lie; she knows that much is "wrong."

2. Ibsen seems to suggest that "masculine society" lives by the letter of the law and will not take into account extenuating circumstances, such as Nora's altruistic reasons for forging her father's signature on the loan. This is a correct assessment of Helmer, but whether it is also an accurate observation of today's society is a subject of debate.

3. When Nora heads for the door, getting past Helmer is perhaps easy compared with facing the disapproval she will meet on the other side. The social pressures she will have to endure as a wife and mother who has abandoned her family will be formidable.

ANTON CHEKHOV, *The Cherry Orchard* (p. 1375)

In Chekhov's last play, he reiterates familiar themes of human isolation and grief caused by the failure of people to look at themselves or listen to one another. In *The Cherry Orchard*, these failures cause not only personal grief, but societal grief as well. Yet the play is not ultimately a clear tragedy. Some good works dealing with this play are Jean–Pierre Barricelli's

"Counterpoint of the Snapping String: Chekhov's *The Cherry Orchard*" in *Chekhov's Great Plays: A Critical Anthology*, J. P. Barricelli, ed. (New York: New York UP, 1981, 111–28); R.L. Jackson, ed. (Englewood Cliffs: Prentice, 1967); and *Chekhov: A Collection of Critical Essays*, David Magarshak's *Chekhov the Dramatist* (New York: Hill, 1960).

Considerations (p. 1411)

1. Most of the characters of *The Cherry Orchard* do not cope well with everyday life. To take but a few examples: Madame Ranevsky was extremely unhappy with her lover in Paris, yet still needed to be rescued from the situation by her daughter. She gives away gold and throws a party when she is nearly bankrupt. Her words reveal a preoccupation with the past which affects her ability to and her *interest* in dealing with the present. She talks about her drowned son, about the orchard when she was a girl, but refuses to talk about the money needed for the estate's survival.

    Madame's brother, Gaev, is no more practical than his sister about real-life situations. He manages to miss the train to town for the auction that will determine his future and his family's as well. His inappropriate, sometimes nonsensical comments show how out of touch with reality he is.

    Firs can only manage everyday life if it remains as it was a half-century before, so his thoughts and actions reflect a man who still wishes to be a serf. His words often refer to duties he had years before; he still feels the need to take care of the family, although because of his physical condition, the family at this point needs to take care of him.

    Even Lopahin, who handles his business affairs well enough to become a wealthy man, cannot handle his personal relationship with Varya. His speech betrays him, for each time he tries to ask Varya to marry him, he either makes a joke or changes the conversation to another topic in order to avoid the issue.

2. Like the first question, this one is very broad and can be dealt with in as many ways as there are characters in the play. The "new order" characters are especially interesting, since each gives a rather philosophical speech at some point in the play.

    Lopahin finds the meaning of life in work. As he says on two occasions (p. 1392 and p. 1405) he feels fulfilled only when he is working; work lets him know "what I exist for". He gets what he wants in the short run — wealth — but he has no one with whom to share it, and even what he has may be tenuous, for the revolution is not far off.

    In Trofimov's case, the meaning of life is to be "free and happy . . . . [as] We go forward irresistibly" (p. 1394). Trofimov has more of a chance to realize his goal than many of his fellow intellectuals who merely theorize, for he recognizes the need for hard work. However, he still does not seem to have a clear-cut idea of how to achieve this goal. The selling of the orchard is an important first step toward his goal, because it will start his march forward; his ultimate success will depend on whether he can support his dreams with solid foundations.

    Anya is perhaps the most likely to realize her dream, for she has some concrete ideas of how to start. For her, creating a cherry orchard no matter where they are in Russia is to bring to a "new garden" the beauty of the old. Anya plans to get an education as a step toward the fulfillment of her dream, so she does base some part of her dream in reality. Further, because her dream depends more on her own ability to find joy than on anything else, it is possible to believe that she will find what she seeks.

3. A cherry orchard is a more fitting symbol of the "old order" than uncultivated woods because pre-revolutionary Russia did have a form, a cultivation. The forward-looking characters are not pioneers in an untamed land, as were the first American settlers. Russia already had a long history, a history of great cultivation and beauty. Chekhov's contention is that the old life has outlived its usefulness. Madame Ranevsky clings to the orchard as a symbol of the past; like herself, it is beautiful but not useful. The cherries are not even harvested any more, for the recipe to preserve them for sale has been lost. The new owner,

Lopahin, cares nothing for the past. He values only his own wealth, not even caring to cultivate Varya's love. It is Anya who is most realistic about the orchard, and therefore the most hopeful character. She values the beauty of the orchard and the family life it signifies to her; however, she also is aware of the negative aspects of the old life. She urges her family to press forward to create a "new garden" (p. 1403) elsewhere.

4. Life outside the orchard is represented by two different places, Paris and the city. Despite its claim to culture, Paris is depicted as a place of immorality and dissipation. It is favored by the most unsympathetic characters in the play, Yasha and Madame Ranevsky's free-loading lover.

   The town stands in a more ambiguous relation to the orchard. It looms (literally) in the background as the destroyer of the agrarian life; yet it is also the place of the future, a place free of the constraints of class-bound society, where even the child of a peasant, Lopahin, can become wealthy and powerful.

5. Yasha, Lopahin, and Trofimov each embody aspects of the "new order." Yasha, the young valet, stands in contrast to the old valet Firs. Neither of them will be part of the Russian future, because Firs clings exclusively to the past, and dies with it; on the other hand, Yasha's complete denial of his heritage as he makes plans to leave for Paris, indicates that he will not be a part of any *Russian* future, either.

   Lopahin's "old order" counterparts are Madame Ranevsky and Gaev; he is the one who will assume the position of power and wealth in the future. He is able to plan and to work diligently toward his goals, unlike Madame Ranevsky and Gaev, who grasp at the most preposterous schemes to save the orchard, but never consider any practical plans. They give parties and make loans when they need loans themselves. Lopahin is an opportunist, which makes it even more clear how incapable Gaev and Madame Ranevsky are of making use of their opportunities. However, Chekhov also indicates that Lopahin's single-minded concern for making money has left him poor in other ways. The denial of the past and of connections leaves him alone at the end of the play, while Madame Ranevsky and Gaev still have the love of their family.

   Trofimov, the third proponent of the "new order," is a foil for the old-style landowner, Pishtchik but also for the forward-looking Lopahin. Trofimov is surprised to learn that Pishtchik has read Nietzsche, but chagrined to learn that the most important thing Pishtchik has learned from the great philosopher is that "one can make forged bank notes (p. 1396). Pishtchik's deficiency, like Lopahin's, is that he has given up his spiritual side for the material. Twice he sells rights to alter the farmland drastically, first to the railroad, and later to the English for mining. One might consider Trofimov too idealistic, as when he claims to be "above love." Yet he realizes the error of his fellow intellectuals who "seek nothing, do nothing," (p. 1392), and while he and Lopahin represent opposite sides of the new order, they both realize the need for constant work in order to achieve it.

6. Chekhov uses his characters' responses to the past, present and future as an indication of how much hope there is for them at the end of the play. For Firs, who clings entirely to the dead past, all that remains is death. Madame Ranevsky idealizes the past and lives completely for what brings her joy in the present, never planning for the future. Her future is in doubt unless one of the more forward-looking characters, such as Anya, is able to take care of her. She might survive, but she will never be an integral part of the future.

   Yasha and Lopahin place no value on the past, except as an error not to be repeated. Yasha is like Madame Ranevsky in his refusal to think and plan for the future; he simply does whatever is expedient at the moment. Since he does not value the past (the only one who mourns his departure is his mother, whom he treats despicably), it is unlikely he will be cared for in the future. Lopahin's refusal to value the past may well result in his repeating it; if he forgets that oppressors are eventually overthrown, and becomes an oppressor, he too will be overthrown.

The characters Chekhov presents most optimistically are Anya and Trofimov, who honor the past but also see its deficiencies, and seek to learn from the past as they plan their future. Importantly, Trofimov perceives history as a continuum; even as he plans his career on the "front ranks" of those striving toward "highest truth," he realizes that his part in the advancement is not everything: "I shall get there, or I shall show others the way to get there" (p. 1405).

7. David Mamet's comments (see p. 1412) notwithstanding, *The Cherry Orchard* is an appropriate title. In its beauty but present uselessness, it symbolizes a system of living which does not work any longer. Like the orchard, the Russian aristocracy is about to fall, but the future is tenuous because the destroyers have no appreciation for the beauty about to be destroyed, no direction for the journey about to begin. The larger human issue involved is the importance of valuing the past while creating a future, and the characters who ignore the orchard's beauty or its problems also have difficulty working out their present relationships. Love, like the cherry blossoms, is idealistically beautiful, but has no value in a material sense. Those who will not appreciate it for its idealistic, spiritual value, risk losing it altogether.

8. The sound of the ax is a death knell for the orchard and for the way of life it represents. Besides representing the specific death of the Russian aristocracy, the destruction of the orchard signifies the end of the simple agrarian life as the world becomes more modern, complex, and urban.

9. Despite the undeniable sadness of leaving the past behind, the ending is more hopeful than pessimistic. Firs, after all, dies peacefully of old age; he is not murdered. The young people, Anya and Trofimov, look forward to the future. On the other hand, the family is separating and the trees are being chopped down. Perhaps the ending might be considered fatalistic; it is not possible to stop history. Gaev calls nature "beautiful and indifferent" (p. 1392). It will endure regardless of human acts. The play ends before the Russian revolution begins. Times are likely to get worse for the wealthy, the landowners, but they could be times of great joy and dedication for Anya and Trofimov.

10. The play certainly has moments of comedy, even farce: Epihodov's creaking boots; Gaev's conversation with the bookcase; Petya's fall down the steps. And the characters of Trofimov and especially Anya leave great hope for the future. These aspects, combined with undeniable moments of sadness, death, and destruction at the end could support consideration of the play, like *A Doll's House*, as a tragicomedy. Chekhov believed in people's ability to change for the better, if as Madame Ranevsky says, "you should look at yourselves" (p. 1390). This play, with its varied characters, is Chekhov's attempt to get all kinds of people to look at themselves. As Chekhov wrote, the artist's job is "to put the right questions, but the answers must be given by the jury according to their own lights" (p. 1412).

ANTON CHEKHOV, *On What Artists Do Best* (p. 1412)

As a development of Consideration 2, ask students to define the task Chekhov sets himself in *The Cherry Orchard*. What are "the right questions" Chekhov asks — through the characters and the action — to explore this problem?

DAVID MAMET, *Notes on* The Cherry Orchard (p. 1412)

In a less formal writing assignment, students might imagine Chekhov's response to Mamet.

29. Experimental Trends In Drama

SAMUEL BECKETT, *Krapp's Last Tape* (p. 1423)

A single character on a stage with a tape recorder does not sound like a very promising dramatic situation, but Beckett manages to evoke the essence of Krapp's life in a brief, concentrated period of time, an essence that Krapp barely articulates or understands. Krapp's surprised, bewildered, and even contemptuous response to his earlier selves on the tapes serves as a dramatic reminder of how we are changed by time and experience. Beckett's Krapp is a comic figure, whose serious purpose is to remind us that we are often strangers to ourselves. For a discussion of how this type of theater makes us "aware of man's precarious and mysterious position in the universe" see Martin Esslin, *On the Theater of the Absurd* (p. 1430).

Considerations (p. 1429)

1. The play is set "in the future" rather than the present because tape recorders for home use became available in the 1950s, and Krapp tells us he made his first tapes thirty years ago (p. 1428).

2. Krapp's present physical condition — his purple nose (ravaged by alcohol), short trousers, baggy pockets, white face — makes him look like a clown or music-hall tramp. He can hardly hear, see, or walk. Although he is a shabby, ridiculous figure, the tape recordings and his reactions to them provide us with a serious look at his inner life that is both intriguing and puzzling.

3. The recordings serve as Krapp's journal. Each year he records his impressions of important events; these are then reviewed on subsequent birthdays. The tapes give him access to a memory that he appears to have lost, and because of that loss he frequently seems surprised by his own words, which come from an earlier self he no longer knows or understands.

4. The many pauses show Krapp responding to himself. They range from simple reflections, meditations, regret, and nostalgia to incredulity at his own naïveté.

5., 6. The sixty-nine-year-old Krapp regards his thirty-nine-year-old self as a "young whelp" full of "resolutions" and "aspirations" (p. 1425), while the thirty-nine-year-old finds his twenty-eight-year-old self to be callow (p. 1428). The older Krapp is revolted by the pretentiousness of his thirty-nine-year-old revelations about himself; he refuses to listen to them and fast-forwards the tape to a lyrical moment when he had made love in a boat and then renounced love in favor of a "fire" in him. Writing, he believed, would become his life's work. Sadly, he had rejected love and life for the sale of "seventeen copies" (p. 1428) of his work.

7. Krapp sees his life as blank. He was wrong about rejecting love, and he is now paying the price as he faces the rest of his life. Instead of discovering meaning in his recordings, he is confronted with a record of painful errors that have led him to isolation, alienation, and a sense of futility.

8. Krapp is not heroic in any conventional sense, but he does fit the general definition of an antihero who is "bewildered, ineffectual, deluded, and lost" (p. 1420).

9. "Farewell to love" is an appropriate subtitle because it helps explain why Krapp has recorded his last tape at the age of sixty-nine. At thirty-nine Krapp recorded what he thought was a moment of insight when he rejected love to explore his inner "dark," but he now sees

that he recorded the moment when he turned from the possibilities of love and life, which have been permanently lost.

10. At the end of the play Krapp is more conscious of his loneliness. This recognition does appear to have changed his present life, because instead of behaving clownishly he now sits motionless, staring into space and listening to silence. He has nothing more to say.

MARTIN ESSLIN, *On the Theater of the Absurd* (p. 1430)

The essential difference between the absurdists' assumptions about "ultimate realities" and earlier perspectives is, according to Esslin, that the absurdists posit a world devoid of absolute values, in which there is no common agreement on what is true or false. No doctrines, no myths, no system of values provides ready answers to the disturbing questions the absurdists raise concerning human existence. Because individuals in absurdist dramas can take no comfort in shared values and identities, they are, like Beckett's Krapp, thrown upon their own experiences. Whatever meaning there is in their lives is derived from their own situations. Unlike a Sophocles, Shakespeare, or Ibsen play, in which community expectations represent powerful forces and values, absurdist drama presents "one man's descent into the depths of his personality, his dreams, fantasies, and nightmares."

HAROLD PINTER, *The Dumb Waiter* (p. 1432)

In a BBC interview with Kenneth Tynan in 1960, Pinter described the typical situation his characters find themselves in:

Two people in a room — I am dealing a great deal of the time with this image of two people in a room. The curtain goes up on the stage, and I see it as a very potent question: What is going to happen to these two people in the room? Is someone going to open the door and come in?

The anxiety Gus and Ben experience derives from this situation. They don't know what will happen next, but whatever it is they will have little control over the arbitrary power that exercises its will upon them. These two professional killers await the arrival of a victim who turns out to be one of them. We don't know why this happens, but we do know there is reason to feel dread in this ominous atmosphere.

Considerations (p. 1457)

1. Not until Gus pulls a revolver from under his pillow (p. 1443) do we realize that these two men are not typical workers. Since we are given a chance to get to know them a bit before they can be categorized as organization killers, Pinter preserves some mystery while simultaneously drawing us into the characters.

2. Neither man is a cool professional; each is pathetic and confused about what goes on around him. Nothing seems to make very much sense to them — not the newspaper stories, their orders, or any of the trivial details they discuss about the basement room.

3. Ben, "the senior partner," is clearly smarter and more competent than Gus, who is less disciplined and asks questions about Wilson and their working conditions. Gus resents being kept in the dark, and his sense of powerlessness is expressed when he shouts "WE'VE GOT NOTHING LEFT! NOTHING! DO YOU UNDERSTAND?" (p. 1455).

4. Apparently Gus's behavior has become too unpredictable for the organization. He asks too many questions; he stopped the car when he thought Ben was asleep; he seems to feel sympathy for the victims; and he's beginning to sound rebellious about following orders he cannot fathom. When Gus becomes the victim at the end of the play, we see that the organization does not tolerate such individualism.

5. If Ben does not shoot his partner, he too will have to be eliminated. Given Ben's previous willingness to go along with the organization's orders, it seems likely that he will kill Gus.

We do not know that for a fact, however, because the play ends with the two staring at each other. Does this indicate some hope, or is it a sign that each knows what must happen?

6. The silences and pauses focus attention on even the most trivial exchanges and charge them with meaning, the meaning being the characters' emotions — their fear, bewilderment, and inability to identify what troubles them.

7. The dumbwaiter makes increasingly ridiculous demands on the two characters as they scramble, Laurel and Hardy fashion, to fill the bizarre orders sent down to them. The humor of this episode sets us up for the ending, when Gus's question ("What's the idea? What's he playing these games for?" [p. 1455]) is answered, and the game turns deadly serious.

8. When Gus and Ben talk about ball cocks or some other trivia, we witness their willingness or inability to express their real concerns about their vulnerability. If they come even close to doing so, the conversations either lapse into silence or quickly veer off onto yet another unrelated subject.

9. The title refers, of course, to the mechanical dumbwaiter that gives the men their orders, but it also puns on *dumb* as "mute" and "stupid"; these waiters-servants-killers are victims of the organization and their own inability to break free from it. The dumbwaiter cannot be reduced to a specific agent, such as society, government, or God. Its arbitrary power can mean all these things and more — whatever insatiable demands are made on human beings without rhyme or reason.

10. Despite the realistic surface of what happens, this play presents an absurd vision of life because we cannot know *why* things happen. Nothing makes very much sense because we don't really know the reasons for Ben's and Gus's behavior or why events turn out as they do (see the discussion of the theater of the absurd in the text, pp. 1420–22).

JANE MARTIN, *Twirler* (p. 1458)

April March's brief monologue takes her well beyond the national baton twirling competition. Her story of humble and tacky beginnings at the Dainty Deb Dance studio is poignant as well as funny. She has "flown high and known tragedy both," the latter from having her hand crushed by Big Blood Red, a horse whose name is a fitting phrase to describe the kinds of nasty surprises that can clip anyone's wings.

Severely injured by Big Blood Red, she discovers "glory" despite a cruel twist of fate. What a fellow twirler once called "blue-collar zen" is a means of transcendence for April. When she's twirling she feels as if her "insides spin and rise and leave the ground." She draws beauty and energy from the sky and understands how Charlene Ann Morrison "could see the face of the Lord God Jesus," because April has experienced the same degree of committed intensity. As a result, April knows that "twirling is the physical parallel of revelation." She doesn't expect most people to understand this, but public misperception and ridicule do not matter to her because she feels the truth in her heart (p. 1459).

April's description of a bloody mystical union with God (the true Big Blood Red) in the snow is her promise, her gift, along with her baton, to us: we can also fly high above the tragedy of life if we do not perversely make fun of spiritual beauty — even if it is in the shape of a spangled baton twirler.

Twirling is an unlikely source for a religious revelation, but students of Flannery O'Connor's stories will recognize April's ability to redeem the commonplace. A comparison of April's revelations with those of one of O'Connor's protagonists in, say, "Revelation" (p. 327) or "A Good Man Is Hard to Find" (p. 342) will yield significant similarities.

30. A Collection of Plays

TENNESSEE WILLIAMS, *The Glass Menagerie* (p. 1462)

Williams depicts a fragile world founded on illusions. Amanda, Laura, Tom, and Jim indulge their own illusions, but so does the world at large as it rushes toward the devastation of total war. Instead of sensing danger, society steeps itself in drink, dance, music, movies, sex, and anything else that pushes reality aside. This tendency characterizes the general tenor of things both inside and outside the family. The play dramatizes a family and a culture trapped in its dreams of self-fulfillment.

Considerations

1. Describe the significance of the setting. How is it related to the major concerns developed in the play?

2. Is Amanda merely a pitiful character? Does she possess any admirable qualities?

3. Who is the protagonist? Can a case be made for more than one?

4. Compare Tom's narrative function in the play with that of the Chorus in Antigone or Oedipus the King. *How is Tom's language different when he speaks as a character instead of as a narrator?*

5. In what sense is Jim O'Connor "a nice, ordinary young man"? How is he similar to and different from the Wingfields?

6. To what extent do all the characters live in a world of illusions? Describe the nature of their individual illusions.

7. Consider the symbolic value of the glass menagerie and the unicorn. What other objects, actions, or characters convey symbolic meanings?

8. Discuss the nonrealistic techniques used in the play. What effects do they achieve?

9. Explain whether you think Williams's reliance on extraliterary devices such as the screen indicates a lack of faith in his own writing.

10. Discuss whether the play is primarily a comedy or a tragedy.

ARTHUR MILLER, *Death of a Salesman* (p. 1508)

Willy Loman's intentions are the best; he wants what the "American Dream" of success promises: in addition to security, comfort, and possessions, he longs for love and respect. Unfortunately, he is all too willing to sacrifice the highest human values to achieve his dreams. He is a salesman who, ironically, sells himself; he fails to realize that he loses much more than he can possibly gain by lying, cheating, or stealing. His aspirations reflect everyone's longings, but his dream falls far short of the kind of idealism associated with his father's hard work and perseverance. He mistakes brand names for true values and in doing so earns the name of *Loman*.

Considerations

1. Discuss Miller's use of realistic and nonrealistic techniques. What is the effect of blending them? How does Miller make Willy's thoughts accessible to us?

2. *Is Willy responsible for his failure, or is some force outside him the cause of his downfall?*

3. *Explain how Willy can be characterized as representing a tragedy of the "common man" (see Miller's essay on this subject, p. 1763). Is Willy a tragic figure?*

4. *What is Ben's function in the play? What does he mean to Willy?*

5. *To what extent do Biff and Happy embody Willy's traits? How do they incorporate into each of their lives some of their father's values?*

6. *How does the relationship between Charley and Bernard differ from that of Willy and his sons?*

7. *At the conclusion of the play, what kind of future seems to be in store for Biff and Happy? Explain whether you think they will live similar lives.*

8. *Why is it especially appropriate that Willy is a salesman rather than, for example, a factory worker or schoolteacher? (See the student essay on p. 1768.)*

9. *What does the Requiem contribute to our understanding of the characters?*

10. *Read Delmore Schwartz's poem "The True-Blue American" (p. 843) and compare its treatment of the American dream with the one in* Death of a Salesman. *How does the tone of each work differ?*

AN ALBUM OF WORLD LITERATURE

WOLE SOYINKA, *The Strong Breed* (p. 1577)

Soyinka learned his stagecraft firsthand. After attending University College in Ibadan, Nigeria, for two years, he graduated with honors in 1957 from Leeds University in England. He taught school and became a script reader for Royal Court Theatre in London, learning the mechanics of play direction and stage production. During this period he also participated in a writers' group and acted in dramatic improvisations. Success came quickly: Soyinka's first three plays — *The Swamp Dwellers* (1958), *The Invention* (1959), and *The Lion and the Jewel* (1959) — were all produced in London, and *The Swamp Dwellers* and *The Lion and the Jewel* were both staged in Ibadan to enthusiastic response.

After studying African traditional drama on a Rockefeller Foundation grant, Soyinka became a lecturer in English at the University of Ife in 1962, only to resign the next year in protest against the imprisonment of Chief Awolowo, a western Nigerian tribal leader. For the next two years, Soyinka devoted himself to various forms of social protest and to the development of a Nigerian theater. His writing during this time reflected even more deeply the influence of the traditional dramatic form of Yoruba tribal ritual, especially harvest festivals.

Soyinka returned to academic life as senior lecturer at the University of Lagos in 1965. In August, 1967, just before becoming chair of the Drama Department at the University of Ibadan, he was arrested on suspicion of supporting Biafran rebels. He spent the next twenty-six months in prison, fifteen of them in solitary confinement. His autobiographical *The Man Died* (1972) records much of this experience.

Soyinka's most important Western influences include Samuel Beckett and Bertolt Brecht (he based his comedy *Opera Wonyosi*, 1977, on Brecht's *Three Penny Opera*), but even his most satiric or absurdist work expresses some affirmation of traditional values, albeit sometimes in terms of the bitter cost of their disintegration.

Soyinka's plays include *A Dance of the Forests* (1960), *The Trials of Brother Jero* (1961), *Kongi's Harvest* (1965), *Madmen and Specialists* (1970), and *Death and the King's Horseman* (1976).

When *The Strong Breed* opened in New York, author Wole Soyinka was in prison in Nigeria for aiding Biafran leaders in the civil war against the Nigerian government. Soyinka said at the time that he was trying to arrange a cease-fire between the warring factions. In Eman, Soyinka creates a central character whose life is sacrificed in the attempt to negotiate a balance between tribal customs and the larger world.

Considerations

1. *In his insightful essay "Tribal Patterns" in* The Reporter *38:3 (February 8, 1968): 39–40, Gerald Weales states that at least four dramas take place in* The Strong Breed. *According to Weales, a sacrificial melodrama, a psychological drama, and an ironic inheritance drama all finally merge into a larger social play. How do the first three combine to create the fourth?*

   Eman enacts an archetypal scapegoat story, with similarities to both the Christian myth and ancient African tribal customs. His powerful sense of mission, and his response to Sunma's charge that he is inhuman with "I am very much my father's son" (p. 1585) echo the Christian story. The rite enacted by the villagers is a scapegoat ritual of several African tribes, among them the Yorubas, whose home is in Soyinka's native Nigeria.

   The psychological drama involves Eman's attempts to find a place for himself in society. Eman's puberty rites ironically result in his leaving his community rather than being fully accepted into it, after he defends Omae from the lecherous tutor. He returns home twelve years later, hoping to find a peaceful life there with Omae; but when she dies, he leaves again, to become a teacher in Sunma's village. He still finds no sense of belonging until he gives himself up in sacrificial ritual; his last words indicate his sense of finally going home to his father.

   The inheritance drama is ironic because Eman leaves his own tribe, where he would have inherited his father's role as carrier, yet he becomes the carrier for Sunma's tribe. He follows his father figuratively and also literally, since he is chasing a vision of his father when he steps into the trap at the end. Thus he cannot ultimately escape his legacy.

   The issues of the past (ritual, custom, inheritance) combine with the psychological conflicts Eman faces as a man educated in the modern world to create the social drama which then unfolds — that of the primitive tribe coming into contact with modern sensibilities.

2. *What functions do the flashbacks serve?*

   The first, the scene between Eman and his father, identifies Eman to the audience as a member of the "strong breed" of carriers, and indicates that he is fully aware of the risks of the ritual from which Sunma attempts to protect him.

   The second flashback is a tender scene of young love between Omae and Eman, a scene rendered all the more striking by its place in the center of the horrible events of the evening. It further clarifies Eman's character, indicating his capacity for involvement which was challenged by Sunma earlier, and providing insight into the guilt he feels concerning her suffering for his sake. The future scapegoat sees in his own life the process of suffering for the deeds of another.

3. *Why do you think Soyinka is so insistent that "there can be no break in the action" (p. 1577)?*

   One possible reason is that the action of the play is the enactment of a ritual which, according to Jaguna and Oroge, must be completed without interruption or deviation if the "magic" is to work. Further, the continuity enables the playwright to work somewhat like the writer of a short story, creating a powerful effect from which there is no escape.

4. *Who are the "strangers" in the play?*

   While the idiot boy Ifada and Eman, both of whom come from other villages, are the only strangers recognized by Jaguna and Oroge, there is a sense in which all the female characters are also strangers. The Girl is an outcast because of her never-defined sickness, which the villagers seem to think will contaminate them; Sunma's education has caused her to "wonder if I really sprang from here. . . . they are nourished in evil and unwholesomeness in which I have no part" (p. 1582). Even Omae became a stranger in her own village by defiling the puberty rites; only Eman's father's intercession shielded her after Eman left the village.

5. *What are the indications that the modern world is encroaching upon the village?*

    The presence of the lorry indicates a link between the village and the larger world. Also, Sunma and Eman, through their professions as health worker and teacher, bring the modern world to the village.

6. *Discuss the play's ironic ending.*

    The villagers catch Eman in their trap, but refuse to hurl curses at him, thus failing to complete the ritual. Eman is a man to them, not just a ritualistic symbol. Ironically, this means that Eman is a successful carrier, for he has assumed the ritual unto himself, leaving the villagers free to abandon some portion of their superstition and open themselves up to a world beyond themselves.

AN ALBUM OF CONTEMPORARY PLAYS

CARYL CHURCHILL, *Top Girls* (p. 1603)

Caryl Churchill said in an interview (see p. 1769) that one of the important ideas in *Top Girls* is "that achieving things isn't necessarily good, it matters *what* you achieve." Her characters, ancient and modern, all claim various achievements; nevertheless, Churchill finds little to praise when achievement allows — or forces — people to remain apart as "us" and "them". The character Marlene anticipates the new decade with delight, but Churchill terms the decade "frightening".

Considerations

1. *To what (or whom) does the title*Top Girls *refer? Is it meant to be taken seriously or ironically?*

    "Top Girls" is the employment agency of which Marlene has just become managing director. Since Marlene herself is the "top girl" in the agency, it refers to her as well. Finally, since Marlene claims kinship with the various women at dinner in the first scene, celebrating their mutual "courage and the way we changed our lives and our extraordinary achievements" (p. 1612), these women are "top girls" also. In view of the somewhat pessimistic ending of the play, the title is ironic. One can almost hear Churchill saying, "Is this the best we can do?" Simply using the words "girls" here implies immaturity and a lack of respect regarding the characters.

2. *What is the relationship among the six dinner guests in the first scene?*

    At first it might appear that Churchill has simply made an effort to bring together "active" women from as diverse backgrounds, cultures, and time periods as possible— which, on one level, she has. Upon closer examination, however, we see that the women are carefully chosen to be foils for one another and for Marlene. Nijo and Isabella, for instance, both spent a large portion of their lives traveling; for Isabella, it was the joy of her life, but for Nijo, travel meant penitence and regret. Dull Gret and Joan are presented as intellectual opposites: Gret's life is completely earth-bound, her concerns totally physical; Joan's is a life of the soul — she is so unaware of the physical, in fact, that her lover has to tell her that she is pregnant, for she has no idea what is happening to her own body. Griselda is the only guest who has lived in complete acquiescence to the patriarchy, and thus she is a touchstone for the others to measure how far they have (or haven't) come in their rebellion against patriarchy.

    Additionally, all the women's stories are linked by issues concerning the role of women in society, although the characters' perspectives on these issues vary. Some of the issues addressed by everyone at dinner are fulfillment, children, clothes, and the men in their lives.

3.   *Churchill creates a technique for dialogue in* Top Girls *in which the characters frequently talk over one another's speeches. What is the effect?*

    One effect is a heightened sense of realism, which is important for Churchill to achieve, since the premise of her bringing these particular characters together is so unrealistic. The interruptions and talking simultaneously is what actually happens when a group of close friends gets together. The interruptions gradually disappear as the characters enter more deeply into the painful circumstances of their lives. After the excited camaraderie of the first part of the scene, each character retreats more into herself toward the end. Joan's comments here (spoken in Latin, which further distances her from the others) clarify what is going on: The women abandon mutual empathy for the feeling of peace they gain from regarding each other, and their sufferings, as something separate from themselves.

4.   *How do the three scenes of Act I relate to one another?*

    In these scenes, the audience views the "top girls" of the past, the present, and the future. Churchill seems to find many of the same unresolved problems no matter where she looks in time.

5.   *Carefully examine the cast of characters. Can you discern any pattern in the shared roles?*

    While it is not unusual for cast members with minor roles to take on other roles, particularly in companies such as the Joint Stock Theater Group with which Churchill was familiar, there are specific patterns in the "reincarnations" of the dinner group. In fact, given her presentation of the "top girls" as a problem for past, present, and future, we may well be expected to consider the modern characters as new versions of their predecessors. For instance, Nijo, whose entire life was based on sexual relationships, one being a forbidden liaison with a Buddhist priest, re-enters the play as Win, who is engaged in a relationship with a married man. Isabella, with all her regrets about her sister Hennie who stayed home while she wandered, appears as Marlene's sister who does stay home and becomes burdened with life-draining responsibilities. The earthly Dull Gret becomes Angie, a school dropout who plays ritualistic games with menstrual blood. The careful matching of characters past and present emphasizes Churchill's contention that hoped-for progress in the condition of women has not come about.

6.   *Discuss the men in the play.*

    Not a single male figure appears in Top Girls, *yet male-female relationships are an important aspect of all the females' lives. In general, the men who are all positively portrayed die quickly: among these are Nijo's priest, Joan's friend, and Isabella's husband, as well as her former lover. The men who do not die make existence difficult for the women: Joyce's and Griselda's husbands, and Marlene's boyfriends who are threatened by her success, for example. Sometimes the men make life difficult and then die, such as Nijo's emperor and Marlene's father. Students might wish to discuss whether Churchill is being anti-male, or whether she is trying to consider the liberation of women as an issue separate from women's relationships with men. If they think Churchill regards liberation as a separate issue, is this consistent with her linking feminism and socialism?*

7.   *How does Churchill characterize Marlene?*

    Marlene is a modern woman who has "made it" in a man's world; that is, she has competed on economic terms and has become a financial success. However, Churchill suggests the price of success has been enormous. She has alienated her sister, abandoned her child, adopted "male" bad habits (including drinking), and intimidates any man who wishes to have a relationship with her. Churchill stresses that what has doomed her is her capacity to distance herself from anyone who gets in her way, to attend exclusively to her own struggles and separate herself from those of others. She divides people into "us" and "them," "us" being the Reagans and Thatchers and all the materially successful people, and "them" being anyone who is "stupid or lazy or frightened" — even her own daughter. What Churchill thinks of this kind of success is well put in Marlene's words in the first scene— "Oh God, why are we all so miserable?" — and in Angie's in the last— "Frightening""(p. 1656).

8. *Is there any cause for optimism in this play?*

Top Girls is Churchill's warning that people— particularly women— are in deep trouble. While she seems to respect Joyce more than the other characters, she sees little hope or joy as long as people look upon their struggles as separate from one another. If students see some reason for hope in Marlene and Angie's togetherness as the play ends, point out that (1) Marlene has just denied her motherhood, and also that, (2) chronologically, this is not the last scene. According to stage directions, it has taken place a year earlier. The chronological end of the play is on page 1644, with Marlene saying of her daughter, the one who should be the hope for the future, "She's not going to make it."

AUGUST WILSON, *Fences* (p. 1657)

Troy Maxson's struggles in Wilson's 1985 play make comparisons to Arthur Miller's *Death of a Salesman* inevitable. Nevertheless, *Fences* stands on its own as a work specific to the black struggle in America and, at the same time, one which has a larger, more universal context. Troy Maxson attempts to use his large hand to take the world and "cut it down to where I could handle it" (p. 1683). Although the world proves to have forces more powerful than Troy can manage, he finally does what he considers most important in the baseball game which is his life: He "goes down swinging."

Considerations

1. *What are some of the fences to which the title of the play refers?*

The physical fence Troy builds in his yard has different meanings for Troy and Rose: Rose considers it a means of keeping herself and her loved ones in and protected, while Troy finally completes it in hopes of keeping out those with whom he does not wish to deal, "Mr. Death" and Troy's son Cory. This fence also serves to confine the play as a whole, for every scene takes place within the Maxson house and yard.

Other characters in the drama deal with their own fences. The penitentiary walls contain Troy, Bono, and Lyons; Uncle Gabe is confined in a mental institution. According to the playwright (see interview on pp. 1770–1773), all the major characters become "institutionalized," since Rose becomes involved in a church and Cory joins the Marines. The specific fences are contained in the larger metaphor of white America as a fence confining black hopes.

Finally, the fence is the boundary for home runs in a baseball park; this meaning becomes more crucial because of the pervasiveness of the baseball metaphor in the play.

2. *How does Wilson develop the idea of Troy's life as a baseball game? Why is the metaphor appropriate?*

A baseball bat and rag ball hanging from a tree are visible onstage from the first moments of the play. Troy uses the fact that he had talent but never could play in the major leagues as a symbol of how white America has prevented black achievement (even though, as Rose reminds him, he was forty years old when he left prison and wanted to play). He describes his life to Rose in terms of a baseball game in the important scene on page 1691. Later, Troy "calls strikes" on Cory in demanding his obedience, and Cory swings a bat at his father twice before hesitating in their final confrontation. Troy dies swinging a baseball bat.

In baseball, Wilson chooses a sport which has been highly symbolic of working-class America throughout the twentieth century, but also one which has fueled arguments about the respective talents of black and white athletes due to the prohibition against black players until 1947.

3.   What details does Wilson use to make Fences specific to black experience?

Among these details are the version of American history which precedes Act I, the choices of athletics and music by Troy's sons (Wilson maintains these are the only places fully open to blacks), and the story with which Wilson begins the play. Troy's narrative about their co-worker getting away with stealing a watermelon by acting dumb is a "High John the Conqueror story, a type of story slaves told to one another (but not to whites) which often involved a slave appearing ridiculous while he was stealing from the white master with impunity.

4.   As a writing assignment, you might ask students to discuss the function and importance of Wilson's stage directions.

The section prior to Act I entitled "The Play" reveals Wilson's outrage over the discrepancy between the treatment of European immigrants and the treatment of black Americans. It also notes that, in 1957, "The Milwaukee Braves won the World Series" (p. 1658), a detail which prepares the reader for the importance of baseball imagery in the work to come. Also, the stage directions for Gabriel's final scene make clear the inadequacy of traditional white Christianity and the "life-giving" quality of Gabe's return to primitive African ritual (the "black church").

5.   Rose tells Troy, "The world's changing around you and you can't even see it," (p. 1677). What are some of the things Troy does not recognize?

Troy never accepts that his failure to become a major-leaguer was due to his age as well as to racism; he refuses to recognize his monetary reasons for having Gabe committed; he does not accept his sons' maturity or notice their need for his approval; and he never appreciates his wife's desperation, which matches his own.

6.   Troy describes his maturing process as an attempt to cut the world "down to where I could handle it" (p. 1683). That is, he wants to control his life, no matter how narrow a definition of life he must accept in order to have that control. Up to what point in the play does Troy seem to be in control?

At first, Troy seems to be in control of his life. He risks his job by objecting to the policy of all-white garbage truck drivers, but he is rewarded by becoming the company's first black driver (even though he does not have a driver's license!). He is authoritative with Rose, controls Cory's life by removing him from the football team, and keeps Lyons under his control by his refusal to recognize his career.

His relationship with Alberta, which enables him to see the life of "quiet desperation" he has been leading, is the turning point for Troy; his confession to Rose is the turning point of the play. During the argument with Rose, Cory defies his father for the first time. After it, Troy becomes isolated from Rose, Cory, Bono and his other friends from work, and Gabe; in a futile gesture to control his life by controlling Death, he completes the fence which confines his life.

7.   Discuss the relationship between the fathers and sons in the play. Are sons, according to Wilson, always doomed to repeat their fathers' lives?

Troy has repeated his father's dedication to responsibility even at the expense of many of the joys in life, and also his father's violent behavior toward his maturing son. Wilson believes that sons do inherit many of their fathers's traits, and can only improve their lives by making these "tools" work for them. Bono's long-term relationship with Lucille after his own father left his family demonstrates Wilson's belief in the possibility of improvement.

8.   What is the role of the women in Fences?

While the play and its central metaphor are masculine in orientation, the most hope and the greatest successes lie with the women. Lucille inspires Bono to abandon his wanderlust; Rose is a member of a black church, an affiliation which Wilson approved, and is given a "second chance" at life in raising Raynell. Raynell herself is a sign of hope at the play's end.

Even Alberta, whom we never see, is positive in the joy she brings into Troy's life, and for giving birth to Raynell, the new hope.

9. *Is the end of the play optimistic or pessimistic?*

    Both moods are present. Troy dies isolated from family and friends, but he also dies swinging the bat, which in baseball terms is infinitely more heroic than taking a called third strike. He dies smiling. Gabe's last dance is "life-giving." The optimism of the women has already been discussed.

    On the other hand, Cory's role as a Marine in 1965 is surely an ironic touch. Is Wilson suggesting that Cory is repeating Gabe's life, but in a war that America was to lose? Or is Cory's comment to Lyons, that six years in the military is enough, our cue that he will make a life beyond the fences?

DAVID HENRY HWANG, *M. Butterfly* (p. 1707)

   M. Butterfly opened on Broadway in March 1988 with John Lithgow in the role of Gallimard and B. D. Wong (an actor whose name does not give away his gender) portraying Song Liling. Students may find themselves carried far into the play by the absurdity of the premise, a man in love with another man, before realizing the seriousness of Hwang's larger themes.

Considerations

1. *How does the structure of the play help to reinforce its themes?*

    By overlapping scenes from present and past, reality and fantasy, and even from two separate plays, Hwang reinforces the interconnectedness of his themes. The play is not merely an attempt to address separate problems — sexism, racism, and imperialism — all within the confines of a single work. Hwang's contention is that these attitudes are all part of the same problem: the need to dominate another in order to feel complete — a need that has disastrous consequences.

    Further, Hwang has the characters move in and out of the various plays being enacted, with many of them taking on two or three roles, and even having them move out of their participation in the action on stage to relate directly to the audience. This shifting of roles and direct address of the audience constantly reminds the audience that it is watching a play; M. Butterfly *thus becomes a metadrama, a drama about drama, about role-playing, about the illusions we are capable of creating — and believing in.*

2. *Is Gallimard a sympathetic or a despicable character?*

    Certainly we are meant to despise Gallimard's arrogance in cultural, sexual, and diplomatic matters; we cheer Song's assessment of his superficiality in Act I, scene vi. Throughout the play, the audience has reasons to dislike him. Nevertheless, the self-deprecating sense of humor he displays in his speeches to the audience ("I've become a patron saint of the socially inept") and the vulnerability so obvious in his dealings with his old friend Marc make us sympathize and perhaps identify with him. Further, he does eventually fall in love with Song and loses everything because of the relationship. Final judgment of the character is an open question.

3. *Besides Gallimard, who else in this play reveals prejudice?*

    Nearly all the characters display at least one kind of prejudice. There is sexism on both sides of the Bamboo curtain, as Marc and Song ("only a man knows how a woman is supposed to act") demonstrate. Helga is biased against Chinese culture, Chin against homosexuals, to name but a few examples.

4. *Discuss what Gallimard's response to Song's letters reveals.*

    Gallimard's reactions to Song's letters reveal his motivations at the beginning of their relationship. He will not respond to dignified begging, to the asexual (and therefore more equal) term "friend," or to anger. Only complete submission and humiliation make him feel powerful enough to return. Gallimard does not want to exercise his power over Song (i.e., by tearing her clothes off); he does, however, want to be sure that he can.

5. *What purpose do Marc and Helga serve in the play?*

Both are essentially foils who help to further define Gallimard. There is a point at which Marc and his friend have similar sexual attitudes, but Gallimard shows a greater capacity for growth. For instance, Marc considers Gallimard "crazy" when he feels ashamed of his behavior regarding Song's letters. Marc makes Gallimard seem much less despicable by virtue of comparison; it is Marc, not Gallimard, who finally fits the Pinkerton role.

Helga is slightly more sympathetic. Gallimard admits he married her for ambition, not love; this and his cold announcement that he wants a divorce, display a side of him that counterbalances some of his positive qualities. On the other hand, the complete lack of feeling with which Hwang presents Helga helps the audience to comprehend what was missing in Gallimard's life when he became involved with Song.

6. *What are some of the explanations offered for this incredible situation and for Gallimard's ignorance? Which is the most plausible?*

The real "Gallimard" claimed that his meetings with the actor always took place hastily and in the dark, a claim Hwang at least partially reinforces by the way he presents their first meetings and by the fact that Gallimard never sees Song naked. Chin suggests homosexuality as the explanation; the scene between the two toward the end of the play (Act III, scene ii) gives credence to this interpretation. Song claims Gallimard believed because he wanted so much to believe, and that his Western attitude toward Orientals dictated that "being an Oriental, I could never be completely a man" (p. 1749). Since this is the last explanation offered, and Gallimard essentially agrees with at least the first part of it, this is possibly the most convincing. However, the question is intended to provoke discussion more than conclusion.

7. *Why does Gallimard link magazine centerfold models with Oriental women?*

Early in the play (p. 1713), Gallimard equates Oriental women and centerfold models because both are "women who put their total worth at less than sixty-six cents." Further, both appeal to his sense of power: The centerfold is a fantasy figure and will perform whatever Gallimard's imagination dictates. This provocative submissiveness is also an important part of Gallimard's fantasy about Oriental women.

Later, Gallimard's centerfold reappears as Renee, with whom he has an "extra-extra-marital" affair. At this point, he discovers that Renee's total lack of inhibition renders her almost "masculine" to him; nevertheless, he continues to see her to force Song into further submissiveness.

8. *Discuss the role reversal which takes place in the final scene.*

In fact, the role reversal begins taking place gradually before the final scene, once Gallimard falls in love with Song and wants to marry him/her. Prior to that time, Gallimard controlled the relationship; afterward, Song assumes more and more power, so the final reversal is a culmination rather than a sudden reversal. Both Gallimard and the audience come to realize the depth of Madame Butterfly's love, a love which has little to do with a stereotypical vision of Oriental submissiveness. This love raises the play beyond all of its "isms" to a story of love and loss which finally touches even Song.

9. *Is M. Butterfly a comedy or a tragedy?*

The absurd situation upon which the play is based is enough to elicit embarrassed laughter from the outset. Hwang's quotation from the song lyrics of David Bowie and Iggy Pop further augment the light mood. Gallimard portrays himself as a clown in his first speech. Throughout the play, there are hilarious moments — Renee's discussion of Gallimard's "weenie," the revolutionary rhetoric of Chin's meetings with Song, Song's repartee with the trial judge. Nevertheless, the drama's themes and ultimate outcome are tragic. True to tragic form, Gallimard becomes enlightened only when it is too late for him to do anything about it except die. Perhaps the play should be considered a tragicomedy.

10. Despite the many awards M. Butterfly has garnered, the play has not received universal acclaim. Some critics have faulted it for the heavy-handed way in which Hwang links Western sexism to the events in Vietnam rather than letting the audience draw its own conclusions. Others claim that Hwang himself reinforces racial stereotypes: that his use of a Japanese character for a story based in China says that "all Orientals are alike," and that the play as a whole reinforces a "Mata Hari" image of Oriental women — beautiful but dangerous. In a writing assignment, you might ask students to respond to these criticisms.

31. Perspectives on Drama

OWEN DAVIS, *On Formulaic Melodrama* (p. 1756)

Davis's primary objection to melodrama is that the plots are always racing toward the next climax, so that there is no time to develop characterizations or themes. This problem is still evident in many television series and films. Students should recognize that serious works can use some melodramatic elements (see Shakespeare's *Hamlet* or Chekhov's *The Cherry Orchard* for examples) without pandering or producing an insatiable appetite for high anxiety and excitement in an audience.

SUSAN GLASPELL, *From the Short Story Version of* Trifles (p. 1758)

Considerations (p. 1760)

1. The play's opening description immediately gives us information about the Wrights' "gloomy" kitchen; the story, however, can take us beyond the kitchen so that we get a larger view of the house from a little hill. We are told that to Mrs. Hale the house looked "lonesome." The story, of course, can provide more details by way of the narrator.

2.–4. The story begins with characterizations of Mr. and Mrs. Peters ("she didn't seem like a sheriff's wife") as well as Mrs. Hale. The women take more central roles earlier on in the story than in the play. The story also permits us to get inside Mrs. Hale's mind to learn her feelings of guilt for not having visited Mrs. Wright earlier. This intimacy emphasizes Mrs. Hale's perspective and suggests why Glaspell uses the title "A Jury of Her Peers." The story seems to focus more on justice than on the "trifles" overlooked by the men. Perhaps this slight shift in emphasis occurs because the trifles — the sewing, bird cage, and dead canary — make for good stage business.

TENNESSEE WILLIAMS, *Production Notes to* The Glass Menagerie (p. 1760)

Williams's assertion that the "theater of realistic conventions" is "exhausted" is overstated, at least insofar as audiences are concerned. The perennial popularity of realistic plays indicates that although many gifted playwrights are impatient with realistic conventions, audiences find them entertaining and rewarding. Indeed, the decision to drop the screen owing to the "extraordinary power of Miss Taylor's performance" suggests that an effective actress speaking Williams's dialogue does not require such a device. The nostalgia, fragility, and radiance that Williams seeks to evoke with the music and lighting are a useful summary of the play's tone.

ARTHUR MILLER, *Tragedy and the Common Man* (p. 1763)

Considerations (p. 1766)

1. Miller argues that our modern scientific understanding of human behavior makes tragedy less accessible to us, because we tend to approach behavior from a clinical or sociological perspective rather than from an individual's "total compulsion to evaluate himself justly." This, coupled with the apparent "paucity of heroes among us," seems to limit the possibilities for tragedy.

2. Unlike Aristotle, who argued that the tragic hero must be an extraordinary person, Miller makes a case for the "common man." Such a person knows "the underlying fear of being

displaced, the disaster inherent in being torn away from our chosen image of what and who we are in this world."

3. The final paragraphs of the excerpt make a distinction between pathos and tragedy. Unlike a tragic character, a pathetic one is to be pitied because he could not possibly have won against superior forces. A tragic figure is someone who might have succeeded but did not.

ARTHUR MILLER, *On Biff and Willy Loman* (p. 1766)

As a development of Miller's remarks, ask students to comment on why the self-realization of Biff is not a weightier counterbalance to Willy's disaster. Does this "flaw" compromise the play as tragedy? If not, why not?

ERIC BENTLEY, *On Drama as Literature and Performance* (p. 1767)

Bentley wisely argues that "literary" and "theatrical" perspectives on drama could complement rather than compete with each other. Both are valid positions, but neither tells the whole story. Bentley would point out to students that reading a play and watching a performance of it offer a fuller experience than either activity can provide by itself. That's only common, and good, sense.

JOHN WAGNER, *A Student Essay on* Death of a Salesman (p. 1768)

This relatively unsympathetic treatment presses Willy's own logic on him as a means of accounting for his failure. Despite Willy's selling himself, some readers find his aspirations, albeit trivial and corrupt (not unlike those of Fitzgerald's Jay Gatsby), almost noble. Students who understand that Willy represents cultural (perhaps universal) values as well as an individual's desires are more likely to see the tragic dimensions of his failure.

KATHLEEN BETSKO, RACHEL KOENIG, AND EMILY MANN, *An Interview with Caryl Churchill* (p. 1769)

You might ask students to look up British and American reviews of *Top Girls* to see if there are ways other than the ones Churchill describes in which the play has been misunderstood. Other questions to pursue: Do American reviews of the play recognize Churchill's interest in socialism? Do British reviews differ substantially from American reviews in their analysis and assessment of the play?

DAVID SAVRAN, *An Interview with August Wilson* (p. 1770)

Wilson says that "the process of assimilation to white American society was a big mistake" (p. 1771). He suggests that African-Americans should demand "to participate in society as Africans." Ask students to find reflections of these beliefs in *Fences* or in another play by Wilson. If they read one of Wilson's earlier or later plays, ask them to write an essay (or report to the class) comparing the plays in terms of changes in conditions for blacks in America and changes in black responses to these conditions.

DAVID SAVRAN, *An Interview with David Henry Hwang* (p. 1775)

Savran notes that "Shi turns out to be Pinkerton" at the end of the play, and Hwang seems to agree when he says that this reversal is "the axis on which the play turns" (p. 1775). You might ask students to discuss this choice. Does it make sense — not just dramatic sense, but sense in terms of the world students know? Or is this choice too manipulative? Ask students to consider the play's representation of Western projections on the East and Eastern projections on the West in answering these questions.

32. Critical Strategies For Reading

Although there is an emphasis upon critical strategies for reading throughout the second edition of *The Bedford Introduction to Literature*, this chapter brings into focus an increasing tendency in introductory literature classes to make students aware of critical approaches to literature used by contemporary theorists. The treatment of the eight major approaches discussed in this chapter — formalist, biographical, psychological, historical, sociological (including Marxist and feminist strategies), mythological, reader-response, and deconstructionist — is designed to supplement the more general kinds of Questions for Responsive Reading that are provided in each genre section (for fiction see p. 362, for poetry see p. 742, for drama see p. 954). These critical strategies range from longstanding traditional approaches such as those practiced by biographical and historical critics to more recent and controversial perspectives represented, for example, by feminist and deconstructionist critics.

By introducing students to competing critical strategies, you can help them to understand that there are varying strategies for talking about literary works. A familiarity with some of the basic assumptions of these strategies and with the types of questions raised by particular ways of reading will aid students in keeping their bearing during class discussions as well as in the deep water of the secondary readings they're likely to encounter for their writing assignments. After studying this chapter, students should have a firmer sense that there can be many valid and interesting readings of the same work. Their recognition should open up some of the interpretive possibilities offered by any given text while simultaneously encouraging students to feel more confident about how their own reading raises particular kinds of questions and leads them into the text. In short, this chapter can empower students to think through their own critical interpretations in relationship to a number of critical contexts.

This chapter can be assigned at any point during the course. Some instructors may find it useful to assign the chapter at the start of the course so that students are aware of the range of critical approaches from the very beginning. Many students are likely to raise more informed and sophisticated questions about texts for having been exposed to these critical strategies. Other instructors may prefer to lead up to the critical perspectives and assign the chapter later in the course as a means of pulling together the elements of literature taken up during the preceding weeks in the course. Whatever your preference, you can assign this chapter (or portions of it if, for example, you want to discuss a biographical reading of a particular work and just want students to read the few pages in the chapter about that kind of approach) whenever you think it most appropriate for your students and your teaching style. When you do assign the chapter, however, remind students to read first the very brief short work by Kate Chopin, "The Story of an Hour" (p. 12), since each of the critical approaches is applied to that particular work, as well as to other texts.

The purpose of this chapter is not to transform students into Stanley Fishes or Northrup Fryes (although the chapter's Selected Bibliography might serve to introduce those critics to students); instead, the purpose is to suggest how texts can be variously interpreted by looking through different critical lenses. Despite the intimidating fact that literary criticism is an enormous and complex field, it can be usefully introduced as part of the intellectual landscape to even beginning students.

The Perspectives provide a small sampling of some of the issues that can be raised about the critical strategies discussed in the chapter. Sontag's objections to interpreting texts (p. 1798) should strike a familiar chord (if for different reasons) among students who are more comfortable leaving works of art "alone" rather than interpreting them. But Sontag's claim that interpretation makes art "manageable" and "comfortable" can be challenged by having students read Fetterley's feminist treatment of "A Rose for Emily" (p. 1799), a reading that's worth connecting to the ideological commitments articulated by Kolodny, who demands that criticism reject "intellectual neutrality" (p. 1802).

Before asking students to wrestle with Debicki's helpful distinction between New Criticism and deconstructionism (p. 1803), you might have them read Fish's piece on what makes an interpretation acceptable (p. 1800), because Fish's essay provides some fascinating as well as controversial groundwork for the idea that readers should be open to a variety of approaches to texts. The final Perspective by Thomas (p. 1806) offers a politically sensitive reading of "Ode on a Grecian Urn" as a "social text" that suggests how a new historical approach to a work enriches both our understanding of the past and present.

Selected Bibliographies for Authors Treated in Depth

FICTION

Selected References for the Study of Nathaniel Hawthorne

Baym, Nina. *The Shape of Hawthorne's Career*. Ithaca: Cornell UP, 1976.
Bloom, Harold, ed. *Nathaniel Hawthorne*. New York: Chelsea, 1986.
Cameron, Kenneth W. *Hawthorne among His Contemporaries*. Hartford: Transcendental, 1968.
Cantwell, Robert. *Nathaniel Hawthorne: The American Years*. New York: Hippocrene, 1971.
Crews, Frederick C. *The Sins of the Fathers: Hawthorne's Psychological Themes*. New York: Oxford UP, 1966.
Crowley, J. Donald. *Hawthorne: The Critical Heritage*. New York: Barnes, 1970.
Hall, Lawrence S. *Hawthorne: Critic of Society*. New Haven: Yale UP, 1944.
Hawthorne, Nathaniel. *The Complete Novels and Selected Tales of Nathaniel Hawthorne*. Ed. Norman Holmes Pearson. New York: Modern, 1965.
———. *Complete Short Stories of Nathaniel Hawthorne*. Garden City: Hanover, 1959.
———. *The Letters of Nathaniel Hawthorne, 1813–1843*. Vol. 15 of *The Centenary Edition of the Works of Nathaniel Hawthorne*. Ed. Thomas Woodson et al. 18 vols. Columbus: Ohio State UP, 1985.
———. *The Letters of Nathaniel Hawthorne, 1843–1853*. Vol. 16 of *The Centenary Edition of the Works of Nathaniel Hawthorne*. Ed. Thomas Woodson et al. 18 vols. Columbus: Ohio State UP, 1985.
———. *The Letters of Nathaniel Hawthorne, 1857–1864*. Vol. 18 of *The Centenary Edition of the Works of Nathaniel Hawthorne*. Ed. Thomas Woodson et al. 18 vols. Columbus: Ohio State UP, 1987.
———. *The Portable Hawthorne*. Ed. Malcolm Cowley. New York: Viking, 1969.
Mellow, James. *Nathaniel Hawthorne in His Times*. Boston: Houghton, 1980.
Stubbs, John Caldwell. *The Pursuit of Form: A Study of Hawthorne and the Romance*. Urbana: U of Illinois P, 1970.

Selected References for the Study of Flannery O'Connor

Bloom, Harold, ed. *Flannery O'Connor*. New York: Chelsea, 1986.
Feeley, Kathleen. *Flannery O'Connor: Voice of the Peacock*. New Brunswick, NJ: Rutgers UP, 1972.
Grimshaw, James A. *The Flannery O'Connor Companion*. Westport, CT: Greenwood, 1981.
O'Connor, Flannery. *The Complete Stories*. New York: Farrar, 1971.
———. *Conversations with Flannery O'Connor*. Ed. Rosemary M. Magee. Jackson: UP of Mississippi, 1987.
———. *The Habit of Being: The Letters of Flannery O'Connor*. Ed. Sally Fitzgerald. New York: Farrar, 1979.
———. *Mystery and Manners*. Ed. Sally and Robert Fitzgerald. New York: Farrar, 1969.
———. *The Violent Bear It Away*. New York: Farrar, 1960.
———. *Wise Blood*. New York: Harcourt, 1952.

POETRY

Selected References for the Study of John Keats

Bates, Walter Jackson. *John Keats*. Cambridge, MA: Harvard UP, 1963.
Dickstein, Morris. *Keats and His Poetry: A Study in Development*. Chicago: U of Chicago P, 1971.
Ende, Stuart. *Keats and the Sublime*. New Haven: Yale UP, 1976.
Keats, John. *Complete Poems and Selected Letters*. Ed. Clarence DeWitt Thorpe. Indianapolis: Bobbs, 1976.
———. *The Essential Keats*. Ed. Philip Levine. New York: Ecco, 1987.
———. *Letters of John Keats: A Selection*. Ed. Robert Gittings. New York: Oxford UP, 1987.
———. *The Letters of John Keats*. Ed. Hyder Edward Rollins. Cambridge, MA: Harvard UP, 1958.
———. *The Poems of John Keats*. Ed. Jack Stillinger. Cambridge, MA: Harvard UP, 1978.
Ryan, Robert K. *Keats: The Religious Sense*. Princeton: Princeton UP, 1976.
Ward, Aileen. *John Keats: The Making of a Poet*. New York: Farrar, 1986.

Selected References for the Study of Robert Frost

Bloom, Harold, ed. *Robert Frost*. New York: Chelsea, 1986.
Cox, James Melville. *Robert Frost: A Collection of Critical Essays*. Englewood Cliffs: Prentice, 1962.
Frost, Robert. *Interviews with Robert Frost*. Ed. Edward Connery Lathem. New York: Holt, 1966.
———. *The Poetry of Robert Frost*. Ed. Edward Connery Lathem. New York: Holt, 1979.
———. *Robert Frost on Writing*. Ed. Elaine Barry. New Brunswick: Rutgers UP, 1973.
———. *Robert Frost: A Time to Talk*. Ed. Robert Francis. Amherst: U of Massachusetts P, 1972.
———. *Selected Letters*. Ed. Lawrance Thompson. New York: Holt, 1964.
———. *Selected Prose*. Ed. Hyde Cox and Edward Connery Lathem. New York: Holt, 1966.
Pritchard, William H. *Frost: A Literary Life Reconsidered*. New York: Oxford UP, 1984.
Squires, James Radcliffe. *The Major Themes of Robert Frost*. Ann Arbor: U of Michigan P, 1969.
Thompson, Lawrance. *Fire and Ice: The Art and Thought of Robert Frost*. New York: Russell, 1970.
———. *Robert Frost: The Early Years, 1874–1915*. New York: Holt, 1966.
———. *Robert Frost: The Years of Triumph, 1915–1938*. New York: Holt, 1970.
Thompson, Lawrance, and R. H. Winnick. *Robert Frost: A Biography*. New York: Holt, 1982.

DRAMA

Selected References for the Study of Sophocles

Bloom, Harold. *Sophocles's Oedipus Rex*. New York: Chelsea, 1988.
Bowra, Sir Maurice. *Sophoclean Tragedy*. Oxford: Clarendon, 1944.
Brown, Andrew. *A New Companion to Greek Tragedy*. Totowa, NJ: Barnes, 1983. [Antigone]
Edmonds, Lowell. *Oedipus: The Ancient Legend and Its Later Analogues*. Baltimore: Johns Hopkins UP, 1985.
Fergusson, Francis. *The Idea of a Theater*. Princeton: Princeton UP, 1949. 14-53. [Oedipus Rex]
Gardiner, Cynthia P. *The Sophoclean Chorus: A Study of Character and Function*. Iowa City: U of Iowa P, 1987.
Knox, Bernard M. *Sophocles at Thebes: Sophocles' Tragic Hero and His Time*. New York: Norton, 1971.
Linforth, I. M. *Antigone and Creon*. Berkeley: U of California P, 1961.
Woodard, T. M., ed. *Sophocles: A Collection of Critical Essays*. Englewood Cliffs: Prentice, 1966.

Selected References for the Study of William Shakespeare

Barber, C. L. *Shakespeare's Festive Comedy*. Princeton: Princeton UP, 1968.

Bloom, Harold, ed. *William Shakespeare's Hamlet*. New York: Chelsea, 1986.

Bradley, A. C. *Shakespearean Tragedy*. New York: Meridian, 1955.

Dusinberre, Juliet. *Shakespeare and the Nature of Women*. London: Macmillan, 1975.

Frye, Northrop. *On Shakespeare*. New Haven: Yale UP, 1986.

Gardner, Helen. "The Noble Moor." Ed. Anne Ridler. *Shakespeare Criticism: 1935–1960*. Oxford: Oxford UP, 1970.

Goddard, Harold C. *The Meaning of Shakespeare*. Chicago: U of Chicago P, 1951.

Granville-Barker, Harley. "Preface to *Othello.*" *Prefaces to Shakespeare*. Vol. 2. Princeton: Princeton UP, 1947.

Heilman, R. B. *Magic in the Web: Action and Language in* Othello. Lexington: U of Kentucky P, 1953.

Kermode, Frank, ed. *Four Centuries of Shakespearean Criticism*. New York: Avon, 1974.

Mack, Maynard. "The World of Hamlet." *Yale Review* 41 (1952): 502–523.

Neely, Carol Thomas. "Women and Men in *Othello*: 'What should such a fool/Do with so good a woman?' " *Shakespeare Studies* 10 (1978).

Prosser, Eleanor. *Hamlet and Revenge*. Stanford, CT: Stanford UP, 1967.

Righter, Anne. *Shakespeare and the Idea of the Play*. Harmondsworth, England: Penguin Ltd. in association with Chatto and Windus, 1967.

Schoenbaum, Samuel. *William Shakespeare: A Documentary Life*. New York: Oxford UP, 1975.

Spivak, Bernard. *Shakespeare and the Allegory of Evil: The History of a Metaphor in Relation to His Major Villains*. New York: Columbia UP, 1958.

Wilson, John Dover. *What Happens in Hamlet*. Cambridge: Cambridge UP, 1967.

Selected References on the Teaching of Literature

Adler, Mortimer J., and Charles Van Doren. *How to Read a Book*. New York: Simon, 1972.

Bunge, Nancy L. *Finding the Words: Conversations with Writers Who Teach*. Athens: Ohio UP, 1985.

Guerin, Wilfred L., et al. *A Handbook of Critical Approaches to Literature*. New York: Harper, 1979.

Koch, Kenneth. *Rose, Where Did You Get That Red?* New York: Vintage, 1974.

Lipschultz, Geri. "Fishing in the Holy Waters." *College English* 48.1 (1986): 34–39.

Ponsot, Marie, and Rosemary Deen. *Beat Not the Poor Desk*. Upper Montclair: Boynton, 1982. 154–80.

Pound, Ezra. *ABC of Reading*. New York: New Directions, 1960.

Young, Gloria L. "Teaching Poetry: Another Method." *Teaching English in the Two-Year College*. Feb. 1987: 52–56.

Film, Video, and Audiocassette Resources

The following list of resources is organized by genre (Fiction, Poetry, and Drama), and within each genre section the listings are alphabetically arranged by author. Film and video resources are followed by audiocassette listings for Fiction and Poetry. The list of distributors (following the Drama section) can help you locate these films of theatrical performances, tapes of poets reading their own work and talking about poetry, and videos of short stories adapted for film and for the stage. The list is not exhaustive by any means. It is meant as a list of exciting possibilities for supplementing and provoking class discussion.

FICTION: FILM AND VIDEO RESOURCES

Margaret Atwood: Once in August
60 min.,1988.
From the Creative Process Series.
Distributed by Brighton Video.

Anton Chekhov —
Gielgud's Chekhov (Part I)
60 min., color.
VHS, Beta.
Hosted by John Gielgud. Stories on the theme of escape, both literal and figurative.
Distributed by MasterVision.

Anton Chekhov — Gielgud's Chekhov (Part II)
60 min., color.
VHS, Beta.
Hosted by John Gielgud. Two of Chekhov's best-loved works.
Distributed by MasterVision.

Anton Chekhov — Gielgud's Chekhov (Part III)
60 min., color.
VHS, Beta.
Hosted by John Gielgud. An examination of the themes of avarice and revenge.
Distributed by MasterVision.

Anton Chekhov — The Lady with the Dog
86 min., b&w, 1960.
In Russian with English subtitles.
Distributed by Corinth Video

Kate Chopin : The Joy That Kills
56 min., 1985.

A dramatization of the author's "The Story of an Hour."
Distributed by Films for the Humanities.

Colette
13 min., 1979.
Narrated by Israel Berman. Examines the author's life and works.
Distributed by Perspective Films and Video.

Stephen Crane — The Bride Comes to Yellow Sky
29 min., b&w, 1965.
Videotape from the American Short Stories Classics Series.
Distributed by Michigan Media (University of Michigan).

Charles Dickens
see *Introducing Great Authors,* p. 246.
see also *England: Background of Literature,* p. 246.

Louise Erdrich — A Conversation with Louise Erdrich
30 min., color.
VHS, 3/4" U-Matic.
Hosted by Martha Satz.
Distributed by Eidos Productions.

William Faulkner — Barn Burning
(movie title: *The Long, Hot Summer*)
115 min., color, 1958.
With Orson Welles, Paul Newman, Joanne Woodward, Lee Remick, Tony Franciosa.
Distributed by Films, Inc.

244

William Faulkner — A Life on Paper
120 min., color, 1980.
VHS, Beta, 3/4" U-Matic.
A documentary in which Lauren Bacall, Howard Hawks, Anita Loos, George Plimpton, Tennessee Williams, and daughter Jill Faulkner Summers give their recollections of the author.
Distributed by Films, Inc.

William Faulkner's Mississippi
49 min., color, 1965.
VHS, Beta, 3/4" U-Matic.
Background and conflicts of Faulkner's life explained, selections from several of his works read.
Distributed by Benchmark Films.

Gabriel García Márquez: Magic and Reality
60 min., 1982.
A study of the novels **One Hundred Years of Solitude** and **The Autumn of the Patriarch.**
Shot on the Colombian coast of Aracataca. Available in Spanish or English.
Distributed by Films for the Humanities.

Nathaniel Hawthorne — The Birthmark
15 min., 1978.
Distributed by Indiana University AV Center.

Nathaniel Hawthorne: Light in the Shadows
23 min., 1982.
The author's background and view of the world explored through scenes of his youth.
Distributed by International Film Bureau.

Nathaniel Hawthorne — Literature Appreciation: Analyzing Characters
14 min., color, 1970.
VHS, Beta, 3/4" U-Matic.
Characters from the works of Thurber, Hart, and Hawthorne come to life and rate themselves in terms of development and complexity.
Distributed by Coronet/MTI Film and Video.

Nathaniel Hawthorne — Young Goodman Brown
30 min., color, 1973.
Directed by Donald Fox.
Distributed by Pyramid Film and Video.

Ernest Hemingway: Grace Under Pressure
55 min., color, 1982.

VHS, Beta, 3/4" U-Matic.
Narrated by Anthony Burgess. Carefully constructs an overview of the author's life through photographs, newsreel footage, and film clips to parallel his personal experiences and his work.
Distributed by Films for the Humanities.

Ernest Hemingway — Rough Diamond
30 min., color, 1978.
VHS, Beta, 3/4" U-Matic.
A revealing look at Hemingway's life-style, novels, and philosophy.
Distributed by Centron Films.

James Joyce's Dublin
22 min., color.
VHS, Beta, 3/4" U-Matic.
Covers the artist as a young man, his self-exile, his life on the continent, and his death in Zurich.
Distributed by Carousel Film and Video.

James Joyce's Women
91 min., color, 1983.
VHS, Beta.
With Fionnula Flanagan, Timothy E. O'-Grady, Chris O'Neill. Acclaimed film, adapted and produced by Flanagan. Features enacted portraits of real-life Joyce associates, his wife, and three of his famous characters, including Molly Bloom.
Distributed by MCA Home Video.

D. H. Lawrence as Son and Lover
52 min., 1985.
Biography told through excerpts from the author's letters, essays, and autobiographical pieces.
Distributed by Films for the Humanities.

Herman Melville — Bartleby
28 min., color, 1969.
Distributed by Encyclopedia Britannica.

Herman Melville — Bartleby
29 min., b&w, 1965.
Video from the American Short Stories Classics Series.
Distributed by Michigan Media.

Edgar Allan Poe
see **Introducing Great Authors,** p. 246.

Katherine Anne Porter — Short Story: Katherine Ann Porter
30 min., 1968.
Interview
Distributed by NETCHE.

Mark Twain
see **Introducing Great Authors,** p. 246.

Eudora Welty
29 min., 1979.
From the Writer in America Series. Examines the author's style.
Distributed by Perspective Films and Video.

Eudora Welty — A Conversation with Eudora Welty
30 min., 1973.
The author talks about her commitment to the South and the way she draws on it for material.
Distributed by NETCHE.

England: Background of Literature
11 min., 1962.
Presents the works of English writers including Charles Dickens, William Shakespeare, and Alfred, Lord Tennyson, against the settings that inspired them.
Distributed by Coronet/MTI Film and Video.

Introducing Great Authors
50 min.
Depicts and analyzes the lives and works of Charles Dickens, Edgar Allan Poe, William Shakespeare, Jonathan Swift, and Mark Twain.
Distributed by Video Knowledge; Bennu Productions.

FICTION: AUDIOCASSETTE RESOURCES

Toni Cade Bambara — Interview
58 min.
Distributed by American Audio Prose Library.

Raymond Carver — Interview
51 min.
Distributed by American Audio Prose Library.

John Cheever
"The Swimmer" and "The Death of Justina" read by the author.
Distributed by American Audio Prose Library; Caedmon.

Colette Reads Colette
68 min.
In French.
Distributed by Jeffrey Norton Publishers.

Stephen Crane — The Bride Comes to Yellow Sky
50 min.
Distributed by Jimcin Recordings.

Stephen Crane — The Red Badge of Courage and Other Stories
6 hrs. 39 min., 6 cass., 1976.
Unabridged edition, includes "Mystery of Heroism," "The Open Boat," and "The Bride Comes to Yellow Sky."
Distributed by Listening Library.

Louise Erdrich — Interview
50 min.
Erdrich and her husband, Michael Dorris, discuss the nature of their collaboration as mixed-blood Native Americans. Excellent discussion of the imagery, symbolism, and Native American elements in the author's fiction.
Distributed by American Audio Prose Library.

William Faulkner Reading
1 cass.
Includes "As I Lay Dying," "Tull, Darl, and Vardaman," "Fable," "Old Man," Nobel Prize acceptance speech.
Distributed by Caedmon.

Gail Godwin — Interview
56 min.
The author discusses the recurring themes and aesthetic concerns that inform her fiction, her creative process, and her characters.
Distributed by American Audio Prose Library.

Nathaniel Hawthorne — The Great Stone Face
Distributed by Esstee Audios.

Nathaniel Hawthorne — The Minister's Black Veil and Young Goodman Brown
82 min., 1980.
Dramatizations.
Distributed by Jimcin Recordings.

Nathaniel Hawthorne — Young Goodman Brown
Distributed by Esstee Audios.

Alice Munro — Interview
72 min.
The author discusses artists who have influenced her, her relationship with

feminist critics, the emergence of Canadian literature, and more.
Distributed by American Audio Prose Library.

Joyce Carol Oates
The author reads *Marya* and "Where Are You Going, Where Have You Been?" and discusses the unchanging author's voice and the autobiographical impulse in her work.
Distributed by American Audio Prose Library.

Tillie Olsen
1 hr. 17 min., 2 cass., 1981.
The author reads "I Stand Here Ironing" and excerpts from her other work.
Distributed by American Audio Prose Library.

Tillie Olsen — Interview
51 min., 1 cass.
Distributed by American Audio Prose Library.

Tillie Olsen — A Profile
30 min., 1 cass.
Distributed by National Public Radio.

Grace Paley — A Conversation with My Father
42 min., 1 cass., 1986.
The author reads "A Conversation with My Father" and "Friends."
Distributed by American Audio Prose Library.

Grace Paley — Interview
43 min., 1986.
Distributed by American Audio Prose Library.

Katherine Anne Porter — Collected Stories of Katherine Anne Porter
2 hrs. 50 min., 2 cass., 1986.
Abridged edition.
Distributed by Audio Partners.

John Updike
169 min.
The author reads six stories selected by him.
Distributed by Random House Audiobooks; American Audio Prose Library.

John Updike — Interview
25 min., 1978.
A rare interview.
Distributed by American Audio Prose Library.

Eudora Welty
1956.
The author reads "Why I Live at the P.O.," "A Worn Path," and "A Memory."
Distributed by Caedmon; Poets' Audio Center; American Audio Prose Library.

Eudora Welty — On Story Telling (alternate titles: Learning to Write Fiction, Writing a Short Story)
53 min., 1961.
The author discusses ingredients necessary for creative and successful writing.
Distributed by American Audio Prose Library; Audio Forum.

POETRY: FILM AND VIDEO RESOURCES

John Ashbery
see *Potpourri of Poetry — From the Jack Kerouac School of Disembodied Poetics, Summer 1975,* p. 259.

Elizabeth Bishop — Voices and Visions: Modern American Poets
60 min.
VHS, 3/4" U-Matic.
Distributed by ABC-CLIO.

William Blake
57 min., 1976.
Documentary of the author's life.
Distributed by Time-Life Video.

Essay on William Blake
52 min., 1969.
Distributed by Indiana University AV Center.

Robert Bly

see *Poets Talking,* p. 259.

Gwendolyn Brooks
30 min., 1966.
The author discusses her poetry and the Chicago environment that inspired it.
Distributed by Indiana University AV Center.

Robert Creeley — Poetry: Robert Creeley
30 min., b&w, 1966.
3/4" U-Matic.
Interview.
Distributed by Indiana University AV Center.

E. E. Cummings
17 min., 1979.
Exposition of several poems shows how reading can clarify Cummings's unusual structure.
Distributed by Churchill Films.

E. E. Cummings — The Making of a Poet
24 min.
A profile as told through the author's words and works.
Distributed by Films for the Humanities.

E. E. Cummings — Poetry for People Who Hate Poetry
15 min., color, 1980.
VHS, Beta, 3/4" U-Matic.
Lecturer, performer, and poet Roger Steffens selects "poetry for people who hate poetry" and presents it in a contemporary, easily understandable style.
Distributed by Churchill Films.

Emily Dickinson
22 min., color, 1978.
VHS, Beta, 3/4" U-Matic.
Ancillary materials available.
Distributed by Journal Films.

Emily Dickinson: A Certain Slant of Light
29 min., color, 1984.
VHS, Beta, 3/4" U-Matic.
Distributed by International Film Bureau.

Emily Dickinson — Voices and Visions: Modern American Poets
60 min.
VHS, 3/4" U-Matic.
Distributed by ABC-CLIO.

T. S. Eliot — Voices and Visions: Modern American Poets
60 min.
VHS, 3/4" U-Matic.
Distributed by ABC-CLIO.

Robert Frost: A First Acquaintance
16 min., color.
VHS, Beta, 3/4" U-Matic.
A look at the author's life, as told through his poems.
Distributed by Films for the Humanities.

Robert Frost — An Interview with Robert Frost
30 min., b&w, 1952.
Interview by Bela Kornitzer. Reads some poetry.
Distributed by Social Studies School Service (NBC).

Robert Frost's New England
22 min., color, 1976.
VHS, Beta, 3/4" U-Matic.
A selection of the author's poetry relating to New England and its seasons.

Exquisite photography.
Ancillary materials available.
Distributed by Churchill Films.

Robert Frost — Voices and Visions: Modern American Poets
60 min.
VHS, 3/4" U-Matic.
Distributed by ABC-CLIO.

Allen Ginsberg
see ***Potpourri of Poetry — From the Jack Kerouac School of Disembodied Poetics, Summer 1975,*** p. 259.

Nikki Giovanni — A Conversation with Poet Nikki Giovanni
30 min., color.
VHS, 3/4" U-Matic.
Hosted by Emma Rodgers.
Distributed by Eidos Productions.

Donald Hall
see ***Poets Talking,*** p. 259.

Robert Hayden
see ***Poets Talking,*** p. 259.

Langston Hughes
24 min., 1971.
A biographical look, providing examples of his works.
Distributed by Carousel Film and Video.

Langston Hughes — Voices and Visions: Modern American Poets
60 min.
VHS, 3/4" U-Matic.
Distributed by ABC-CLIO.

John Keats: His Life and Death
55 min., 1973.
Extended version of John Keats: Poet, which explores in greater depth the author's love affair with Fanny Brawne and the events surrounding his death.
Distributed by Britannica Films.

John Keats: Poet
31 min., 1973.
Written by Archibald MacLeish. Dramatizes the author's life and includes excerpts from his letters and poems.
Distributed by Britannica Films.

Galway Kinnell
see ***Poets Talking,*** p. 259.

Denise Levertov — Poetry: Denise Levertov and Charles Olson
30 min., b&w, 1966.
3/4" U-Matic.

Interviews.
Distributed by Indiana University AV Center.

Robert Lowell — Poetry: Richard Wilbur and Robert Lowell
30 min., b&w, 1966.
3/4" U-Matic.
Interviews.
Distributed by Indiana University AV Center.

Robert Lowell — Voices and Visions: Modern American Poets
60 min.
VHS, 3/4" U-Matic.
Distributed by ABC-CLIO.

W. S. Merwin
see ***Poets Talking,*** p. 259.

Marianne Moore — Voices and Visions: Modern American Poets
60 min.
VHS, 3/4" U-Matic.
Distributed by ABC-CLIO.

Frank O'Hara — Poetry: Frank O'Hara and Ed Sanders
30 min., b&w, 1966.
3/4" U-Matic.
Interviews.
Distributed by Indiana University AV Center.

Sylvia Plath
30 min., color, 1974.
VHS, Beta, 1/2" reel, 3/4" U-Matic, 2" Quad.
A four-part examination of the author's life and work.
Distributed by New York State Education Department.

Sylvia Plath: Letters Home
90 min., color, 1985.
VHS, Beta, 3/4" U-Matic.
With June Brown and Anna Nigh. A staged portrayal of the author's letters to her mother, outlining her day-to-day life and psychological descent.
Distributed by Films for the Humanities.

Sylvia Plath — Part I: The Struggle
30 min., color, 1974.
VHS, Beta, 1/2" reel, 3/4" U-Matic, 2" Quad.
The Royal Shakespeare Company presents dramatizations of the author's best-known poems.
Distributed by New York State Education Department.

Sylvia Plath — Part II: Getting There
30 min., color, 1974.
VHS, Beta, 1/2" reel, 3/4" U-Matic, 2" Quad.

Michele Collison sings a selection of Plath's poems, set to music by Elizabeth Swados.
Distributed by New York State Education Department.

Sylvia Plath — Voices and Visions: Modern American Poets
60 min.
VHS, 3/4" U-Matic.
Distributed by ABC-CLIO.

Edgar Allan Poe
see ***Introducing Great Authors,*** p. 246.

Edgar Allan Poe: Background and His Works
13 min., 1979.
Paintings created in the style of Poe's writings bring to life scenes of his works and background of his life. Some excerpts are presented.
Distributed by Coronet/MTI Film and Video.

Ezra Pound: Poet's Poet
29 min., 1970.
Distributed by Films for the Humanities.

Ezra Pound — Voices and Visions: Modern American Poets
60 min.
VHS, 3/4" U-Matic.
Distributed by ABC-CLIO.

William Shakespeare
see ***England: Background of Literature,*** p. 246.
see also ***Introducing Great Authors,*** p. 246.

William Shakespeare — Poetry and Hidden Poetry
53 min., color, 1984.
VHS, Beta, 3/4" U-Matic.
With the Royal Shakespeare Company. An examination of Shakespeare's poetry, various monosyllabic and polysyllabic phrases, and hidden poetic significance.
Distributed by Films for the Humanities.

William Shakespeare — Poetry for People Who Hate Poetry
15 min., color, 1980.
VHS, Beta, 3/4" U-Matic.
Lecturer, performer, and poet Roger Steffens selects "poetry for people who hate poetry" and presents it in a contemporary, easily understandable style.
Distributed by Churchill Films.

William Shakespeare — Selected Sonnets
40 min., 1984.
Readings by Ben Kingsley and Jane Lapotaire.
Distributed by Films for the Humanities.

William Shakespeare's Sonnets
150 min., color, 1984.
VHS, Beta, 3/4" U-Matic.
With Ben Kingsley, Roger Reese, Claire Bloom, Jane Lapotaire. An in-depth look at fifteen of Shakespeare's sonnets performed by actors and analyzed by A. L. Rowse and Stephen Spender.
Distributed by Films for the Humanities.

Wallace Stevens — Voices and Visions: Modern American Poets
60 min.
VHS, 3/4" U-Matic.
Distributed by ABC-CLIO.

Alfred, Lord Tennyson
see ***England: Background of Literature,*** p. 246.

Dylan Thomas
25 min., 1982.
Produced by BBC.
Distributed by Films, Inc.

Dylan Thomas: A Child's Christmas in Wales
26 min., b&w, 1960.
VHS, Beta, 3/4" U-Matic.
Narrated by the author. A moody realization of this story, augmented by a score of Welsh harp music.
Distributed by McGraw-Hill.

A Dylan Thomas Memoir
28 min., color, 1972.
VHS, Beta, 3/4" U-Matic.
A character study that won Blue Ribbon at the American Film Festival.
Distributed by Pyramid Film and Video.

Dylan Thomas — The Days of Dylan Thomas
21 min., 1965.
Distributed by McGraw-Hill.

Walt Whitman: Poet for a New Age
26 min., 1972.
A study of the author's beliefs, his conflicts with contemporaries, and how they influenced his poetry.
Distributed by Britannica Films.

Walt Whitman — Voices and Visions: Modern American Poets
60 min.
VHS, 3/4" U-Matic.
Distributed by ABC-CLIO.

Richard Wilbur — Poetry: Richard Wilbur and Robert Lowell
30 min., b&w, 1966.
3/4" U-Matic.
Interviews.
Distributed by Indiana University AV Center.

William Carlos Williams — Voices and Visions: Modern American Poets
60 min.
VHS, 3/4" U-Matic.
Distributed by ABC-CLIO.

William Wordsworth: William and Dorothy
52 min., 1985.
Directed by Ken Russell. A dramatization of the poet's life, work, and relationship to his famous sister.
Distributed by Films for the Humanities.

William Butler Yeats — Yeats Country
18 min., 1965.
The author's poetry, with scenes of the places in western Ireland that inspired him. Includes some biographical info.
Distributed by International Film Bureau.

POETRY: AUDIOCASSETTE RESOURCES

Claribel Alegria (with Carolyn Forché) — Who Raised Up This Prison's Bars?
58 min., 1988.
Alegria reads her poems in Spanish, with Forché reading in English her own translations as well as new ones by Alegria's husband.
Distributed by Poets' Audio Center.

Maya Angelou
30 min., 1979.
The author reads her poetry, talks about her memoir, and discusses a three-year period when she refused to speak.
Distributed by American Audio Prose Library.

Maya Angelou — I Know Why the Caged Bird Sings
179 min., 2 cass.

The author reads excerpts from her autobiography, about growing up black in a small town in Arkansas in the 1930s and '40s and about her sensitivity to sound and language.
Distributed by American Audio Prose Library.

John Ashbery
see *The Poet's Voice,* p. 259.

John Ashbery
39 min., 1967.
Reading at the YMHA New York Poetry Center.
Distributed by Poets' Audio Center.

John Ashbery — The Songs We Know Best
60 min., 1973 and 1989.
Recorded performance at the Folger Shakespeare Library, 1988, and studio recordings from the Library of Congress, 1973.
Distributed by Poets' Audio Center.

Margaret Atwood
59 min., 1977.
Studio recording of selected poems.
Distributed by Caedmon; Poets' Audio Center.

Margaret Atwood — Interview
56 min.
Conducted by Jan Castro, editor of *River Styx.*
Distributed by American Audio Prose Library.

Margaret Atwood — The Poetry and Voice of Margaret Atwood
1 cass.
Distributed by Caedmon.

W. H. Auden
see *Caedmon Treasury of Modern Poets Reading Their Own Poetry,* p. 258.
see also *Poems Set to Jazz,* p. 259.
see also *The Poet's Voice,* p. 259.

W. H. Auden
59 min., 1966.
Reading at the YMHA New York Poetry Center.
Distributed by Poets' Audio Center.

W. H. Auden — Selected Poems
48 min.
A retrospective reading of seventeen poems prepared and recorded by the author for the Spoken Arts Archives.

Distributed by Caedmon; Poets' Audio Center.

W. H. Auden — Selected Poems
51 min., 1954.
Caedmon studio recording supervised by the author with notes by him.
Distributed by Caedmon; Poets' Audio Center.

John Berryman
see *The Poet's Voice,* p. 259.

William Blake — The Poetry of William Blake
1 cass.
Distributed by Caedmon.

Robert Bly — Fairy Tales for Men and Women
90 min., 1987.
"Stretch a prose-poem to its limits, frame it with Jungian archetypes, and you get those fascinating explorations of psycho-sexual development."
Distributed by Poets' Audio Center.

Robert Bly — For the Stomach: Selected Poems, 1974
64 min.
The author reads his own work, from all phases of his career.
Distributed by Poets' Audio Center.

Robert Bly — Poetry East and West
140 min., 1983.
A lecture, leaning heavily on examples, comparing and contrasting poetry. Accompanied by the dulcimer.
Distributed by Poets' Audio Center.

The Poetry of Robert Bly
38 min., 1 cass., 1966.
Distributed by Jeffrey Norton Publishers.

Robert Bly — Poetry Reading: An Ancient Tradition
145 min., 1983.
The author reads his own work and the work of others. Includes commentary on the oral tradition of poetry throughout the centuries.
Distributed by Poets' Audio Center.

Robert Bly — The Six Powers of Poetry
75 min., 1983.
Lecture recorded at the San Jose Poetry Center. Focuses on the vital components of poetry and is interspersed with readings of the author's and others' poems.
Distributed by Poets' Audio Center.

Louise Bogan — The Eight-Sided Heart
58 min., 1948–1968.
Compiled from several master recordings in the collections of Yale University and the Library of Congress.
Distributed by Poets' Audio Center.

Gwendolyn Brooks Reading Her Poetry
52 min., 1 cass., 1973.
Caedmon studio recording.
Distributed by Caedmon.

Elizabeth Barrett Browning — Sonnets from the Portuguese
1 cass.
Distributed by Caedmon; Spoken Arts.

Elizabeth Barrett Browning — Sonnets from the Portuguese
46 min., 1 cass., 1979.
Unabridged edition.
Distributed by SBI Publishers Sound.

Amy Clampitt — The Dahlia Gardens
56 min., 1986.
The author reads poems from each of her books in a studio recording.
Distributed by Poets' Audio Center.

Lucille Clifton — The Place for Keeping
45 min., 1974 and 1979.
A retrospective compiled from two live readings.
Distributed by Poets' Audio Center.

Robert Creeley
25 min., 1966.
Reading at the YMHA New York Poetry Center.
Distributed by Poets' Audio Center.

Countee Cullen — The Poetry of Countee Cullen
1 cass.
Distributed by Caedmon.

E. E. Cummings
see *Caedmon Treasury of Modern Poets Reading Their Own Poetry,* p. 258.

E. E. Cummings — Collected Poems, 1920–1940
79 min., 2 cass.
Caedmon's engineers spent years putting this set together; it's the best of many concert readings the author gave over thirty years.
Distributed by Caedmon; Poets' Audio Center.

E. E. Cummings — Nonlecture I: I & My Parents
II: I & Their Son
III: I & Selfdiscovery

IV: I & You & Is
V: I & Now & Him
VI: I & Am & Santa Claus
6 separate cass.
Distributed by Caedmon.

Poems of E. E. Cummings
60 min., 1 cass.
Unabridged edition.
Distributed by Summer Stream.

E. E. Cummings Reads His Collected Poetry: 1943–1958
2 cass.
A second set, covering the latter half of the author's work.
Distributed by Caedmon; Poets' Audio Center.

Emily Dickinson
1 cass.
Distributed by Recorded Books.

The Poems of Emily Dickinson
1 cass., 1989.
Distributed by Knowledge Unlimited.

Poems and Letters of Emily Dickinson
1 cass.
Distributed by Caedmon.

Emily Dickinson Recalled in Song
30 min., 1 cass.
Distributed by Jeffrey Norton Publishers.

John Donne
see *Palgrave's Golden Treasury of English Poetry,* p. 258.

John Donne — Essential Donne
1 cass.
Includes a paperback book.
Distributed by Listening Library.

John Donne: The Love Poems
1 cass.
Distributed by Recorded Books.

H. D. — Helen in Egypt
39 min., 1955.
A rare recording made available by Yale's Collection of American Literature, Beinecke Rare Book and Manuscript Library. The author reads excerpts from this work.
Distributed by Poets' Audio Center.

John Dryden
see *Palgrave's Golden Treasury of English Poetry,* p. 258.

T. S. Eliot
see *Caedmon Treasury of Modern Poets Reading Their Own Poetry,* p. 258.

see also *The Poet's Voice,* p. 259.

T. S. Eliot and George Orwell
41 min., 1 cass., 1953.
Distributed by Jeffrey Norton Publishers.

T. S. Eliot — Poems Choruses
50 min., 1955.
A studio reading of twelve poems, including "Prufrock" and "Ash Wednesday."
Distributed by Caedmon; Poets' Audio Center.

T. S. Eliot — Reading "Four Quartets"
56 min.
BBC recording licensed to Caedmon.
Distributed by Caedmon; The Poets' Audio Center.

T. S. Eliot — Selected Poems
49 min., 1971.
Caedmon posthumous compilation of the author reading selected poems, including "Waste Land."
Distributed by Caedmon; Poets' Audio Center.

T. S. Eliot — 20th Century Poets in English: Recordings of Poets Reading Their Own Poetry, No. 3
29 min.
Distributed by New Letters on Air.

Lawrence Ferlinghetti — Into the Deeper Pools
58 min., 1984.
Composed of two live recordings, which include poems from 1955 to the author's most recent volume, *Over All the Obscene Boundaries: European Poems.*
Distributed by Poets' Audio Center.

Carolyn Forché — Ourselves or Nothing
58 min., 1981–82.
Reading from *The Country Between Us,* nominated for a Pulitzer Prize. Recorded live at the Folger Shakespeare Library, 1981, and at Watershed Studio, 1982.
Distributed by Poets' Audio Center.

Robert Frost
see *Caedmon Treasury of Modern Poets Reading Their Own Poetry,* p. 258.
see also *The Poet's Voice,* p. 259.

Robert Frost
49 min., 1956.
The author reads selected poems at home.

Distributed by Caedmon; Poets' Audio Center.

Robert Frost
55 min., 1953–54.
Compilation from three readings at the YMHA New York Poetry Center.
Distributed by Caedmon; Poets' Audio Center.

Robert Frost in Recital
1 cass.
Includes "Desert Places," "Fire and Ice," "Gift Outright," "Need of Being Versed in Country Things," "Once by the Pacific," "Stopping by Woods on a Snowy Evening," and many other poems.
Distributed by Caedmon.

Robert Frost Reads "The Road Not Taken" and Other Poems
1 cass.
Includes "Acquainted with the Night," "After Apple-Picking," "Birches," "Departmental," "Mending Wall," "Pasture," "Provide, Provide," and many other poems.
Distributed by Caedmon.

Robert Frost — 20th Century Poets in English: Recordings of Poets Reading Their Own Poetry, No. 6
cass., LP also available.
Includes "Acquainted with the Night," "Departmental," "Gift Outright," "Pasture," "Provide, Provide," "Stopping by Woods on a Snowy Evening," and many other poems.
Distributed by Library of Congress.

Allen Ginsberg
see *The Poet's Voice,* p. 259.

Allen Ginsberg and Anne Waldman
48 min., 1975.
Ginsberg and Waldman reading together at the Naropa Institute. Ginsberg's complete recording of "Howl."
Distributed by Poets' Audio Center.

Nikki Giovanni
see *Black Literature and Poetry,* p. 258.

Robert Graves
see *Caedmon Treasury of Modern Poets Reading Their Own Poetry,* p. 258.

Donald Hall
29 min., 1987.
Distributed by New Letters on Air.

Donald Hall — Names of Horses
55 min., 1985.
Composed of a recording at Eagle Pond Farm and an outstanding performance at the Folger Shakespeare Library. Includes poems from all the author's books as well as work in manuscript.
Distributed by Poets' Audio Center.

Donald Hall — The Poetry of Donald Hall
26 min., 1 cass., 1964.
Distributed by Jeffrey Norton Publishers.

Robert Herrick
see **Palgrave's Golden Treasury of English Poetry,** p. 258.

A. E. Housman: A Shropshire Lad and Other Poetry
1 cass.
Distributed by Caedmon.

Langston Hughes
see **Black Literature and Poetry,** p. 258.

Langston Hughes — Poetry and Reflections
47 min., 1962–64.
Includes BBC recordings of 1962 and 1964. The author reads his poetry and discusses his life and work.
Distributed by Caedmon; Poets' Audio Center.

Langston Hughes — The Poetry of Langston Hughes
2 cass.
Distributed by Caedmon.

Langston Hughes Reads and Discusses His Poetry
43 min.
Rare — earliest available tape of the author. With commentary.
Distributed by Poets' Audio Center.

Langston Hughes Reads and Talks about His Poems
1 cass., 1989.
Distributed by Knowledge Unlimited.

Langston Hughes: Simple Stories
1 cass.
Distributed by Caedmon.

Randall Jarrell
see **The Poet's Voice,** p. 259.

Randall Jarrell
67 min., 1963.
Reading at the YMHA New York Poetry Center.

Distributed by Poets' Audio Center.

John Keats — Essential Keats
1 cass.
Includes paperback book.
Distributed by Listening Library.

John Keats: Odes
1 cass.
Distributed by Jeffrey Norton Publishers.

John Keats — The Poetry of Keats
1 cass.
Distributed by Caedmon.

Galway Kinnell
1 hr., 1975.
The author selected poems from **The Book of Nightmares** in a Caedmon studio recording.
Distributed by Caedmon; Poets' Audio Center.

Etheridge Knight
29 min., 1 cass.
Distributed by New Letters on Air.

Maxine Kumin — Progress Report
42 min., 1986.
Recorded in performance at the Folger Shakespeare Library.
Distributed by Poets' Audio Center.

Denise Levertov — The Acolyte
63 min., 1985.
A retrospective that spans forty years' work.
Distributed by Poets' Audio Center.

Philip Levine
49 min., 1975.
Caedmon studio recording of selected poems.
Distributed by Caedmon; Poets' Audio Center.

Philip Levine — Hear Me
62 min., 1977.
Taken from two public performances; does not duplicate any poems in the Caedmon recording.
Distributed by Poets' Audio Center.

Audre Lorde
Distributed by New Letters on Air.

Audre Lorde — Shorelines
55 min., 1984.
Composed of both live and studio recordings. Retrospective encompassing the entire breadth of the author's work.
Distributed by Poets' Audio Center.

Robert Lowell — The Poetry of Robert Lowell
28 min., 1 cass., 1968.
Distributed by Jeffrey Norton Publishers.

Robert Lowell — A Recital
1976.
The author's last reading, December 8, 1976, at YMHA New York Poetry Center.
Distributed by Caedmon; Poets' Audio Center.

Archibald MacLeish
see *Caedmon Treasury of Modern Poets Reading Their Own Poetry,* p. 258.

Archibald MacLeish
54 min.
Studio recording.
Distributed by Caedmon; Poets' Audio Center.

James Merrill — Reflected Houses
60 min., 1986.
Studio recording. Includes selections from *Mirabell: Books of Number.*
Distributed by Poets' Audio Center.

W. S. Merwin Reading His Poetry
1 cass.
Distributed by Caedmon.

Czeslaw Milosz — Fire
65 min., 1986.
Retrospective includes "Parting with my Wife Janina," a poem never read in public. Recorded in studio and at the Hirshhorn Museum in Washington, DC. A few selections in Polish.
Distributed by Poets' Audio Center.

John Milton
see *Palgrave's Golden Treasury of English Poetry,* p. 258.

Marianne Moore
see *Caedmon Treasury of Modern Poets Reading Their Own Poetry,* p. 258.
see also *The Poet's Voice,* p. 259.

Marianne Moore
28 min., 1954.
Studio recording.
Distributed by Caedmon; Poets' Audio Center.

Howard Nemerov
74 min., 1962.
Reading at the YMHA New York Poetry Center.
Distributed by Poets' Audio Center.

Pablo Neruda
59 min., 1971.

The author reads selected poems in Spanish.
Distributed by Poets' Audio Center, Spoken Arts.

Sharon Olds — Coming Back to Life
59 min., 1984.
Recorded at the Folger Shakespeare Library and in the studio. Includes poems from *The Dead and the Living* and *Satan Says* as well as newer work.
Distributed by Poets' Audio Center.

Linda Pastan — Mosaic
51 min., 1986.
The author reads selections from all her books and newer work.
Distributed by Poets' Audio Center.

Marge Piercy — At the Core: Selected Poems
58 min., 1986.
Distributed by Poets' Audio Center.

Marge Piercy — Interview
50 min.
Discussion includes the author's response to those who criticize her for writing out of a political and social vision.
Distributed by Poets' Audio Center.

Sylvia Plath
see *The Poet's Voice,* p. 259.

Sylvia Plath
55 min., released 1976.
A compilation from BBC and Poetry Room, Harvard College Library, tapes.
Distributed by Poets' Audio Center.

Sylvia Plath — Plath
48 min., 1962.
Historic recording made in late October 1962, probably the most prolific month of the poet's life. Readings of fifteen poems, including "Ariel," "Daddy," and "Lady Lazarus." Also an interview with Peter Orr of the BBC.
Distributed by Poets' Audio Center.

Sylvia Plath — Poetry of Sylvia Plath: Literary Criticism
60 min., 1 cass.
Distributed by Gould Media.

Ezra Pound
see *Caedmon Treasury of Modern Poets Reading Their Own Poetry,* p. 258.
see also *The Poet's Voice,* p. 259.

Ezra Pound
89 min., 2 cass., 1960.
Studio recording, made just after the author

was released from St. Elizabeth's Hospital.
Distributed by Caedmon; Poets' Audio Center.

Adrienne Rich
30 min., 1968.
Reading at the YMHA New York Poetry Center.
Distributed by Poets' Audio Center.

Adrienne Rich — Planetarium: A Retrospective, 1950–1980
63 min., 1986.
The author traces each of her books up to 1980, including **Diving into the Wreck, Necessities of Life** and **Hunger** in a studio recording.
Distributed by Poets' Audio Center.

Adrienne Rich — Tracking the Contradictions: Poems 1981–1985
55 min., 1986.
A live reading that includes the entire poem "Sources" and several selections from **Your Native Land, Your Life.** Produced as a companion to **Planetarium.**
Distributed by Poets' Audio Center.

Rainer Marie Rilke
51 min., 1 cass., 1953.
Distributed by Caedmon; Poets' Audio Center

Theodore Roethke
see **The Poet's Voice,** p. 259.

Theodore Roethke
48 min., released 1972.
The author reads selected poems. Compiled posthumously.
Distributed by Caedmon; Poets' Audio Ctr.

Theodore Roethke — The Poetry of Theodore Roethke
36 min., 1 cass.
Distributed by Jeffrey Norton Publishers.

Theodore Roethke Reads His Poetry
1 cass.
Distributed by Caedmon.

Christina Rossetti
see **Poems Set to Jazz,** p. 259.

Carl Sandburg Reading Fog and Other Poems
1 cass.
Distributed by Caedmon.

Anne Sexton
35 min., 1964.

Reading at the YMHA New York Poetry Center.
Distributed by Poets' Audio Center.

Anne Sexton
30 min., 1968.
Interview with the poet and critics about her readings accompanied by "chamber rock" orchestra. Includes selections from live performance, recorded 1968.
Distributed by Poets' Audio Center.

Anne Sexton
52 min., 1973.
Studio recording.
Distributed by Caedmon; Poets' Audio Ctr.

William Shakespeare
see **Palgrave's Golden Treasury of English Poetry,** p. 258.
see also **Poems Set to Jazz,** p. 259.

William Shakespeare — Complete Collection of Sonnets
2 cass., abridged edition.
Distributed by Cassette Book.

William Shakespeare — Great Sonnets and Soliloquies
1 cass.
Distributed by CMS Records.

William Shakespeare Sonnets
2 hrs., 2 cass., 1988.
Distributed by Caedmon.

William Shakespeare — Sonnets of Shakespeare
1 cass., 1989.
Distributed by Knowledge Unlimited.

Gary Snyder
60 min., 1989.
Retrospective reading.
Distributed by Poets' Audio Center.

Wallace Stevens
see **Caedmon Treasury of Modern Poets Reading Their Own Poetry,** p. 258.
see also **The Poet's Voice,** p. 259.

Wallace Stevens
51 min., 1955.
Studio recording.
Distributed by Poets' Audio Center.

May Swenson
Studio recording.
Distributed by Caedmon; Poets' Audio Center.

Alfred, Lord Tennyson — Portrait of a Poet
53 min., 1890 and 1970.

Includes a salvaged excerpt from the historic wax cylinder recording made in 1890 of Tennyson reading from "Maud." On most of the tape, C. Day Lewis, John Gielgud, Sybil Thorndike, and others read selections. Sir Charles Tennyson recalls boyhood memories of his grandfather. A 1970 BBC broadcast.
Distributed by Poets' Audio Center.

Dylan Thomas
see **Caedmon Treasury of Modern Poets Reading Their Own Poetry,** p. 258.

Dylan Thomas — A Child's Christmas in Wales
46 min., 1 cass.
Unabridged edition. Includes "Ballad of the Long-legged Bait," "Ceremony After A Fire Raid," "Do not go gentle into that good night," "Fern Hill," "In the white giant's thigh."
Distributed by Caedmon.

Dylan Thomas — The Complete Recorded Poetry
110 min., released 1975.
Includes all the studio sessions the author completed in his lifetime.
Distributed by Caedmon; Poets' Audio Center.

Dylan Thomas — An Evening with Dylan Thomas
1 cass.
The author reads his own poetry, as well as that of Auden, Hardy, and Yeats.
Distributed by Caedmon.

Dylan Thomas Reading A Visit to America
1 cass.
Includes "A Visit to America" — Dylan Thomas; "The Bards" — Walter de la Mare; "Master and Bos'n Song," "As I Walked Out One Evening" — W. H. Auden; "Chard Witlow: Mr. T. S. Eliot's Sunday Evening Broadcast Postscript," "Naming of Parts" — Henry Reed; "The Owl" — Edward Thomas; "Broken Appointment," "To Lizbie Brown," "In Death Divided," — Thomas Hardy.
Distributed by Caedmon.

Dylan Thomas Reading Quite Early One Morning
1 cass.
Includes "Holiday Memory," "Reminiscences of a Childhood," "Visit to Grandpa's."

Distributed by Caedmon.

Dylan Thomas Reads a Personal Anthology
1 cass.
The author reads works by other poets, including Vernon Watkins, W. H. Davies, Alun Lewis, Edward Thomas, Wilfred Owen, W. B. Yeats, Gerard Manley Hopkins, D. H. Lawrence, John Milton.
Distributed by Caedmon.

John Updike
1967.
Reading of poetry and prose at the YMHA New York Poetry Center.
Distributed by Poets' Audio Center.

Edmund Waller
see **Palgrave's Golden Treasury of English Poetry,** p. 258.

Robert Penn Warren — Reads Selected Poems, 1923–1978
53 min.
Studio recording.
Distributed by Caedmon, Poets' Audio Center.

Walt Whitman: As a Disciple of Emerson
60 min., 1 cass.
Distributed by Gould Media.

Walt Whitman — Crossing Brooklyn Ferry and Other Poems
1 cass.
Distributed by Caedmon.

Walt Whitman — Essential Whitman
1 cass.
Includes paperback book.
Distributed by Listening Library.

Walt Whitman — Leaves of Grass
— 1 hr. 45 min, 2 cass., abridged ed.
Distributed by Cassette Book.
— 1 cass., 1989.
Distributed by Knowledge Unlimited.

Walt Whitman — Leaves of Grass: I Hear America Singing and Song of the Open Road
Distributed by Caedmon.

Walt Whitman — Leaves of Grass: Literary Criticism
60 min., 1 cass.
Distributed by Gould Media.

Walt Whitman — Orson Welles Reads "Song of Myself"
1 cass.
Distributed by Jeffrey Norton Publishers.

Walt Whitman — 20th Century Poetry in English, No. 13: Whitman the Man
From the Leaves of Grass Centennial Series.
Distributed by Library of Congress.

Walt Whitman — 20th Century Poetry in English, No. 14: Whitman the Poet
From the Leaves of Grass Centennial Series.
Distributed by Library of Congress.

Walt Whitman — 20th Century Poetry in English, No. 15: Whitman the Philosopher
From the Leaves of Grass Centennial Series.
Distributed by Library of Congress.

Walt Whitman — 20th Century Poetry in English, No. 16: Walt Whitman Speaks for Himself
From the Leaves of Grass Centennial Series.
Distributed by Library of Congress.

Richard Wilbur
see *Caedmon Treasury of Modern Poets Reading Their Own Poetry,* p. 258.

Richard Wilbur
55 min., 1967.
Studio recording which the author supervised.
Distributed by Caedmon, Poets' Audio Center.

William Carlos Williams
see *Caedmon Treasury of Modern Poets Reading Their Own Poetry,* p. 258.
see also *The Poet's Voice,* p. 259.

William Carlos Williams
42 min., 1957.
Studio recording.
Distributed by Caedmon; Poets' Audio Center.

William Carlos Williams Reads His Poetry
1 cass.
Distributed by Caedmon.

William Wordsworth — The Poetry of William Wordsworth
1 cass.
Distributed by Spoken Arts.

James Wright
57 min., 1977.
Studio recording.
Distributed by Caedmon; Poets' Audio Center.

James Wright — The Poetry and Voice of James Wright
1 cass.
Distributed by Caedmon.

William Butler Yeats
see *Caedmon Treasury of Modern Poets Reading Their Own Poetry,* p. 258.
see also *Dylan Thomas Reads the Poetry of W. B. Yeats and Others,* p. 257.

William Butler Yeats
42 min.
On a rare BBC tape, the author reads several of his favorite poems and discusses modern poetry. Several other Yeats poems read by Siobhan McKenna and Michael MacLiammoir.
Distributed by Poets' Audio Center.

William Butler Yeats — An Approach to the Poetry of Yeats
1 cass., 1986.
Distributed by Jeffrey Norton Publishers.

William Butler Yeats — Dylan Thomas Reads the Poetry of W. B. Yeats and Others
1 cass.
Mostly Yeats poems, plus works by Louis MacNeice, George Barker, Walter de la Mare, W. H. Auden, and D. H. Lawrence.
Distributed by Caedmon.

William Butler Yeats: Poetry
60 min., 1 cass.
Distributed by Gould Media.

William Butler Yeats — The Poetry of William Butler Yeats
1 cass.
Distributed by Caedmon.

POETRY COLLECTIONS: FILM AND AUDIOCASSETTE RESOURCES

Black Literature and Poetry
25 min., color, 1980.
VHS, Beta, 3/4" U-Matic.
Hosted by Roscoe Lee Brown and Abbey Lincoln. An examination of black literature and poetry. Includes readings from the works of Frederick Douglass, Nikki Giovanni, Langston Hughes, James Weldon Johnson, and Richard Wright.
Distributed by Salzburg Enterprises.

Caedmon Treasury of Modern Poets Reading Their Own Poetry
95 min., 2 cass.

Includes T. S. Eliot, W. B. Yeats, W. H. Auden, Edith Sitwell, Dylan Thomas, Robert Graves, Gertrude Stein, Archibald MacLeish, E. E. Cummings, Marianne Moore, Stephen Spender, Conrad Aiken, Robert Frost, William Carlos Williams, Wallace Stevens, Ezra Pound, Richard Wilbur, and a few others.
Distributed by Caedmon.

Palgrave's Golden Treasury of English Poetry
2 cass.
Includes William Shakespeare, John Donne, John Dryden, Robert Herrick, Edmund Waller, John Milton, Thomas Gray, and other.
Distributed by Caedmon.

Poems from Black Africa
1 cass.
Many poets and poems from Africa, including oral traditionals from various parts of the continent (Nigeria, South Africa, Ghana, and others).
Distributed by Caedmon.

Poems Set to Jazz
30 min., 1 cass.
Includes "Stop All the Clocks" and "Underneath the Abject Willow" — W. H. Auden; "We'll Go No More A-Roving" — Lord Byron; "Timothy Winters" — Charles Causley; "When I Am Dead, My Dearest" — Christina Rossetti; "Sigh, No More, Ladies" — William Shakespeare; "Lesbos" — Lawrence Durrell; "The Housewife" — Michael Baldwin.

Distributed by Gould Media.

Poets Talking
Donald Hall, Galway Kinnell, Gregory Orr, Carolyn Kizer, Robert Bly, Louis Simpson, Marvin Bell, Jerome Rothenberg, Wendell Berry, Larry Fagin, W. S. Merwin, Robert Hayden, Howard Norman, Lawrence Raab, Joyce Peseroff.
29 min. each, color, 1975.
3/4" U-Matic.
American poets read their works and discuss the process of poetry and such things as the effect of translation on their poems. All programs available individually.
Distributed by Michigan Media.

The Poet's Voice
6 cass.
From the tape archive of the Poetry Room, Harvard University. Includes John Ashbery, W. H. Auden, John Berryman, T. S. Eliot, Robert Frost, Allen Ginsberg, Randall Jarrell, Robinson Jeffers, Marianne Moore, Sylvia Plath, Ezra Pound, Theodore Roethke, Wallace Stevens, William Carlos Williams.
Distributed by Poets' Audio Center.

Potpourri of Poetry — from the Jack Kerouac School of Disembodied Poetics, Summer 1975
60 min., 1975.
Allen Ginsberg, Dianne DiPrima, John Ashbery, Ted Berrigan, Philip Whalen, and others.
Distributed by Poets' Audio Center.

DRAMA: FILM AND VIDEO RESOURCES

Anton Chekhov — The Cherry Orchard
43 min., color and b&w, 1967.
16-mm film.
Distributed by Encyclopaedia Britannica.

Anton Chekhov — The Cherry Orchard I
22 min., color, 1968.
VHS, Beta, 3/4" U-Matic.
Distributed by Encyclopaedia Britannica.

Anton Chekhov — The Cherry Orchard II, Comedy or Tragedy?
22 min., color, 1968.
VHS, Beta, 3/4" U-Matic.
Distributed by Encyclopaedia Britannica.

Henrik Ibsen — A Doll's House
89 min., b&w, 1959.
VHS, Beta, 3/4" U-Matic, 8 mm.
With Julie Harris, Christopher Plummer, Jason Robards, Hume Cronyn, Eileen Heckart, and Richard Thomas.
Distributed by MGM/UA Home Video; Video Yesteryear.

Henrik Ibsen — A Doll's House
98 min., color, 1973.
VHS.
With Jane Fonda, Edward Fox, Trevor Howard, and David Warner.
Distributed by Prism Entertainment.

Arthur Miller — Death of a Salesman
115 min., b&w, 1951.
16-mm, film.
With Fredric March and Mildred Dunnock.
Distributed by many rental agencies.

Arthur Miller — Death of a Salesman
135 min., color, 1985.
VHS, Beta, laser, stereo.
Emmy Award–winning made-for-TV movie,
with Dustin Hoffman, Charles Durning,
Stephen Lang, John Malkovich, Kate
Reid.
Distributed by Image Entertainment; Laser-
Disc; Warner Home Video.

William Shakespeare
see *Introducing Great Authors,* p. 246.
see also *England; Background of Literature,* p. 246.

**William   Shakespeare — William
Shakespeare's Art**
29 min., b&w, 1961.
VHS, Beta, 3/4" U-Matic.
Examines Shakespeare's art, craftsmanship,
and techniques.
Distributed by Michigan Media (University
of Michigan).

William Shakespeare
25 min., color, 1955.
Recounts the life of Shakespeare from his
early boyhood to his time as a
playwright and actor in London.
Distributed by Britannica Films.

**William Shakespeare: Background for
His Works**
14 min., color, 1955.
Examining the time and elements of English
life that gave Shakespeare his language
and shaped his characters.
Distributed by Coronet/MTI Film and Video.

**William Shakespeare and His Stage:
Approaches to Hamlet**
45 min., color.
VHS, Beta, 3/4" U-Matic.
John Barrymore, Laurence Olivier, John
Gielgud, and Nicol Williamson. A look
at how four great actors have portrayed
Hamlet.
Distributed by Films for the Humanities.

William Shakespeare — Hamlet
155 min., b&w, 1948.
VHS, Beta, laser.
Academy Awards for best picture and best
actor, with Laurence Olivier as Hamlet.

Directed by Olivier.
Distributed by Paramount Home Video.

William Shakespeare — Hamlet
114 min., color, 1969.
VHS, HiFi.
With Anthony Hopkins, Marianne Faithful,
Anjelica Huston, Nicol Williamson.
Distributed by RCA/Columbia Pictures
Home Video.

William Shakespeare — Hamlet
104 min., color, 1970.
16-mm film.
With Richard Chamberlain and Michael
Redgrave. Directed by Peter Wood.
Distributed by Films, Inc.

William Shakespeare — Hamlet
150 min., color, 1979.
VHS, Beta, 3/4" U-Matic.
With Derek Jacobi. British.
Distributed by Time-Life Video.

**William Shakespeare — Hamlet: The
Age of Elizabeth, I**
30 min., color, 1959.
VHS, Beta, 3/4" U-Matic.
An introduction to Elizabethan theater.
Distributed by Encyclopaedia Britannica.

William Shakespeare — Otello (based on
the play by William Shakespeare)
135 min., color, 1982.
VHS, Beta.
Verdi's opera, with Vladimir Atlantov and
Kiri Te Kanawa, taped at the Arena di
Verona in Rome.
Distributed by HBO Video; Home Vision.

William Shakespeare — Otello
123 min., color, 1986.
VHS, Beta, laser.
Lush, opulent film of the Verdi opera,
directed by Franco Zeffirelli. Placido
Domingo plays Otello.
Distributed by Image Entertainment; Kultur
Video.

William Shakespeare — Othello
81 min., 1922.
VHS, Beta, 3/4" U-Matic, 8-mm film.
German silent version, with Werner Krauss.
Titles in English.
Distributed by Discount Video Tapes; Video
Yesteryear.

William Shakespeare — Othello
120 min., color, 1982.
VHS, Beta.

BBC version with Anthony Hopkins.
Distributed by Time-Life Video.

William Shakespeare — Shakespeare and His Theatre
52 min., color, 1977.
VHS, Beta, 3/4" U-Matic.
Examines the life and times of Shakespeare and the theater he created.
Distributed by Gould Media.

William Shakespeare — Shakespeare and the Globe
31 min., color, 1985.
VHS, Beta, 3/4" U-Matic.
A look at Shakespeare's life and historical significance, with emphasis on his plays, motifs, and interpretations.
Distributed by Films for the Humanities.

William Shakespeare — The Shakespeare Collection
1. *Macbeth* 2. *King Richard II* 3. *Antony and Cleopatra* 4. *The Tempest* 5. *Othello*
170 min., color, 1983.
VHS, Beta.
Simon McCorkindale, Piper Laurie, Lynn Redgrave, David Birney, Ron Palillio, Ted Sorel, Efrem Zimbalist, Jr., Ron Moody, William Marshall, Jenny Agutter.
A series of full-length productions.
Distributed by Kultur Video.

William Shakespeare — Shakespeare of Stratford and London
32 min., color, 1978.
3/4" U-Matic.
A tour of Shakespeare's birthplace and hometown.
Distributed by National Geographic Society.

William Shakespeare — Shakespearean Tragedy
40 min., color, 1984.
VHS, Beta, 3/4" U-Matic.
Tackles the basics in theme and motif of the tragedies, particularly Hamlet and Macbeth.
Distributed by Films for the Humanities.

William Shakespeare — Shakespeare's World
29 min., b&w, 1961.
Examines Shakespeare's view of humanity and the universe, as well as the thoughts and ideas prevailing in his world and time, as revealed in excerpts from *As You Like It, Othello, Troilus and Cressida,* and *King Lear.*
Distributed by Michigan Media (University of Michigan).

William Shakespeare — Understanding Shakespeare: His Stagecraft
20 min., 1972.
Staging of scenes from Hamlet, Romeo and Juliet, and Henry V.
Distributed by Coronet/MTI Film and Video.

Sophocles — Antigone
120 min., 1987.
Staged version.
Distributed by Films for the Humanities.

Sophocles — Oedipus Rex
90 min., color, 1956.
VHS, Beta.
An authentic recreation of the author's original intent, in which the actors wear masks throughout.
Distributed by Corinth Video.

Sophocles — Oedipus Rex
90 min., color, 1959.
VHS, Beta, 3/4" U-Matic.
3 parts. Important scenes with discussion.
Distributed by Encyclopaedia Britannica.

Sophocles — Oedipus Rex
1987.
VHS, Beta.
A dance version, choreographed by George Balanchine and composed by Igor Stravinsky. Recorded at the Carre Theatre in Amsterdam.
Distributed by Home Vision.

Sophocles — Oedipus the King
29 min., color, 1976.
3/4" U-Matic.
Examines the classical Greek theater in general and *Oedipus the King* in particular.
Distributed by Films for the Humanities.

Sophocles — Oedipus the King
97 min., color, 1968.
16-mm film.
With Christopher Plummer and Orson Welles.
Distributed by Swank Motion Pictures.

Sophocles — Oedipus Tyrranus
60 min., color, 1978.
VHS, Beta, 3/4" U-Matic.
Hosted by José Ferrer. Shown from the point when Oedipus is told of his father's death.
Distributed by Films, Inc.

Tennessee Williams
1956.
The author reads a selection from his poems and excerpts from **The Glass Menagerie** and his story "The Yellow Bird."
Distributed by Caedmon; Poets' Audio Center.

Tennessee Williams — The Glass Menagerie
134 min., color, 1988.

Video.
With John Malkovich, Joanne Woodward, and Karen Allen.
Distributed by MCA Home Video.

Tennessee Williams — Interview
25 min., 1978.
The author discusses his plays and his bouts with drugs.
Distributed by American Audio Prose Library.

DISTRIBUTORS

ABC-CLIO
Video Division: Intellimation
2040 Alameda Padre Serra
P.O. Box 4397
Santa Barbara, CA 93140-4397
1-800-422-2546

American Audio Prose Library
P.O. Box 842
1015 E. Broadway, Suite 284
Columbia, MO 65205
1-800-447-2275

Audio Forum
see **Jeffrey Norton Publishers, Inc.**

Audio Partners
P.O. Box 6930
Auburn, CA 95603
1-800-982-8319

Benchmark Films
145 Scarborough Rd.
Briarcliff Manor, NY 10510
(914) 762-3838

Bennu Productions
165 Madison Ave.
New York, NY 10016
(212) 213-8511

Brighton Video
250 West 57th St., Suite 916
New York, NY 10019
1-800-542-5554

Britannica Films
see **Encyclopaedia Britannica Education Corp.**

Caedmon
(Division of Harper & Row)
1995 Broadway
New York, New York 10023
(212) 580-3400

Carousel Film and Video
241 East 34th St., Room 304
New York, NY 10016
(212) 683-1660

Cassette Book Company
P.O. Box 7111
Pasadena, CA 91109
(818) 799-4139

Centron Films
see **Coronet/MTI Film and Video**

Churchill Films
662 Oral Roberts Blvd.
Los Angeles, CA 90060

CMS Records Inc.
226 Washington St.
Mt. Vernon, NY 10553
(914) 667-6200

Corinth Video
(Division of Corinth Films Inc.)
34 Gansevoort St.
New York, NY 10014
1-800-221-4720

Coronet/MTI Film and Video
Coronet American Short Story and Video Series
108 Wilmot Rd.
Deerfield, IL 60015
1-800-621-2131

Dallas County Community College
Center for Telecommunications
4343 North Highway 67
Mesquite, TX 75150
(214) 324-7988

Discount Video Tapes
3711B West Clark Ave.
P.O. Box 7122
Burbank, CA 91510
(818) 843-3366

Eidos Productions, Inc.
3404 South Ravinia Dr.
Dallas, TX 75233

Encyclopaedia Britannica Educational Corp.
425 North Michigan Ave.
Chicago, IL 60611
1-800-558-6968

Esstee Audios
3635 Glengyle Ave., Suite 5E
Baltimore, MD 21215
(301) 764-3343

Films for the Humanities
P.O. Box 2053
Princeton, NJ 08540
(609) 452-1128
1-800-257-5126

Films, Inc.
4420 Oakton St.
Skokie, IL 60076
(312) 878-2600, ext. 44
1-800-323-4222, ext. 44

Gould Media
44 Parkway West
Mount Vernon, NY 10552
(914) 664-3285

HBO Video
1370 Avenue of the Americas
New York, NY 10019
(212) 977-8990

Home Vision
5547 North Ravenwood Ave.
Chicago, IL 60640-1199
1-800-826-3456

Image Entertainment
6311 Romaine St.
Hollywood, CA 90038
(213) 468-8867

Indiana University AV Center
Bloomington, IN 47405
(812) 885-8087

International Film Bureau, Inc.
332 South Michigan Ave.
Chicago, IL 60604
(312) 427-4545

Jeffrey Norton Publishers, Inc.
On-the-Green
Guilford, CT 06437
1-800-243-1234

Jimcin Recordings
P.O. Box 536
Portsmouth, RI 02871
1-800-626-3333

Journal Films
930 Pitner Ave.
Evanston, IL 60202
1-800-323-5448

Knowledge Unlimited
P.O. Box 52
Madison, WI 52701
(608) 836-6660

Kultur Video
121 Highway 36
West Long Branch, NJ 07764
(201) 229-2343

LaserDisc Corp. of America
200 West Grand Ave.
Montvale, NJ 07645
(201) 573-1122

Learning Corp. of America
1350 Avenue of the Americas
New York, NY 10019
(312) 940-1260
1-800-621-2131

Library of Congress
(Division of the U.S. Government)
Washington, DC 20540
(202) 287-5000

Listening Library, Inc.
1 Park Ave.
Old Greenwich, CT 06870
1-800-243-4504

MasterVision Inc.
969 Park Ave.
New York, NY 10028
(212) 879-0448

MCA Home Video
70 Universal City Plaza
Universal City, CA 91608
(818) 777-4300

McGraw-Hill Book Co.
Continuing Education Program
1221 Avenue of the Americas
New York, NY 10020
(212) 997-6572

MGM/UA Home Video
10000 West Washington Blvd.
Culver City, CA 90232-2728
(213) 280-6000

National Geographic Society
17th and M Strs., NW
Washington, DC 20036
(202) 857-7378

National Public Radio
2025 M. St., NW
Washington, DC 20036

NETCHE (Nebraska Educational TV Council for Higher Education)
Box 83111
Lincoln, NE 68501
(402) 472-6833

New Letters on Air
5216 Rockhill
Kansas City, MO 64110

New York State Educational Department
Center for Learning Technologies, Media Distribution Network
Room C7, Concourse Level, Cultural Education Center
Albany, NY 12230
(518) 474-3168

Paramount Home Video
5555 Melrose Ave.
Los Angeles, CA 90038
(213) 468-5000

Perspective Films and Video
65 East South Water St.
Chicago, IL 60601
1-800-621-2131

Poets' Audio Center
P.O. Box 50145
Washington, DC 20004-0145
(202) 722-9106

Prism Entertainment
1888 Century Park East, Suite 1000
Los Angeles, CA 90067
(213) 277-3270

Pyramid Film and Video
P.O. Box 1048
Santa Monica, CA 90406
1-800-421-2304

RCA/Columbia Home Video
3500 W. Olive Ave.
Burbank, CA 91505
(818) 953-7900

Random House Audiobooks
Random House
201 East 50th St.
New York, NY 10022
1-800-638-6460

Recorded Books, Inc.
270 Skipjack Rd.
Prince Frederick, MD 20678
1-800-638-1304

SBI Publishers, Sound
Willow Street
South Lee, MA 01260

Social Studies School Service
(Division of NBC)
10000 Culver Blvd.
Culver City, CA 90232-0802
1-800-421-4246

Spoken Arts Records
310 North Ave.
New Rochelle, NY 10801
(914) 636-5482

Summer Stream
P.O. Box 6056
Santa Barbara, CA 93160
(805) 962-6540
also, 359 Ft. Washington Ave., Suite 4H
New York, NY 10033
(212) 795-3262

Swank Motion Pictures, Inc.
201 South Jefferson Ave.
St. Louis, MO 63166
(314) 534-6300

Time-Life Video
1271 Avenue of the Americas
New York, NY 10020
(212) 484-5940

University of Michigan Media Library
R4440 Kresge 1, Box 56
Ann Arbor, MI 48109
(313) 763-2074

Video Knowledge Inc.
29 Brambel La.
Melville, NY 11747
(516) 367-4250

Video Yesteryear
Box C
Sandy Hook, CT 06482
1-800-243-0987

Warner Home Video
4000 Warner Blvd.
Burbank, CA 91522
(818) 954-6000

Connections Between Selections Suggested by *Connections* Questions in Text

FICTION: LIST OF CONNECTIONS BETWEEN STORIES

(Please note: A degree symbol (°) following a story's title in the "Connected To" column indicates that the connections questions are located with that story, and not with the story in the first column. A "§" indicates that there are connections questions listed with both stories.)

AUTHOR, STORY	CONNECTED TO:
Kate Chopin, *The Story of an Hour*	Eudora Welty, *Livvie*° Nathaniel Hawthorne, *The Wives of the Dead*° Yukio Mishima, *Patriotism*° Stevie Smith, *How Cruel Is the Story of Eve*° (Poetry) Susan Glaspell, *Trifles*° (Drama)
Gail Godwin, *A Sorrowful Woman*	Herman Melville, *Bartleby, the Scrivener*° Colette [Sidonie Gabrielle], *The Hand*° Tillie Olsen, *I Stand Here Ironing*° Henrik Ibsen, *A Doll's House*° (Drama)
William Faulkner, *A Rose for Emily*	Grace Paley, *A Conversation with My Father*° William Faulkner, *Barn Burning*° Ralph Ellison, *Battle Royal*° Eudora Welty, *Livvie*° Flannery O'Connor, *Everything that Rises Must Converge*° Yukio Mishima, *Patriotism* Louise Erdrich, *Fleur*°
Grace Paley, *A Conversation With My Father*	William Faulkner, *A Rose for Emily* Tim O'Brien, *How to Tell a True War Story*
William Faulkner, *Barn Burning*	William Faulkner, *A Rose for Emily* Flannery O'Connor, *A Good Man Is Hard to Find*° Louise Erdich, *Fleur* §
Herman Melville, *Bartleby, the Scrivener*	Gail Godwin, *A Sorrowful Woman* Gabriel García Márquez, *A Very Old Man with Enormous Wings*° Nathaniel Hawthorne, *Young Goodman Brown*§ Franz Kafka, *A Hunger Artist*

265

Suggested Connections Between Selections

AUTHOR, STORY	CONNECTED TO:
Herman Melville, *Bartleby, the Scrivener* (cont.)	Liliana Heker, *The Stolen Party* ° Robert Frost, *Mending Wall* ° (Poetry)
Eudora Welty, *Livvie*	Kate Chopin, *The Story of an Hour* William Faulkner, *A Rose for Emily* Ernest Hemingway, *Soldier's Home*
Ernest Hemingway, *Soldier's Home*	Eudora Welty, *Livvie* ° Flannery O'Connor, *Good Country People* ° John Updike, *A & P* Yukio Mishima, *Patriotism* Tim O'Brien, *How to Tell a True War Story§*
Alice Munro, *How I Met My Husband*	Ralph Ellison, *Battle Royal* Toni Cade Bambara, *The Lesson*
Anton Chekhov, *The Lady with the Pet Dog*	Joyce Carol Oates, *The Lady with the Pet Dog* °
Joyce Carol Oates, *The Lady with the Pet Dog*	Anton Chekhov, *The Lady with the Pet Dog* Raymond Carver, *Boxes* ° Fay Weldon, *IND AFF, or Out of Love in Sarajevo* °
Colette, *The Hand*	Gail Godwin, *A Sorrowful Woman* Katherine Anne Porter, *The Grave* ° Nathaniel Hawthorne, *The Wives of the Dead* ° Nathaniel Hawthorne, *The Birthmark§* John Updike, *A & P*
Ralph Ellison, *Battle Royal*	William Faulkner, *A Rose for Emily* Alice Munro, *How I Met My Husband* ° Katherine Anne Porter, *The Grave* ° Mark Twain, *The Story of the Bad Little Boy* ° James Joyce, *Araby* M. Carl Holman, *Mr. Z* (Poetry) August Wilson, *Fences* (Drama)
Katherine Anne Porter, *The Grave*	Colette, *The Hand* Ralph Ellison, *Battle Royal* Toni Cade Bambara, *The Lesson* James Joyce, *Araby*
Stephen Crane, *The Bride Comes to Yellow Sky*	Joseph Conrad, *An Outpost of Progress* ° Mark Twain, *The Story of the Bad Little Boy* ° Katherine Mansfield, *Miss Brill*
Joseph Conrad, *An Outpost of Progress*	Stephen Crane, *The Bride Comes to Yellow Sky* Flannery O'Connor, *Revelation* ° R. K. Narayan, *Trail of the Green Blazer* ° Tim O'Brien, *How to Tell a True War Story* °

AUTHOR, STORY	CONNECTED TO:
Jospeh Conrad, *An Outpost of Progress* (cont.)	Michael Harper, *The Militance of a Photograph in the Passbook of a Bantu Under Detention* ° (Poetry)
Gabriel García Márquez, *A Very Old Man with Enormous Wings*	Herman Melville, *Bartleby, the Scrivener* Flannery O'Connor, *A Good Man Is Hard to Find* ° and Nathaniel Hawthorne, *The Birthmark* Flannery O'Connor, *A Good Man Is Hard to Find* ° Franz Kafka, *The Hunger Artist* Louise Erdich, *Fleur* °
Tillie Olsen, *I Stand Here Ironing*	Gail Godwin, *A Sorrowful Woman* John Updike, *A & P*
Mark Twain, *The Story of the Bad Little Boy*	Ralph Ellison, *Battle Royal* Stephen Crane, *The Bride Comes to Yellow Sky* R. K. Narayan, *Trail of the Green Blazer* ° Edwin Arlington Robinson, *Richard Cory* (Poetry)
Nathaniel Hawthorne, *The Wives of the Dead*	Kate Chopin, *The Story of an Hour* Colette, *The Hand* Nathaniel Hawthorne, *Young Goodman Brown* °
Nathaniel Hawthorne, *Young Goodman Brown*	Herman Melville, *Bartleby, the Scrivener* § Nathaniel Hawthorne, *The Wives of the Dead* Nathaniel Hawthorne, *The Birthmark*§ Nathaniel Hawthorne, *The Minister's Black Veil* ° Nathaniel Hawthorne, *The Birthmark* and *The Minister's Black Veil*
Nathaniel Hawthorne, *The Birthmark*	Colette, *The Hand*§ Gabriel García Márquez, *A Very Old Man with Enormous Wings* and Flannery O'Connor, *A Good Man Is Hard to Find* ° Nathaniel Hawthorne, *Young Goodman Brown* § Nathaniel Hawthorne, *The Minister's Black Veil* ° Nathaniel Hawthorne, *Young Goodman Brown* and *The Minister's Black Veil* ° Yukio Mishima, *Patriotism*
Nathaniel Hawthorne, *The Minister's Black Veil*	Nathaniel Hawthorne, *The Birthmark* Nathaniel Hawthorne, *Young Goodman Brown* Nathaniel Hawthorne, *Young Goodman Brown* and *The Birthmark*
Flannery O'Connor, *Good Country People*	Ernest Hemingway, *Soldier's Home*

AUTHOR, STORY	CONNECTED TO:
Flannery O'Connor, *Good Country People* (cont.)	Flannery O'Connor, *Everything that Rises Must Converge* ° Flannery O'Connor, *Revelation* §
Flannery O'Connor, *Everything that Rises Must Converge*	William Faulkner, *A Rose for Emily* Flannery O'Connor, *Good Country People* Flannery O'Connor, *Revelation* § Raymond Carver, *Boxes* °
Flannery O'Connor, *Revelation*	Joseph Conrad, *An Outpost of Progress* Flannery O'Connor, *Good Country People* § Flannery O'Connor, *Good Country People; Everything that Rises Must Converge; and A Good Man Is Hard to Find* Jane Martin, *Twirler* (Drama)
Flannery O'Connor, *A Good Man Is Hard to Find*	William Faulkner, *Barn Burning* Gabriel García Márquez, *A Very Old Man with Enormous Wings* Gabriel García Márquez, *A Very Old Man with Enormous Wings* and Nathaniel Hawthorne, *The Birthmark* Flannery O'Connor, *Revelation* °
Toni Cade Bambara, *The Lesson*	Alice Munro, *How I Met My Husband* ° Katherine Anne Porter, *The Grave* ° R. K. Narayan, *Trail of the Green Blazer* °
John Cheever, *Reunion*	Robert Phillips, *Running on Empty* ° (Poetry)
James Joyce, *Araby*	Ralph Ellison, *Battle Royal* ° Katherine Anne Porter, *The Grave* °
Franz Kafka, *A Hunger Artist*	Herman Melville, *Bartleby, the Scrivener* ° Gabriel García Márquez, *A Very Old Man with Enormous Wings*
D. H. Lawrence, *The Horse Dealer's Daughter*	Yukio Mishima, *Patriotism* ° Fay Weldon, *IND AFF, or Out of Love in Sarajevo* °
Katherine Mansfield, *Miss Brill*	Stephen Crane, *The Bride Comes to Yellow Sky* ° Liliana Heker, *The Stolen Party* °
John Updike, *A & P*	Ernest Hemingway, *Soldier's Home* ° Colette, *The Hand* ° Tillie Olsen, *I Stand Here Ironing* °
Yukio Mishima, *Patriotism*	Kate Chopin, *The Story of an Hour* William Faulkner, *A Rose for Emily* ° Ernest Hemingway, *Soldier's Home* ° Nathaniel Hawthorne, *The Birthmark* ° D. H. Lawrence, *The Horse Dealer's Daughter* Tim O'Brien, *How to Tell a True War Story* Marge Piercy, *A Work of Artifice* (Poetry)

AUTHOR, STORY	CONNECTED TO:
R. K. Narayan, *Trail of the Green Blazer*	Joseph Conrad, *An Outpost of Progress* Mark Twain, *The Story of the Bad Little Boy* Toni Cade Bambara, *The Lesson* Liliana Heker, *The Stolen Party*°
Raymond Carver, *Boxes*	Joyce Carol Oates, *The Lady with the Pet Dog* Flannery O'Connor, *Everything that Rises Must Converge*
Louise Erdich, *Fleur*	William Faulkner, *A Rose for Emily* William Faulkner, *Barn Burning* § Gabriel García Márquez, *A Very Old Man with Enormous Wings*
Tim O'Brien, *How to Tell a True War Story*	Grace Paley, *A Conversation with My Father*° Ernest Hemingway, *Soldier's Home* § Joseph Conrad, *An Outpost of Progress* Yukio Mishima, *Patriotism* °
Fay Weldon, *IND AFF, or Out of Love in Sarajevo*	Joyce Carol Oates, *The Lady with the Pet Dog* Nathaniel Hawthorne, *The Birthmark* D. H. Lawrence, *The Horse Dealer's Daughter*

POETRY: LIST OF CONNECTIONS BETWEEN POEMS

AUTHOR, POEM	CONNECTED TO:
John Updike, *Dog's Death*	Seamus Heaney, *Mid-term Break*°
William Hathaway, *Oh, Oh*	Robert Frost, *Design*°
Robert Francis, *Catch*	Emily Dickinson, *The thought beneath so slight a film* and *Portraits are to daily faces*°
Regina Barreca, *Nighttime Fires*	Nikki Giovanni, *Nikki-Rosa*°
Tracy Chapman, *Fast Car*	Robert Phillips, *Running on Empty*°
Mary Oliver, *The Black Snake*	Emily Dickinson, *A narrow Fellow in the Grass* William Stafford, *Traveling through the Dark*
Nikki Giovanni, *Nikki-Rosa*	Regina Barreca, *Nighttime Fires* M. Carl Holman, *Mr. Z*
Emily Dickinson, *To make a prairie it takes clover and one bee*	Robert Frost, *Mending Wall*°
e e cummings, *she being Brand*	Sharon Olds, *Sex without Love*°
Emily Dickinson, *If I shouldn't be alive*	Emily Dickinson, *Because I could not stop for Death* °
Andrew Marvell, *To His Coy Mistress*	Stevie Smith, *How Cruel Is the Story of Eve* °

Suggested Connections Between Selections

AUTHOR, POEM	CONNECTED TO:
Andrew Marvell, *To His Coy Mistress* (cont.)	John Keats, *Ode on a Grecian Urn* °
Richard Wilbur, *A Late Aubade*	Stevie Smith, *How Cruel Is the Story of Eve* ° Sharon Olds, *Sex without Love* °
Edna St. Vincent Millay, *Never May the Fruit Be Plucked*	Stevie Smith, *How Cruel Is the Story of Eve* ° John Keats, *Ode on a Grecian Urn* e e cummings, *since feeling is first* Emily Dickinson, *Wild Nights — Wild Nights!* §
Thomas Hardy, *The Convergence of the Twain*	David R. Slavitt, *Titanic* °
David R. Slavitt, *Titanic*	Thomas Hardy, *The Convergence of the Twain*
Marge Piercy, *A Work of Artifice*	Yukio Mishima, *Patriotism* (Fiction) Stevie Smith, *How Cruel Is the Story of Eve* Henrik Ibsen, *A Doll's House* (Drama)
Stevie Smith, *How Cruel Is the Story of Eve*	Kate Chopin, *The Story of an Hour* (Fiction) Andrew Marvell, *To His Coy Mistress* Richard Wilbur, *A Late Aubade* Edna St. Vincent Millay, *Never May the Fruit Be Plucked* Marge Piercy, *A Work of Artifice* °
Theodore Roethke, *Root Cellar*	Richard Eberhart, *The Groundhog* ° John Keats, *To Autumn* °
Matthew Arnold, *Dover Beach*	Wilfred Owen, *Dulce et Decorum Est* Thomas Hardy, *The Oxen* Anthony Hecht, *The Dover Bitch*
H. D., *Heat*	John Repp, *Cursing the Hole in the Screen, Wondering at the Romance Some Find in Summer* °
William Blake, *London*	Claribel Alegria, *I am Mirror* °
Sally Croft, *Home-Baked Bread*	Cathy Song, *The White Porch* °
Wilfred Owen, *Dulce et Decorum Est*	Matthew Arnold, *Dover Beach* °
Margaret Atwood, *Dreams of the Animals*	Rainer Maria Rilke, *The Panther* °
John Repp, *Cursing the Hole in the Screen, Wondering at the Romance Some Find in Summer*	H.D., *Heat* William Shakespeare, *Shall I compare thee to a summer's day?* Louise Bogan, *Dark Summer*
Dylan Thomas, *The Hand that Signed the Paper*	Rita Dove, *Parsley* °
Sylvia Plath, *Mirror*	Claribel Alegria, *I am Mirror* °
Emily Dickinson, *The thought beneath so slight a film —* and *Portraits are to daily faces*	Robert Francis, *Catch* Robert Frost, *Mending Wall* Robert Frost, *Birches*

AUTHOR, POEM	CONNECTED TO:
Dylan Thomas, *Do not go gentle into that good night*	Theodore Roethke, *The Waking* ° John Donne, *Death Be Not Proud* Sylvia Plath, *Daddy* Robert Creeley, *Fathers* °
Emily Dickinson, *I know that He exists*	Emily Dickinson, *Lightly stepped a yellow star* ° Robert Frost, *Design* °
Robert Frost, *Acquainted with the Night*	Octavio Paz, *The Street* °
Edwin Arlington Robinson, *Richard Cory*	Mark Twain, *The Story of the Bad Little Boy* (Fiction) °
e e cummings, *next to of course god america i*	Robert Frost, *The Gift Outright* °
Stephen Crane, *A Man Said to the Universe*	Robert Frost, *Out, Out* °
William Stafford, *Traveling through the Dark*	Mary Oliver, *The Black Snake* ° Richard Eberhart, *The Groundhog* §
William Stafford, *Traveling through the Dark* and Richard Eberhart, *The Groundhog*	D. H. Lawrence, *Snake*
Richard Eberhart, *The Groundhog*	Theodore Roethke, *Root Cellar* William Stafford, *Traveling through the Dark*§
D. H. Lawrence, *Snake*	William Stafford, *Traveling through the Dark* and Richard Eberhart, *The Groundhog* °
Emily Dickinson, *Lightly stepped a yellow star*	Emily Dickinson, *I know that He exists* Gerard Manley Hopkins, *God's Grandeur*
May Swenson, *A Nosty Fright*	Lewis Carroll, *Jabberwocky* °
Emily Dickinson, *A Bird came down the walk—*	Rainer Maria Rilke, *The Panther* °
Galway Kinnell, *Blackberry Eating*	Pablo Neruda, *Sweetness, Always* °
Robert Southey, *The Cataract of Lodore*	Federico García Lorca, *Somnambule Ballad* °
Gerard Manley Hopkins, *God's Grandeur*	Emily Dickinson, *Lightly stepped a yellow star* ° William Wordsworth, *The World Is Too Much with Us* ° Denise Levertov, *Gathered at the River* °
Lewis Carroll, *Jabberwocky*	May Swenson, *A Nosty Fright* Robert Francis, *Glass*
Thomas Hardy, *The Oxen*	Matthew Arnold, *Dover Beach* °
Robert Francis, *The Pitcher*	Lawrence Ferlinghetti, *Constantly risking absurdity* Robert Wallace, *The Double Play*
Helen Chasin, *The Word* Plum	Pablo Neruda, *Sweetness, Always* °
Robert Herrick, *Delight in Disorder*	Ben Jonson, *Still to Be Neat* §
Ben Jonson, *Still to Be Neat*	Robert Herrick, *Delight in Disorder*

AUTHOR, POEM	CONNECTED TO:
Emily Dickinson, *Because I could not stop for Death*	Emily Dickinson, *If I shouldn't be alive* Emily Dickinson, *I heard a Fly buzz — when I died —*
William Wordsworth, *The World Is Too Much With Us*	Gerard Manley Hopkins, *God's Grandeur* Amy Clampitt, *Nothing Stays Put* §
William Shakespeare, *Shall I compare thee to a summer's day?*	John Repp, *Cursing the Hole in the Screen, Wondering at the Romance Some Find in Summer* °
Theodore Roethke, *The Waking*	Dylan Thomas, *Do not go gentle into that good night* e e cummings, *since feeling is first*
Seamus Heaney, *Mid-term Break*	John Updike, *Dog's Death* A. E. Housman, *To an Athlete Dying Young*
Walt Whitman, From *I Sing the Body Electric*	Allen Ginsberg, *A Supermarket in California* °
Allen Ginsberg, *A Supermarket in California*	Walt Whitman, From *I Sing the Body Electric* Walt Whitman, *Song of the Open Road* Amy Clampitt, *Nothing Stays Put* °
Carolyn Forché, *The Colonel*	Rita Dove, *Parsley* °
John Keats, *Ode on a Grecian Urn*	Andrew Marvell, *To His Coy Mistress* Edna St. Vincent Millay, *Never May the Fruit Be Plucked* ° John Keats, *To Autumn* Richard Wilbur, *Love Calls Us to the Things of This World*
John Keats, *Ode on Melancholy*	Federico García Lorca, *Somnambule Ballad* °
John Keats, *To Autumn*	Theodore Roethke, *Root Cellar* John Keats, *Ode on a Grecian Urn* ° Robert Frost, *After Apple-Picking*
Robert Frost, *Mending Wall*	Herman Melville, *Bartleby, the Scrivener* (Fiction) Emily Dickinson, *To make a prairie it takes a clover and one bee* Robert Frost, *Neither out Far nor In Deep* Ruth Fainlight, *Flower Feet* °
Robert Frost, *Mending Wall* and *Birches*	Emily Dickinson, *The thought beneath so slight a film — and Portraits are to daily faces* °
Robert Frost, *Home Burial*	Robert Frost, *Out, Out* ° Galway Kinnell, *After Making Love We Hear Footsteps* °
Robert Frost, *After Apple-Picking*	John Keats, *To Autumn*°
Robert Frost, *Out, Out*	Stephen Crane, *A Man Said to the Universe* Robert Frost, *Home Burial*

AUTHOR, POEM	CONNECTED TO:
Robert Frost, *Out, Out* (cont.)	Robert Frost, *The Need of Being Versed in Country Things*
Robert Frost, *The Need of Being Versed in Country Things*	Robert Frost, *Out, Out* °
Robert Frost, *Design*	Robert Frost, *Design* °
	William Hathaway, *Oh, Oh*
	Emily Dickinson, *I know that He exists*
	Robert Frost, *The Need of Being Versed in Country Things*
	Denise Levertov, *Gathered at the River* °
Robert Frost, *Neither out Far nor In Deep*	Robert Frost, *Mending Wall* °
Robert Frost, *Provide, Provide*	Pablo Neruda, *Sweetness, Always* °
Robert Frost, *The Gift Outright*	e e cummings, *next to of course god america i*
	Allen Ginsberg, *America*
	Claude McKay, *America*
Leonard Adame, *Black and White*	Michael Harper, *The Militance of a Photograph in the Passbook of a Bantu Under Detention* °
W. H. Auden, *The Unknown Citizen*	James Merrill, *Casual Wear* °
John Berryman, *Dream Song 14*	Charles Baudelaire, *To the Reader* °
Louise Bogan, *Dark Summer*	Edna St. Vincent Millay, *Never May the Fruit Be Plucked* °
	Theodore Roethke, *The Waking* °
e e cummings, *since feeling is first*	Theodore Roethke, *The Waking* °
	Edna St. Vincent Millay, *Never May the Fruit Be Plucked* °
Emily Dickinson, *I heard a Fly buzz — when I died*	Emily Dickinson, *Because I could not stop for Death* °
Emily Dickinson, *Wild Nights — Wild Nights!*	Edna St. Vincent Millay, *Never May the Fruit Be Plucked* °
John Donne, *Death Be Not Proud*	Dylan Thomas, *Do not go gentle into that good night* °
T. S. Eliot, *The Love Song of J. Alfred Prufrock*	Charles Baudelaire, *To the Reader* °
Lawrence Ferlinghetti, *Constantly risking absurdity*	Robert Francis, *The Pitcher* °
Allen Ginsberg, *America*	Robert Frost, *The Gift Outright* °
	Charles Baudelaire, *To the Reader* °
Donald Hall, *My Son, My Executioner*	Robert Creeley, *Fathers* °
Anthony Hecht, *The Dover Bitch*	Matthew Arnold, *Dover Beach* °
M. Carl Holman, *Mr. Z*	Ralph Ellison, *Battle Royal* ° (Fiction)
	Nikki Giovanni, *Nikki-Rosa* °
Gerard Manley Hopkins, *Pied Beauty*	Denise Levertov, *Gathered at the River* °
A. E. Housman, *To an Athlete Dying Young*	Seamus Heaney, *Mid-term Break* °
Claude McKay, *America*	Robert Frost, *The Gift Outright* °
Edna St. Vincent Millay, *I Too Beneath Your Moon, Almighty Sex*	Sappho, *With his venom* °

AUTHOR, POEM	CONNECTED TO:
Howard Nemerov, *Life Cycle of Common Man*	James Merrill, *Casual Wear* °
Sylvia Plath, *Daddy*	Dylan Thomas, *Do not go gentle into that good night* °
Sylvia Plath, *Morning Song*	Galway Kinnell, *After Making Love We Hear Footsteps* °
Theodore Roethke, *I Knew a Woman*	Li Ho, *A Beautiful Girl Combs Her Hair* °
Delmore Schwartz, *True-Blue American*	Arthur Miller, *Death of a Salesman* ° (Drama)
Robert Wallace, *The Double Play*	Robert Francis, *The Pitcher* °
Richard Wilbur, *Love Calls Us to the Things of this World*	John Keats, *Ode on a Grecian Urn* °
James Wright, *Lying in a Hammock at William Duffy's Farm in Pine Island, Minnesota*	Octavio Paz, *The Street* °
Anna Akhmatova, *Apparition*	Rita Dove, *Parsley* James Merrill, *Casual Wear*
Claribel Alegria, *I am Mirror*	William Blake, *London* Sylvia Plath, *Mirror* Czeslaw Milosz, *A Poor Christian Looks at the Ghetto* °
Charles Baudelaire, *To the Reader*	John Berryman, *Dream Song 14* T. S. Eliot, *The Love Song of J. Alfred Prufrock* Allen Ginsberg, *America*
Federico García Lorca, *Somnambule Ballad*	Robert Southey, *The Cataract of Lodore* John Keats, *Ode on Melancholy*
Li Ho, *A Beautiful Girl Combs Her Hair*	Theodore Roethke, *I Knew a Woman* Cathy Song, *The White Porch*
Muhammad al-Maghut, *Tourist*	Felix Mnthali, *The Stranglehold of English Lit.* James Merrill, *Casual Wear*
Czeslaw Milosz, *A Poor Christian Looks at the Ghetto*	Claribel Alegria, *I am Mirror* Michael Harper, *The Militance of a Photograph in the Passbook of a Bantu Under Detention*
Felix Mnthali, *The Stranglehold of English Lit.*	Muhammad al-Maghut, *Tourist* ° Shinkichi Takahashi, *Explosion* David Henry Hwang, *M. Butterfly* (Drama)
Pablo Neruda, *Sweetness, Always*	Robert Frost, *Provide, Provide* Galway Kinnell, *Blackberry Eating* Helen Chasin, *The Word Plum* Shinkichi Takahashi, *Explosion* °
Octavio Paz, *The Street*	Robert Frost, *Acquainted with the Night* James Wright, *Lying in a Hammock at William Duffy's Farm in Pine Island, Minnesota*

AUTHOR, POEM	CONNECTED TO:
Rainer Maria Rilke, *The Panther*	Margaret Atwood, *Dreams of the Animals* Emily Dickinson, *A Bird came down the Walk*
Sappho, *With his venom*	Edna St. Vincent Millay, *I Too Beneath Your Moon, Almighty Sex* Cathy Song, *The White Porch*
Shinkichi Takahashi, *Explosion*	Felix Mnthali, *The Stranglehold of English Lit.* ° Pablo Neruda, *Sweetness, Always* Robert Phillips, *Running on Empty*
Amy Clampitt, *Nothing Stays Put*	William Wordsworth, *The World Is Too Much With Us* § Allen Ginsberg, *A Supermarket in California* Ruth Fainlight, *Flower Feet* °
Robert Creeley, *Fathers*	Dylan Thomas, *Do not go gentle into that good night* Donald Hall, *My Son, My Executioner*
Rita Dove, *Parsley*	Dylan Thomas, *The Hand that Signed the Paper* Carolyn Forché, *The Colonel* Anna Akhmatova, *Apparition* ° Michael Harper, *The Militance of a Photograph in the Passbook of a Bantu Under Detention* °
Ruth Fainlight, *Flower Feet*	Robert Frost, *Mending Wall* Amy Clampitt, *Nothing Stays Put* James Merrill, *Casual Wear*
Michael Harper, *The Militance of a Photograph in the Passbook of a Bantu Under Detention*	Joseph Conrad, *An Outpost of Progress* (Fiction) Leonard Adame, *Black and White* Czeslaw Milosz, *A Poor Christian Looks at the Ghetto* ° Rita Dove, *Parsley*
Galway Kinnell, *After Making Love We Hear Footsteps*	Robert Frost, *Home Burial* Sylvia Plath, *Morning Song* Peter Meinke, *The ABC of Aerobics* °
Denise Levertov, *Gathered at the River*	Gerard Manley Hopkins, *God's Grandeur* Robert Frost, *Design* Gerard Manley Hopkins, *Pied Beauty*
Peter Meinke, *The ABC of Aerobics*	Galway Kinnell, *After Making Love We Hear Footsteps* James Merrill, *Casual Wear* ° Sharon Olds, *Sex without Love*
James Merrill, *Casual Wear*	W. H. Auden, *The Unknown Citizen* Howard Nemerov, *Life Cycle of Common Man* Ruth Fainlight, *Flower Feet* ° Peter Meinke, *The ABC of Aerobics*

Suggested Connections Between Selections

AUTHOR, POEM	CONNECTED TO:
Sharon Olds, *Sex without Love*	Richard Wilbur, *A Late Aubade* e e cummings, *she being Brand* Peter Meinke, *The ABC of Aerobics* ° Alberto Ríos, *Seniors* ° Cathy Song, *The White Porch* °
Robert Phillips, *Running on Empty*	John Cheever, *Reunion* (Fiction) Tracy Chapman, *Fast Car* Shinkichi Takahashi, *Explosion* °
Alberto Ríos, *Seniors*	T. S. Eliot, *The Love Song of J. Alfred Prufrock* Sharon Olds, *Sex without Love*
Cathy Song, *The White Porch*	Sally Croft, *Home-Baked Bread* Li Ho, *A Beautiful Girl Combs Her Hair* ° Sappho, *With his venom* ° Sharon Olds, *Sex without Love*

DRAMA: LIST OF CONNECTIONS BETWEEN PLAYS

AUTHOR, PLAY	CONNECTED TO:
Susan Glaspell, *Trifles*	Kate Chopin, *The Story of an Hour* (Fiction) Sophocles, *Oedipus the King* William Shakespeare, *Othello the Moor of Venice* Molière, *Tartuffe* ° Henrik Ibsen, *A Doll's House* °
Sophocles, *Oedipus the King*	Susan Glaspell, *Trifles* ° Sophocles, *Antigone* ° William Shakespeare, *Hamlet, Prince of Denmark* William Shakespeare, *Othello the Moor of Venice* Henrik Ibsen, *A Doll's House* Tennessee Williams, *The Glass Menagerie* ° Wole Soyinka, *The Strong Breed* ° David Henry Hwang, *M. Butterfly* °
Sophocles, *Antigone*	Sophocles, *Oedipus the King* ° William Shakespeare, *Hamlet, Prince of Denmark* ° Molière, *Tartuffe* ° Henrik Ibsen, *A Doll's House* ° Tennessee Williams, *The Glass Menagerie* °
William Shakespeare, *Hamlet, Prince of Denmark*	Sophocles, *Oedipus the King* ° Sophocles, *Antigone* William Shakespeare, *Othello the Moor of Venice* °

AUTHOR, PLAY	CONNECTED TO:
William Shakespeare, *Hamlet, Prince of Denmark* (cont.)	Molière, *Tartuffe* Henrik Ibsen, *A Doll's House* Arthur Miller, *Death of a Salesman* ° David Henry Hwang, *M. Butterfly* °
William Shakespeare, *Othello the Moor of Venice*	Susan Glaspell, *Trifles* ° William Shakespeare, *Hamlet, Prince of Denmark* Molière, *Tartuffe*
Molière, *Tartuffe*	Sophocles; Shakespeare (Any Plays) Susan Glaspell, *Trifles* Sophocles, *Antigone* William Shakespeare, *Hamlet, Prince of Denmark* ° William Shakespeare, *Othello the Moor of Venice* ° Henrik Ibsen, *A Doll's House* Anton Chekhov, *The Cherry Orchard*
Henrik Ibsen, *A Doll's House*	Gail Godwin, *A Sorrowful Woman* (Fiction) Marge Piercy, *A Work of Artifice* ° (Poetry) Susan Glaspell, *Trifles* Sophocles, *Antigone* William Shakespeare, *Hamlet, Prince of Denmark* ° Molière, *Tartuffe* ° Anton Chekhov, *The Cherry Orchard* °
Anton Chekhov, *The Cherry Orchard*	Molière, *Tartuffe* ° Henrik Ibsen, *A Doll's House* Samuel Beckett, *Krapp's Last Tape* ° Tennessee Williams, *The Glass Menagerie* § Arthur Miller, *Death of a Salesman* °
Samuel Beckett, *Krapp's Last Tape*	Anton Chekhov, *The Cherry Orchard* Jane Martin, *Twirler* ° Arthur Miller, *Death of a Salesman* David Henry Hwang, *M. Butterfly*
Jane Martin, *Twirler*	Flannery O'Connor, *Revelation* (Fiction) William Shakespeare, *Hamlet, Prince of Denmark* William Shakespeare, *Othello the Moor of Venice* Samuel Beckett, *Krapp's Last Tape*
Tennessee Williams, *The Glass Menagerie*	Sophocles, *Oedipus the King* Sophocles, *Antigone* Anton Chekhov, *The Cherry Orchard* § Arthur Miller, *Death of a Salesman* David Henry Hwang, *M. Butterfly* °
Arthur Miller, *Death of a Salesman*	Delmore Schwartz, *True-Blue American* (Poetry)

AUTHOR, PLAY	CONNECTED TO:
Arthur Miller, *Death of a Salesman* (cont.)	William Shakespeare, *Hamlet, Prince of Denmark* Anton Chekhov, *The Cherry Orchard* Samuel Beckett, *Krapp's Last Tape* ° Tennessee Williams, *The Glass Menagerie* ° Wole Soyinka, *The Strong Breed* ° August Wilson, *Fences* °
Wole Soyinka, *The Strong Breed*	Sophocles, *Oedipus the King* Arthur Miller, *Death of a Salesman* August Wilson, *Fences* °
August Wilson, *Fences*	Ralph Ellison, *Battle Royal* (Fiction) Arthur Miller, *Death of a Salesman* Wole Soyinka, *The Strong Breed*
David Henry Hwang, *M. Butterfly*	Felix Mnthali, *The Stranglehold of English Lit.* ° (Poetry) Sophocles, *Oedipus the King* William Shakespeare, *Hamlet, Prince of Denmark* Samuel Beckett, *Krapp's Last Tape* ° Tennessee Williams, *The Glass Menagerie*

A List of Selections on the Audio Recording of Classic and Contemporary Poems

This audio recording features pairs of poems linked by "Connections" questions in the text; the work of authors treated in depth (Keats, Frost, and Shakespeare); poems that serve as excellent examples of the elements of poetry discussed in the book (sound, imagery, rhythm, form, etc.); and, finally, a rich selection of classic and contemporary poems.

Side 1

Poetry Pairs: poems linked by "Connections" questions in the text.
(Poems are arranged alphabetically by the first author in a pair.)

Matthew Arnold, *Dover Beach* (Chapter 14. Images, p. 549)
Thomas Hardy, *The Oxen* (Chapter 17. Sound, p. 619)

Margaret Atwood, *Dreams of the Animals* (Chapter 14. Images, p. 555)
Rainer Maria Rilke, *The Panther* (Chapter 22. A Collection of Poems, p. 888)

William Blake, *The Lamb* (Chapter 18. Patterns of Rhythm, p. 634)
William Blake, *The Tyger* (Chapter 18. Patterns of Rhythm, p. 635)

Thomas Hardy, *The Convergence of the Twain* (Chapter 13. Word Choice, Word Order, and Tone, p. 539)
David R. Slavitt, *The Titanic* (Chapter 13. Word Choice, Word Order, and Tone, p. 540)

Robert Herrick, *Delight in Disorder* (Chapter 18. Patterns of Rhythm, p. 632)
Ben Jonson, *Still to Be Neat* (Chapter 18. Patterns of Rhythm, p. 633)

John Keats, *To Autumn* (Chapter 21. A Study of Two Poets, p. 701)
Robert Frost, *After Apple-Picking* (Chapter 21. A Study of Two Poets, p. 718)

Li Ho, *A Beautiful Girl Combs Her Hair* (Chapter 22. A Collection of Poems, p. 882)
Cathy Song, *The White Porch* (Chapter 22. A Collection of Poems, p. 904)

Christopher Marlowe, *The Passionate Shepherd to His Love* (Chapter 22. A Collection of Poems, p. 814)
Sir Walter Raleigh, *The Nymph's Reply to the Shepherd* (Chapter 22. A Collection of Poems, p. 834)

Edna St. Vincent Millay, *Never May the Fruit Be Plucked* (Chapter 13. Word Choice, Word Order, and Tone, p. 538)
Emily Dickinson, *Wild Nights — Wild Nights!* (Chapter 22. A Collection of Poems, p. 774)

William Shakespeare, *Shall I compare thee to a summer's day?* (Chapter 19. Poetic Forms, p. 647)
William Shakespeare, *My mistress' eyes are nothing like the sun* (Chapter 19. Poetic Forms, p. 648)

Walt Whitman, *The Soul, reaching, throwing out for love* (Chapter 15. Figures of Speech, p. 574)

Walt Whitman, *A Noiseless Patient Spider* (Chapter 15. Figures of Speech, p. 573)

A selection of classic and contemporary poems arranged alphabetically by author.

Katharyn Machan Aal, *Hazel Tells LaVerne* (Chapter 13. Word Choice, Word Order, and Tone, p. 529)

Anonymous, *Western Wind* (Chapter 12. Reading Poetry, p. 506)

Regina Barreca, *Nighttime Fires* (Chapter 12. Reading Poetry, p. 507)

Elizabeth Bishop, *One Art* (Chapter 22. A Collection of Poems, p. 757)

William Blake, *The Sick Rose* (Chapter 16. Symbol, Allegory, and Irony, p. 590)

Robert Browning, *My Last Duchess* (Chapter 18. Patterns of Rhythm, p. 637)

Side 2

A selection of classic and contemporary poems (continued)

George Gordon, Lord Byron, *She Walks in Beauty* (Chapter 22. A Collection of Poems, p. 763)

Sally Croft, *Home-Baked Bread* (Chapter 14. Images, p. 558)

E. E. Cummings, *next to of course god america i* (Chapter 16. Symbol, Allegory, and Irony, p. 588)

Emily Dickinson, *Much madness is divinest Sense—* (Chapter 22. A Collection of Poems, p. 774)

John Donne, *A Valediction: Forbidding Mourning* (Chapter 15. Figures of Speech, p. 575)

Michael Drayton, *Since There's No Help* (Chapter 22. A Collection of Poems, p. 779)

Carolyn Forché, *The Colonel* (Chapter 20. Open Form, p. 671)

Robert Frost, *The Road Not Taken* (Chapter 21. A Study of Two Poets, p. 711)

Gerard Manley Hopkins, *God's Grandeur* (Chapter 17. Sounds, p. 614)

Langston Hughes, *Harlem (A Dream Deferred)* (Chapter 22. A Collection of Poems, p. 803)

John Keats, *On First Looking into Chapman's Homer* (Chapter 21. A Study of Two Poets, p. 678)

John Keats, *La Belle Dame sans Merci* (Chapter 21. A Study of Two Poets, p. 692)

John Keats, *Ode on a Grecian Urn* (Chapter 21. A Study of Two Poets, p. 698)

Etheridge Knight, *A Watts Mother Mourns While Boiling Beans* (Chapter 22. A Collection of Poems, p. 807)

Denise Levertov, *O Taste and See* (Chapter 20. Open Form, p. 671)

Andrew Marvell, *To His Coy Mistress* (Chapter 13. Word Choice, Word Order, and Tone, p. 534)

John Milton, *When I consider how my light is spent* (Chapter 22. A Collection of Poems, p. 823)

Marianne Moore, *Poetry* (Chapter 22. A Collection of Poems, p. 823)

Sylvia Plath, *Mirror* (Chapter 15. Figures of Speech, p. 570)

Sappho, *With his venom* (Chapter 22. A Collection of Poems, p. 889)

William Shakespeare, *Soliloquy from* Hamlet, III. i. 56–88 (Chapter 26. A Study of William Shakespeare, p. 1108)

Percy Bysshe Shelley, *Ozymandias* (Chapter 22. A Collection of Poems, p. 848)

Wallace Stevens, *The Emperor of Ice-Cream* (Chapter 22. A Collection of Poems, p. 853)

Alfred, Lord Tennyson, *Tears, Idle Tears* (Chapter 22. A Collection of Poems, p. 858)

William Wordsworth, *The World Is Too Much with Us* (Chapter 19. Poetic Forms, p. 646)

William Butler Yeats, *Crazy Jane Talks with the Bishop* (Chapter 22. A Collection of Poems, p. 873)

William Butler Yeats, *The Lake Isle of Innisfree* (Chapter 22. A Collection of Poems, p. 873)